The New Biography

Studies on the History of Society and Culture
Victoria E. Bonnell and Lynn Hunt, Editors

The New Biography

Performing Femininity in Nineteenth-Century France

EDITED BY

Jo Burr Margadant

UNIVERSITY OF CALIFORNIA PRESS
Berkeley · Los Angeles · London

University of California Press
Berkeley and Los Angeles, California

University of California Press, Ltd.
London, England

© 2000 by
The Regents of the University of California

Library of Congress Cataloging-in-Publication Data

Margadant, Jo Burr, 1939–
    The new biography : performing femininity in
nineteenth-century France / Jo Burr Margadant,
editor
        p.   cm. — (Studies on the history of society
        and culture ; 38)
    Includes bibliographical references and index.
        ISBN 0-520-22140-0 (cloth : alk. paper). —
    ISBN 0-520-22141-9 (pbk. : alk paper)
        1. Feminism — France — History — 19th
    century. 2. Feminists — France — Biography.
    3. Motherhood in popular culture — France —
    History — 19th century.   4. Sex role — France —
    History — 19th century.   5. Women in pol-
    itics — France — History — 19th century.
    6. Women authors, French — 19th century —
    Biography.   I. Title. II. Series.

HQ1615.A3 M37 2000
305.42'0944 — dc21   99-048288
                                                 CIP

Manufactured in the United States of America

09   08   07   06   05   04   03   02   01   00

10   9   8   7   6   5   4   3   2   1

The paper used in this publication meets the mini-
mum requirements of ANSI/NISO Z39.48-1992 (R
1997) (Permanence of Paper). ♾

Contents

Illustrations

Preface

This collection presupposes the recent genesis of a new way of writing biography. Nonetheless, in putting it together, I rapidly concluded that the entire project was *creating* as much as *defining* this fresh approach to a well-worn historical genre. That recognition has made the enterprise an exciting one for all of us associated with it. The idea for the project originated in conversations between me and several of the authors who were themselves experimenting with new methods for recounting individual lives. I had been struck by the urgent pedagogical need for such a publication after teaching an undergraduate seminar on the history of biography without the help of any text explaining the origins of the proliferating experiments in biographical writing in terms that students could easily understand. Exceptionally for pioneering scholarship, therefore, I decided to involve students in the first step of our undertaking.

With the generous sponsorship of Santa Clara University, twenty-two undergraduates and graduate students from Santa Clara University, Stanford University, and San Jose State University gathered with the other five contributors and me for a one-day conference in February 1998 to review the first draft of the manuscript. The students had all taken courses similar to those for which this volume is intended. The diversity of such courses produced an equal diversity in the backgrounds of our student interlocutors as well. Some had no knowledge of French history; others had never heard of critical theory or examined gender as an historical concept; many knew nothing about the history of biographical writing. Because the authors wanted to ensure student comprehension without sacrificing the conceptual originality of their work, the feedback produced by this uneven preparation proved indispensable to us all. No one benefited more from suggestions for clarification and elaboration than the editor, and I promptly rewrote my introduction. To the extent that the volume achieves its pedagogical goals, all six contributors incurred a tremendous debt of gratitude to the students listed below whose critical insights also added to our collective recognition that we were truly engaged in something new: Huda Almarashi, Paul Boisvert, Crystal Boyd, Robert Cirvilleri, Gina Dimino, Julie Garcia, Marianne Gregory, Lori Heathorn, Emalie Heinrich, Jennifer Hillier, Susan Jenkins, Jaime Jochums, Saul Morales, Heather Morris, Michele Quinnette, Kimberly Rowley, Lorea Russell, John Salazar III, Joseph Santos, Alyssa Sepinwall, Steve Schloesser, and Andrew Smith. I also wish to thank the provost, the dean of the College of Arts and Sciences, the chair of the History Department and the director of Women Studies at Santa Clara University for underwriting this highly productive and novel experiment in student review.

That conference initiated my own effort to explore the potential in this collection for rethinking French history as well as biographical writing. Each contributor, whether she wrote her essay independently or in dialogue with the others, added new dimensions to what we all eventually agreed the new biography was and might accomplish. But the chronological organization of the volume opened avenues of inquiry that no piece could have generated alone. For encouraging me to expand still further on the implications of our six biographical essays for debates in the history of French women, I wish to thank the two anonymous readers from the University of California Press, who are in no way responsible, of course, for any inadvertent errors and who may not necessarily agree with the conclusions I have drawn. Most of all, I would like to acknowledge the pleasure that I have had in working with the other authors on this project in a spirit of shared adventure and discovery.

Jo Burr Margadant
Santa Clara University

Introduction

Constructing Selves
in Historical Perspective

JO BURR MARGADANT

Biography is once again in fashion, not only for a general reading public that never lost its taste for individual life stories, but also for academic historians who endlessly turn over the debris of earlier generations in search of fresh lessons to tell us about ourselves. The resurrection of biography ends four decades of historical writing, during which — under the weight of interpretive approaches drawn from the social sciences — individual life histories lay nearly as dormant for academic history as the dead.[1] The rare exceptions to that indifference among self-conscious pioneers were adepts of psychobiography who revisited the lives of great historical figures armed with psychological theories.[2] Nonetheless, the "new biographers" do not take their cues for narrating peoples' lives from either psychology or earlier practitioners of the craft, neither of whose epistemological premises they any longer share. An explanation of our common assumptions for writing biography in the late twentieth century and of some of the intellectual paths that led to our approach forms one objective, therefore, for this introductory essay.[3]

A second objective is to show the rich potential of new methods in biography for exploring changes over the course of the nineteenth century in the possibility of a feminine presence in public life. The essays in this volume all present French women from socially elite backgrounds who developed into veritable celebrities within their lifetimes or after they had died. To achieve that goal, each of them had had to craft a feminine self legible to the public and credible to herself that might also win approval in at least some influential circles. The individual acts of self-invention that this search for fame entailed explains the subtitle given our collection.

Performing a self has a long history in Western culture. If we ignore antiquity, self-fashioning as a cultural undertaking for public life dates in Western Europe to the Renaissance.[4] The idea of making oneself over through some combination of education and willful intention would develop, as social and political institutions democratized, into the cultural foundation of a belief in individualism in the West. Significantly, the courtly manuals that launched the concept in sixteenth- and seventeenth-century Europe did not confine the art to the male sex any more than would the nineteenth-century manuals of bourgeois manners and advice that descended from them.[5] But as a bourgeois public sphere developed in eighteenth-century France, separate from the court and critical of aristocratic society and privilege, feminine and masculine personae became ever more sharply differentiated for the elite in ways that limited where and how females might present themselves respectably in public.[6] All the women in this volume had to perform their public selves against opposition to their presence created by that cultural trend. Among other things, the contributors to this volume examine how each woman met that challenge.

The difficulties the women encountered should not be underestimated. No one "invents" a self apart from cultural notions available to them in a particular historical setting. Often the unconventional is a collage of familiar notions merged in unfamiliar ways. But piecing a novel feminine self together was a risky business in nineteenth-century France. Accepted models for women in public life were few and circumscribed in polite society. Women who ignored or sought to expand existing stereotypes faced a daunting and never-ending task controlling others' opinions of their femininity. Several essays in this volume consider how friends and enemies depicted unconventional women who ventured into public life. All of them explore, in greater or less detail, how each celebrity composed a public self.[7] Some fashioned selves eclectically in a pastiche of possibilities drawn from conventional feminine behavior in domestic settings transplanted to the public sphere; others built on female models drawn from history, theater, and novels. In intention at least, whether they controlled the effect that they produced, the public selves these women fabricated were necessarily subversive. That being the case, choosing arenas for staging their personae required ingenuity. Several authored novels and plays with heroines caught up in dilemmas similar to their own. Some wrote histories or commentaries on contemporary events in an authorial voice that placed them, in keeping with their readers' expectations, on the periphery of whatever they described. More than half staged their private lives as provocative, though perfectly legal, alternatives to what elite propriety imposed on wives and mothers. Five women ventured directly into politics, but always in situations where they could project established signs of femininity for their observers.

Since, like everyone, these celebrities fashioned selves from cultural material they had at hand, the parade of femininities they performed suggests new possibilities as the century advanced. That observation figures importantly in our shared commitment to situating these biographies within a feminist history that could alter the way historians recount the past. Gendered systems in a particular time and place have great power, feminist theorists argue, to shape men and women in established ways. Those who break the mold do so by exploiting unsuspected fissures that over time may shatter prevailing gendered notions altogether. To identify the fissures exploited by these women, therefore, while offering some explanation for their presence, constitutes another goal of this introduction and the whole collection.[8] For readers familiar with the gendering of nineteenth-century public life in other national settings, distinctive features in the French case will become apparent. French historians may discover in the shifting parameters of the feminine in public life another way of mapping change in modern France.

THE NEW BIOGRAPHY

Since the intended audience for this volume includes undergraduates in courses ranging from biography to modern French history to the history of women and gender, a general introduction to the origins of our reconceptualization of biography seems appropriate. Roughly speaking, the demise of biography on the front line of academic history dates from post–Second World War, when leading historians shifted the plot line of the past away from acts by major figures in public life to external forces identified as shaping influences on the actions and choices of agglomerated individuals. Grouped under collective rubrics representing their presumed social identity, these new historical actors included classes; occupational groups; women; ethnic, racial and religious minorities; sometimes whole communities or societies, sometimes simply crowds. Initially, interpretations of collective experience located the origin of shared identities in the material circumstances of life, a position identified with but not monopolized by Marxist historians.[9] More recently, a challenge (that I would describe as "ethnographic") to that position has sought to show that social identities take shape within an historically specific cultural setting that imparts meaning to the materiality of life and not the other way around. In other words, to understand how people assume the identity that situates and motivates them in relation to others, it is necessary to grasp the symbolic world from which they construct meaning in their lives.[10] Explaining how an ethnographic turn in studies of collective behavior sparked a renewed interest in biography among historians, however, leads our inquiry to an epistemological conundrum that developed within cultural studies itself.

Although the study of culture or ethnography resides as an academic field in anthropology, some of the principal theorists of a cultural approach to interpreting human experience have also come from linguistics, philosophy, and literary criticism. The variety of positions defended by theoreticians as different as Jacques Derrida, Michel Foucault, and Hayden White, to name some of the best known, tends to bewilder historians by their complexity and disagreements.[11] Still more troubling are the implications of their cultural approach to understanding for any claim to objective knowledge. If meaning derives entirely from culture as some postmodern epistemologists would have it, then the way we appropriate and understand the world merely reports or, at the very least, is filtered through the meanings that our own culture makes available to us. By training, historians respect the principle of cultural relativism, since unique developments in highly particular settings constitute the very object of historical study. However, because the new epistemological relativism specifically includes the way we think about the world, its relativist implications extend to historians' own claims to expertise.[12] If narrating the past always involves a frame that is culturally produced, how, some theorists ask historians, does writing history differ from the exercise of writing fiction? Though this radical espistemological position does not reflect the views of contributors to this collection, something of this self-critical stance encourages Susan Grogan and Mary Pickering to present their respective portraits of Flora Tristan and Clotilde de Vaux as merely one of several possible versions of each woman. Self-critique, however, is not the only reason for historians to admit that a biographical subject has many profiles, since another aspect of the epistemological revolution underway in cultural studies is to call into question what constitutes identity.

Initially the shift from a materialist to a cultural interpretation of the origin of group identity did nothing to undermine the importance attached by historians to such collective studies or to rehabilitate biography. A case in point was the seminal reconsideration of the origins of working-class identity undertaken by E. P. Thompson in *The Making of the English Working Class* that appeared in 1966.[13] Thompson jettisoned the essentially Marxist notion that the origins of the English working classes lay in economic forces and material conditions unleashed by the industrial revolution; he replaced it with a working-class identity forged from values drawn from an existing artisanal culture and in response to the challenge raised to traditional ways by the new industrial order. He retained, however, the concept of a working class that came to know itself through shared experience. The certainty that shared experience formed the bedrock of class identity received a serious blow in a subsequent debate between two other historians of the working classes, Gareth Stedman Jones and Joan Scott, over when and how the term "working class" entered the language of English politics.[14] The upshot of their exchange was to suggest a then radical idea that the origin of class identity lay in language, to wit in naming, categorizing, and assigning meaning to an otherwise disparate group of individuals, rather than in experience itself. Of course this discussion echoed the epistemological issues raised by those cultural theorists who maintained that all experience was constructed and acquired meaning only through discursive practices. The logical corollary for some historians was to raise doubts about the use of categories like class as the fundamental building blocks for studying the past without considering how historians themselves might be implicated in their construction. Such doubts opened the first breach in the wall of indifference that had placed biography off limits for many historians who aspired to be on the cutting edge of historical inquiry.

Just as important for the return of biography for American historians were theoretical issues raised by the inability of political activists in the 1960s and 1970s, united by convictions about the historical oppression of their sex, ethnic group, race, or sexual orientation, to sustain their sense of shared oppression as a rallying point into the 1980s and 1990s. The feminist movement offers just one example, but a prodigiously fruitful one from the point of view of theory.[15] Confronted with a highly heterogeneous population of women activists whose priorities differed radically from one ethnic, racial, or otherwise distinctive social milieu to another, feminist theorists had to reconsider the category of woman both as an identifying marker for individual women and as a position from which to wage a political struggle.[16] The crisis over how to configure politically empowering identities provoked important theoretical debates that also drew insights from the epistemological revolution going on elsewhere in cultural studies.[17]

One of these debates questioned the intellectual soundness and political utility of the category "woman."[18] The term itself suggested an essential likeness between women that defied culture and, therefore, many activists would argue, opened the way for foes of feminist aspirations to use the notion of an essential female nature to lock the female sex into a permanently disadvantaged social position. Feminists convinced by radical theories of cultural construction believed, in any event, that "woman" was a fictional category that had its origin not in any physical determinism but rather in a system of assigning meaning based on binary oppositions associated with the way that humans think. Such social constructionists recognized only one commonality between females: everywhere and always women had lived their lives within cultures that gendered social worlds. No society had ever treated women as unique individuals without a significant cultural meaning attached to their belonging to a sex that also regulated social power. The cultural anthropologist Sherry Ortner further claimed that in almost all societies studied by ethnographers, female tasks carried less prestige than those the men performed, while the feminist historian Gerda Lerner argued that all historically documentable societies had already developed patriarchal cultural practices before they entered historical time.[19] The impact of these considerations for historians was to encourage feminist scholars to shift their focus of analysis from women as a biologically identifiable group to the way cultural definitions of femininity and masculinity, which is to say gender, work in different settings to situate females in relationship to social power. This approach to investigations of oppression had for feminist politics the great advantage of posing questions that encompassed all women without privileging one group's social experience over any another. It also allowed feminists to sidestep the issue of whether there is anything outside culture that defines a woman. Equally significant, studying gender put feminist studies into the mainstream of historical writing since everyone feels the effects of gendering, a recognition that has recently sparked interest in the historical construction of masculinity and "queerness" alongside the history of femininity as a culturally defined and consequently mutable set of attributes.[20]

But if gender constitutes a marker of identity through which everyone organizes and understands their worlds, it is far from the only one. Multiple other categories of likeness to and difference from others make up the social identities of individuals. Potentially the list of categorizing labels is endless since people continually create new meaningful associations for themselves and others. Practitioners of identity politics have discovered this repeatedly since the 1960s as they have sought to organize people around one aspect of their identity based on their lack of power relative to outsiders only to find them splintering into factions based on other, contrasting identities among themselves. [21]

Some historians find confirmation of this social process in the philosophical position advanced by Jacques Derrida, who identifies in the species' way of constructing meaning a continuous fission whereby each new binary opposition that the human mind comes up with suggests other differences that generate yet other binaries in an endless dialectic of assigning meaning and significance. Other historians see in the multiplicity of identities assumed by individuals a new, more open-ended method for connecting the material conditions of life to the way people choose to categorize themselves.[22] Recently, a number of scholars have sought insights into the process and politics of identity formation in the cross-cultural encounters produced historically by imperial conquest, colonialism, migrating populations, or centralizing states.[23] But whatever the origin of this new interest in the politics of identity construction, the effect in historical studies is to return biography to center stage since cultural politics are most easily examined as well as empathetically imagined in the individual life.

Obviously, therefore, the logic that the new biography pursues and the questions that it asks will differ greatly from what biographers assumed to be their task before the recent epistemological revolution took hold. One of the key goals of biography since Lytton Strachey transformed the genre in the early twentieth century was to identify in a person's life an underlying pattern or motif that could serve as the organizing theme for a biography meant to tell a coherent story about an identifiably unified, though not necessarily unconflicted, individual. Given the new self-consciousness of historians about their own role as creators of the history that they write, a narrative strategy designed to project a unified persona has become for the new biographer nearly as suspect as claims to a "definitive" biography. The subject of biography is no longer the coherent self but rather a self that is performed to create an impression of coherence or an individual with multiple selves whose different manifestations reflect the passage of time, the demands and options of different settings, or the varieties of ways that others seek to represent that person.

In some ways this approach appears to echo that of psychologically

informed investigations. For when psychobiographers are not also looking, as Strachey did, for a single psychic conflict that unlocks a person's
life, they may look for evidence of multiple selves born of repressed
desires in the unconscious. The kind of detective work that psychobiography involves often relies, however, on a premise that the new episte-
mology rejects, namely that there exists a psychic process that operates
independently of culture and produces universal psychic symptoms. A
postmodern approach might well assume that within a particular culture,
psychic tensions could arise in individuals involving relations to their
parents, their bodies, or the symbolic universe of patriarchy that can be
studied through the historically contingent terms that brought those tensions into being in the first place. Understood that way, psychology
remains a powerful tool for relating individual biography to particular
social conditions and cultural practices in which a sense of self evolved.
But even then, for practitioners of the new biography, psychobiography
is merely one more construction in the universe of multiple possibilities
that they embrace.

But does that mean that practitioners of the new biography accept the
view that experience or reality does not exist outside the meanings
imparted to it by our culturally limited understandings, as Joan Scott has
recently argued is the case, and that we cannot, therefore, make physical
experience or material conditions a starting point for interpreting historical change?[24] This remains an open question for the authors in this collection because the new biography implies first and foremost, not a
totalizing theory of cognition, but a method of analysis that recognizes
the constructed nature of our conscious selves and views of others.[25] It
does not require of its adepts a radical postmodern epistemological posture as a necessary premise of their enterprise.

All the same, for those interested in theories of cognition, the new
biography could potentially serve as a laboratory for testing or, at the
very least, examining the implications for lived experience of one or
another theory, a classic exercise within the empirical discipline of history. Though none of the articles in this collection pursues this possibility, Elinor Accampo's essay, "Private Life, Public Image: Motherhood
and Militancy in the Self-Construction of Nelly Roussel, 1900–1922"
might provoke debate on the connection between experience and altered
consciousness, since Roussel's insistence on the rights of women to control their reproduction and her construction of herself as an apostle for
that cause originated in the pain and fear she experienced in giving birth
herself. One might equally well inquire how much Roussel's tuberculosis

and Flora Tristan's frail health shaped the metaphoric language of martyrdom that they adopted for representing and justifying their radical politics and transgressive public selves. My own suggestions later in this introduction about the material and legal conditions within which these eight French women explored their options embed their stories in a kind of social history, minus any deterministic features. The evidence presented here cannot resolve the disagreements that currently divide radical from moderate epistemological positions in postmodern thought over the links between experience and change, but it can launch a fruitful conversation.[26]

The new biography can potentially fulfill two further classic goals of the historian's craft. The object of study for the new biographers is not just the construction of identities but also and inevitably, the contested nature of inventing selves. Every social location offers a limited number of possibilities from which individuals can create a possible self. Options do exist, however, and individuals may combine alternatives in distinctive ways. But since all social identities imply positioning within a network of relationships of power, claiming an identity often produces conflict. The eight women featured in this collection encountered more resistance than most people in establishing who they were and what they wanted, since their ambitions took them into public life, and several of the authors display their subjects in the heat of battle. This in turn makes possible, though certainly not compulsory, a narrative line that engages readers empathetically in a gripping story, just as certain older forms of biography are meant to do. To the extent that the essays presented here exploit that possibility, they execute in new ways some of the most appealing aspects of biographical writing generally.

There is another equally important possibility for the new biography as practiced in this collection. The methods of this new genre of biographical writing might apply to anybody, male or female, prominent or not. But the particular visibility of the eight female celebrities presented here and the significance of the conflicts over gender that their lives embodied and their representations expressed carry the potential for changing historians' "master narratives" for nineteenth-century France.[27] The conflicts in which these eight women were involved turned on issues that excited intense public debate: Where ought women to figure in the public eye? Which civil and civic rights might they legitimately have? Who should control women's reproductive choices? And what constituted femininity anyway? Recent accounts by historians of such debates have stressed the rigidity of the boundaries delimiting the possibilities for

women. William Reddy and Robert Nye describe an elite culture of
honor in nineteenth-century France in which women had no honor to
protect outside their reputation for sexual virtue, making them highly
vulnerable to slanderous attacks and barred from politics on that
account.[28] Joan Scott has argued that French feminists, whether or not
they acknowledged gendered differences themselves, were forced to articulate demands for women from a position outside the universality
defined as male by liberalism.[29] That discursive location trapped them in
a logical contradiction that feminism could not resolve. Geneviève
Fraisse finds many logical contradictions as well in the philosophical
defense made for male privilege in men's writings in the early part of the
century, but she, too, finds universal resistance to equality between the
sexes, an opposition she attributes to a phantasmic fear of women.[30]
Finally, Michèle Riot-Sarcey has traced the disenchantment of leading
feminist spokeswomen from the working classes who joined the radically
liberationist Saint-Simonian movement in the 1830s, only to find that
male privilege reigned implacably even there.[31] This collection offers a
different slant to those depressing tales.

   All eight of the women under examination accepted the duality of sexual difference that opinion across the political spectrum from monarchists
to socialists endorsed, but they did not necessarily either approve or tolerate the social, civic, or civil consequences that misogynists and the law
derived from that idea. What we learn from watching their performances
is that for audacious women from the elite who were determined to have
a hearing in the public forum and to liberate themselves from the worst
consequences of family law under the Napoleonic Civil Code, empowering personae did exist. Their use of accepted notions of femininity in
unconventional places did more than create new opportunities for themselves, however, since other women inspired by their examples could
imagine new possible selves as well. As for our own historical understanding, because their stories expose the cracks in what has often been
presented as a monolithic separation of gendered spheres in nineteenth-
century bourgeois France, they challenge historians to rethink their own
assumptions. The effect of that reevaluation could bring such women
from the margins of the historical record into history's mainstream.

A SUMMARY OF THE ARTICLES

A brief description of the six essays in the collection will whet the
appetite for what's ahead and introduce those readers unfamiliar with

French political history in the nineteenth century to some of its com-
plexities. Our volume opens with four articles that present women grap-
pling in the 1820s through the 1840s with the implications for their own
ambitions of the discursive triumph among the French elites of a version
of femininity that celebrated women in the role of nurturing and moralizing mother. This was not a new idea. As early as the seventeenth century, the playwright Molière had sought in his satirical attacks on women
intellectuals to distinguish between women at the court and other elite
Parisian women who in his view should have been devoting their lives to
domesticity and the happiness of their families instead of trying to rival
literary men. A century later, the republican theorist Jean Jacques Rousseau made domesticity the ideal condition for all women in his hugely
successful sentimental novel *Émile* that also imagined maternal love and
chaste wives at the center of a morally regenerated social and political
order. When Rousseau's political heirs, the Jacobins, adopted his views
on women during the radical republican phase of the French Revolution,
a page in the history of French women turned. Ten years later the
Napoleonic Civil Code of 1804 consolidated the domestic power of husbands by giving them control over the sexuality, property, and civil
actions of their wives.

The first piece in our collection, entitled "The Duchesse de Berry and
Royalist Political Culture in Postrevolutionary France," explores the
impact of this sea change in cultural ideals and jurisprudence on the way
French royalty represented mothers in the royal family. As its author, I
sought to explain the curious resistance to this cultural trend in the representation of maternity for royalty through the 1820s and to highlight
simultaneously the pivotal role that the young mother of the Bourbon
heir to the throne played, unwittingly for the most part, in modernizing
this aspect of royalist political culture in the 1830s. Her story is deeply
implicated in the political conflicts born of the revolution that would
trouble France throughout the nineteenth century and already during
the revolutionary period itself, produced a constitutional monarchy, a
democratic republic, a popular dictatorship, and an imperial despotism
under Napoleon I. The duchesse de Berry entered this embattled political theater in 1816 after victorious European powers had twice defeated
Napoleon and twice replaced him on the throne of France with the
brother of Louis XVI, executed in 1793 by republicans who believed
they had abolished monarchy in France forever. Obviously, the restoration of the Bourbon throne was not applauded in all quarters. Historians
have often noted the difficulty the Bourbons had, after a quarter century

spent in exile, in fabricating a royal image that resonated with the general public, but none have focused on their difficulties in depicting motherhood. This is the untold story that my biography of the duchesse de
Berry sets out to relate.

Married at sixteen to the only Bourbon likely to produce an heir to the
throne, widowed in 1820 by an assassin's knife while pregnant with that
heir, the duchesse de Berry lived a life worthy of a melodramatic novel.
She embroidered considerably on that possibility when, after a popular
revolution in 1830 had overthrown the Bourbons and replaced them on
the throne with their cousin Louis-Philippe, she returned secretly from
political exile to lead an abortive insurrection on her son's behalf. This
heroic maternal gesture eventually landed her in prison, where, most
inopportunely, she gave birth again. The ludicrous finale to her political
ambitions has for too long obscured the real political significance of this
royal mother in precipitating a striking transformation in the way French
royalists imagined a royal family. Her efforts to recast the role of
royal mother during and after the Restoration monarchy, together with
responses of supporters and detractors who read politically potent meanings into all her public acts, provide the basis for recovering the several
stages of that transformation for the historical record.

While my article contrasts the efforts of a woman to project a self
onto the public stage with what others said about her, Susan Grogan
explores the imagined selves fantasized by another famous female activist
under the regime of Louis-Philippe, Flora Tristan, in a melodrama of her
own making. The problem that Grogan probes in this striking portrait
turns on several recent studies of the Enlightenment and revolution that
make sweeping claims about the influence on the republican Left of Jean
Jacques Rousseau's insistence on confining women to domestic duties.
Several biographies in this collection, including Grogan's of Tristan, find
rather more flexibility among the intellectual heirs to Rousseau's thought
regarding what might constitute a civic role for women than Rousseau
himself foresaw. The legitimacy of any such activity, however, rested first
and foremost for the women in this study, as for their admirers, on rec-
ognizably feminine signs associated with their public profile. Flora
Tristan's published and private writings are particularly revealing in that
regard. A single mother legally separated from her husband, who sought
to support her family as a writer, Tristan also hoped to solve the desperate poverty of workers by inspiring them to organize a national welfare
fund, and undertook an illegal lecture tour to major cities in France for
this purpose. Tristan had no ready-made way to package herself for this

unusual undertaking, even in her own imagination. Her solution, as Grogan sensitively unveils it, was to create a kaleidoscope of selves drawn from history, melodrama, and the Bible that allowed her to envision her own transgressions in ways that also justified them. Whether observers understood her performances as Tristan did is not Grogan's concern. Instead, she shows how this spectacularly novel female activist composed a feminine self by artful borrowings of respected feminine and feminized personae from the cultural baggage of her times.

Whitney Walton's article, "Republican Women and Republican Families in the Personal Narratives of George Sand, Marie d'Agoult, and Hortense Allart," extends the investigation of the way ambitious, talented women dealt with the legacy of Rousseau's thought to three famous women writers from the period, all mothers and all republican in their political convictions. Each experienced an unhappy marriage that ended in a legal separation; two bore illegitimate children. Walton's stunningly original approach to their biographies asks how such liberated women made peace between, on the one hand, a republican ideology that embraced patriarchy and domesticity for women and, on the other, the personal independence that their own life choices required. She concludes from reading their autobiographies that each of them, having lost her natural father, created an imagined father who would have condoned her choices. In other words, Sand, d'Agoult, and Allart escaped the confining implications of republican patriarchy by constructing fathers who would have ratified their lifestyles and authorized their political opinions. In their writings and friendships with politically active men, they also each created a new version of republican women that endorsed equality in marriage and imagined intellectual women like themselves actively questioning the status quo and contributing to reform. Criticized in their day and often remembered by biographers separately from their politics, these three luminaries of the Parisian literary scene appear in Walton's essay freshly resurrected within a storyline that undercuts any hegemonic conception of republican motherhood.

If Rousseau dominated historians' accounts of republican patriarchy in the first half of the nineteenth century, the philosopher Auguste Comte, inventor of positivism and prophet of the dawn of social science, has worn the mantle of founding father for a more progressive republicanism after 1870 that linked a massive program of educational reform for girls to the survival of a French republic.[32] Mary Pickering's probing essay, "Clotilde de Vaux and the Search for Identity," offers a startling reassessment of Comte's relations with the woman around whose memory he would build his own profoundly gendered vision of human progress. Comte identified three stages of intellectual development in his account of humankind's historical search for truth that progressed from religious explanations through metaphysics to science. Only the last of these stages promised positive knowledge now and for the future. In Comte's sociology of knowledge, men took charge of enlightening the world through scientific discovery, but they needed intelligent women for spiritual and moral inspiration. After de Vaux's death in 1846, Comte's writings turned her into his ideal of womanhood for the positivist age. In striking contrast with Comte's Clotilde de Vaux, however, Pickering discovers a de Vaux performing in her private letters and her published novels in the guise of a belligerently independent, aspiring writer, locked in mortal combat with her famous admirer as well as with the members of her family for control over who she "really" was. In an ironic twist to which history often lends itself, de Vaux may win the battle in the end, with Pickering's help, but only by remaining indecipherable. As for Auguste Comte, his story emerges from this particular battle between the sexes embedded in another largely unknown tale about the singular importance women writers had within the Parisian literary, intellectual, and political elite in the 1830s and 1840s in exploring alternative relations of love and power between men and women with intellectual talent.[33]

After another popular revolution in 1848 that overturned Louis-Philippe and his July monarchy, the French experimented for the next thirty years with various means of governing themselves in the deeply divisive aftermath of the French Revolution. For a short time after 1848, France became a republic, until its elected president, the nephew of Napoleon, staged a coup d'état to create a second Napoleonic empire with himself as emperor. Louis-Napoleon's military defeat during the Franco-Prussian War led to the proclamation of another republic by Parisian revolutionaries in 1870. This Third French Republic teetered precariously on the edge of political collapse for nearly a decade while social democrats, moderate republicans, and supporters of three different dynastic claimants to the throne of France battled for supremacy. Finally, in 1877, the majority of Frenchmen opted definitively in national legislative elections for candidates supporting a republic.

The two final articles in our collection present women who developed public careers after this republican success. Their strategies for fashioning a female public self each reflect options and obstacles specific to the four decades leading up to World War I, when republican politicians, inspired partially by Comte's work, embraced a vast expansion of girls' public education to insure the loyalty of French women to the Republic only to discover, as an unintended effect, a dramatic increase in ambition among young bourgeois women. Beginning in the 1880s and 1890s, the presence of women from the elite in the work force or in public life threatened to deepen an already serious crisis of confidence in French masculinity born of military defeat in 1871. In her brilliantly argued "Acting Up: The Feminist Theatrics of Marguerite Durand," Mary Louise Roberts examines the tactics of the feminist journalist Marguerite Durand for overcoming the anxiety provoked by the "new woman" even as she defied the prevailing gendered social order by founding a daily newspaper with an entirely female staff. To disarm the fears of men in the profession, Durand performed her challenge to their prerogatives as men in the guise of a seductive bourgeois woman. Much criticized at the time by other feminists for her "feminism by seduction," Durand succeeded all the same in projecting a subversive version of the feminine. Her very seductiveness made it possible for contemporaries to tolerate the female journalist she invented, Roberts shows, while her professional performance undercut conventional views about the meaning of femininity. The larger project within which this essay fits asks a critically important question: how did the vast expansion of the commercialization of feminine images in the press and theaters of Paris from the 1880s on transform the possibilities for ordinary women to imagine a feminine self?

Elinor Accampo closes our collection with a sensitive portrait of the way one such outwardly conventional matron exploited the unprecedented range of doors open to audacious bourgeois women after the turn-of-the-century. A leading advocate of birth control, Nelly Roussel lectured all over France without a scandal, largely, Accampo claims, because she performed herself in the persona of a bourgeois mother concerned with improving marital relations and enriching family life and because her beauty, dress, and theatrical style also projected coded signs of femininity. This strategy was all the more important because her plea for the right to control fertility flew in the face of a widespread concern over the declining birthrate of the French that had produced both a multisided social policy focused on the family and a national discourse that connected motherhood with femininity. Even self-declared feminists accepted the importance of mothers to the nation. And yet the woman whom Accampo's discerning eye uncovers in "Private Life, Public Image: Motherhood and Militancy in the Self-Construction of Nelly Roussel, 1900–1922," faces yet another and more private issue. Roussel had to somehow harmonize her message with the fact that to deliver it, she had to spend months of every year apart from both her husband and her children. That she succeeded in this perceptual sleight-of-hand depended on the way she defined herself in relation to her cause and to attitudes toward mothering within her extended family that were far more common, I suspect, than historians have led us to believe. Roussel's example shows how various the possibilities for unconventional choices sometimes were in the actual living of a life and how little we often learn from generalizations about the feminine condition. Biography as a tool for breaking through our own encrusted expectations comes into its own with this bravura performance by both the author and her subject.

CONTEXTUALIZING CONSTRUCTIONS OF A FEMININE SELF IN FRANCE

All the same, generalizations do have a role to play in advancing our broader understanding of how men and women in historically specific times and particular social settings conceived the selves that they composed. We can even heuristically draw out from these essays some of the possibilities available to elite French women for performing selves in public that derive from the peculiarities of French political culture, from social and familial practices among the French elite, and from images and metaphors that were available to women at particular historical junctures in French politics. This discussion will suggest to some readers comparisons with options open to socially elite women elsewhere in Europe and in the United States in the nineteenth century. For those with knowledge of French history, this section seeks also to demonstrate the particular advantages offered by the new biography for integrating individual life stories over an entire century into the grand historical narratives familiar to us. The new biography will expand our historical understanding insofar as it contextualizes and historicizes the identities individual women put together to reveal their connection with established themes in the history of the period.

One characteristic feature of French political culture that affected the way several women in this study imagined themselves turns on a way of defining women in relation to the state that crystallized during the French Revolution and distinguished French conceptions of civic life from English liberalism. The radical nature of the French Revolution in 1789 partly explains this specificity. English rebels at the time of the

Glorious Revolution of 1688 simply took for granted the exclusion of women from English liberties that dated to the Magna Carta. French revolutionaries, by contrast, under the necessity of rewriting from scratch the legal script for society and state had to justify excluding women from the vote by theorizing the civic implications of sexual difference.[34] This they accomplished by imagining the family rather than the individual as the basic unit in the nation, jettisoning in the process the liberal version of a civil order based on individual rights, which might have one day applied to women as well. Instead, in this familial and gendered construction of the state, men performed the part of active citizens as voters and armed defenders of the nation, while women served the nation either indirectly through their roles in families or directly in civic life through tasks associated with domestic feminine work. This way of construing the nation, far from excluding women from civic life, positively legitimated their presence, if in very particular ways. Originating in the eighteenth century in a political outlook associated with Rousseau, this familial civic outlook in French liberalism underwent constant reinterpretations in the following century, as several articles in this collection suggest. But through all real or imaginary transformations, no artificial or conceptual barrier arose between the private duties and civic responsibilities of French women — only a prescriptive difference buttressed by the law in the way men and women were expected to behave and function in each setting.[35]

French familial culture also assisted elite women who wished to move from private into public life in the nineteenth century. In the first place, French inheritance law and testamentary practices often made elite French women exceedingly wealthy. Under the Napoleonic Civil Code, parents were obliged to give a share of their estates to daughters as well as sons; and though as wives, women lost control of this wealth unless otherwise stated in their marriage contracts, a widow not only regained control of her dowry but also received use rights to her deceased husband's properties if he so stipulated in his will, a common practice in the nineteenth century.[36] George Sand, about whom Walton writes, broke initially with her husband in 1830 when she discovered that due to his personal ire he left this customary stipulation out of his testament.[37] Separated, widowed, or divorced, therefore — the last not a choice between 1816 and 1884 — elite women were often independently wealthy, a fact crucial to crafting a public persona for Sand and d'Agoult, and, to a lesser extent for Allart, Tristan, and Durand.[38] As the deserted and defrauded de Vaux knew all too well when she turned, helpless in her poverty, to Comte, some independent wealth was the usual precondition for pursuing fame among respectable women.

Three other features of elite family life could assist women from the propertied elite seeking public prominence in this period. The small size of French families (by comparison to American and other European households), also reflected in the lives of women in this study, made mothering a less time-consuming task for French women than for mothers of the larger families elsewhere. By the 1870s, moreover, republican prescriptions for family life encouraged active parenting by fathers, which should have also lightened maternal burdens for some women.[39] Most important of all, perhaps, the overwhelming presence of family enterprises in all sectors of the economy meant that no sharp division existed between the world of business and the family in the way many husbands and wives defined their interests, whatever tasks they may have performed. Consequently, if the patriarchal rights given husbands over wives by Napoleon could lead to the brutality that Tristan, Allart, and Sand encountered in their marriages, some unpredictable mix of factors, conditioned by the particularities of French family practices, could also lead to the companionate marital style of Roussel and her husband for whom work and family, the private and the civic seemed to merge in a seamless expression of equality, free of some of the more expected gendered stereotypes.

No history of performing femininity in nineteenth-century France would be complete without considering the effect of the leisure pastimes of the French elite on that performance. Everywhere, but especially in Paris, leisure, whether pursued in private homes sheltered from the uninvited eye or displayed publicly at theaters or balls, involved elite women staging feminine selves before an audience made up partly, and sometimes predominantly, of men. In that regard, the tradition of the *salonnière* in Paris, which dated to the seventeenth century and retained legitimacy in political and literary circles until World War I, was particularly flush with possibilities.[40] The Parisian salon had never functioned for the performance of male talents only. However famous in the history of the Enlightenment for creating a mainly masculine space for philosophical discussions, from early on such gatherings also featured the hostess as a woman of ideas and often as a writer. Certainly d'Agoult, and to some degree Tristan, Sand, Allart, and Durand as well, situated themselves within the tradition of the *salonnière* who invited influential men and occasional women into their homes for conversations. De Vaux may have been too poor for such ambitions, but Comte clearly envisioned their relationship within that mold.

Like the salon, a long-standing love of theater also favored feminine performances among the French elite, though as the panoply of evidence presented here makes clear, the relationship between women and the stage evolved during the nineteenth century.[41] The professional actress, for example, however lionized for her talent by an admiring public, suffered long from the ostracism of polite female society. Under the Old Regime, the Catholic Church, with the full compliance of the state, had even prohibited marriage and sacred burial for such women. Nonetheless, no such taboo prevented well-bred women from performing on the stage at the French court, which was the royal household, or in other domestic settings for entertainment.[42] Despite Jean Jacques Rousseau's famous condemnation of the fictions of the stage, described by Roberts, this sort of private entertainment survived the revolution. In the 1820s, under the restored Bourbon monarchy, aristocratic hostesses and their guests often performed in theatrical productions presented in their country homes, sharing the stage with professional actors. During the regular social season in the capital, a passion for seeing and being seen took some women several times a week out to the theater.[43] Moreover, a related pastime of high society, masked balls, spread contagiously down the social scale after the Revolution of 1830 had displaced the aristocracy from political power.[44] The several disguises donned by the duchesse de Berry while in hiding in the Vendée and Tristan's brazen presence in the all-male galleries of the British Parliament, dressed up as a Turk, reflected this widely shared Parisian taste for masquerades that swept up women as well as men in the first half of the century.

The exceptional popularity of theater-going in Paris eventually prompted a few women writers to try to build a professional reputation of playwriting. Sand, d'Agoult, and, much later, Roussel, each experimented with this genre, though only Sand had any recognized success. Through the first half of the century, a career in acting remained unthinkable for upper-class women, lest they resemble in their own version of a Bohemian lifestyle, the kinds of lower-class women who frequented the Bohemian circles created in this period by impoverished bourgeois men.[45] Near the end of the century, however, as the youthful ambitions of Durand and Roussel suggest, acting, though still not quite respectable, had become an option for bourgeois women who wanted a professional career. It was a natural evolution in a leisure culture where playacting had long held a fascination for elite women and only awaited a change in social attitudes to permit a few of them to ascend to the professional stage.

In the course of that development, Roberts argues, the actress joined the woman writer in constructing fictional female characters through whom elite women might rethink their lives. Throughout the nineteenth century, fear that novels might seduce young women into acts of rebellion or sexual experimentation had obsessed conservative opinion.[46] The works of several women writers who appear in this collection were frequently accused of corrupting the morals of their female readers. At the end of the century, when theater-going in Paris reached the zenith of its popularity, the actress added something new to the critical reassessment that an artist's "fictions" might encourage in her audience. By performing with equal verisimilitude several feminine types, stars like Sarah Bernhardt could break down the idea of an essential woman for her adoring fans. The artifice involved in what it meant to be a woman, Roberts claims, could at last become apparent to her audience through the actress's own dramatic transformations. Of course, such a perception would not determine how any particular woman chose to represent her sex, whether in dialogue with herself or in relationship to other people, as Bernhardt's own deliberately excessive femininity attests.

One final way of contextualizing the performance of femininity by these eight women takes us to the metaphors through which they chose to present themselves and through which contemporaries interpreted their behavior. Here we enter the domain of historical analysis par excellence, tracking change over time. There is, however, nothing automatic or easy about that undertaking. The chronological organization adopted in this collection suggests the possibility of tracing continuity and change in the crafting of a public profile for a woman as the century advanced; but because a single metaphor will not carry the same meaning for different generations, for diverse contemporary audiences, or even for individual performers, a comparison over time is as potentially misleading as it is potentially productive of new insights. Having noted the risks, I shall proceed to some historical reflections, however provisionally advanced, on two striking images that some of these women used to project their voices into the public forum.

The first proclaimed a woman of especially remarkable literary talent to be a "genius." The very rarity of such individuals assured a woman so described by her intellectual peers and friends certain liberties denied to other women as unseemly. "Genius" stretched the boundaries of acceptable feminine behavior for women writers, without eliminating them altogether. George Sand, like her literary predecessor and only female rival for celebrity in the first half of the nineteenth century, Germaine de

Staël, used a recognition of her genius to justify her life and work.[47] Doing so, of course, did not protect either de Staël or Sand from the malice of their enemies.[48] All the same, alone among the numerous women writers of their day, these two publicly acknowledged female "geniuses" joined the pantheon of contemporary writers who had indisputable stature. Therein lies a paradox. For if genius, once acknowledged in a woman writer, gave her unofficial entree to the academy of great men that dominated French high culture, it also served to bar the way to other women. The rivalry with Sand that Clotilde de Vaux sought to establish through her novels, about which Pickering writes, originated in a logic adopted by male literary critics who guarded the gates to literary fame that pitted all women novelists and playwrights against the unique woman genius rather than against the work of noted writers of the other sex.[49]

"Genius" as a rhetorical device for honoring female writers did not survive into the second half of the nineteenth century in France. One might seek the explanation in the new and deeply gendered science of neurology that made it quite impossible for its adepts to imagine a female brain with the properties of genius.[50] But we can also trace the demise of the woman genius in the history of the literary salon. Without ever disappearing, this institution, which had sustained the fiction of the uniquely exceptional woman in the company of men, lost much of its importance once a vast expansion of the popular press had undercut the symbiotic relationship that existed between a highly concentrated world of writers, journalists, and publishers and a few notable salons. And once the avenues for literary self-promotion multiplied beyond what the salons of a few prominent individuals controlled, "genius" lost its efficacy as a label for defining women of accomplishment. It could no longer operate in the exclusionary way it had before, celebrating both the woman genius and the men whose company she kept. The infrastructure necessary for this transformation included a rebuilt Paris, crisscrossed with avenues and fancy apartments; the first department stores; daily papers with a mass circulation; and eventually, trains to every medium-sized town in France. This was the world that in the 1890s brought Marguerite Durand out of a political salon into journalism for the masses. Unwilling to depend on a small coterie of well-connected male friends to orchestrate her rise to prominence, Durand forced the world of journalists to take her measure by moving directly into the limelight as the editor of a daily paper of her own. A law passed in 1881 that ended a prohibition slapped on female journalists in 1851, denying them the right to direct a paper, paved the way for this unprecedented step as well.

This new France with its modern transportation system also permitted Nelly Roussel to take her lectures all over France throughout the Belle Epoque, a dream that in the unhealthy conditions of travel in the 1840s killed Flora Tristan within a few years. But Roussel and Tristan shared more than their embrace of causes that forced them into itinerant lifestyles. Each adopted an apostolic or similarly messianic idiom to describe her political activities. This strategy provides the second metaphor used to justify the presence of a woman in the public eye that leaps out of the biographies in this collection. Moreover, like the claim to "genius" for a woman, "apostolate" had a history as an enabling feminine descriptor linked to broader trends in French society and culture.

The idea of an apostolate outside the Catholic Church made its first appearance in the language of French civic life in the 1820s and early 1830s with the Saint-Simonians. From that time through the Second Republic, a succession of messianic movements of social and spiritual reform periodically inflamed French public life.[51] Flora Tristan did not have to create the idea of a socialist reformer in the guise of an "apostle" in the 1840s. She merely had to perform that persona in the body of a woman. By the 1890s, however, within a political lexicon that was otherwise still loaded with religious imagery, the rhetorical options for republicans denied certain sacred metaphors to men that women might continue to use. Thus, a political vocabulary that imagined schoolteachers for the republic carrying on the "sacred fire" or inspired by a "sacred faith" applied equally well to men and women as they advanced French civilization by teaching love for the republic in state schools. But within the civic vocabulary of republicans, "apostle" apparently acquired feminine connotations. The anticlericalism of republican politics, born of Catholic support for dynastic rule, could partly explain this taboo, but it also reproduced in political rhetoric the feminization of active religious practice in republican families, according to which only women and children went regularly to church. In contrast to "genius," which by the end of the century no longer could apply to women, in the metaphoric language of the republican Left, it appears that only females might perform "apostolates" in public life, an idea also expressed in the extraordinary popularity in this period of Joan of Arc, resurrected in the role of French patriot by even the republican Left. However emotionally satisfying the idea of her "apostolate" became for Nelly Roussel, it also served to sanction yet one more transgressive version of a feminine presence in civic life by associating her with a feminized symbolic order.

One final aspect of the performances recounted in these essays that also linked these women to their times involves the way they told their stories. A number of them used a melodramatic narrative line to dramatize themselves, whether they chose for their self-staging a novel, an autobiography, a diary, private letters, a photograph, or a carefully choreographed public act. Whatever the universe they imagined, they assumed one of two classic roles in melodrama for themselves: the heroic victim or the messenger bearing truths that others would deny. Only Marguerite Durand adopted irony to stage her public self, no doubt to soften and thereby render more effective her decidedly feminist challenge. Certainly in establishing who they were and what they wanted, the women featured here attracted controversy, but if we look carefully at their self-constructions, we also see in their embattled selves heroic postures of their own creation. The new biography does not require distance from the sympathy that such self-narrations might enlist, but it does not insist on an emotional response in readers either. What counts in this new form of telling people's lives is the recognition of the culturally constructed notion of a self and others and, also, of the fluidity of those constructions.

However coolly analytical our tone, as feminist historians, we do care how the story of individual women's struggles to disrupt and alter conventional notions of feminine behavior in the public eye turned out, for them and for later generations. Recently a major controversy has erupted between the American scholar and declared feminist Joan Scott and the self-styled antifeminist French scholar Mona Ozouf, each of whom has also authored a volume of essays on famous French women in modern France.[52] One dimension of their debate concerns the effectiveness of the republican notion of "equality in difference" to secure for French women real equality as individuals in public life. Scott maintains, both in her argument with Ozouf and in her study of the failure of French feminists to gain equality for women in civic life from the revolution through the 1930s, that the contradictions between liberalism's claim to speak for universal principles and feminists' unavoidable necessity of speaking for a distinct category of persons has produced an historical impasse in the arguments defending women's rights during the past two hundred years that may never be resolved as long as gender retains its cultural power to differentiate and categorize individuals in the discourse of public life.

Ozouf disagrees with that assessment. She claims that the principle of universality that public education spread and is now reflected in all French law, if not yet in social and political practice, can cohabit successfully with a national rhetoric that places gendered differences, together with heterosexual love and seduction, at the heart of what it means culturally to be French. Feminism, which she imagines crudely to be a club for bludgeoning men in the hands of American academics, is, also, in her view intrinsically foreign to the French. It should be apparent from this introduction that Ozouf's quest for a quintessential French identity is a scholarly enterprise at odds with the new biography as well as with the epistemological revolution from which it springs. And yet, all the women whose lives figure in our biographical essays would have agreed with Ozouf about the necessity of preserving gendered differences while expanding women's options, and they developed their public persona in accordance with that logic. Naturally, then, the questions raised by this debate are significant to the contributors to this collection of essays, but not in the same way they are for Ozouf and Scott because the scholarly issues we address differ in important ways from theirs.

As practitioners of the new biography, neither our methods nor our premises resemble those adopted by Ozouf. Whereas her vignettes sum up each woman in a single controlling attribute or outlook, our narratives take shape in keeping with our premises, namely that identities are mobile, contested, multiple constructions of the self and others that depend as much on context as any defining traits of character. We seek to mirror the reality of that proposition in the way we tell our stories. Furthermore, as biographers, we are concerned with the way individual women lived their lives creatively given the alternatives presented to them, which is not the subject of Scott's study because she focuses on the fate of leading feminists' ideas. Rather than debate the consequences since the revolution for women's rights of an ideological commitment to both universalism and sexual difference, which is what the debate between Ozouf and Scott concerns, our essays reflect upon the process of redefining what femininity meant along the way.

Collectively, the objectives of the authors are twofold. On the one hand, we seek to understand how the gendering of the settings in which these eight elite French women moved shaped their sense of self and the possibilities for performing feminine personae under public scrutiny. On the other hand, we propose to show how conceptualizing biography as constructions of selves pieced together by individuals and their observers from culturally legible notions of the feminine in a particular time and place can once again insert biography into general histories. In our conception of them, these famous women appear on the historical stage liberated from a storyline that confines them to the status of "exceptional women" to become, as well, prisms for observing shifts in the gendering of their worlds. In that configuration, biography can potentially alter the content of the master narratives we create in writing history. Should this collection of biographical essays change how historians of France recount the nineteenth century, it will fulfill our most ambitious goal.

NOTES

Our student collaborators and the two anonymous referees engaged by the University of California Press to critique earlier versions of this introduction were immensely helpful in producing the final product. I am particularly indebted to my co-contributors for the thoughtful dialogue in which we engaged as I crafted and recrafted these reflections on the significance of our collective effort. Bonnie Smith's and Ted Margadant's generosity, insights, and editorial advice were indispensable throughout the process. I am also grateful to Timothy Tackett for the opportunity to discuss my introduction with his graduate students at the University of California, Irvine, and with Helen Chenut and Caroline Ford, who participated in that seminar. Lynn Hunt's invaluable suggestions arrived just in time for my final revisions. I also wish to thank several colleagues at Santa Clara University who read this introduction as it progressed and continually refreshed my sense of the importance of the collection: Catherine Montfort, Nancy Unger, Robert Senkewicz, Sita Raman, and Barbara Molony. The enthusiasm for this project of two other friends and colleagues, Susan Mann and Barbara Metcalf, spurred me on as well. None of these several commentators nor the Press can be held responsible, of course, for any factual errors or questionable interpretations. Fortunately, the satisfaction did not conclude with the completion of the manuscript. The much anticipated pleasure of working with Sheila Levine as the editor for this book turned out to be everything her reputation led me to expect, while in Suzanne Knott and Ellen Browning I found, respectively, a model project editor and meticulous copyeditor.

    1. For reflections on the marginalization of biographers in the profession in the 1960s and 1970s and what has happened since, see Lloyd Moote, "New Bottles and New Wine: The Current State of Early Modernist Biographical Writing" *French Historical Studies,* Special Issue: Biography, 19, no. 4 (fall 1996), 911–26 and the introduction to Lloyd Kramer's *Lafayette in Two Worlds: Public Cultures and Personal Identities in an Age of Revolutions* (Chapel Hill: University of North Carolina Press, 1996), 1–16.
    2. This point is not to meant to dismiss the importance in laying the groundwork for the "new biography" of a few pathbreaking biographies of women in the 1970s and 1980s that examined the construction of gendered identities in relation to a range of activities, social organizations, and historically specific cultural

representations. See for example, Kathryn Kish Sklar, *Catharine Beecher: A Study in American Domesticity* (New Haven, Conn.: Yale University Press, 1973); Mary A. Hill, *Charlotte Perkins Gilman: The Making of a Radical Feminist, 1860–1896* (Philadelphia: University of Pennsylvania Press, 1980); and Jacqueline Dowd Hall, *Revolt against Chivalry: Jesse Daniel Ames and the Women's Campaign against Lynching* (New York: Columbia University Press, 1974).

3. For other discussions of the new biography, see Jo Burr Margadant, "The New Biography in Historical Practice," *French Historical Studies*, Special Issue: Biography, 19, no. 4 (fall 1996), 145–58; Linda Wagner-Martin, *Telling Women's Lives: The New Biography* (New Brunswick, N.J.: Rutgers University Press, 1994); Robert Folkenflik, ed., *The Culture of Autobiography: Constructions of Self-Representation* (Stanford: Stanford University Press, 1993); "Special Issue on Autobiography and Biography," *Gender and History* 2, no. 1 (spring 1990), 1–78; Carolyn Steedman, "La Théorie qui n'en est pas une: or Why Clio Doesn't Care," in *Feminist Revision History*, ed. Ann-Louise Shapiro (New Brunswick, 1994), 73–94; Bella Brodski and Celeste Schenck, eds., *Life/Lines: Theorizing Women's Autobiography* (Ithaca: Cornell University Press, 1988); Ira Bruce Nadel, *Biography: Fact, Fiction and Form* (New York: St. Martin's Press, 1984).

4. Stephen Greenblatt, *Renaissance Self-Fashioning; From More to Shakespeare* (Chicago: Chicago University Press, 1990); Natalie Zemon Davis, *The Return of Martin Guerre* (Cambridge, Mass.: Harvard University Press, 1983), and Natalie Zemon Davis, "On the Lame." In AHR Forum: "The Return of Martin Guerre" *American Historical Review* 93 (June 1988): 572–603.

5. Kali A. K. Israel, "Style, Strategy, and Self-Creation in the Life of Emilia Dilke," in *Constructions of the Self*, ed. George Levine (New Brunswick, N.J.: Rutgers University Press, 1992), 213–48; Jonathan Dewald, *Aristocratic Experience and the Origins of Modern Culture: France, 1570–1715* (Berkeley and Los Angeles: University of California Press, 1993), 69–145; Norbert Elias, *The Court Society*, trans. Edmund Jephcott (New York: Pantheon Books, 1983), 78–116; Michèle Longino Farrell, *Performing Motherhood: The Sévigné Correspondence* (Hanover, N.H.: University Press of New England, 1991).

6. Jürgen Habermas, *Transformation of the Public Sphere*, trans. Thomas Burger (Cambridge, Mass.: M.I.T. Press, 1989); Joan Landes, *Women and the Public Sphere in the Age of the French Revolution* (Ithaca: Cornell University Press, 1988); Dena Goodman, *The Republic of Letters: A Cultural History of the French Enlightenment* (Ithaca: Cornell University Press, 1994), 53–135, 253–280; Geneviève Fraisse, *Reason's Muse: Sexual Difference and the Birth of Democracy*, trans. Jane Marie Todd (Chicago: University of Chicago Press, 1994); William M. Reddy, *The Invisible Code: Honor and Sentiment in Postrevolutionary France, 1814–1848* (Berkeley and Los Angeles: University of California Press, 1997), 65–113; Geneviève Fraisse and Michelle Perot, eds. *A History of Women in the West*, vol. 4. *Emerging Feminism from Revolution to World War* (Cambridge, Mass.: Harvard Press, 1993), 9–114, 319–442.

7. For theoretical discussions of the way women have constructed public selves see Kali A. K. Israel, "Writing inside the Kaleidoscope: Re-Representing Victorian Women Public Figures," *Gender and History* 2, no. 1 (spring 1990):

40–48; Kali A. K. Israel, "Kaleidoscopic Lives and Genres of Biography" in "Drawing from Life: Art, Work, and Feminism in the Life of Emilia Dilke (1840–1940), Ph.D. diss., Graduate School-New Brunswick, Rutgers, the State University of New Jersey, 1992, 1–52; Carolyn G. Heilbrun, *Writing a Woman's Life* (New York: Norton, 1988); Linda Wagner-Martin, *Telling Women's Lives;* Brodzki and Schenck, eds., *Life/Lines;* The Personal Narratives Group, Jay Webster et al., *Interpreting Women's Lives: Feminist Theory and Personal Narratives* (Bloomington: Indiana University Press, 1989); Shari Benstock, ed., *The Private Self: Theory and Practice of Women's Autobiographical Writing* (Chapel Hill: University of North Carolina Press, 1994).

8. We are indebted in a general way for this approach to the suggestive work of Judith Butler, especially her *Gender Trouble: Feminism and the Subversion of Identity* (New York: Routledge, 1990), but as historians attuned to the weight of changing material conditions, traumatic events, cultural borrowing, and even memory on the historical possibilities for mutable cultural meanings, we emphasize the multiplicity of the conditions within which individuals assume identities for themselves and in the eyes of others.

9. For the effects of this materialist interpretation on the Annales school of historical writing under the influence of Fernand Braudel, see several articles in Jacques Revel and Lynn Hunt, eds., *Histories: French Constructions of the Past,* vol. 1, *Postwar French Thought,* trans. Arthur Goldhammer and others (New York: New Press, 1995).

10. The two most influential anthropologists who shaped the way cultural historians now conceptualize the past are Marshall Sahlins, *Islands of History* (Chicago: University of Chicago Press, 1985) and Clifford Geertz, "Deep Play: Notes on the Balinese Cockfight," *The Interpretations of Cultures* (New York: Basic Books, 1973) and Clifford Geertz, "Blurred Genres: The Refiguration of Social Thought," *Local Knowledge: Further Essays in Interpretive Anthropology* (New York: Basic Books, 1983). See also "The Fate of 'Culture': Geertz and Beyond," Special Issue, ed. Sherry B. Ortner, *Representations* 59 (summer 1997).

11. Jacques Derrida, *Of Grammatology,* trans. Gayatri Chakravorty Spivak (Baltimore: Johns Hopkins Press, 1974); Hayden White, *The Content of the Form: Narrative Discourse and Historical Representation* (Baltimore: Johns Hopkins Press, 1987); Michel Foucault, *The Order of Things: An Archaeology of the Human Sciences* (New York: Vintage, 1973) and *The History of Sexuality,* vol. 1, *An Introduction,* trans. Robert Hurley (New York: Pantheon Books, 1978). See also by Foucault, *Language, Counter-Memory, Practice,* trans. Donald F. Bouchard and Sherry Simon (Ithaca: Cornell University Press, 1977); *Discipline and Punish: The Birth of the Prison,* trans. Alan Sheridan (New York: Pantheon Books, 1979); *Power/Knowledge: Selected Interviews and Other Writings, 1972–1977,* trans. Colin Gordon (New York: Pantheon Books, 1980).

12. For lucid discussions of the implications of critical studies for historians, see Joyce Appleby, Lynn Hunt, and Margaret Jacob, *Telling the Truth about History* (New York: Norton, 1994), and Joyce Appleby, "The Power of History," Presidential Address, *American Historical Review* 103, no. 1 (February 1998): 1–14.

13. E. P. Thompson, *The Making of the English Working Class* (New York: Vintage, 1966).

14. Gareth Stedman Jones, *Languages of Class: Studies in English Working-Class History, 1832–1982* (Cambridge, Eng.: Cambridge University Press, 1983); Joan Scott, "On Language, Gender, and Working-Class History," in *Gender and the Politics of History,* edited by Judith Butler and Joan Scott (New York: Columbia University Press, 1988), 53–67. See also Dror Wahrman, *Imagining the Middle Class: The Political Representation of Class in Britain, c. 1780–1840* (Cambridge, Eng.: Cambridge University Press, 1995).

15. Ann-Louise Shapiro, "History and Feminist Theory," *Feminists Revision History* (New Brunswick, N.J.: Rutgers University Press, 1994), 1–23.

16. Lorraine Bethel, "What Chou Mean *We,* White Girl? or the Colored Lesbian Feminist Declaration of Independence (Dedicated to the Proposition that All Women are Not Equal, i.e., Identically Oppressed," *Conditions: Five* 2, no. 2 (autumn 1979): 86–92.

17. Jennifer Terry, "Theorizing Deviant Historiography," in *Feminist Revision History,* ed. Ann-Louise Shapiro, 276–303.

18. Joan Scott, "Introduction," *Gender and the Politics of History,* 1–11; Denise Riley, *Am I That Name? Feminism and the Category of 'Woman'* (Minneapolis: University of Minnesota, 1988); Marianne Hirsch and Evelyn Fox Keller, *Conflicts in Feminism* (New York: Routledge, 1990); Laura Lee Downs, "If 'Woman' Is Just an Empty Category, Then Why Am I Afraid to Walk Alone at Night? Identity Politics Meets the Postmodern Subject," *Comparative Studies in Society and History* 35 (1993): 414–43; Joan W. Scott, "The Tip of the Volcano," *Comparative Studies in Society and History,* 35 (1993): 438–43; Laura Lee Downs, "Reply to Joan Scott," *Comparative Studies in Society and History* 35 (1993): 444–51.

19. Sherry B. Ortner, "Rank and Gender," *Making Gender: The Politics and Erotics of Culture* (Boston: Beacon Press, 1996); Gerda Lerner, *The Creation of Patriarchy* (New York: Oxford University Press, 1986), 212–17.

20. Joan Scott, "Gender: A Useful Category of Historical Analysis," *Gender and the Politics of History,* 28–52; R. W. Connell, "The Big Picture: Masculinities in Recent World History," *Theory and Society* 22 (1993): 597–623; David M. Halperin, "Is There a History of Sexuality?" in *The Lesbian and Gay Studies Reader,* Henry Abelove, Michèle Aina Barale, and David M. Halperin (New York: Routledge, 1993), 416–31.

21. Teresa de Lauretis, ed. *Feminist Studies/Critical Studies* (Bloomington: Indiana University Press, 1986). Mary Childers and Bell Hooks, "A Conversation about Race and Class" and Katie King, "Producing Sex, Theory, and Culture: Gay/Straight Remappings in Contemporary Feminism," in *Conflicts in Feminism,* ed. Marianne Hirsch and Evelyn Fox Keller, 60–81, 82–101.

22. I am indebted for this point to Lynn Hunt's and Victoria Bonnell's suggestive introduction to their edited volume *Beyond the Cultural Turn* (Berkeley and Los Angeles: University of California Press, 1999), which I was able to consult before its publication.

23. For examples of this rapidly developing scholarship, see Michael T. Taussig, *Mimesis and Alterity: A Particular History of the Senses* (New York:

Routledge, 1993); Barbara D. Metcalf, "What Happened in Mecca: Mumtaz Mufti's 'Labbaik,'" in *The Culture of Autobiography: Constructions or Self-Representation*, ed. Robert Folkenflik (Stanford: Stanford University Press, 1993), 149–67; Gina Buijs, ed., *Migrant Women: Crossing Boundaries and Changing Identities* (Oxford: Berg, 1993); Simon Gikandi, *Maps of Englishness: Writing Identity in the Culture of Colonialism* (New York: Columbia University Press, 1996); Hilary Pilkington, *Migration, Displacement and Identity in Post-Soviet Russia* (New York: Routledge, 1998); Peter Sahlins, *Boundaries: The Making of France and Spain in the Pyrenees* (Berkeley and Los Angeles: University of California Press, 1989); Linda Colley, *Britons: Forging the Nation, 1707–1837* (New Haven: Yale University Press, 1992); Patrick Williams and Laura Chrismen, eds., *Colonial Discourse and Post-Colonial Theory: A Reader* (New York: Harvester Wheatsheaf, 1993); Jean Comaroff and John L. Comaroff, *Of Revelation and Revolution: Christianity, Colonialism and Consciousness in South Africa* (Chicago: University of Chicago, 1991); Inderpal Grewal and Caren Kaplan, "Introduction: Transnational Feminist Practices and Questions of Postmodernity," in *Scattered Hegemonies. Postmodernity and Transnational Feminist Practices* (Minneapolis: University of Minnesota, 1994), 1–33.

24. Joan W. Scott, "The Evidence of Experience," *Critical Inquiry*, 17, no. 4 (summer 1991): 773–97.

25. George Levine, ed., *Constructions of the Self* (New Brunswick, N.J.: Rutgers University Press, 1992). For other references see notes 2, 3, and 5 above. For theorizing the performance of gender, see Judith Butler, *Gender Trouble: Feminism and the Subversion of Identity; Bodies that Matter: On the Discursive Limits of 'Sex'* (New York: Routledge, 1993), and *The Psychic Life of Power: Theories in Subjection* (Stanford: Stanford University Press, 1997).

26. See the recent forum "Critical Pragmatism, Language, and Cultural History: on Roger Chartier's *On the Edge of the Cliff* in *French Historical Studies*, 21, no. 2 (spring 1998): 231–64; Gérard Noiriel, *Sur la "crise" de l'histoire* (Paris: Belin, 1996); and Victoria Bonnell and Lynn Hunt, eds. *Beyond the Cultural Turn*.

27. On the need for gendered master narratives in European history, see Lynn Hunt, "Deconstruction of Categories and Reconstruction of Narratives in Gender History," in *Gender History and General History*, ed. Anne-Charlotte Trepp and Hans Medick (Göttinger Gespräche zur Geschichtswissenschaft) (forthcoming). If we acknowledge, as Hunt does, that in historical writing, master narratives are always provisional, incomplete, and constructed to a political purpose, then it is high time that the mounting evidence from scholarship on women and gender begin to reshape the stories that we tell about the past. Several of the articles in this collection present new material that could be incorporated into a revision of the history of nineteenth-century France.

28. Robert A. Nye, *Masculinity and Male Codes of Honor in Modern France* (New York: Oxford University Press, 1993), 47–71; Reddy, *The Invisible Code*, 65–113.

29. Joan Scott, *Only Paradoxes to Offer: French Feminists and the Rights of Man* (Cambridge, Mass.: Harvard University Press, 1996).

30. Geneviève Fraisse, *Reason's Muse: Sexual Difference and the Birth of Democracy*.

31. Michèle Riot-Sarcey, *La démocratie à l'épreuve des femmes. Trois figures critiques du pouvoir, 1830–1848* (Paris: Albion, 1994).

32. Zeldin, *France 1848–1945, vol. 1, Ambition, Love and Politics* (Oxford: Oxford University Press, 1973), 260, 345, 353, 624, 658 and 2; vol. 2, *Intellect, Taste and Anxiety* (Oxford: Oxford University Press, 1977), 27, 157, 215, 595–600; Mary Pickering, *Auguste Comte: An Intellectual Biography*, vol. 1 (Cambridge, Mass.: Harvard University Press, 1993); Sarah Kofman, *Aberrations: Le devenir-femme d'Auguste Comte* (Paris: Aubier-Flammarion, 1978).

33. See Reddy, *The Invisible Code*, 3, 38–40, 46, 51–71, 230. Reddy argues that women novelists assumed this role as early as the seventeenth century.

34. Jean Bethke Elshtain, *Public Man, Private Woman: Women in Social and Political Thought* (Princeton: Princeton University Press, 1981), 147–70; Carole Pateman, *The Sexual Contract* (Stanford: Stanford University Press, 1988), 97–102; Mona Ozouf, *Women's Words: Essay on French Singularity*, trans. Jane Marie Todd (Chicago: University of Chicago Press, 1997), 229–83; Joan Scott, "The Uses of Imagination: Olympe de Gouges in the French Revolution," in *Only Paradoxes to Offer*, 19–56. The specificity of the French case has been noted repeatedly by Karen Offen and most recently in her comparative European study *European Feminisms, 1700–1950: A Political History* (Stanford: Stanford University Press, forthcoming). Jan Lewis argues that early republicanism in the United States at the time of the revolution resembled that of France but that a rhetoric of separate male and female spheres came to dominate American political ideology and rhetoric in the nineteenth century. "Motherhood and the Construction of the Male Citizen in the United States, 1750–1850" in *Constructions of the Self*, ed. George Levine, 143–64.

35. I agree entirely with this point in Mona Ozouf's controversial concluding chapter, "Essay on French Singularity," in *Women's Words*, 229–83. See also Suzanne Desan, " 'War between Brothers and Sisters': Inheritance Law and Gender Politics in Revolutionary France," *French Historical Studies*, 20, no. 4 (fall 1997): 632–34.

36. See Margaret H. Darrow, *Revolution in the House: Family, Class, and Inheritance in Southern France, 1775–1825* (Princeton: Princeton University Press, 1989) and Adeline Daumard, *La Bourgeoisie parisienne de 1815 à 1848* (Paris: S.E.V.P.E.N., 1963), 335–36.

37. Whitney Walton, *Eve's Proud Descendants; Four Women Writers and Republican Politics in Nineteenth-Century France* (Stanford: Stanford University Press, 2000). I am indebted to Whitney for allowing me to read this important manuscript before its publication.

38. In 1792 the revolutionaries introduced a liberal divorce law that made incompatibility a grounds for divorce and did not privilege men's rights over children or property in the dissolution of a marriage. The Napoleonic Civil Code also permitted divorce but made seeking a divorce much more difficult for women than for men and privileged fathers' rights over maternal rights to children. In 1816, under the Bourbon Restoration, divorce became once again illegal, though men or women could sue for a separation that included a legal separation

of their properties. In 1884, divorce became legal again, although not easy to obtain. See Roderick Phillips, *Putting Asunder: A History of Divorce in Western Society* (Cambridge, Eng.: Cambridge University Press, 1988).

39. Philip Nord, *The Republican Moment: Struggles for Democracy in Nineteenth-Century France* (Cambridge, Mass.: Harvard University Press, 1995), 218–44.

40. Ozouf, *Women's Words*; Dena Goodman, *The Republic of Letters*, 53–135; Carolyn C. Lougee, *"Le Paradis des Femmes": Women, Salons, and Social Stratification in Seventeenth-Century France* (Princeton: Princeton University Press, 1976); Londa Schiebinger, *The Mind Has No Sex? Women in the Origins of Modern Science* (Cambridge, Mass.: Harvard University, 1989); William M. Reddy, *The Invisible Code*, 1–64.

41. The English upper class also pursued this pastime with a passion in the nineteenth century.

42. Thomas E. Kaiser, "Madame de Pompadour and the Theaters of Power," *French Historical Studies*, 19, no. 4 (fall 1996): 1025–44. Under Louis XVI, even Marie Antoinette took part in theatrical performances at the court.

43. Anne Martin-Fugier, *La vie élégant ou la formation du Tout-Paris, 1815–1848* (Paris: Fayard, 1990), 291–324.

44. Alain Faure, *Paris Carême-prenant: du carnaval à Paris au XIXe siècle* (Paris: Hachette, 1978).

45. Jerrold Seigel, *Bohemian Paris: Culture, Politics, and the Boundaries of Bourgeois Life, 1830–1930* (New York: Viking, 1987). For the most recent scholarship on French actresses, see Lenard R. Berlanstein, "Women and Power in Eighteenth-Century France: Actresses at the Comédie Française," *Feminist Studies*, 20, no. 3 (fall 1994): 474–506 and "Britches and Breeches: Cross-Dressed Theater and the Culture of Gender Ambiguity in Modern France," *Comparative Studies in Society and History*, 38 (April 1996): 338–70.

46. Jann Matlock, *Scenes of Seduction: Prostitution, Hysteria, and Reading Difference in Nineteenth-Century France* (New York: Columbia University Press,, 1994), 199–219.

47. See Bonnie G. Smith, "History and Genius: The Narcotic, Erotic, and Baroque Life of Germaine de Staël," *French Historical Studies*, Special Issue: Biography, 19, no. 4 (fall 1996), 1059–81 and *The Gender of History: Men, Women and Historical Practice* (Cambridge, Mass.: Harvard, 1998).

48. Janis Bergman-Carton, *The Woman of Ideas in French Art, 1830–1848* (New Haven, Conn.: Yale University Press, 1995).

49. Using George Sand as a measure of other women writers' merits was a regular feature of journalists' reviews of books and plays from the late 1830s through the 1840s in literary reviews in *les Débats* and *le National*.

50. I am grateful to Susan Ashley for the following references: J. (de Tours) Moreau, *La psychologie morbide dans ses rapports avec la philosophie de l'histoire ou de l'influence des neuropathies sur le dynamisme intellectuel* (Paris, 1859) and Moreau, *De la folie hystérique et de quelques phénomènes nerveux propres à l'hystérie* (Paris, 1865); Max Nordau, *Psycho-physiologie du génie et du talent*, trans. Auguste Dietrich (Paris, 1897) and Nordau, *Degeneration*, 7th ed. (New York, 1895).

51. Riot-Sarcey, *La démocratie à l'épreuve des femmes;* Christopher Johnson, *Utopian Communism in France* (Ithaca: Cornell University Press, 1974).

52. Scott, *Only Paradoxes to Offer;* and Ozouf, *Women's Words.* The debate among several French and American historians of France, including Joan Scott, was occasioned by Ozouf's book and appeared in *Le Débat,* no. 87, (Nov.–Dec. 1995), 117–46.

The Duchesse de Berry
and Royalist Political Culture
in Postrevolutionary France

JO BURR MARGADANT

After an exceedingly shaky start, interrupted by the brief return of Napoleon in 1815, the restored Bourbon dynasty managed to hold onto the throne of France for a mere decade and a half. In July of 1830, a popular revolution brought it down in three days of street fighting in Paris. The very rapidity of that collapse exposed the shallow roots of the monarchy's support within the capital. Of course, a foolhardy plan to alter the constitution by royal fiat had triggered the uprising, but the isolation of the court and dynasty in Paris, notably from the upper classes, arose as well out of longer-term miscalculations. Both in configuring their court and in representations of the royal family, the Bourbons sought to legitimate their rule with outdated cultural scripts. In the first place, the strategy they adopted for representing the cultural world of the court undermined it as a fashionable center for the capital's elite, reopening a rift between the court and Paris that had destroyed the Old Regime. Equally damaging, though less obviously so, the Bourbons projected a dynastic image out of keeping with the domesticity of the upper classes, including even the aristocracy. In particular, mothering, the most powerful of the domestic symbols of bourgeois culture, eluded the Bourbons' version of a royal household.[1] As a result, familial metaphors deployed by the dynasty to legitimate its rule resonated only weakly with the wider public.

Through the life of the duchesse de Berry, the mother of the heir to the Bourbon throne, both shortcomings of the regime's self-presentation come sharply into focus. As a young widow in the 1820s, the duchess set out to create a personal following for herself within the Parisian upper classes. This project distinguished her in cultural style from her in-laws. At the same time, she performed her role as royal mother within the limits that an outdated maternal role imposed upon her. Her popular success throughout the Restoration and her complete political inconsequence at the moment of the July Revolution suggest at once the possibilities for a royal style more open to the fashions of the city and the limitations of the part assigned to royal mothers by the Bourbons. Later, after the fall of the regime, when the duchesse de Berry returned from exile to France to raise an insurrection on her son's behalf, her life became a story, written and rewritten by rival political factions as well as by herself, about what constituted royal motherhood. Only at this point did she become a politically potent royal symbol, dangerous for the new regime and compelling for supporters of the Bourbons. To follow the trajectory of her life and the efforts of various voices to give it meaning, therefore, is to discover afresh not only the failings of the Restoration monarchy but also the opportunities missed. This essay shows how attention to the meanings of gender and cultural life revealed through the life of the duchesse de Berry both reshapes the history of the Restoration monarchy and turns the Revolution of 1830 into a watershed for the meaning of motherhood in royalist political culture in nineteenth-century France.

   The problem of how to situate the court in relation to Paris was not a new development in royal history. Louis XIV concluded from the eruption of the Fronde in Paris in the 1650s that the court needed protection from the city. Having moved to Versailles, he created there a court society so exclusive and prestigious that no other social center could challenge its prerogative as an arbiter of taste.[2] Paris successfully disputed this monopoly in the Enlightenment. Later, the revolution returned the court to Paris and then destroyed the monarchy, but that ephemeral republican triumph did not alter expectations about the functioning of a court. During the empire, with Paris now the capital, Napoleon revived the court as a locus of fashionable display, this time for a composite elite made up of new aristocrats, high military officers, and those among the prerevolutionary nobles whom he managed to win over.[3] Glamour at the court remained an indispensable tool of domination over Parisian high society. Despite a widely held contrary impression, Louis XVIII and Charles X apparently understood the necessity of linking a socially diverse elite to court society.[4] They failed to grasp, however, the singular importance of exploiting both the court and city as venues for parading the social world of high society in Paris under royal auspices in a way that would identify the monarchy with the cultural dynamism of its own elite. The same could not be said for the duchesse de Berry, whose own strategy for representing royalty would temporarily overcome the cultural gulf between the monarchy and the more self-consciously inventive urban culture of the city. In the end, though, this difference played into the hands of critics of Charles X as a confirmation in cultural style of his hopelessly reactionary political views.[5]

The second, and this time almost totally unexamined, weakness in the Bourbons' self-presentation lay in the realm of family symbols. Recent research on the uses of familial metaphors for state building in France has produced two major new interpretations. Sarah Hanley argues that the absolutist monarchy of the sixteenth century evolved out of a family pact between the monarch and the nobility to consolidate control over patrilineal property by excluding women from the inheritance of land as well as from the throne and to justify their exclusion from the throne under a supposedly ancient but, in fact, entirely fictitious Salic law. This family pact rested on the belief that semen alone produced a child and, hence, provided physical legitimization for patrilineal descent. No discovery in eighteenth-century reproductive science at variance with that view could dislodge such a politically useful claim.[6] Lynn Hunt's work on familial metaphors in the French Revolution, by contrast, links mutating images of the father to new expectations for monarchical rule in France.[7] As a paternalistic image replaced a patriarchal ideal in eighteenth-century literary versions of fatherhood, kings had to become good fathers to be accepted as "real" fathers in the eyes of the French people. The execution of Louis XVI occurred metaphorically, therefore, within a family romance that pitted ill-treated sons against a bad father who had failed the paternity test by conspiring with counterrevolutionary and foreign enemies. With the father gone, moreover, all brothers and sisters had a right to inherit some portion of the family property. The execution of the queen, interpreted by Hunt as the resolution of a psychocultural crisis triggered by the killing of the father, permitted a return to patriarchy within each legally equal household of the Republic. Precisely how Napoleon picked his way through this minefield of familial metaphors under the empire has yet to be researched, but Louis XVIII and Charles X took the throne of France in the belief that nothing fundamental in benevolent dynastic patriarchy had changed, least of all the position of a royal mother.

The traditional Bourbon script for royal mothers imagined them exclusively as birth mothers, never as caretakers for their sons and daughters. Once delivered of a child, a royal mother relinquished the task of nourishing and nurturing to female guardians chosen by the king, until at the age of five, sons passed from the supervision of women into the hands of men. The one exception to this familial arrangement might occur when a king left his realm temporarily to wage war or a son fell heir to the throne while under age. In such cases, if selected to be regent, a royal mother would acquire along with royal power ultimate authority over royal offspring.

This version of motherhood contrasted sharply with the image of the nurturing mother that Rousseau had sponsored and that had spread in Germany and England by the early nineteenth century from the bourgeoisie to the aristocracy and even into royal households.[8] Although Simon Shama concluded from official portraits in the empire that Napoleon, like French kings before the revolution, eschewed a domestic style of royal iconography to avoid the ridicule of the old aristocracy in Paris, Margaret Darrow has argued, based on memoirs from the 1820s, that the aristocrats who went into exile with the Bourbons returned converted to mothering as a feminine ideal.[9] Thus, in her diary from the 1820s, the duchesse de Maillé recorded with unabashed pride her presence at the prize ceremony ending her sons' academic year and reminisced about tender summers spent together in the family château; similarly, the memoirs from the 1830s of the comtesse de Boigne allude to aristocratic hostesses in the Faubourg Saint-Germain whose salons were filled with children.[10] A powerfully emotive new persona had clearly made her way into the homes of high-placed Parisian families whom the Bourbons' familial symbols would patently ignore. Using gender as a category of analysis, to repeat Joan Scott's now famous admonition, exposes unsuspected tensions, therefore, in the monarchical alternative offered by the Restoration.[11]

The duchesse de Berry offers more than a mere barometer for tracking cultural change: she herself imparted a distinctive inflection to conflicts over royal images.[12] Too often recent studies of political culture in monarchical Europe have lost sight of the contingency of personality in shaping public battles over royal persons and the narratives or metaphors that they embody.[13] As argued here, the contradictions between the Restoration monarchy's self-presentation and the expectations of its varied publics opened a space in which the young duchess could act. Nonetheless, the duchesse de Berry's own intentions for her actions are not the main issue in this essay. Its focus rests on the interplay between her actions and the meanings varied audiences sought to give them. That she could only partially influence how others perceived her demonstrates an important underlying premise, namely, that public space is always a dynamic intersection where various participants strive to fasten meaning on individuals and events. In such contests, public figures cannot control the meanings assigned to their persona, but they do set the parameters of plausible interpretations for their actions. Throughout this analysis, therefore, the duchesse de Berry appears in a dual guise, both as creator of her public self and as a mutable symbol of royal motherhood that supporters and opponents of the Bourbons manipulated to define themselves and disparage rivals.

When the seventeen-year-old Neopolitan princess from the Kingdom of Two Sicilies arrived in France in April 1816, already married by proxy to the duc de Berry, a man twenty-one years her senior, she unquestionably embodied memories of past Bourbon brides. Like them, and even more than most, she brought to France a womb on which all hopes for continuing the dynasty depended. Royalist prints sold in Paris before she came depicted her within a botanical metaphor as the rose on a lily's stem, the Bourbons' emblem, announcing her reproductive role.[14] As potential mother for a sacred birth, she also starred in a long ritual of welcome that began in the towns and cities through which she passed on her northward journey from Marseilles, continued when she met the royal family in the forest of Fontainebleau, and culminated with a royal entry into Paris. Throughout this ritualized greeting, gestures on all sides conformed to carefully prescribed rules as if to emphasize her coming as a consecrated act.[15] To that end also, the king arranged for the royal family to greet Marie-Caroline in the same clearing where, as the comte de Provence, he had met his own bride in 1773. On this occasion as on all others, the Bourbons relied on royal etiquette drawn from the repertoire of Versailles to reinstate the sacred nature of their dynasty.

However, parallel to this public version of Marie-Caroline's arrival and unbeknownst to the king, the duc de Berry had been inventing secretly for his new bride another scenario of welcome. In private letters crafted in a romantic style of courtship, the duke had been wooing her by courier for weeks. Highly stylized at first, these courtly letters rapidly assumed another tone as specific details about her personal tastes began to reach him.[16] Having heard that she liked hunting, he wrote that he had purchased horses for her and promised that they would hunt together. When he also learned that she enjoyed the theater and music, he offered Paris as a continual source of entertainment. He worried that she would find him older and uglier than his portrait and once even used the familiar "tu" form of address. Drawing back from such audacity, he apologized for revealing his feelings toward her so forthrightly. When she replied in kind, the royal couple sealed themselves into a romantic pact. Very quickly the rules of outdated royal forms became its target. The duke warned that the king forbade such intimacy in his presence. Etiquette honored by the court kept him from rushing south to meet her as his heart urged him to do. Worse still, at their initial meeting as precedent prescribed, the king, smelling of tobacco, would kiss her first. Such warnings and avowals, however artfully contrived, spoke from a register of feeling far removed from the prerevolutionary expectations for a royal marriage. Theirs, the duke appeared to promise, would be a sentimental union and, as such, a mock conspiracy against the Restoration court.

The personal histories of both the teenage princess and the middle-aged duke had prepared each in different ways for this manner of self-dramatization. Neither had been raised in the hothouse atmosphere of a ceremonious court. The duc de Berry escaped at age twelve into exile, where, after several years vagabonding from court to court in search of military action and pleasure, he ended up in London. There he made a name for himself as a womanizer and fan of opera. He also established a quasi-domestic relationship with an English woman named Amy Brown who, with two daughters fathered by the duke, followed him after 1814 to Paris.[17] Marie-Caroline's childhood was in some ways equally tumultuous.[18] Her mother, the wife of the heir to the throne of Two Sicilies, died when she was three. In 1798, fearing a French invasion, the court fled briefly to Sicily. Forced to flee Napoleonic armies once again in 1805, this time the court remained in Palermo several years. Growing up in Sicily, the young Marie-Caroline learned the local dialect, avoided her studies whenever possible, and developed a deep love for the sea.[19] Napoleon's defeat by the concert of Europe in 1814 took the Sicilian Bourbons back to Naples. For all their difference in age, then, the Berrys shared remarkably similar personal histories born of war and revolution that placed them in sensibility and outlook in the romantic generation.

That generation had no other representative at the Bourbon court. The rest of the royal family consisted of the childless Louis XVIII; the comte d'Artois, his brother and father of the duc de Berry; the duc d'Angoulême, Berry's impotent older brother; and Angoulême's wife, who was also the daughter of Marie-Antoinette and Louis XVI and the only member of the former royal family to have escaped alive from prison. Collectively, these four Bourbons also formed a generation marked by war and revolution. However, trauma rather than a sense of personal autonomy accompanied the shattering of the prerevolutionary world for them. Under the influence of a Catholic revival that swept up many deeply shaken members of the aristocracy, the comte d'Artois, a hedonistic prince before the revolution, had vowed himself to celibacy in 1804. The duchesse d'Angoulême, the other devout member of the Restoration court and, in her friends' eyes, the incarnation of Catholic charity, was also the family member whose unsmiling demeanor most visibly manifested the emotional wounds inflicted by the revolution's fury on them all.[20] As for the king, he defended himself against the upturning of a world he had known into his forties by reinstating it, which meant resurrecting at the Tuileries the rituals and etiquette of the court of Versailles. To say that the Berrys defined themselves against this elaborately ceremonial court and its commitment to remembering would exaggerate the particularity of their position. Nonetheless, the personal style of both husband and wife as well as of the life they chose to lead together placed them in a distinctive orbit around the court linked to the spectacle of pleasure staged by high society in Paris.

It was not only in relation to the court that the Berrys situated them-selves in their pursuit of pleasure in the capital. The theatricality of Parisian leisure in the 1820s derived to a considerable extent from divi-sions within the upper class that pitted rival social groups against each other in a daily competition for social turf and fashionable display. The character of different residential neighborhoods inscribed these rivalries onto the city's map.[21] On the left bank of the Seine, the Faubourg Saint-Germain still housed, as it had since the seventeenth century, the aristo-cratic families most closely connected to the court. It was this social circle which, under much of the Restoration monarchy, set the fashion-able pace for Paris.[22] On the right bank of the Seine, the Faubourg Saint-Honoré remained an aristocratic stronghold as it had been since the eighteenth century, while the once opulent but now unstylish Marais in the city's center boasted just a few aristocratic families. The most dynamic residential quarter lay to the north of the western boulevards on the Chaussée d'Antin where banking families like that of James de Rothschild built lavish homes alongside other magnates of the capital's growing wealth on the lookout for a smart address. The occasional salon or private party might bring the social worlds of the Faubourg Saint-Germain and the Chaussée d'Antin together. Festivities at court, remark-ably infrequent under Louis XVIII, included representatives from all these worlds but did not fuse them, since specially honored guests invariably came from old aristocratic families.[23] Only the pursuit of pleasure in the city and the performance it involved brought these diverse social circles into frequent visual contact, which is where they might also frequently have encountered the duc and duchesse de Berry.

Just as promised in their courtship, the duke led his eager bride into a world of pleasurable diversions outside the confines of the court.[24] Their residence facilitated such a lifestyle, for though the king insisted on their presence at the Tuileries for dinner and ceremonial occasions, the Berrys made their home at the Elysée-Bourbon Palace in the middle of the Faubourg Saint-Honoré. Inevitably, as socialites within the city, the Berrys had to locate themselves in relation to the rival coteries that graced it. Social markers depended only partly on the company they kept. Where and how the royals entertained themselves also emitted signals to a finely tuned Parisian public, which quickly recognized their bid for fashionable ascendance. Occasionally, the duke appeared on horseback alongside the duchess when she joined the daily afternoon parade of fashionable carriages along the avenue de Neuilly, later named the Champs-Elysées. At other times, in a spectacularly new style of royal intimacy, the Berrys strolled arm in arm in the public gardens of the Tuileries.[25] As host and hostess, the Berrys gave balls unrivaled for their gaiety and glamour that also produced no adverse comment about the guest list from aristocratic socialites sensitive to possible intrusions.[26] More adventuresome were their evenings out together as a couple. Regular invitations to parties at the d'Orléans, the duke's politically liberal cousin, introduced the Berrys to a social circle broader than the one in favor at the court.[27] More conspicuous, and therefore more remarked, were their habits as enthusiasts of theater that took them regularly to the four royal theaters in the capital but also to popular theaters on the boulevards where the other Bourbons never ventured.[28]

Inevitably, the Berrys' lifestyle attracted adverse comment from members of the old aristocracy, who regularly passed judgment on the royal family. In particular, memoirs by aristocratic women from the Faubourg Saint-Germain faulted the duke for his hot temper, his continued womanizing, and his use of the familiar "tu" to address his wife in public. Commentary on the teenage duchess was, if anything, still harsher. Untrained and ill-adapted temperamentally to the formal etiquette exacted by the Bourbons, she appeared under the cruel eyes of one elderly *grande dame* to be more suited to a girls' boarding school than to court. Her inattentiveness at mass also offended the sensibilities of certain courtiers. Court gossip and her doctor blamed an early miscarriage on her vigorous dancing and explained the postnatal death of a son in 1818 as the consequence of the mother's gorging herself on Neopolitan sweets.[29] When the duchess did, finally, produce a viable infant on September 21, 1819, it proved to be a girl and another disappointment for the court. For her part, the duchesse de Berry simply ignored her critics or, after the duke had purchased a château for her at Rosny-sur-Seine, left town for frequent brief excursions.

Her reputation in Paris produced few traces from this period, though police investigations following the duke's assassination turned up a florist who admired the sociable royal princess to whom she sold her flowers.[30] On the whole, though, before her husband's death, few outside the intimates of the court knew much about her. By contrast, afterward, the widowed duchess would develop into the one persona at the court of whom a broad Parisian public more or less approved.

The harrowing evening of the duke's assassination outside the Royal Opera on February 12, 1820, by a supporter of Napoleon named Louis-Pierre Louvel, placed the duchesse de Berry for the first time since her marriage in the dual limelight of the court and city.[31] Staged by the two principals in the melodramatic style long in vogue in popular theaters on the boulevard, the death scene, which took six hours to complete, received multiple recountings in the press.[32] The entire royal family took part in the night-long vigil in an anteroom of the royal entry to the theater. As dawn broke, the king himself appeared just in time to hear his nephew's plea for royal mercy for his attacker. Berry's request to spare the villain's life, in the mistaken belief that his murder revenged some personal insult, won wide approval among his courtly audience for its royal grandeur, even though the king refused to grant his wish. Equally arresting for those same observers were his gestures of solicitude for his wife and children, legitimate and illegitimate alike. In the eyes of his critics, like the duchesse de Maillé and the comtesse de Boigne, the duke had fashioned a better death than he had lived a life.[33] The key figure in the death scene whose presence made the drama successful as propaganda in the popular press, however, was the heartbroken, twenty-year-old duchess.

Genuinely inconsolable, Marie-Caroline displayed throughout the tragedy a highly tuned sensibility for the heroic act. From her unassisted leap from the carriage in response to her husband's cry, to her bloodied white gown, which first cradled her husband and then provided a makeshift bandage for his wound, to her final swoon when the doctors pronounced her husband dead, the duchess offered an array of striking postures that engravers for both refined and popular tastes promptly captured in a flood of prints.[34] For some, an equally touching scene, less well known to the general public, occurred when the dying duke's two illegitimate daughters by his English mistress, Amy Brown, suddenly appeared in the middle of the night at his request. The duchess, to whom her husband presented the girls as offspring of a relationship that preceded theirs, promised that she would be their second mother and embraced them.[35] The last scene of this real-life melodrama hawked by print sellers in the streets of Paris caught the grief-stricken new widow in the act of shearing off her long blond locks, which the duke had particularly admired.[36] Dozens of cheap prints and pamphlets recounting the death scene in the weeks after the event attested to its commercial success among a Parisian public attuned, like the duchess herself, to a romantic notion of the self.

All the same, this theatrical performance did not carry the same resonance for all observers. Firsthand accounts reported that the duchesse d'Angoulême voiced approval for her sister-in-law's behavior only at the point when Marie-Caroline embraced her dying husband's illegitimate daughters.[37] In this instance, Marie-Caroline seemed to incarnate an ideal of noble condescension to which the duchesse d'Angoulême herself had remained deeply attached. By contrast, the Neapolitan's passionate display of feeling shocked this princess, for whom the veiling of emotions still expressed the essence of nobility, as it had for the aristocracy of the Old Regime. Such temperamental differences, at another moment in French history, might have carried no political charge. But the contrasting style of these two women, one aloof and brusque, the other sociable and expressive, offered the material for others to align them with alternative visions of the court's relationship to the nation and, more especially, to the diverse social groups in Paris vying for social standing and a political voice. Any friction within the royal family that appeared to echo such divisions could metamorphose into judgments on the monarchy itself. First, though, the duchesse de Berry had to develop into a personality of importance, however much contested, at the court.

That possibility originated in the startling revelation by the dying duke that his wife was pregnant. Inevitably, such an announcement invited disbelief from cynics. Too much rode on such fortuity, since the Bourbons' dynasty would otherwise die out, for their enemies not to suspect the pregnancy was faked. To counter that impression, the royalist press flooded the Parisian market with illustrations of the grieving widow holding her year-old daughter, Louise, beside a memorial for her husband

The Assassination of the duc de Berry (1820). Bibliothèque Nationale de France, Cabinet des Estampes. Photo Bibliothèque Nationale de France, Paris

or praying at his tomb.[38] Presumably such images increased the plausibility of the event while winning public sympathy for the mother. As doubts about her pregnancy subsided, suspicions rose that the mother might switch infants at the birth. In this case, the duchess displayed a flair for silencing the skeptics. First, she made a well-advertised pilgrim-

The Death of the duc de Berry (1820). Bibliothèque Nationale de France,
Cabinet des Estampes. Photo Bibliothèque Nationale de France, Paris

age to Notre Dame de Liesse, where French queens since the Middle Ages
had prayed for sons. Then, writing herself into the tradition of supernat-
ural intervention, she dreamed in the fourth month of her pregnancy that
Saint-Louis appeared before her, accompanied by a boy to whom he gave
his crown. After the birth, royalists would publish her signed description
of this dream.[39] The real test, however, would come with the sworn testimony of reliable witnesses to the birth.[40]

As it turned out, plans for a carefully orchestrated, well-documented
delivery were all for naught. The duchesse de Berry gave birth at night
with only one sharp labor pain to warn her. By the time a lady-in-wait-
ing and a chambermaid, who were sleeping close at hand, could even
light the room, her son had exited the womb.[41] The circumstances could
hardly have been more propitious for derision. Acutely sensitive to the
danger, Marie-Caroline's response bore the imprint of her training as a
royal princess who understood that like the king, but in an entirely dif-

Louis XVIII closes the eyes of the duc de Berry (1820). Bibliothèque Nationale de France, Cabinet des Estampes. Photo Bibliothèque Nationale de France, Paris

ferent way, French royal women also had two bodies, one personal and private, the other maternal and communal.[42] If not sacred like the king's, the body of a royal woman giving birth belonged to the community for whom her offspring might one day be king. The duchess, therefore, ordered her lady to invite any national guardsmen whom she could find in the vicinity of her apartments to verify the authenticity of the birth. Each of four guardsmen apprehended, as well as two officially designated witnesses who did finally appear, found Marie-Caroline naked, legs apart, and still attached to the infant at her side. After waiting several minutes for the second of two official witnesses to arrive, her physician held up the umbilical cord still attached to the placenta in her womb and cut it.[43] The gout-ridden and enormously fat Louis XVIII arrived an hour later.

This time royalist accounts would be less literal than they had been on the occasion of her husband's death in representing the intrepid princess in heroic action. All the same, the publication in newspapers the next day of a certificate of birth signed by a grocer, a pharmacist, an employee, and a wholesale merchant left considerable room for imagining the

event.[44] Members of the royal family veiled their reactions to the audacious actions of their in-law, though the king's refusal to reward her doctor generously revealed his royal pique. More interesting were the
divergent views within the aristocracy. Unwittingly, the duchess had
exposed with the immodest inspection of her body the cultural gap that
divided the contemporary social practices of this old elite from its rever-
ently held political memories. Under the Old Regime, a socially mixed
public birthing by a royal mother had enhanced the image of a king as
father to his subjects.[45] By 1820, such an extraordinary application of
royal insouciance risked the opposite effect. Some members of the aristocracy avowed respect for Marie-Caroline's thoroughly royal lack of
prudery under duress. But the comtesse de Boigne recorded a different,
more prescient reaction to this exaggerated version of traditional royal
births when she referred to the "disgusting" official testimonials in the
press.[46] The one aristocratic witness, the duc d'Albuféra, chosen for his
Napoleonic background, felt his part in the event ridiculously out of step
with contemporary mores. "I am surer that the duc de Bordeaux . . . is
the child of Madame la duchesse de Berry," he quipped ironically to the
duc d'Orléans, "than I am that my son is the child of his mother."[47]

Behind these discomfited reactions in the aristocracy lay a serious contradiction for a monarchy wedded to its past traditions. On the one
hand, dynasticism under the Old Regime viewed a royal mother's womb
as the vessel for a sacred reproductive act and, therefore, subject to policing by the public. On the other hand, a new, postrevolutionary culture
that Napoleon's patriarchal civil code also expressed, turned wives' sexual parts into the hidden, private property of husbands. Arguably, legal
policing of the sexual parts of licensed prostitutes may even have
increased the ambiguities inherent in public royal birthing. In one way,
the context for this particular royal birth favored the ruling family,
nonetheless. The duchesse de Berry's well-established ardor for her husband made gossip questioning her sexual reliability unlikely. By contrast,
accusations of child swapping filled the rumor market. Heir to the throne
himself should the Bourbons die out, the duc d'Orléans was not convinced of the legitimacy of the birth nor were many of the liberals who
supported him.[48] An apparently unauthorized denunciation even
appeared in an English paper under the duc d'Orléans's name.[49] Popular
skepticism found expression in the satirical verses of the celebrated
republican singer Béranger and in caricatures hawked surreptitiously in
the streets of Paris.[50]

To defend the monarchy against such libels, royalists flooded Paris with images culled from the Bourbon family's past. The child's title, the duc de Bordeaux, and his Christian name, Henri, set the stage for a popular recovery of Bourbon family history. The title rewarded the loyalty to the Bourbons of the city of Bordeaux in 1814; the Christian name recalled Henri IV, the founder of the Bourbon dynasty. From Béarn came the traditional accessories for a Bourbon birth, a bottle of Jurançon and a bulb of garlic.[51] After the birth, Louis XVIII thanked the duchesse de Berry with a bouquet of diamonds, several bank notes and the same cryptic observation that the grandfather of Henri IV addressed to Jeanne d'Albret when she delivered him an heir: "That is for you; and this is for me."[52] For the devout or merely superstitious among supporters of the monarchy and certainly for the duchesse de Berry herself, the most important interpretation of the event was given by the papal nuncio in Paris who proclaimed Henri a "miracle child" because his coming had, against all odds, preserved and restored the Bourbon dynasty from extinction in its senior branch. Meanwhile, in the French capital, market women called the *poissardes* who, before the revolution, had traditionally proclaimed their admiration for the queen after the delivery of a son, found themselves resurrected ritually as a corporation with a special royal dinner in their honor.[53] Seven months later at the baptism of Henri, the carriage of the royal mother stopped to receive the *poissardes*' compliments on the way to Notre Dame Cathedral. Memorialists for the Bourbons later claimed that the birth of an heir and the favorable impression made on Paris by the courage of the duchesse de Berry boosted the popularity of the monarchy greatly.[54]

Nonetheless, except for ceremonial occasions, memoirs from the 1820s rarely report the royal mother in the company of her children. Prints and portraits leave the same impression. After a flurry of prints in 1820 and 1821 representing the royal widow consoled, like France itself, by Henri's birth, official artists and the popular press ignored the duchess in her role as mother.[55] Neither incidental nor accidental, this omission accurately reflected daily life at court, where, in accordance with an etiquette inherited from Versailles, the royal family left precious little mothering to their royal mother. Winters, when the royal family resided at the Tuileries, she spent thirty minutes every morning with her children.[56] In the summer and autumn, when the king took the children with him to Saint-Cloud, often the duchess drove out to see them, but only when she was herself in Paris. Just once did she gain permission to take her daughter to Rosny, and Henri never visited at all. Moreover, all decisions about the proper rearing of her children escaped her. In his memoirs, the eldest son of the duc d'Orléans described how, under Charles X, the official governess for the royal children, the duchesse de Gontaut, virtually replaced their mother as a maternal influence. "Whenever there was a difference of opinion between her and the duchesse de Gontaut, the king always decided in favor of the latter, and the most the mother of the duc de Bordeaux knew about his education was whatever she could surmise from his answers to her questions."[57]

All the same, as the widowed mother of the Bourbons' heir, the duchesse de Berry soon developed into a royal personage of singular importance. Beneath her naturally gay exterior, which reappeared at the end of her required year of mourning, lay an absolute conviction of her royal rights and her own resolute determination to assert them. As expected, the death of Louis XVIII in 1824 reassigned positions in the royal family. With Charles X now king of France, the duc and duchesse d'Angoulême took the titles of "Dauphin" and "Dauphine," reflecting their proximity to the throne. Had he lived, the duc de Berry as brother to the dauphin would have assumed the title of "Monsieur" and his wife that of "Madame." His death, his widow believed, did not affect her claim, and she insisted, over the objections of both the king and the dauphine, that her own attendants address her with that title, even when her sister-in-law's escort refused to do so. Consequently, as the duchesse de Berry strove to make the most of her position at the court, controversy around her person sharpened. The widowed duchess possessed another trump, however. Despite the informality of her manners and occasionally even of her dress, she applied herself with artistry to entertaining.[58] That talent greatly magnified her value to her in-laws, since under Charles X, the court tried for the first time to become a fashionable center for the capital's elite.[59]

Unfortunately, the favorite form of royal entertainment, the king's games, got mixed reviews. Only the likes of deputies enjoyed such royal spectacles *La Mode,* a fashionable monthly read by aristocrats, insinuated, while the youthful duchesse de Maillé reported that for her circle in the Faubourg Saint-Germain, court gatherings held slight appeal.[60] Etiquette weighed too heavily on gala evenings hosted by the king, and the political nature of the list of guests displeased the snobs. For a more select Parisian set, what saved the court from social tedium were the parties presided over by the duchesse de Berry in the apartments of her children where etiquette relaxed and the presence of the duchesse de Gontaut as official hostess permitted more exclusive invitations.[61] On such occasions, under the expert eye of the merry royal widow, whose passion for dancing often kept her balls alive till dawn, the hospitality of Charles X's court scored its only recognized success.[62]

Had she confined her socializing to the court, the duchesse de Berry's presence would have left few traces on the Restoration. That was never her intention. Instead, under the title of "Madame," she initiated a veritable campaign to win approval from the most dynamic elements in the capital. When the first vehicle for mass transit, the omnibus, arrived in Paris, she bet the king 10,000 francs to be given to the poor that she would ride it. (The company's owner promptly renamed his fleet the "Carolines" in a plug for both the princess and his business.)[63] To build her reputation also as a benefactor of the arts, she published at great expense a folio of her husband's and her own collected paintings.[64] The artists who benefited most from her support, however, worked in theater. "As far as anyone knows," wrote one admirer, "she never refused to attend a benefit performance for an actor or actress, and she went with the same alacrity to theaters on the boulevards as to royal theaters . . . one had only to notify her the night before."[65]

Her presence at the theater had political implications far beyond promoting leading artists in the city, though. Theaters in the Restoration were political arenas par excellence.[66] Spectators regularly vented their opinions by applause or hoots for actors' lines in which they saw political allusions. Even going to one or another theater constituted an act of class allegiance with political intent. The key to the popularity of Marie-Caroline lay in her refusal to confine her outings to the royal theaters. Indeed, in 1824, she became a patron for the most successful private theater on the boulevard, the Gymnase dramatique.[67] With its audience drawn mainly from the financial district of the city and a repertoire based largely on domestic dramas by the playwright Eugène Scribe, the "theatre of Madame" visibly linked the royal mother to the capital's rising bourgeoisie. For all the fashionable circles of the city, her glamour found no rivals.[68]

Still, her greatest social triumphs occurred not in Paris but at the tiny port of Dieppe, where, beginning in 1824, her own love of the sea brought seabathing and holidays at the shore into vogue among Parisian socialites.[69] By 1826, with a new jetty in the harbor, a theater and library founded by the duchess, hot baths that bore her name, and five hundred freshly constructed homes, Dieppe would metamorphose into a personal court for the duchesse de Berry every summer.[70] Free of royal etiquette and of her in-laws, Marie-Caroline gave full rein at Dieppe to her own calculated royal style, at once artful, audacious, fun-loving, and socially inclusive. The season opened with the spectacle of the duchess, dressed in her bathing costume, walking into the waves on the arm of the formally attired Medical Inspector of the Baths. On succeeding days, while bemused spectators looked on, she entered the water unceremoniously, accompanied by the youngest, most daring women in her train.[71] Just as in the capital, she blurred the lines that separated royalty and aristocracy from other social worlds. At the theater, local dignitaries were invited to her box, and she readily danced with officials from a bourgeois background for municipal balls.[72] Her controversial reputation followed her to Dieppe, of course, along with intimates of the court. Predictably, also, the rest of the royal family kept its distance.[73] Only once did the duchesse d'Angoulême visit, and when she did, her welcome celebrated not the coming of summer or the town's prosperity but her own return to France in 1815 by way of Dieppe.[74]

As the liberal opposition to Charles X grew in Paris, such disparities in royal style would develop a political spin, but not one imparted by the duchess herself. Instead of winning supporters for the monarchy as she certainly expected, her persona became a convenient foil for criticizing a court and royal family so unlike her. The first to exploit the prospect were her publicists at the Gymnase dramatique. In late June of 1828, with the duchesse de Berry out of town, her theater performed a frankly political play entitled "Before, During, and After." As usual, Scribe's plot revolved around a domestic drama but one that contrasted aristocratic matchmaking before the revolution with a bourgeois courtship in contemporary France.[75] The audience easily understood the political message of the satire, and when word of the resulting scandal reached her, so would the duchesse de Berry. Her threat to withdraw her patronage promptly closed the play.[76] The incident augured ominously for the potential uses of her distinctive royal image in an ever more divided city.

Tensions between aristocratic and bourgeois Paris were not the only currents of dissatisfaction that the youthful duchess would embody. Within the society of the court itself, friction with her aging in-laws duplicated a tension in the Faubourg Saint-Germain that pitted an older generation of women, who had returned from exile committed to moralizing aristocratic manners, against a younger generation eager to define themselves more freely.[77] If the dauphine and her intimates shared the outlook of this older generation, those who accompanied the duchesse de Berry into the sea at Dieppe clearly associated with the second. Thus, to champion the duchesse de Berry as a fashionable pacesetter raised a subtle challenge to the cultural program emanating from the court. Late in

1829, Émile de Girardin began his career in journalism by engaging in just such cultural politics when he founded, under the patronage of the duchesse de Berry, a fashion review called *La Mode* addressed to the Faubourg Saint-Germain.[78] Unbeknownst to her and far more explicitly than the Gymnase dramatique, *La Mode* set out to use her fashionable persona to attack the culturally outdated court and by implication, the reactionary political views that it defended.

Behind the plan lay a developing constitutional crisis born of ever greater electoral successes for liberals and the intransigence of a reactionary king. In August 1829, Charles X cast his lot definitively with the "ultra" royalists, eager to extend the powers of the king, when he asked Jules de Polignac, his old comrade-in-exile, to form a government. Eleven months later, Polignac would precipitate a revolution in Paris by attempting to overturn the constitution of 1814 by decree. In the interim, Émile de Girardin and his associates sought unsuccessfully to turn *La Mode* into a recognized voice for moderate opinion in the Faubourg Saint-Germain.[79]

That a fashion magazine might serve as a vehicle for this ambition testifies to the way the cultural codes imposed at court had come to symbolize the king's reactionary views. It also hints at the potential for reading the duchesse de Berry into political debates simply on the basis of her style. The fact that she shared the outlook of the "ultras" complicated *La Mode*'s maneuvers but not insurmountably, as it turned out.[80] Its campaign opened on December 19, 1829, with a lampoon entitled "Assemblée Législative de la mode." Subtly aimed at both the elderly Council of Ministers under Polignac and Charles X's archaic court, the satire pitted young women of the Faubourg Saint-Germain against women born before the revolution in an imaginary feminine assembly legislating fashion under a constitutional monarchy. With *La Mode* as sovereign, it was decided that only young women could serve on the Council of Ministers. Although the piece never mentioned the duchesse de Berry, the presence on the imaginary Council of Fashion Ministers of the youngest member of her official escort positioned the duchess on the side of the "new order," just as the exclusion of the elderly intimates of the dauphine identified her with those whose fashion sense recalled the Old Regime. Not surprisingly, the next issue of *La Mode* published a letter from the court withdrawing the duchesse de Berry's patronage.

Despite this royal pique, *La Mode*'s satirical strategy did not change. Throughout the winter of 1830 and into the late spring, it used the gay and fashionable duchesse de Berry for sly denunciations of an outdated

court personified in the pages of *La Mode* by the dauphine. Several articles contrasted the stylish clothes of the young duchess with the dress
codes of the court or with her sister-in-law's outdated apparel on her
return to France. Others focused on the younger woman's love of pleasure, especially dancing, and the fact that the dauphine, like the king,
always left a party early.[81] In one particularly racy description of an
"unforgettable" ball honoring the duc de Chartres at a newly opened
dance hall in the city, the review noted that all the women had come
masked as dominoes and, therefore, incognito.[82] It went on to say that
although a great number of fashionable men attended, fewer women
came than had received an invitation. The explanation, which all insiders in the faubourg knew, was that the "prudes" of the Faubourg Saint-
Germain, as Rudolphe Apponyi described them, had opposed such a
scandalous pastime. Many readers would have also heard the rumor,
reported by Apponyi as well, that the duchesse de Berry had slipped into
the ball.[83]

Charles X made his own position clear when a few weeks later, he
refused to take his family to a charity ball at the Royal Opera because he
disliked "masked balls of that sort."[84] The duchesse de Maillé considered
his decision a political gaffe with major import.[85] Anne Martin-Fugier
dates the emancipation of fashionable Paris from the social leadership of
the court to that event. The ball, which a committee of women from all
the fashionable milieux of the city had organized for the benefit of victims of the capital's terrible winter, would have displayed the royal family in the city for the first time amidst the full panoply of its social elite.
Instead, their absence exposed their distance from the city's sociable pleasures, a distance placed in even sharper relief by the presence of the duc
d'Orléans and his family.[86] Such contrasting signals from the king and his
only possible rival inevitably eroded the position that the royal mother
had carved out for the Bourbons in Paris. By late spring, in response to
the shift in political winds, even *La Mode* no longer consistently flattered
her parties.[87]

As it turned out, though she had no role in the decision that precipi-
tated the Revolution of July 1830, her reputation did affect how major
players in the crisis viewed her. In Paris, her popularity protected her
from most attacks directed against other members of the royal family.
During three days of battling for the capital, rampaging crowds left
shops carrying her insignia alone.[88] Later, after the fall of the monarchy,
caricatures lampooning the Bourbons rarely targeted the royal mother.[89]
Only doubts over the birth of her son resurfaced to disturb an otherwise

mildly favorable memory of her in the city.[90] At the court, by contrast, her frivolous reputation undermined her efforts to be taken seriously as a political player. First, the king turned down her request on July 29 to go alone or with her son to Paris, where she imagined that the possibility of a regency would calm the popular storm.[91] Second, on abdicating in favor of his grandson a few days later, Charles X preferred his nephew, the duc d'Orléans, to the duchesse de Berry as regent, a hopeless strategy since the duke had already decided to assume the crown himself.[92] One of the architects of the revolution, the banker Jacques Lafitte, briefly entertained the idea of a regency under the royal mother because of her popularity in Paris.[93] At the time, however, there was no chance of convincing Charles X to consider such a part for the duchesse de Berry, whose opinions even as a mother he ignored.

Over the next twelve months, her position in the Bourbons' political calculations changed dramatically. Most Bourbon loyalists, following the passive lead of the former king himself, were willing after 1830 to leave the future of this sacred dynasty to God; but not all those faithful to the exiled royal family favored resignation. In Paris, a young generation of activists, allied with most of the legitimist press, organized a conspiratorial society called *Amis de l'ordre* that determined to reverse the verdict of July.[94] Those who visited the exiled royal family at the château of Holy-Rood in Scotland, where Charles X spent his first years in exile, found the duchesse de Berry to be the only member of the royal family favorable to their plans.[95] By the spring of 1831, the conspirators had cajoled a reluctant Charles X into accepting her secret return to France with the argument that the arrival of Henri's mother would spark a legitimist uprising in the Midi and the Vendée which, in the event of popular disturbances in Paris and the threat of foreign intervention, might produce another restoration. In fact, the military logistics of the plan had a quixotic character from the outset that several months of delay would only heighten. By the time the duchess arrived in May of 1832, the new regime had the bureaucratic and military apparatus of the state in firm control.[96] Neither in the Midi nor the Vendée could an uprising succeed. Meantime, in Paris, the discovery on February 2, 1832, of a legitimist plot to assassinate Louis-Philippe had devastated their underground society, while popular hatred for the Bourbons, furiously displayed the year before in an attack on the Église Saint-Germain-l'Auxerrois and the archbishop's palace following a mass on February 13 in commemoration of the duc de Berry, precluded any hope of broadening legitimist support beyond the narrow confines of the already committed.[97]

Among those faithful to the Bourbons, though, the duchesse de Berry possessed a powerful new trump. Since the Revolution of 1830, motherhood had come explicitly into vogue in Paris. Even feminine fashions made the point. Quite suddenly, over the spring and summer of 1830, a slight but significant shift occurred in women's apparel, dropping hemlines below the ankle and adding shawls to cover shoulders for their day excursions. Over the next few years, shawls would grow in size to cover ever greater portions of the body while hat brims deepened as if to shade the face from view. Visibly, bourgeois respectability had come to France in feminine wear.[98] Its arrival announced the triumph of a sea change in domestic relations underway in the Restoration even among the aristocracy but with little official recognition from the Bourbon court. That would no longer be the case under the July monarchy, when Queen Marie-Amélie turned mothering her eight children into her personal royal cameo both at court receptions and on her many outings in the city.[99] Much about the cultural politics of Louis-Philippe as "citizen-king" became the immediate butt of ridicule from all his enemies. The image of the queen, however, uninterested in politics and absorbed in her maternal and charitable duties, proved unassailable between 1830 and 1832 from either Left or Right.[100] The entire political class accepted the cultural nexus of feminine signs that she projected. Similarly maternal gestures from the duchesse de Berry had the potential to transform the Bourbon royal mother for legitimists into an object of special veneration, too.

Unfortunately for her publicists, remaking the duchesse de Berry over as a royal mother encountered major problems. Legitimists all recalled the extraordinary courage that she had shown at the duc de Berry's death and the birth of the "miracle child," Henri, but in the absence in the 1820s of any mothering role, her social image had largely overwhelmed that memory, at least in Paris. Once in exile, the royal family only magnified the problem. Charles X had no intention of altering the terms of motherhood already established for the duchess, while she, bored with her position, soon deserted her children and the court at Holy-Rood for a residence in Edinburgh and, later, for the English resort of Bath.[101] *La Mode*, now under new ownership and still the foremost champion of the duchess, set out all the same to present this peripatetic princess as a committed royal mother.[102] To open its campaign, the editors published a letter postmarked Bath reporting that a grave illness had brought the duchess to the spa. In fact, a rumor circulating in the Faubourg Saint-Germain imagined that she was pregnant.[103] With surprising candor, the letter next alluded to the conspiracy underway and the duchess's involvement: "Some grand idea . . . has taken over her soul; she is no longer the person whom we followed with our eyes on our outings, from whom we took all our fashions . . . ; this is a solemn woman who wants to believe in a better future because she is the mother of a child called Henri."[104]

The portrait did not entirely misrepresent the duchess from the spring of 1831 up to her arrest a year and a half later. Whether inspired by royal examples from the past or simply by a sense of sacred duty, she believed that widowhood and the pusillanimity of the Bourbons forced her to defend the son that Berry had fathered and God had blessed.[105] Throughout the course of the conspiracy, that conviction shaped her actions. Astonishing even her accomplices, she engaged actively in plotting her return and made her own adjustments to setbacks, once she arrived in France. When the expected uprising in Provence fizzled out, rather than retreat, she decided on her own to proceed to the Vendée where, over the objections of legitimists from Paris, she chose to go ahead with the rebellion.[106] Afterward, from June until November, she resisted all appeals to leave the country, much to the consternation of both the government and her own supporters. Some legitimists rightly feared that a royal mother at the head of a military insurrection and then hiding in disguise in the Vendée threatened to confirm in the public's mind the reputation for archaism already attributed to the Bourbons. It could be just as risky for the government to arrest and imprison the Bourbon royal mother, who was also the niece of Queen Marie-Amélie, when bourgeois domesticity, along with its protected place for mothers, had become a defining cultural code for the regime.

Paradoxically, therefore, the government's discovery and arrest of the duchesse de Berry on November 7, 1832, in her hiding place at Nantes temporarily brightened legitimists' fortunes.[107] Locked in prison where supporters could imagine her pining for her children, the duchesse de Berry became a powerful political weapon in the hands of publicists for the Bourbons. Even her escapade in the Vendée metamorphosed into a drama of exemplary virtue. Dozens of prints spewed off legitimist presses depicting a thoroughly feminized royal mother giving solace to a peasant family, caring for a hurt companion, innocently receiving the blackguard who would betray her, and, finally, imprisoned in a government fortress with only portraits of her children and a letter to sustain her.[108] The melodramatic framing of her story clearly capitalized on a narrative style adopted widely by Parisian theater in the 1830s, but the real force of the legitimists' campaign derived from their portrait of the duchess as beleaguered mother.[109] Invariably, those wielding the pen in her defense

The duchesse de Berry in prison at Blaye (1833). Bibliothèque
Nationale de France, Cabinet des Estampes. Photo Bibliothèque
Nationale de France, Paris

extolled her maternal heroism. "Since her recent misfortunes," one biographer gushed, "Madame the duchesse de Berry . . . has seemed to me to
be an ideal mix of everything that is touching and beautiful on earth,
an ideal example of a woman, wife, and mother."[110] "Only the heart of
a mother," readers of *La Gazette de France* were told, "can, at this
moment, be in perfect harmony with hers and feel all that is both sweet
and cruel in seeing the portraits of these two children for whom her
tenderness has not spared her the most painful sacrifices. . . ."[111] The
most electrifying of these panegyrics to the captive duchess, written by
Chateaubriand, concluded with the war cry: "Madame, Your son is my
king."[112] Women as well as men signed petitions for her release.[113] Several

asked to join her or to take her place.[114] Hostesses in the Faubourg Saint-
Germain, in a gesture of solidarity with the royal mother, refused to entertain.[115] So completely did the barrage of criticism place the government
on the defensive that Adolphe Thiers, the interior minister, having dared
to arrest her now asked for a reassignment to the Ministry of Commerce
to protect his own career.[116]

Then, as rumors of a royal pregnancy in prison began to spread, new
possibilities surfaced in the press war that swirled about the Bourbons'
royal mother. Hoping to discredit all hereditary regimes, republican
papers also joined the fray.[117] Legitimist dailies responded by deepening
the lugubrious hues around their long-suffering royal mother with claims
that she was seriously ill. Several young legitimist hotheads challenged to
duels editors who dared besmirch their royal mother's name.[118] Pressed
into action by her swelling girth, the duchess finally signed an official
declaration on February 22, 1833, revealing a secret marriage but without the husband's name.[119] Most people concluded that only a pregnancy
could have induced such an avowal.[120] Many, including the exiled
Bourbons, also assumed that the child was illegitimate.[121] Publicly,
though, the legitimist press adopted one of two positions. Either editors
proclaimed a government hoax and imagined their royal mother dying in
the hands of her oppressors, a tactic pursued by *La Gazette de France*
and *La Quotidienne;* or they argued more judiciously, as *La Mode* ultimately would do, that if the duchess produced a child, she had surely
married.[122] Right up to the astonishing finale of a birth in prison of a
daughter on May 10, 1833, the press turned reporting on the duchesse de
Berry into a deeply embittered battle over honor, in a classic example of
journalistic practices recently described by William Reddy as endemic
under both the late Bourbon and Orléanist monarchies.[123]

Remarkably, in this high-stakes contest to control her image, the
duchesse de Berry won the final round, at least among legitimists.[124] Not
only did she produce a father for her daughter in time to grace the birth
certificate, but did so with the name of Hector Lucchesi-Palli, an Italian
count.[125] An accommodating Catholic Church would later provide a
record of their marriage dated December 1831, which would also convince a reluctant Charles X to permit her once again to see her Bourbon
children.[126] Equally important, after the debacle of her pregnancy at
Blaye, she devised a life that positioned her firmly within the ascendant
cultural configuration of bourgeois motherhood.[127] Her union with
Lucchesi-Palli proved a happy one, producing numerous offspring.[128]
Although her relations with Charles X never recovered and the Bourbons

refused to receive her husband at their exiled court, the Lucchesi-Palli family chose to live in Austria close to the relocated Bourbon household so that the duchess could visit Henri and Louise.[129] Inconsequential as a maternal influence, she managed by this presence to retain symbolic weight of great significance for legitimists. Her own actions counted only marginally in that outcome, a necessary but not sufficient cause of the importance that she retained as a vector of legitimist memory. Instead, her significance lay in the connection between legitimist politics and the practice of everyday life among the faithful. Above all, it speaks to the important role that women played after 1830 in keeping legitimacy alive as a political culture.

An episode at Dieppe in the summer of 1837 illuminates the continuing popularity of the Bourbon royal mother among legitimist women. In the annual ladies' charity bazaar that year, two shirt buttons turned up among the handicrafts, one carrying a bust of the duchesse de Berry, the other emblazoned with a crown and scepter and the words "Madame, Your son is my king."[130] A dismayed subprefect advised his superiors to ignore the insult, even though Queen Marie-Amélie and her daughters, who were vacationing in their nearby château at Eu, had also contributed handicrafts to the event. In a resort where bathers "gathered *in memory of the former dynasty*," the subprefect warned, any reprisal would "instantly" produce "five hundred similar objects and eight thousand green and white bouquets," the colors of the Bourbons' royal mother. The offender was the wife of a former mayor of Dieppe who had lost his post in 1830. Behind that biographical detail lay a social reality that explains the mobilizing power of the duchesse de Berry's memory. Officials loyal to the Bourbons, like the mayor of Dieppe, left public office in droves in 1830, and most Bourbon loyalists waited to reenter politics until the Second Empire or even the 1870s. In the interim, a political culture constructed exclusively around memory took shape in legitimist homes. In that setting, under the vigilance of aristocratic women in their dual roles as curators of family histories and overseers of family piety, stories about the duchesse de Berry lived on.[131]

Once again, as when she returned to France in 1816, the duchesse de Berry became under the July monarchy a vehicle for preserving memories of the royal family. Suzanne d'Huart tells us that small pieces from the bloodied dress worn by the duchess on the night her husband died were a highly prized possession in legitimist families.[132] A.-J. Tudesque discovered that among legitimist women in Bordeaux, admiration for the duchesse de Berry produced a quasi cult. In the Parisian legitimist press, her rehabilitation began in 1834 with a new version of *La Vendée et*

Madame, a memoir written originally by the general who arrested her at Nantes but penned this time by an anonymous legitimist intent on justifying the duchesse de Berry as a mother.[133] In 1837, she returned to the pages of *La Mode* as mother to Henri and Louise, hostess for aristocratic visitors from France, and generous patron for her loyal followers, past and present.[134] Much that lent her notoriety in the Restoration would be forgotten. The fashionable duchess who built a bridge from the royal court to Paris in the 1820s faded from public memory. The Gymnase effaced her name from its marquis. Dieppe renamed its baths. Even the muckraking press ignored the duchess, once the wider public lost interest in the Bourbons and the press laws of September 1835 silenced all attacks on members of the reigning royal family. Her eclipse in the larger public's eye made it all the easier for her memorialists within legitimist circles to recall the duchesse de Berry in her now primary guise as a royal mother of exemplary zeal. Under the Restoration monarchy, motherhood, as fashioned by her in-laws, had inscribed her inescapably in the antiquated ceremonials of the Bourbon court. Reconfigured after her sacrifices for her son at Blaye, she could exemplify what the dominant classes now imagined mothers were or ought to be.

Political historians almost universally dismiss the duchesse de Berry's adventure in the Vendée as a devastating fiasco for the legitimist cause. Given the high esteem in which legitimists and particularly women held this royal mother afterward, I reinterpret the episode at the level of cultural symbols as a resounding and irreversible success. For if the Bourbons never again came to power and if the ideology of legitimism served to isolate supporters of the dynasty into a political subculture under later regimes, legitimists could finally imagine their royal family in terms familiar to their own lives and in keeping with bourgeois ideals. To that extent, after 1833 they entered rather than left the cultural mainstream of national political life.

NOTES

Guide to References and Abbreviations

A.F.   Archives of the Orléans royal family
A.N.   National Archives, Paris
A.P.P.P.   Archives of the Prefecture of Police, Paris.
B.N.F.   National Library of France, Paris
Estampes   Salle des Estampes, National Library of France

A slightly different version of this article appeared in *History Workshop Journal* 43 (spring 1997): 23–52. A fellowship from the American Council of Learned Societies and the generosity of Santa Clara University made the research for this article possible. My debt extends to several friends and scholars who read earlier versions and suggested mutiple ways to improve it. They include Bonnie Smith, Margaret Darrow, John Merriman, Rachel Fuchs, Susanna Barrows, Jann Matlock, and several anonymous reviewers. Throughout the creative process, Ted Margadant's insights and editorial advice were indispensable.

The Photographic Service of the B.N.F. kindly provided all illustrations. I am particularly grateful to Santa Clara University for a grant to help defray the cost of copyright fees.

1. I am using the term "bourgeois" to refer to a cultural outlook among the urban elites in postrevolutionary France analyzed in Robert A. Nye's pathbreaking study, *Masculinity and Male Codes of Honor in Modern France* (Oxford: Oxford University Press, 1993). I have also taken seriously William Reddy's admonition regarding the imprecision of the term "bourgeois" and never use the term with a transitive verb, i.e., the bourgeoisie did such and such. For reasons given in the introduction to this collection, the concept of the bourgeoisie as a self-conscious, identifiable social group having historical agency has been put in question by postmodern theories of identity. See William M. Reddy, "The Concept of Class," in *Social Orders and Social Classes in Europe since 1500: Studies in Social Stratification*, ed. M. L. Bush (London: Longman, 1992), 13–25.

2. Norbert Elias, *The Court Society*, trans. Edmund Jephcott (New York: Pantheon Books, 1983), 66–68, 186–88.

3. Philip Mansel, *The Eagle in Splendour: Napoleon I and his Court* (London: G. Philip, 1987), 79–98.

4. Philip Mansel, *The Court of France, 1789–1830* (Cambridge, Eng.: Cambridge University Press, 1988).

5. In her otherwise fine study, Anne Martin-Fugier fails to recognize the importance of the duchesse de Berry's forging links to the city's diverse elite. Martin-Fugier, *La Vie élégante ou la formation du Tout-Paris, 1815–1848* (Paris: Fayard, 1990).

6. Sarah Hanley, "Engendering the State: Family Formation and State Building in Early Modern France," *French Historical Studies* 16 (spring 1989): 4–27; "Les Visages de la loi salique dans la quête pour le droit des hommes et l'exclusion des femmes du gouvernement monarchique," introduction to *Les Droits des femmes et la Loi Salique* (Paris: Indigo Côté-femmes, 1994), 7–20; "The Monarchic State in Early Modern France: Marital Regime Government and Male Right," in *Politics, Ideology, and the Law in Early Modern Europe*, ed. Adrianna E. Bakos (Rochester: University of Rochester Press, 1994), 107–26; "Mapping Rulership in the French Body Politic: Political Identity, Public Law, and the *King's One Body*," *Historical Reflections/Réflections historiques* 23, no. 2 (1997): 129–49.

7. Lynn Hunt, *The Family Romance of the French Revolution* (Berkeley and Los Angeles: University of California Press, 1992).
8. George L. Mosse, *Nationalism and Sexuality: Middle-Class Morality and Sexual Norms in Modern Europe* (Madison: University of Wisconson Press, 1985), 1–22; and Linda Colley, *Britons: Forging the Nation, 1707–1837* (New Haven, Conn.: Yale University Press, 1992), 195–216, 237–82.
9. Simon Shama, "The Domestication of Majesty: Royal Family Portraiture, 1500–1850," *The Journal of Interdisciplinary History*, 17 (summer 1986): 155–84. Margaret Darrow, "French Noblewomen and the New Domesticity, 1750–1850," *Feminist Studies* 5 (spring 1979): 41–65.
10. Duchesse de Maillé, *Souvenirs des deux restaurations* (Paris: Perrin, 1984), 223. Comtesse de Boigne, *Mémoires de la comtesse de Boigne. Récits d'une tante* (Paris: Mercure de France, 1986), 2: 245. A.-D. Tolédano found that active mothering was of great importance in aristocratic households in Paris beginning with the Restoration Monarchy. *La Vie de famille sous la Restauration et la Monarchie de Juillet* (Paris: A. Michel, 1943), 177–78. According to Alan Spitzer, a defining feature of the young male elite in the 1820s was their "deification of mothers." *The French Generation of 1820* (Princeton: Princeton University Press, 1987), 188.
11. Joan Wallach Scott, "Gender: A Useful Category of Historical Analysis," in *Gender and the Politics of History* (New York: Columbia University Press, 1988).
12. Useful biographies of the duchess consulted for this study include the works of Guillaume de Bertier de Sauvigny, *Documents inédits sur la conspiration légitimiste de 1830 à l832* (Paris: A. Hatier, 1951); André Castelot, *La Duchesse de Berry d'après des documents inédits* (Paris: Librairie académique Perrin, 1963); Hugues de Changy, *Le Soulèvement de la duchesse de Berry, 1830–1832: les royalistes dans la tourmente* (Paris: Albatros and Diffusion-Université-Culture, 1986); General Dermoncourt, *La Vendée et Madame* (Paris, 1833); Etienne Léon Lamothe-Langon, baron de (Alfred Nettement, pseud.), *Mémoire historique de S.A.R. Madame, duchesse de Berri depuis sa naissance jusqu'à ce jour*, 3 vols. (Bruxelles, 1837); Louis-Charles comte de Mesnard, *Souvenirs intimes de M. le Cte de Mesnard, premier écuyer et chevalier d'honneur de S.A.R. Mme la duchesse de Berry*, 3 vols. (Paris, 1844); H. Thirria, *La Duchesse de Berry (S.A.R. Madame), 1798–1870* (Paris, 1900); Jacques Vidal de la Blanche, *Marie-Caroline duchesse de Berry* (Paris: France-Empire, 1980).
13. For a recent study that does examine the creation of a royal figure as a dynamic process, see Michael Marrinan, *Painting Politics for Louis-Philippe* (New Haven, Conn.: Yale University Press, 1988).
14. D 110771, Estampes, B.N.F.
15. *Le Moniteur universel*, April 28, 1816. See also Françoise Waquet, *Les Fêtes royales sous la Restauration ou l'ancien régime retrouvé* (Geneva: Droz, 1981), 71–72.
16. Excerpts from these letters published after the duc de Berry's assassination appear in François-René, Vicomte de Chateaubriand, *Mémoires, lettres et pièces authentiques touchant à la vie et à la mort de S.A.R. monseigneur Charles-*

Ferdinand-d'Artois, fils de France, duc de Berry (Paris, 1820), 157–87. Further excerpts appeared in Lamothe-Langon, *Mémoires*, 105–39. The letters using "tu" and referring to the king's tobacco can be found in Lucas-Dubreton's *La Duchesse de Berry*, 12–13 and Vidal de la Blanche's, *Marie-Caroline*, 28–29.

17. Tony Henri Auguste vicomte de Reiset, *Les Enfants du duc de Berry: d'après de nouveaux documents*, 3d ed. (Paris, 1905). André Castelot contends that the duke secretly married the protestant Amy Brown in England; *Le Duc de Berry et son double marriage, d'après des documents inédits* (Paris: S.F.E.L.T., 1950).

18. Lamothe-Langon, *Mémoires*, 36–64, 1: 90.

19. The duchesse de Berry claimed that her education had left her "ignorant as a carp." Prosper Ménière, *La Captivité de madame la duchesse de Berry à Blaye 1833: journal du Docteur P. Ménière, médecin envoyé par le gouvernement auprès de la princesse*, (Paris, 1882), 1: 110 and 2: 26.

20. Maillé, *Souvenirs*, 163; Boigne, *Mémoires*, 1: 18, 128–33.

21. Martin-Fugier, *La Vie élégante*, 100–112.

22. Jean Nagle, *Luxe et charité: le Faubourg Saint-Germain et l'argent* (Paris: Perrin, 1994).

23. Waquet, *Les Fêtes royales*, 147.

24. Lamothe-Langon, *Mémoires*, 1: 159–70.

25. Lucas-Dubreton, *La Duchesse de Berry*, 18.

26. Honoré de Balzac, *La Duchesse de Langeais* (Paris: Librarie générale française, 1983). During the first restoration, the duc de Berry imitated his liberal cousin, the duc d'Orléans, and invited guests from various political circles. After 1815, following Napoleon's Hundred Days, he discontinued the practice. Boigne, *Mémoires*, 2: 20.

27. Comtesse d'Agoult (pseudonym Daniel Stern) *Mes Souvenirs, 1806–1833* (Paris, 1877), 284, 287.

28. Duchesse de Gontaut-Biron, *Mémoires de madame la duchesse de Gontaut* (Paris, 1891), 183.

29. Gontaut-Biron, *Mémoires*, 180, 183–84; Maillé, *Souvenirs*, 52, 247, 257; Boigne, *Mémoires*, 1: 423, 453–55; d'Agoult, *Mes souvenirs*, 280. For police reports on the duke's love affairs before and after his marriage, see Castelot, *La Duchesse de Berry*, 67–75.

30. A A/344, document 381, and E A/119, A.P.P.P.

31. For documents relating to the assassination, BB18 1057–65, A.N.

32. For anonymously authored accounts of these events, see A A/343, A.P.P.P. For songs, Pierre Barbier and France Vernillat, eds., *Histoire de France par les chansons, La Restauration*, 3d ed. (Paris: Gallimard, 1958), 4: 82 and A A/343, A.P.P.P. According to Marie-Pierre Le Hir, the melodramatic situations favored in boulevard theaters during the Restoration always revolved around familial love, unlike those of Pixerécourt, the playwright who introduced melodrama to popular theater in Paris around 1800. This may suggest a shift in Parisian popular culture that helps explain why a popular audience would find the response of the duchesse de Berry to her husband's death so touching. "La Représentation de la famille dans le mélodrame du début du dix-neuvième siècle de Pixerécourt à

Ducange," *Nineteenth-Century French Studies* 18 (fall/winter 1989/1990): 15–24.

33. Boigne, *Mémoires,* 2: 26, 30.

34. P 30714, P 30754, P 30757, Estampes, B.N. See also P 30702, P 30716, P 30718–P 30756.

35. Gontaut-Biron, *Mémoires,* 208.

36. P 30764–30767, Estampes, B.N. For a song with this detail, see E A/119 4, A.P.P.P. For a good example of the starring role assigned to the duchess, see the anonymous *La France éplorée ou Berri n'est plus* (Paris, 1820), A A/343, A.P.P.P. A monarchist Parisian daily reported the lachrymose effect that one such testimonial produced in an elite boarding school for girls in the city. *La Gazette de France,* March 27, 1820, 342.

37. Gontaut-Biron, *Mémoires,* 208. See also Lamothe-Langon, *Mémoires,* 1: 235. A royal ordinance gave Charlotte, the older girl, the title "Mademoiselle d'Issoudun." Louise, the younger daughter, became Mademoiselle de Vierzon.

38. P 30939, Estampes, B.N. The duchess eventually had a chapel built at her château of Rosny for the duke's embalmed heart.

39. "In my fourth month of pregnancy, having fallen asleep, I saw Saint Louis come into my bedroom, looking just the way he is painted, with his crown on his head, his royal robe covered with lilies, and his venerable face. I presented my daughter to him; he opened his great robe and presented to me the prettiest little boy, and after that throughout my pregnancy, I had not a single doubt. Marie-Caroline." Quoted in H. de Pène, *Henri de France* (Paris, 1883), P 30871. For images, see P 30872, P 30874–P 30875, Estampes, B.N.

40. The two men named as official witnesses were the Marshal de Coigny, Governor of the Invalides, and Marshal Suchet, duc d'Albuféra.

41. Gontaut-Biron, *Mémoires,* 217–24. For the memoirs of the duchess's personal physician, Dr. Pierre Deneux, see G.-J. Witkowski, *Les Accouchements à la Cour* (Paris, n.d.), 287–340.

42. See E. H. Kantorowicz, *The King's Two Bodies* (Princeton: Princeton University Press, 1957).

43. Lamothe-Langon, *Mémoires,* 2: 65. A letter to their superior from the four royal grenadiers who witnessed this display is quoted in Henri d'Alméras, *La Vie parisienne sous la Restauration* (Paris, 1910), 233–35.

44. Newspaper accounts quickly appeared as reprints. See "Détails intéressants sur l'accouchement de S.A.R. Madame la duchesse de Berry, extrait de *La Gazette de France* du 30 septembre, 1820" (Marseilles, n.d.) and "Suite des bulletins sur l'accouchement de S.A.R. Madame la duchesse de Berry. Extrait du *Moniteur* du 2 octobre 1820" (Marseilles, n.d.).

45. Witkowski, *Les Accouchements,* 228–30, 311, 320, 331–32.

46. Boigne, *Mémoires,* 2: 42. The duchesse d'Abrantès recounts a witticism making the rounds of the Faubourg Saint-Germain about the birth in *Mémoires sur la Restauration,* 5: 322. Quoted in d'Alméras, *La Vie parisienne,* 211.

47. Gontaut-Biron, *Mémoires,* 221.

48. On the Orléans' initial doubts, see "Marie-Amélie, reine des français," *Journal de Marie-Amélie, reine des français,* ed. Suzanne d'Huart (Paris: Perrin,

1981), 280 and Ferdinand-Philippe d'Orléans, duc d'Orléans, *Souvenirs, 1810–1830,* ed. Hervé Robert (Geneva: Droz, 1993), 289.

49. Reprinted in Witkowski, *Les Accouchements,* 342.

50. Béranger, "L'Enfant du Mystère" and "C'est le Roi, le Roi, le Roi" in *Histoire de France par les chansons,* ed. Pierre Barbier and France Vernillat, 4: 83, 91, 340; P 30879, Estampes, B.N.

51. Witkowski, *Les Accouchements,* 308–11.

52. Lucas-Dubreton, *La Duchesse de Berry,* 46–47. In the birth announcement of the duc de Bordeaux, *La Gazette de France* referred to his mother as "the new Jeanne" and the child as "a new Henri." Quoted in Vidal de la Blanche, *Marie-Caroline,* 19. The duchesse de Berry reportedly sang the same song for Louis XVIII that Jeanne d'Albret had sung at the birth of her son. See P 30935, Estampes, B.N.

53. D'Alméras, *La Vie parisienne,* 218.

54. Lamothe-Langon, *Mémoires,* 67.

55. For popular prints, see P 30915, P 30937; P 30963; P 30950. For portraits see N 2 Berry, C 54956, D 089713, D 089715; D 089694; D 089728; D O8964; D 008969; D 08971. F. Gérard painted the last portrait of the widowed mother alone with her children when Henri was two, in remembrance of the duc de Berry. It appeared at the salon exhibition of 1823. Portrait N 2 Berry, B 50630. For a description, see P 30964–P 30965, Estampes, B.N.

56. Lamothe-Langon, *Mémoires,* 181–82.

57. Duc d'Orléans, *Souvenirs,* 107.

58. Even some of her personal attendants gossiped savagely about her. Maillé, *Souvenirs,* 247–48, 272. Boigne, *Mémoires,* 2: 93–94, 100–101.

59. Waquet, *Les Fêtes royales,* 60, 165–78.

60. *La Mode* (Jan.-March 1830), 18. Maillé complained especially about the Bourbons' efforts to "separate the two sexes as much as possible" in order to avoid the racy reputation of Versailles. *Souvenirs,* 174, 205–6.

61. The duchesse de Gontaut credits the idea for these occasions entirely to the royal mother, who warned the king: "It is necessary to entertain the French." *Mémoires,* 265–66.

62. Duponchel, "Des Bals costumés de S.A.R. Madame Duchesse de Berri, comparés aux diverses mascarades qui ont eu lieu en cour depuis le 14e siècle." *Revue de Paris,* vol. 1, 2d ed. (Paris, 1829); Maillé, *Souvenirs,* 171, 198, 268–69; Boigne, *Mémoires,* 2: 138–39, 167; Rodolphe Apponyi, *Vingt-cinq ans à Paris, 1826–1850, journal du comte Rodolphe Apponyi,* 2d ed. (Paris: Plon-Nourrit, 1913), 1: 44–46.

63. D'Alméras, *La Vie parisienne,* 106.

64. F. Bonnemaison, *Galerie de Son Altesse Royale Madame, duchesse de Berry: École française, peintres modernes et lithographies par d'habiles artistes,* 2 vols. (Paris, 1828).

65. Quoted from Brazier, *Chroniques des petits théâtres de Paris* in D'Alméras, *La Vie parisienne,* 226.

66. Odile Krakovitch, *Les Pièces de théâtre soumises à la censure (1800–1830)* (Paris: Archives nationales, 1982), 1–39.

67. When it opened in December 1820, the Gymnase dramatique had the

legal right to present only excerpts from plays performed in other theaters. Efforts by the Minister of Culture to enforce that limitation in 1824 led the theater's director, Delêstre Poirson, to appeal to the duchesse de Berry for her protection. Lamothe-Langon, *Mémoires*, 2: 103–6. The audience for the Gymnase included clerks as well as financiers, according to *La Mode*, Jan.-March 1830, 18.

68. Martin-Fugier estimates that four thousand people made up "Tout-Paris." Around eight hundred people normally attended the largest parties at the court.

69. Alain Corbin, *The Lure of the Sea: The Discovery of the Seaside in the Western World, 1750–1840*, trans. Jocelyn Phelps (Berkeley and Los Angeles: University of California Press, 1994), 273–75.

70. Isabelle Taillandier, "La villégiature à Dieppe sous la Restauration" (Maîtrise, University of Paris I, 1988), 23, 35, 40.

71. She used her mourning as a pretext to choose some young women for her royal entourage. Boigne, *Mémoires*, 2: 100. Her personal circle of intimates included a "bizarre" mixture of women drawn from "all classes, all periods, all courts, from the Directory to that of Charles X," according to the Baron d'Haussez, *Mémoires de baron d'Haussez*, (Paris, 1896), 2: 123. The duchesse d'Agoult remembered her delight with the opportunity as a seventeen-year-old to join the royal mother for her sea dip; *Mes souvenirs*, 281–83.

72. Her partners at a ball held in Dieppe in 1826 included the commissioner of the ball, a vicomte; the mayor of Gonneville, a member of the local gentry; a local wholesale merchant; and the engineer who had drawn up the plans for the theater and hot spa at Dieppe. Cited from the *Journal de Rouen* in Taillandier, "La Villégiature," 70.

73. Louise visited once in six summers; Gontaut-Biron, *Mémoires*, 256, 286, 300.

74. Taillandier, "La Villégiature," 44.

75. Eugène Scribe and Roger de Rougemont, "Avant, pendant et après, esquisses historiques" (Paris, 1828).

76. Accounts differ regarding which aspect of the play's plot outraged the court. See d'Alméras, *La Vie parisienne*, 167 and Vidal de la Blanche, *Marie-Caroline*, 54.

77. Maillé, *Souvenirs*, 1, 4, 238.

78. The first issue of *La Mode: revue des modes, galeries de moeurs, album des salons* appeared in October 1929.

79. René Mazedier, *Histoire de la presse parisienne de Théophraste Renaudot à la IVe République, 1631–1945* (Paris: Editions du Pavois, 1945), 87–90. The editors claimed to have twenty-six hundred subscribers; *La Mode*, April-June 1830, 184.

80. The duchesse de Maillé observed: "Popular because of her tastes and lifestyle, she is no closer to the country in her views than is her sister-in-law." *Souvenirs*, 289.

81. See Auger, "Piédestal, notice sur L. H. Leroy" and "Revue de la semaine," *La Mode*, Jan.-March, 1830, 146–56, 260, 349–55.

82. "Causerie du monde," *La Mode*, Jan.-March, 1830, 164–65.

83. Apponyi, *Vingt-cinq ans*, 1: 226–29.

84. Martin-Fugier, *La Vie élégante*, 9–12. The official explanation for the absence of the royal family was the tenth anniversary of the duc de Berry's death of the week before.

85. Maillé, *Souvenirs*, 294–307.

86. "Bal de l'Opéra au profit des indigens," *La Mode*, Jan.-March, 1930, 188–89.

87. "Revue et causeries du Monde," *La Mode*, April-June, 1830, 328.

88. Lamothe-Langon, *Mémoires*, 2: 212–13.

89. Only one caricaturist mocked her fondness for dancing. Qb1 M 110910, Estampes, B.N. Most satirical artists ignored her or presented her as simply an observer.

90. See for example, the anonymous publications *L'Accouchement de la duchesse de Berry ou comment les princesses font les enfants, dialogue entre la duchesse de Berry, le duc et la duchesse d'Angoulême* (Paris, 1831) and *Histoire scandaleuse politique, anecdotique et bigote des duchesses d'Angoulême et de Berry: formant le complement indispensable de l'histoire scandaleuse de Charles X. . . .* (Paris, 1830). In a speech before the Chamber of Deputies, the Orléanist de Bricqueville referred to "the partisans of that suspicious child, to whom they give the name of Henri V." Quoted in Witkowska, *Les Accouchements*, n. 1, 341.

91. Gontaut-Biron, *Mémoires*, 337; Boigne, *Mémoires*, 2: 247. See also Jacques Dinfreville, "La duchesse de Berry et les 'Trois Glorieuses,'" *Écrits Paris* (Feb. 1983), 32–41.

92. See Charles X's letter of August 2 to the duc d'Orléans in 300 AP III 32, A.F., A.N.

93. Lucas-Dubreton, *La Duchesse de Berry*, 59–60. Although no fan of the duchesse de Berry, the comtesse de Boigne nevertheless believed that de Berry's appearance on the streets of Paris might have saved the monarchy. *Mémoires*, 2: 146–47.

94. Ferdinand de Bertier, *Souvenirs d'un ultra-royaliste* (Paris: Tallandier, 1993), 434–35.

95. See her letters to de Bertier in Guillaume de Bertier de Sauvigny, ed., *Documents inédits sur la conspiration légitimiste de 1830 à 1832*, 45–51, 89–91. Bertier made the education of Henri V under a more politically liberal guardian a key objective. The duchesse de Berry became a convert to that cause.

96. For an official assessment of the overall weakness of the legitimists dated May 3, 1832, see "Rapport au Roi sur l'intérieur du royaume," 300 AP III 32, A.F., A.N.

97. For police reports on this popular anticlerical and antilegitimist riot on February 12, 1831, see AA 421, A.P.P.P.

98. Restoration fashions featured skirts above the ankle which also suited the slight frame and tiny stature of the duchesse de Berry. Vidal de la Blanche, *Marie-Caroline*, 32. Accused by a competitor in August 1830 of still championing the skirt length associated with the Restoration court and the duchesse de Berry, now in exile, *La Mode* claimed that their fashionable clientele in the Faubourg Saint-Germain had long since given up wearing short skirts. "Fausses Indications," *La Mode*, July-Sep., 1830, 137.

99. Anne Martin-Fugier, *La Vie quotidienne de Louis-Philippe et de sa famille, 1830–1848* (Paris: Hachette, 1992).

100. I base this conclusion on evidence from the major satirical papers: *La Mode* for the legitimists and *Le Charivari* and *La Caricature* for the republicans.

101. Mesnard, *Souvenirs intimes,* 2: 245–300.

102. Girardin sold the paper in 1831. Under the direction of vicomte Edouard Walsh, *La Mode* pursued an aggressive attack on the July monarchy.

103. Boigne, *Mémoires,* 2: 246, 249, 266. During the Restoration, a rumor, started by members of the duchesse de Berry's suite or by the duchesse de Gontaut, linked her romantically with her first *écuyer* (her principal male attendant), the comte de Mesnard, who was nearly thirty years her senior, extremely thin, plagued by fetid breath, and without a tooth in his mouth, according to an incredulous duchesse de Maillé. *Souvenirs,* 178.

104. "Correspondance. Bath 16 Mai 1831," *La Mode,* July 2, 1831, 6–7.

105. In 1830, at Rambouillet, the duchesse de Berry had given a rousing speech to the royal troops before the family set off for exile. Sailing into exile, she wore a man's military hat in another gesture of the androgynous royal role that events had forced on her.

106. The legitimist lawyer and deputy Pierre-Antoine Berryer's failure to persuade her to leave France is recounted in a letter from the Procureur du Roi at Nantes dated June 12, 1832, after Berryer's arrest; BB30 964, A.P.P.P. To a member of his own party, Berryer confided, "There is in the head and heart of that princess what it takes to make twenty kings." Quoted in Thirria, *La Duchesse de Berry,* 61, 119–28. Among the papers seized at the time of her arrest and presented at the trial of the women who hid her at Nantes, the du Guiny sisters, was a letter from the duchesse de Berry explaining her motive: "I considered my cause lost forever if I were forced to flee the country." Document #267, BB 30 964, A.P.P.P.

107. The legitimist papers ran regular stories on the prisoner at Blaye. With fourteen thousand subscribers, *La Gazette de France* was the leading legitimist paper. About thirty provincial gazettes had come into being after 1830. Vidal de la Blanche, *Marie-Caroline,* 110. A letter addressed to the president of the Council and Minister of War from the military commander who arrested her assured his superiors: "All the respect due her sex and her high rank has been and will be observed"; BB4 1030, A.N.

108. Qb1 M 112118, Estampes, B.N. See also in series QB1: M 111937–8, M 111955, M 111959–60, M 112096, M 112098–100, M 112102–4, M 112101I, M 112107–11, M 112113–16, M 112119–22, M 112203, M 112279.

109. On melodrama in Parisian theaters, see "Revue et Causeries du Monde," *La Mode,* April-June 1830, 310. Le Hir notes a dramatic shift in 1830 in the plots of Victor Ducange, the leading Parisian author of melodramas; women characters now dominated his plots, and mothers became the symbol of the harmony necessary for a happy ending; "La Représentation de la famille," 21.

110. Émile Lefranc, *La Duchesse de Berri en dix-sept tableaux* (Paris, 1832).

111. Reprinted from *Le Journal de la Guienne* in *La Gazette de France,* Feb.

12, 1833, 2. A description of her emotional reaction to finding portraits of her children hidden in a bouquet of flowers appeared in *La Gazette de France,* Feb. 13, 1833, 2 and Feb. 17, 1833, 3. However, memoirs of two men who became her confidants in prison report that she spoke rarely of her children. Lieutenant Ferdinand Petitpierre, *Journal de la captivité de la duchesse de Berry à Blaye, 1832–1833* (Paris, 1904) and Ménière, *La Captivité.*

112. "Mémoire sur la captivité de Madame la Duchesse de Berry" (Paris, 1833). This pamphlet appeared on Dec. 24, 1832, in thirty-five thousand copies. See also Théodore Anne, *La Prisonnière de Blaye* (Paris, 1832) and Cyprien Desmarais, *La Révolution de juillet à S.A.R. la duchesse de Berry, captive à Blaye* (Paris, 1832).

113. *La Gazette de France* and *La Quotidienne* announced petitions repeatedly. A list of around 1,350 names appeared on a petition published as a supplement for *Le Mémorial bordelais,* 1 M 356, Departmental Archives, Bordeaux. Documents relating to petitions and protests on her behalf addressed to the Ministry of the Interior, Ministry of the Marine, Ministry of Justice, and the Chamber of Deputies or published by the press are located in BB18 1331–36, A.N. Petitions sent directly to the king or queen appear in 300 AP III 33, A.F., A.N. An article in *Le Courrier anglais* described the initial positive response to the duchess's maternal sacrifice, reprinted in *Le Constitutionnel,* March 8, 1833, 1.

114. Several of these offers were reported by *La Gazette de France.* For offers made directly to Queen Marie-Amélie, see 300 AP III 33, A.F., A.N.

115. "Paris de cet hiver," *La Mode,* Oct.-Dec., 1932, 111–15, 163–64.

116. Lucas-Dubreton, *La Princesse captive, la duchesse de Berry, 1832–1833* (Paris: Perrin, 1925), 93. The government avoided bringing the duchess to trial, but without a trial or the publication of the correspondence found in her possession, it was difficult to confirm the most damning charges leveled against her of complicity with foreign governments. Legitimists often presented their heroic royal mother as having come to France unarmed and alone to reclaim the rights of her son. See "Réclamation sur la captivité de Madame, Duchesse de Berri" in *L'Orléanais: journal politique, littéraire et commercial,* Feb. 6, 1833, 1, recorded as document 8511 a7 in BB18 1334–36, A.N. *La Gazette de France,* Jan. 26, 1833, 3, even claimed that the uprising in the Vendée preceded her arrival and that she came to stop the bloodshed.

117. On Dec. 10, 1832, *Le Charivari* published six explicit caricatures. In two of them, Mayeux, the fantastical hunchbacked truth-sayer invented by Traviès de Villers, measured the front and backside of the duchesse de Berry. The captions read, "In front two" and "Madame's back is a bit too flat." Another depicted the duchess carrying a baby with the caption, "It's not yours? the beautiful baby?"

118. *Le Constitutionnel,* Feb. 4, 1833, 2. *Le National,* Jan. 31, Feb. 2, Feb. 3, and Feb. 17, 1833. On dueling in this period, see Robert A. Nye, *Masculinity and Male Codes of Honour in Modern France* (New York, Oxford: Oxford University Press, 1993).

119. The declaration appeared in *Le Moniteur* on Feb. 26. The original version of the declaration had included the words, "enceinte de sept mois" (seven

months pregnant). Marie-Caroline substituted the enigmatic phrase "pressée par les circonstances les plus urgentes" (forced by the most urgent circumstances) to explain why she felt compelled to reveal her secret marriage. The implication of a pregnancy was understood by everyone. Cited from the Bordeaux paper *L'Indicateur* in *Le Constitutionnel,* May 8, 1933, 2.

120. The republican editor Philipon ran a lithograph by C. J. Traviès that depicted an astonished legitimist reading *Le Moniteur* with the caption "She is really pregnant!!!!", *La Caricature,* plate 254, March 7, 1833. See also *Le Constitutionnel,* Feb. 26, 1833, 2 and Feb. 27, 1833, 1. An article in *Le Constitutionnel,* Feb. 28, 1833, debunked the idea of the duchesse de Berry as devoted mother and inconsolable widow.

121. Changy, *Le Soulèvement,* 223.

122. The claim that the duchesse de Berry was dying produced a few direct appeals from legitimist women to Marie-Amélie to intervene on her niece's behalf, 300 AP III 33, A.F., A.N. Several legitimist men appealed to the Ministry of the Interior to release the dying prisoner, BB30 964, A.P.P.P. *La Gazette de France* included an article on the duchess, surrounded by a black mourning band, in every issue from March 14 until May 16, 1883, when the government announced her pending release. *La Quotidienne, Le Rénovateur, Le Courrier français, La Gazette de Midi,* and *Le Journal de la Guyenne* also refused to accept the authenticity of the declaration. *Espérance, journal du peuple* published a special supplement on the theme of treachery by the Orléans entitled *"Odieuse Machination de Louis-Philippe et de sa Famille, contre l'Honneur de S.A.R. Madame,"* BB 18, 1333, A.N. After the birth, all the legitimist papers accepted its authenticity except *La Quotidienne,* which published a letter from M. de Kerogorlay, one of the original conspirators, denying that the duchess had been pregnant. Cited in *Le Constitutionnel,* no. 140, May 20, 1833, 2. For other documents claiming disbelief, see 8653-a7 and 9058-a7 in BB18 1334–36, A.P.P.P.

123. William M. Reddy, "Condottieri of the Pen: Journalists and the Public Sphere in Postrevolutionary France (1815–1850)," *American Historical Review,* 99 (Dec. 1994): 1546–70. See also Reddy, *The Invisible Code: Honor and Sentiment in Postrevolutionary France, 1814–1848* (Berkeley and Los Angeles: University of California, 1997). For republican papers' attacks on the dishonorability of Louis-Philippe in this affair, see *Le Charivari,* Feb. 27 and March 3, 1833 and the citation to *Le National* and *Le Courrier Français* in *La Gazette de France,* Feb. 28, 1833, 4–5.

124. Initially, legitimists' private reactions were often hostile to the duchess. Boigne, *Mémoires,* 2: 320. See also the letter dated May 31, 1833, from a judge on the civil tribunal at Gex in the Ain to the Minister of Justice, reporting similar attitudes among legitimists there. BB18 1336, A.N.

125. Madame Cayla, the last favorite of Louis XVIII, is believed to have arranged the marriage with Lucchesi-Palli in a secret correspondence with the duchess while she was in prison. The historian Lucas-Dubreton found, in the archives of the prince de Beauvau, a letter from the duchess, copied in Cayla's handwriting and dated April 12, 1833, addressed from Blaye to Marshal de Bourmont thanking him for conveying to her the sentiments of Comte Lucchesi-Palli. "I will write myself to thank him and to express how touched I am by his

proposal which I accept with the greatest gratitude. My vocation will be to make him happy. I think it important that with the greatest prudence, haste, and secrecy, he go to Naples to register the act of marriage and that he stay there to wait for me." Jean Harteman, *"Une maternité inopinée de Marie-Caroline, duchesse de Berry,"* presented at l'Académie de Stanislas de Nancy, May 16, 1969. Most biographers of the duchess believe that the actual father of the child was the lawyer Achille Guibourg, who, along with the elderly count de Mesnard, was the only man with her in hiding.

126. Pope Gregory XVI invited her to an audience on October 27, 1833, in a spectacular public act of approbation. Thirria, *La duchesse de Berry,* 24. According to the comtesse de Boigne, insiders all knew that on the day selected for the registration of marriage in a little village in the duchy of Modena, Lucchesi-Palli was actually in Holland. *Mémoires,* 2: 322.

127. For aristocratic women, motherhood did not mean giving up their roles as social organizers for a Rousseauian version of domesticity. Nor did it include nursing their infants. See George D. Sussman, *Selling Mothers' Milk. The Wet-Nursing Business in France, 1715–1914* (Urbana: University of Illinois Press, 1982). The duchesse de Berry did not share this sense of feminine propriety. At the Neopolitan court, even queens nursed their offspring. At Blaye, Marie-Caroline wanted to nurse her new infant but was persuaded by Doctor Deneux not to do so.

128. See her correspondence with the comtesse Augustine de Montaigu, 1834–1869, FR 14937, Salle des manuscrits, B.N. The daughter born at Blaye died on November 11, 1833.

129. She eventually purchased the chateau of Brünsee outside Gratz in Styria, Austria, for her principal residence and the palace of Vendramino in Venice for the winter months. As long as Charles X lived, her visits remained infrequent. The death of Charles X on November 6, 1836, did little to improve the royal mother's personal relations with the Angoulêmes. Jean-Paul Bled, *Les Lys en exil ou la second mort de l'Ancien Regime* (Paris: Fayard, 1992), 59–68, 78–80, 83–88, 109–10, 185–91.

130. Cited from BB 18/18/1369/5589, A.N., in Fabrice Lascar, "Cris et chuchotements. Démonstrations séditieuses et injures au Roi ou à la famille royale sous la Monarchie de Juillet (Août 1830-Février 1848)," Maîtrisse, University of Paris I, 1990, 140–41.

131. For a description of that dual role, see David Higgs, *Nobles in Nineteenth-Century France: The Practice of Inegalitarianism* (Baltimore: Johns Hopkins University Press, 1987), 173–74, 182–83.

132. See her introduction to *Journal de Marie-Amélie* and FN 1, 274. Shreds from the dress that de Berry was wearing on the day of her arrest were treasured trophies of remembrance in the Vendée. "Madame, Duchesse de Berry," Exposition Catalogue, Palais Dobrée (Nantes, Dec. 1963-Feb. 1964).

133. *La Vendée et Madame, deuxième édition véritable* (Paris, 1834), 390, 408. The authentic version of Dermancourt's memoir came out in two editions in 1833 with a different publisher. See also T. Morel, *La Vérité sur l'arrestation de Madame, duchesse de Berry, et les mensonges de Deutz dévoilés, . . . augmentée de l'homme qui livre une femme par Victor Hugo* (Paris, 1836); M.L.C. *Mystère dévoilé ou les géoliers de Blaye confondus par eux-memes,* 2d ed. (Paris,

1839); Germain Sarrut and B. Saint-Edmé, *Biographie de Marie-Caroline-Ferdinande-Louise de Bourbon, duchesse de Berri, extraite de la Biographie des hommes du jour* (Paris, 1841); Mesnard, *Souvenirs intimes;* and Lamothe-Langon *Mémoires.*

134. Charles X's death coincided with this revival of attention on the royal mother.

"Playing the Princess"

*Flora Tristan, Performance,
and Female Moral Authority
during the July Monarchy*

SUSAN GROGAN

On the evening of September 22, 1844, Flora Tristan addressed a meeting of workers in an upstairs room on the *rue du Temple* at Agen. She spoke on the major themes of her recent book, *The Workers' Union*, on which she had addressed many similar meetings throughout France over the preceding months. It called for "the universal union of working men and women," and she used her meetings to promulgate the idea and enroll members. Once workers formed a united force, they could pressure the government for reforms, she argued, and begin to remedy the most serious problems confronting the working class. More far-reaching experiments could then be conducted, culminating ultimately in the establishment of a socialist society.[1] But the sixty workers present were clearly nervous and every sound brought anxious glances at the door. The tension reached a climax when a commotion in the street below announced the arrival of a contingent of troops and police officers to shut down the meeting. Flora Tristan described in her diary the events that followed. The workers bolted when ordered to leave, while the troops tried to escape the pouring rain by squeezing into the small room downstairs. In the resulting chaos the "Mother" of this *compagnonnage* establishment, who was in an advanced stage of pregnancy, collapsed and had to be attended to by other women present. The soldiers left standing in the rain became increasingly disgruntled, seeing no sign of the revolution they had been told to expect. "And I, still playing the role of the princess, was standing quietly at the window behind the half-open

Portrait of Flora Tristan. Bibliothèque Nationale de France, Cabinet des Estampes. Photo Bibliothèque Nationale de France, Paris

shutter — watching and listening to everything," Tristan wrote. "The soldiers were furious! . . . One little chap . . . was saying the most amusing
things about the propensity of all police commissioners to see revolutions
everywhere! . . . 'And this Parisian woman who's stirring up revolution,
where the devil is she? At least they could let us see her.' . . . I can't
describe how hilarious it was listening to this Parisian trooper hamming
it up. — He was extremely entertaining."[2]

In recording these events in her diary, Flora Tristan presented the scene
as a performance — as a farce, perhaps — in which she was a leading
player. This illustrates the sense of theatricality that imbued Tristan's view
of the world and that is generally overlooked within standard accounts
focused on her life as feminist and socialist.[3] But it also points to the way
in which the life of an unconventional woman like Flora Tristan might
become or be seen as an extended performance, as she challenged the
norm of female domesticity being promoted in the early nineteenth century. The domestic ideal, which formed one of the pillars of the emergent
bourgeois social order of July monarchy France, defined women's role in
limited terms and in particular denied their right to hold public office or
to exercise public authority. The image of the "domestic woman" was
intended to throw into relief that of the "public man," the citizen who
inhabited the newly articulated public sphere defined as male space.[4] For
a woman like Tristan who aspired to play a key role in political affairs,
who envisaged at one point organizing a provisional government and, at
another, being "at the head of this great European people,"[5] the challenge
was two-fold: to contest both the prohibitions that excluded women from
such roles and the assumptions on which such prohibitions rested. By
drawing on alternate images of womanhood that linked it with authority
and power, and by imagining and representing herself within those traditions, Tristan sought to contest more limited models of woman's potential and justify her own claim to social influence. By observing some of
the personae that Flora Tristan adopted in her venture onto the public
stage then, we can observe one woman's attempt to represent herself as a
figure of public authority in July monarchy France.

DOMESTICATING WOMEN'S INFLUENCE

Flora Tristan's life might well have followed the domestic model idealized
for girls within her culture. Born in 1803, the daughter of an aristocratic
Peruvian father and a French mother, she grew to adolescence nurturing
romantic dreams of love and marriage. But these were shattered by the

discovery of her own illegitimacy, which destroyed any prospect of a good match. Rather than finding happiness in "a passionate and exclusive love for one of those men to whom great devotion attracts great misfortune, who suffer from one of those tragedies that glorify and ennoble the victim they befall,"[6] she married a Parisian engraver shortly before her eighteenth birthday and found instead violence and unhappiness. The conflict continued even after Tristan fled the marital home in 1825 and culminated only with her estranged husband's attempt to murder her in 1838. As Tristan's experience illustrates, the Civil Code was particularly disadvantageous to married women, designed to subject them to the power of their husbands even if a marriage broke down and confirming a patriarchal authority structure by banning divorce. This explains why marriage law reform was a central concern of feminists in this period and why the legalization of divorce was one of Tristan's ongoing political demands.

For any woman, rejection of the marriage in which she was supposed to find her fulfillment was a momentous decision not to be taken lightly. The fact that Tristan had two children to support and was pregnant with her third when she left her husband made her situation particularly challenging, as she realized when she began to seek employment. Having broken with convention in such a public way, she had become a social outcast.[7] She found work by becoming a lady's maid, leaving her children in her mother's care and traveling with her employers to England and throughout Europe. Travel, reading, and general life experience made her increasingly aware of the scope and variety of social injustice, and once back in France in the 1830s, contact with feminists and socialists alerted her to the ideas of others on such matters. She signed petitions for divorce and against capital punishment, subscribed to socialist appeals to finance experiments with collective living, corresponded with other socialists about their ideas for social reorganization, and began to publish political tracts and fiction outlining her own proposals for change. Initially a disillusioned wife, Flora Tristan became a social activist determined to make a difference.

Tristan chose an irregular life, not only by living as a separated wife, but by entering the public arena: earning her living as a writer, speaking out on a variety of social issues, debating ideas for change with other socialists and republicans, seeking to influence public opinion and play a leading role in socialist and working-class politics. Her links with working-class activists from 1843 until her sudden death the following year reflected her conviction that the "largest and most useful class," male

and female, was also the most oppressed, and that their political mobi-
lization was the key to social transformation.[8] She set out to promulgate
this idea in her publications and her speaking tour among French workers: the tour that took her to Agen in September 1844. The problem was
finding the means of legitimizing her position as expert: to have her claim
to public authority, knowledge, and leadership recognized and accepted
by her contemporaries.

The challenge that this undertaking posed can be understood only
within the context of the debate in early nineteenth-century French society about "woman's place," and this debate in turn had its origin in late
eighteenth-century political struggles. During that period, philosophers
and moralists increasingly emphasized the differentiation between the
sexes, and hence between the social roles they should play and the social
spheres they should occupy. Women's role was increasingly defined as a
"private" one, removed from the exercise of public authority or influence, and a variety of arguments was presented to justify their exclusion
from the public arena.[9] Rousseau's writings were particularly influential.
His "republic of virtue" was predicated on women's exclusion from that
republic and their confinement to the domestic sphere. Women's moral
influence was acknowledged, but it was also to be contained and limited
to its "proper" orbit, which was not the world of public debate and
political decision making.[10]

This domestic discourse did not emerge in a vacuum but was partly a
response to the prominent position of aristocratic women in Old Régime
social and political life. By associating the weakness of the Old Order
with the exercise of power by women, its critics simultaneously associated the reshaping of public authority with the removal of women from
political life.[11] A highly gendered notion of revolutionary "virtue" further justified the political authority of men in the new régime. Male
virtue rested on disinterestedness, on adherence to abstract principles,
and pursuit of the general good whatever the personal cost. Female virtue
lay in fostering the happiness of those near and dear to the woman and
in the emotional connectedness that ran counter to dispassionate public
decision making. Whereas man asserted his virtue by his actions within
the public sphere, woman's presence in the public arena was deemed to
destroy her virtue.[12] Consequently, the legitimacy of the new revolutionary régime, particularly the First Republic, was posited on its exclusion
of women. Counterarguments by those like Marquis de Condorcet who
emphasized the essential similarity between women and men were
rejected, and the widespread involvement of women in revolutionary

politics was condemned. Revolutionary leaders idealized the "Republican mother" on one hand and banned women from participation in political debate and activity on the other.[13]

As the events of the revolutionary period demonstrated, the assertion that woman's destiny was essentially domestic was not self-evident but needed constant legitimation. This remained true in the postrevolutionary period also. Conservative theorists stressed the importance of well-ordered families for the creation of a well-ordered society. Claims about women's limited rationality and self-control, and the unruliness of their bodies, justified placing them under male control within the family: a position reflected in the Civil Code.[14] If authority was construed as male within this model, the image of altruism, self-sacrifice, and devotion through which a regenerative social unity would be created was symbolized by the mother, who was attributed the power to inaugurate this new order by her role in shaping the model citizen.[15] Women's role in the moral education of their children was invested rhetorically with enormous power and defined as the underpinning of the public world, which was the domain of men. The "mother-educator" was the ideal to which women were thus encouraged to conform during the July monarchy, and the education of girls of all classes was designed to instill the ideal of domesticity within them.[16]

Both positive and negative representations of womanhood provided arguments for closely defining women's sphere of influence, but the force and frequency with which such demands were reiterated suggest that they were not well heeded. In fact, the July monarchy also witnessed a sustained challenge, both theoretical and practical, to advocates of the domestic ideal. The contrary view considered that, far from creating disorder, the participation of women in public life would end the conflict produced by male competitiveness and aggression. Calls for "moral regeneration" could thus justify a broad definition of woman's place — an idea that permeated the theories of most socialists of the period, including Flora Tristan.[17] Besides, rather than being silent and invisible within the home, women continued to play a range of roles in society. The domestic ideal was irrelevant for working-class and peasant women, the majority of the female population. Many bourgeois women, too, remained actively involved in the affairs of the family business until the second half of the nineteenth century, while philanthropic work gave them an important role in the community.[18] The 1830s also saw the emergence to prominence of female novelists, poets, and journalists whose writings stimulated public debate about such issues as female education and the unequal position of women within marriage. Further-more, in the late 1820s and early 1830s the socialist Saint-Simonian movement briefly provided the spectacle of women as comanagers with men of social services in the poor districts of Paris and as "preachers" of their new socialist religion.[19]

The domestic discourse was clearly not hegemonic as a description of women's lives in the early nineteenth century, therefore, but it could not be ignored. It was the prescription to be contested; the model that simul-taneously defined the *femme révoltée* and condemned her actions. The extent to which radicals — women and men, socialists and feminists — addressed and challenged this model illustrates its prescriptive power. As Flora Tristan's life demonstrates, too, women who lived outside its norms were constantly aware of their own transgression and of the need to explain and justify their lives.

The essence of domesticity lay not in defending a spatial separation of the sexes, but in defining a social hierarchy that enshrined male control of public life and political power. Spatial distinctions mattered because space was political, but the domestic ideal was ultimately about author-ity. Whatever informal power women may have wielded within the fam-ily, for instance, they had few legal grounds for contesting men's decisions even on family matters. And while women did occupy a variety of public roles, these did not include roles of public leadership and authority. There was no recognized political role for women, and political discourse was framed in terms that made it difficult for women to regard themselves, or be regarded by others, as included.[20] In fact, the eruption of women into political life at times of crisis — in protest, rebellion, and revolution — was, for many observers, the hallmark of disorder and of the world gone awry. François Guizot, the leading politician and key theorist of the July monarchy, echoed the views of his revolutionary predecessors in defining the world of politics as a male one, counterposed to the world of women: " . . . there is no doubt that, naturally and in general, neither women nor minors are capable of controlling the interests [of society]. Providence has destined the former for a domestic life; the latter have not yet attained the full development of their individual existence and of their faculties. The first restriction on the right to vote, its legitimacy as well as its necessity, stems from this fact."[21] Moreover, Guizot's Republican opponents excluded women from both the "universal" suffrage they espoused and from the organizations that promoted it.[22]

In a world where views like these were predominant, where politi-cal culture was shaped through images of heroic masculinity and by the exclusion of women, women like Flora Tristan who sought to play a political role faced an enormous task in establishing their legitimacy. They had no positive images of women as political figures that might have justified such an undertaking.[23] However, if political models provided no options, other cultural models of femininity provided images of female authority that might serve to make the woman leader a more familiar and acceptable figure. Both early nineteenth-century melodrama and religious images of the Madonna figure idealized the moral role of women and provided an opening that Tristan could exploit for this purpose. By enacting the archetypal female role as personification of Morality, but placing it within a variety of public contexts, Tristan sought to present herself as a woman leader and claim authority for her message of social transformation.

PERFORMANCE, MELODRAMA, AND THE FEMININE CRITIQUE OF AUTHORITY

The concept of "performance" provides one way of reconceptualizing lives lived in the past, as we grapple with the theoretical challenges posed in recent years to the study of individual lives. The idea that "selves" are "decentered, multiple, or unknowable" rather than fixed, stable, and open to confident interpretation has given rise to a search for new ways to understand such nebulous entities.[24] Moreover, feminist theory has suggested that the historical category "woman" can be understood only as it is created discursively at any given moment, questioning the idea of an essential "womanhood."[25] The notion of a "performed" self or selves, of the continual creation of the self, of the "becoming" rather than the "being" of one's "self," emerges from such considerations. But a woman's "performances" were shaped within specific historical contexts that made available a range of cultural models with which she might engage in perceiving or representing herself. From this perspective, we need to consider not what Flora Tristan was "really like," but how she understood and represented herself as a woman at a given historical moment.

In discussing the life of the late nineteenth-century feminist Marguerite Durand, Mary Louise Roberts argues that Durand's "performance" served to conceal elements of her own perceived identity that did not conform to expected feminine norms. Durand's display of "hyperfemininity," Roberts suggests, served as a critique of "the feminine" and also opened a space for a life lived in "unfeminine" ways by distracting

attention from unconventional aspects of her behavior.[26] But performance can also involve the revelation rather than the concealment of the
self, as Flora Tristan's life demonstrates. It can describe an attempt to
represent, rather than to hide, a self that does not conform to dominant
social expectations. Tristan enacted a womanhood that was powerful
and authoritative in an attempt to mold the feminine norm anew and
expand its parameters. In this sense, she did not so much reject the fet-
ters of a "feminine" life, as seek to extend the conventionally "feminine" in ways that were liberating and fulfilling.

Tristan's writings suggest a woman who frequently conceptualized herself as a performer and who assumed a variety of different characters.
There were moments when she clearly chose to "put on an act," slipping
into a role and in some instances adopting a costume appropriate for the
part.[27] She first represented herself in public in 1838 with the appearance
of her first book, the semiautobiographical *Peregrinations of a Pariah*.
Here, in confessing her status as illegitimate child and separated wife, she
publicly identified with a well-established metaphor for the socially marginalized.[28] Besides, having described herself in her book as "a *Pariah*,
whom people believe they are treating indulgently if they spare her
injury,"[29] she then sought to enact the "Pariah" more completely by having her portrait painted in that guise: as "the *Pariah* . . . the woman born
an Andalusian and condemned by society to spend her youth in tears and
without love!"[30] She reminded the artist that costume and pose would be
all-important in creating this image of the innocent victim and suggested
that he study her physiognomy carefully before putting brush to canvas.
Whether this painting was ever produced is unknown, but the pariah figure was to retain a significant place among Tristan's array of self-images.[31]

Tristan put on another stunning performance when she visited London to study social conditions there. As well as investigating the haunts
of the poor and oppressed, like others interested in "the social question," Tristan also attended a session of Parliament. However, since
women were not admitted to the public galleries, Tristan borrowed a set
of men's clothes and attended dressed as a Turkish diplomat. She
described the scene at length, emphasizing her own starring role in what
was for others a rather disconcerting impromptu performance. While she
assumed "the calm bearing of the true Ottoman," as her character
required, those around her, who saw through the male disguise, were
thrown into confusion. Despite the comic dimensions Tristan gave this
event, however, it was also endowed with a serious moral purpose, facil-

itating her critique of the oppression of women within the self-styled land of liberty and progress.[32]

The "princess" who confronted Police Commissioner Segon at Agen in 1844 was a practiced performer, therefore, and one accustomed to playing the lead. Tristan's report of her encounter with the commissioner also stressed its comic dimension. It suggests that such performances were enormously entertaining for her, particularly when others were required to "ad lib" their lines in a show they had joined unwittingly. In Tristan's version, she took control of the scene and set about making Segon look stupid: "The lengthy silence was becoming tiresome and almost ridiculous . . . I had an idea: 'Champagne,' I said [addressing one of the workers] in the same tone of voice as I would have used in a drawing room, 'do me the pleasure of going downstairs and asking the Mother for a glass of sugared water.' — He had forgotten the spoon, so I asked him with a smile to go back down. — The fat man [Segon] was purple, violet!" After further provocation, Segon finally lashed out verbally at one of the workers, "in such a brutal manner that I could not capture in words his expression, his gesture, or his fury."[33] Similarly, the pretensions of Police Commissioner Boisseneau, whom Tristan had encountered at Toulouse earlier that month, inspired her amused ridicule: "He is the civil servant obsessed with the importance of his office. He is fanatical about his social status, his position, his master L[ouis]-Ph[ilippe]. He is indeed a curiosity. . . . I reproach myself for not having seduced this man with some beautiful and very gentle words but he was so ridiculous that he provoked in me a desire to laugh which I could not control."[34]

These encounters with the authorities, described as comic scenes, were actually far from trivial. By 1844, Tristan had acquired a reputation as a socialist and therefore a politically dangerous person. If *Peregrinations of a Pariah* had been dismissed by the critics as the protest of an atypical woman against marriage, her subsequent publications could not be discounted as comments on her own personal experiences. Her study of London had specifically warned French workers about the dangers they faced as capitalism developed, carrying with it the extremes of wealth and poverty she had detected in England. She had also published a novel whose hero was a "proletarian" struggling against the forces of the old order.[35] Worse still, Tristan had become an associate of well-known socialists and an ally of artisanal militants. Her call for a "workers' union" was therefore viewed by the authorities as a call to revolution, at a time when the July monarchy was increasingly hard-pressed to contain industrial and social protest. As a result, Tristan's speaking tour, like the activities of other troublemakers, was of interest to the police. She was kept under surveillance, her hotel rooms were searched, her papers secretly read and stolen, and her meetings closed down as offenses against public order. This was the situation in which Commissioner Boisseneau at Toulouse forbade her to hold public meetings. This was the situation in which Commissioner Segon descended upon Tristan's gathering in Agen to put a stop to it.

Tristan's "performances" in such situations were presented not simply as moments of comedy, therefore, but as melodrama. Melodrama was the most popular theatrical genre of the period, and it had a strong moral focus. The exaggerated representation of good and evil, personified in the characters of hero and villain, often had a humorous element, but the melodrama was intended primarily as a new-style morality play: clarifying the moral universe in a postrevolutionary world that had witnessed the death of the Sacred and the shattering of the traditional bases of truth and ethics. Its themes made clear that good and evil were at work in the everyday world, which was presented as the site of an ongoing contest between vice and virtue.[36] Melodrama's exploration of moral questions suited a social climate in which the need for moral renewal was generally agreed, although the principles that would characterize the new moral order were hotly debated.[37]

Tristan had a keen interest in the theater and frequently compared incidents and persons to scenes and characters on the Parisian stage. She greatly admired Frédérick Lemaître, one of the leading actors of the day, and was familiar with plays by popular dramatists such as Scribe.[38] Melodrama's moral agenda also appealed to Tristan's interest in moral questions and suited her own sense of the clear polarities between good and bad, right and wrong, justice and injustice. Moreover, like the melodramatists of her day, she regarded the world as upside down. The wicked successfully posed as virtuous, and the virtuous were condemned as evildoers. The hero was awaited who would expose falsity and restore the true moral universe. Flora Tristan envisaged herself in such a role and represented herself in that guise.

The portly Segon in his tricolor sash was a figure of fun because he adopted the exaggerated pomp and posturing of high office, as in contemporary melodramas. But such characterizations also had melodrama's more serious moral dimension. Tristan found it farcical that, while wearing the tricolor sash that symbolized the overthrow of tyranny, Segon should still behave in a tyrannical way: "Oh! it's all done in the name of the king, it's just the same as in [17]88. Lord, it was hardly worth the trouble of guillotining 2 or 3 — or chasing out 4 or 5 — To return 56 years later to the old formula: 'In the name of the king' — what else would they say in Russia? — We must conclude that political revolutions are absolute farces!"[39]

In the melodramatic context, Tristan's confrontation with Segon juxtaposed alternate models of leadership and alternate political priorities and moral qualities. Segon personified for Tristan the powerful figure who was corrupt and unworthy of authority. He was violent, with a reputation for ruthlessness toward the people. His conduct in this incident showed his lack of self-control, as he became angry and lapsed into personal abuse. He had no respect for workers, referring to them as "rabble" and generally bringing his office into disrepute. If Segon was portrayed as the embodiment of despotic behavior, Tristan personified the democratic challenge to injustice, which was also a standard melodramatic theme. Not only was she impervious to the threat that Segon posed, but she defended the workers' rights in this situation. They were obliged to obey the instruction to disband the meeting, but those who belonged to the *Société de l'Union,* on whose premises the meeting was held, were not obliged to leave despite Segon's threats, as she reminded them.[40]

Similarly, the encounter with Boisseneau and his superiors at Toulouse became a scene in which the nature of legitimate authority was examined and contested. For Tristan, Boisseneau and the prefect lacked "the sense of justice, of order, of humanity, which should inspire a public office-holder." Instead, they were driven only by unworthy motives:

> In 1840 the workers triumphed, they forced the *Procureur-général* to flee like a thief — the prefect and the others [too]. — And since then the pride of the prefectural clan has been severely wounded — they want revenge. — But what have things come to, dear God! How can authority, which should represent justice, that is calmness, reason, order, authority [*sic*], dare to proclaim publicly its hatred, its anger, its desire for vengeance? — But that is monstrous! That demonstrates a weakness, an ill-will and a lack of dignity which has never been seen before in any century, in any country.
>
> (This is only a sketch — but I have some wonderful pages to write on this topic!)[41]

By contrast to the motives attributed to Boisseneau, Tristan's account endowed her with moral authority, highlighting her integrity, her respect for the law, her dignity and self-control. Segon and Boisseneau may have been the official power holders, but she also wielded authority in the encounters because authority was recognized in her by those present. The workers were guided by her, not by Segon, while Segon dared not overstep the mark in dealing with her. Similarly, Boisseneau was dismayed by Tristan's audacity as she again assumed the demeanor of the "princess" at Toulouse, affecting an arrogant disregard for his authority and telling him "a few home truths." His subordinates, she noted, "looked at me with an expression of joy[,] of admiration that I can only explain in terms of their disdain for their stupid boss."[42]

Regardless of the accuracy with which Tristan reported these events, the meanings with which she invested them illuminate her sense of self at this time. By constructing them as she did, Tristan claimed for herself an authority that was based not on the privilege of office but on virtue, and, as in melodrama, that virtue was recognized in her by others. The incidents were presented as encounters between the oppressor and the oppressed. As in melodrama, too, the villain was powerful and privileged, corrupt and unworthy, persecuting the powerless who had virtue on their side. If they currently suffered under the weight of the villain's malevolence, the victims could cling to the expectation of eventually overcoming evil.[43] The melodramatic script dictated that the repression of workers' right to organize and to defend their own interests, that the oppression of the weak by the mighty, could not endure. The notes Tristan made in her diary were intended as the basis for a book that would expose the scope and extent of injustice, and give her a heroic and leading role in the process of redress.

PERFORMANCES OF AUTHORITY: FROM MELODRAMATIC HEROINE TO FEMALE MESSIAH

Woman's association with morality in the dominant discourses of femininity provided the basis for her normative role as heart of the family and guardian of its domestic virtues. But insofar as morality was not a purely domestic matter, the confinement of women's moral influence to the home was not straightforward either. Woman's association with the moral realm opened a space for women like Tristan to claim a moral authority that exceeded domestic bounds. This link had provided the basis for the Saint-Simonians' reshaping of gender roles in the early 1830s, as they defended the moral advance to be achieved by bringing women's pacifism, altruism, and love into the public realm. They envisaged the politics of coercion and violence giving way to the politics of persuasion and conciliation.[44] Flora Tristan held a similar view and enacted this transition in her performances as an authoritative public figure.

The genre of melodrama provided one model of femininity in which the moral role attributed to woman was enacted publicly. In the melodramatic tradition, virtue is frequently personified in a woman: a persecuted figure whose courage in adversity and whose challenge to the forces of evil demonstrate her moral superiority to man.[45] This tradition gives added meaning to the melodramatic "performances" of Flora Tristan, linking her claims to authority specifically with her identity as a woman and providing one source of validation for her, as she imagined herself to be a powerful figure.

The role of the heroine of the melodrama, whose very presence expressed virtue as she suffered at the hands of the wicked, suggests a way of reading Tristan's earlier performance as pariah, for instance. As a pariah, she tells us, she was shunned and despised for transgressing social expectations. But this pariah was also the heroine who suffered in the name of a higher set of values, exposing the injustices that women endured. Tristan became "the Pariah" by braving public opinion and urging others to do likewise: "Let women whose lives have been tormented by great adversity recount their sufferings; let them expose the misfortunes that they have experienced as a result of the position in which the laws have placed them and the prejudices that shackle them; but above all let them give their names . . . for, I repeat, reforms will only occur, and there will only be honesty and frankness in social relations as a result of such revelations."[46] From this perspective, a performance as "victim" acquired connotations of grandeur and moral authority, rather than simply of oppression.

Tristan's appearance in court in 1839 during her husband's trial for attempting to murder her can also be interpreted in this light. She entered the courtroom slowly, half an hour late, needing a glass of water before she could begin her evidence and unable to raise her voice sufficiently to be heard as she answered the judges' questions.[47] Her fragile and suffering appearance, her subjection to cross-examination, the fact that her life and writings were examined for signs of immorality although she was the victim of the crime, all combined to make the court scene a reenactment of the heroine's victimization by an unjust world. The pariah, who had fled from a violent husband but had little legal protection against him, was a victim of society and its unjust laws. Her husband, the accused, who had sought to punish his recalcitrant wife and reassert patriarchal authority, was a defender of that society: "The *defender of the husbands* attacked by Flora Tristan," as she observed to a friend.[48] Without diminishing the significance of the injuries she suffered at her husband's hands or the validity of her status as "victim" in the courtroom drama, we might perhaps read her "performance" there, in addition, as another evocation of the pariah figure, and thus of the larger moral issues that the pariah represented.

In her melodramatic performances, Tristan presented herself not just as the heroine, the symbol of innocence oppressed, but as the hero, the character engaged actively in the moral contest. Her encounters with Segon and Boisseneau can be read in this light, for she did not simply endure their persecution, but set out to expose and oppose them. Similarly, she determined to unveil what she regarded as the hypocrisy of Republican militants with whom she frequently found herself in conflict in the towns she visited in 1844. Rather than challenging the perceived weaknesses of Republican theory through her writings, as some of her female contemporaries were doing, Tristan confronted Republican activists directly.[49] She condemned particularly the leaders of secret societies who were prepared to employ violence, and even foment revolution, in order to win power. "The democrats are the same everywhere," she noted at Montpellier, "men with silver tongues who want to make use of the people but who certainly don't wish to serve them!"[50] For her, these "so-called democrats" were driven by naked ambition, and she argued that if a revolution broke out tomorrow ". . . these political men, . . . heeding only factional passion and hatreds, would do what the political men of [17]93 did, they would kill one another" in search of advantage for themselves. What they ought to do, however, was use "all their love, all their intelligence and their energy to serve the people": an agenda that described her own political mission.[51] The revolutionary Republicans' self-interest was contrasted with Tristan's own disinterested altruism; their violence and coercion with her pacifism; the masculinism of their political ideas and practice with an idealized form of politics that she claimed to represent. In confronting them openly and claiming to expose their agenda to workers, Tristan presented herself as an heroic figure representing a superior moral leadership. Furthermore, she claimed for herself as a woman the disinterested defense of the public good that provided one validation for male political authority within the Republican tradition.

The contest between Tristan and the Republicans was perceived by all involved as a gendered contest, adding weight to Tristan's claim that the practice of authority was highly gendered. Republicans in the 1830s and 1840s did not envisage women as citizens and political equals, and their theory of democracy was focused around the representative role of male heads of families.[52] While women contributed to the elaboration of

Republican theory and sought to articulate a political identity for women within the Republican ideal, as Whitney Walton demonstrates in her essay in this volume, this rarely involved direct public challenges to men's political authority. Since women were perceived to be outside the political community, the rules of engagement governing such political challenges were also unclear. Tristan's femininity gave her a tactical advantage in confronting her Republican opponents, because they were uncertain how to respond to her challenge. At Toulouse, for instance, Tristan utilized her feminine charms to good effect against Ribairol, editor of the opposition newspaper *L'Emancipation:* "[He is] endowed with one of those fine male natures that never resist the power of a gentle glance from a woman — and whose male fierceness dissolves completely under the magic influence of a female voice and a caressing smile."[53]

Ribairol claimed to be unable to discuss Tristan's ideas freely because she was a woman, but his constraining chivalry gave her the freedom to criticize his political views unchallenged. Elsewhere, democrats and Republicans had few gentlemanly scruples and attacked her for breaking the rules: the rules that allotted women and men separate and distinct roles within and for the nation. But in accusing her of stepping outside her allotted sphere, and rejecting her claim to play a political role, they were forced to recognize that this was the role she sought and to muster reasons for its unacceptability. The only reason they advanced was that Tristan crossed the invisible gender divide. Saissac, a Montpellier lawyer, "finds that I surpass my womanly functions; that women must not meddle with politics," she complained.[54] At Lyon, the editor of an opposition newspaper insisted that "France cannot follow the orders of a creature in petticoats."[55] She attributed this sentiment, and the efforts of Lyon Republicans to counter her influence among workers there, to "political jealousy, jealousy of the superiority of woman to man."[56]

These incidents were presented by Flora Tristan as encounters, not just between morally flawed and morally sound figures, but between male and female figures who embodied diametrically opposed notions of public authority. The oppositional melodramatic genre within which Tristan constructed them facilitated a contrast between "masculine" modes of authority, which Tristan argued rested on violence and coercion (rather than on the public "virtue" defended by the French Revolutionaries), and an idealized image of female leadership based on women's moral superiority. This was not an argument for women to seek power in male terms. The social damage of a politics of duress would occur regardless of the sex of its practitioners, Tristan argued, and besides, women could not compete successfully with superior male physical force to achieve such a goal.[57] Rather than being a clone of a male leader, a woman leader would represent progress because she would bring a new style, new values, and new purposes to her task. Woman's destiny, Tristan argued, was to be the *"guide of humanity"* who would "[lead] humanity toward perfection by her power of attraction."[58] A model of female authority would therefore depart significantly from its male counterpart, as Tristan explained to the workers of Lyon: "I pointed out to them that we had reached the reign of women — that the reign of war, of brute force had been that of [men] and that now women could achieve more than men because they had more love, and today love alone must govern."[59]

Having already challenged one argument for women's political exclusion by comparing her own disinterested defense of the public good with the self-interest of her male Republican counterparts, Tristan now addressed a second. Whereas women's emotion generally justified disqualifying them from political life, she now claimed the emotional power of womanhood as the basis for a new and superior form of political authority. Embodied in women, authority itself would be transformed.

This formulation of the moral basis for women's authority and social leadership drew its meaning not just from melodrama, but from Tristan's spiritual and religious ideas. Like a number of other socialists of the July monarchy, Tristan gave her politics a religious base, linking religious radicalism and social reform.[60] For socialists of her generation, the Crucified Christ was reborn in the Suffering People, and the message of the Gospels was a message of social justice. A compassionate and humane social agenda, realized through such policies as "the right to work" and the entitlement of the weak to social provision, would ensure dignity to every individual. It would express the necessary link between religious faith and social action for, as Tristan asked rhetorically: "Is a faith that does not act a sincere faith? No indeed. And what makes us act? Passion — love."[61]

Like a number of her contemporaries, too, Tristan believed in divine androgyny and attributed the moral power of femininity to its divine origins.[62] But where the image of the androgyne often surreptitiously suppressed the feminine,[63] Tristan's theory elevated it. She argued that God's femininity manifested itself as "intelligent love," while God's masculinity emerged as "strength" (or "brute strength" as she sometimes described it).[64] Womanhood was thus a superior form of humanity associated with spiritual, rather than physical, predominance, and the assumption of social leadership by woman would represent and ensure progress over the social power of man. This definition of the sexes marked the path to be trodden between current suffering and social disorder in an amoral world and the future harmony of a "feminized" social order. It also marked the distance between Tristan, as a female authority figure, and the current male power holders.

As a woman leader with a message of social transformation, Tristan assumed the role not just of "hero" of the melodrama but of savior and messiah, with an apostolic mission of social regeneration. She presented herself as a redemptive figure, redressing injustice and leading humanity toward perfection like her fictional "woman guide." If her contests with the secular authorities had been presented through scenes that displayed the distance between the female moral leadership she embodied and the flawed "old moral order" of male authority, her encounters with the religious leaders of her society, who were charged with setting its moral standards, defined that distance even more starkly. The Catholic bishops at Dijon, Lyon, Avignon, and Nîmes, whom she visited during her speaking tour in 1844, rejected Tristan's argument that "the duties of the French clergy were to align themselves with the people, to demand rights for them." They emphasized religious observance and alms-giving, she complained, rejecting her message of fraternity and the agenda for social and political change that it required.[65]

In Tristan's account, the contrast between the new morality and the old was articulated most vividly as a confrontation between herself, as a messiah figure bearing a new moral message, and the Church as Antichrist:

> Ah! I must have made a remarkable contrast alongside these two men. — I, who according to the Holy Church, represented Satan — was beautiful with that celestial beauty which faith and love bestow — my emaciated features, my expression of suffering announced the trials of my mission — but my expression, my voice, my resolute, calm bearing, also announced the awareness that I had of my superiority to these two priests who, in my view represented the Antichrist speaking in the Church of Christ, with the crucifix in hand! — and in the name of this same Christ whom they crucified again in my person.[66]

The polarity between good and evil gave this encounter a strongly melodramatic flavor. Like her scenes with Segon and Boisseneau, it counterposed morally upright and morally flawed figures on the same stage. By playing opposite the representatives of Catholicism in this scene, Tristan allowed the melodrama to unfold once more, foreshadowing again the triumph of virtue.

Within this religious and moral framework, too, other cultural images of womanhood, in addition to those of melodrama, became available to her as models of feminine authority. In particular, the celebrated Madonna figure, the highest expression of the mother image, which dominated concepts of French womanhood in the early nineteenth century, offered a powerful image of feminine influence on which she could draw to portray her mission.[67] In the early nineteenth-century Catholic Church, the role of Mary as mediatrix, attributed with a prominent role in human salvation, was receiving heightened attention, while the radical religious sects that flourished in this period reinscribed Mary as a messianic figure in her own right, an active partner in the redemptive enterprise and a new Christ figure.[68] If the Saint-Simonians looked to the coming of a "Woman Messiah" to complete the revelation of the new morality, Flora Tristan found in this figure an image through which she might represent her own authoritative role. Like them, Tristan gave the messiah figure a feminine twist, assuming the character not merely of a savior but of a woman savior.

In her diary Flora Tristan constructed herself and her role in maternal yet suprahuman terms. She portrayed herself as a mother to the oppressed, whose "disciples" became spiritual "children" to whom she gave new life: "When I saw that one of them was ready to receive life, my strength increased a hundredfold to make him great, beautiful, and magnificent."[69] Moreover, she portrayed her spiritual maternity not merely in reproductive terms, but as a new creation, and even envisaged herself giving birth to a new world: "The Jewish people expired in misery and Jesus raised them up. — The Christian people are dead today in misery and Flora Tristan, the first strong woman, will raise them up. — Oh! yes I feel a new world within me — and I will give this new world to the old world that is suffering and dying!"[70] As a maternal figure with spiritual authority, Tristan's self-image evoked the powerful image of the Madonna. But where the Madonna was silent and hidden, nurturing the male Messiah and vicariously enduring his pain (an apposite model for the domestic woman), Tristan, as a messianic woman, claimed the mantle of sacrifice and salvation in her own right.

CONCLUSION

As Stéphane Michaud has argued, nineteenth-century images of woman were shaped largely by male fantasy, since it was generally man who imagined and celebrated woman as Muse, Madonna, and female Messiah.[71] In fact, feminist historians have argued that women were regarded by men as "objects of reflection" not as subjects entitled to speak on their own behalf.[72] They point out further that it was particularly difficult for women to position themselves within the public sphere, creating "public languages and personae" of their own, given that the postrevolutionary public sphere was defined in male terms.[73] As Dorinda Outram notes with reference to Madame Roland, the aspiring political woman needed a "repertoire of images" through which to create herself as a social being, unrestricted by the limits ascribed to her biological body.[74] But idealized images could imprison and restrict women, denying their human needs and desires as it elevated them to the rarefied heights of the ethereal. As the discourse of domesticity illustrates, for instance, rhetorical flights of fancy that attributed to womanhood significant moral influence were not incompatible with a denial of real autonomy and power to real women. In performing or envisaging herself as the embodiment of such idealized figures, Tristan adopted a complex and potentially contradictory stance. At one level, she might be charged with reiterating and reinforcing the abstraction of "woman." But she also attempted to give the idealized woman political substance, to turn her into a figure of public authority, thus participating in the contemporary feminist challenge to women's political exclusion. It was Flora Tristan as Madonna, as messiah figure, as hero of the melodrama, who addressed workers, enrolled them in her "workers' union," urged them to demand their rights and to extend rights to women, encouraged their commitment to socialism, and sought to play a key role within the socialist politics of the July monarchy. In this sense, the metaphorical images that she enacted did not imprison her and limit her to the realms of the imaginary, but provided a language by which she could articulate the possibility and the meaning of a woman leader: a possibility foreign to, or perhaps unimaginable for, many of her contemporaries. In doing so, she both expressed her own sense of self and attempted to open the minds of others to the potentialities of female existence.

In reflecting on Flora Tristan's authoritative performances, we might also reflect on the distinction between the "text" and the "life." As biographical critics have noted, the records that remain of a life are not the "life" itself, but a fragmentary record of the historical figure's attempt to represent herself in writing.[75] The "texts" through which we encounter Flora Tristan today reveal not the essential meaning of her life, but a series of glimpses and reflections, shaped by the mentalities and textual conventions of her day, that we attempt to reconstruct coherently. This account suggests one possible form of coherence for Tristan's life story, by setting her self-representations within the frame of performance and reading her writings through the contemporary discourses of melodrama and messianism. Other frameworks of meaning can also be employed, as the rich historiography on Flora Tristan attests.

While the coherence created by the concept of performance is super-imposed on Tristan's life after the event, however, this framework is not inconsistent with Tristan's own concerns, nor with contemporary per-ceptions of Flora Tristan. Both her allies and her opponents recorded their reactions to some of her "performances," and those reactions were understandably divided. By presenting herself as pariah, for instance, Tristan aroused the scorn of her critics. They saw not the virtuous figure plagued by injustice that she intended, but the woman who stepped out-side her allotted sphere and whose sufferings were therefore deserved and self-imposed.[76] However, for her admirers, Tristan's pariah status marked her as an exceptional figure who deliberately chose the path of the down-trodden.[77] Similarly, Tristan's performance as a messiah figure polar-ized those who witnessed it first hand. The novelist George Sand was exasperated at the antics of the *"comédienne,"* whose performance she judged to be a sham.[78] But for those who shared her religious enthusi-asm, Tristan was recognized as a woman who soared above her kind, a genuine and genuinely inspiring figure of spiritual authority.[79]

Independent testimony supporting Tristan's claims about her spirited engagement with the authority figures of her day is limited.[80] Never-theless, understanding Tristan's sense of self depends less on establishing whether such scenes unfolded exactly as she described them than on exploring why she chose to reconstruct those scenes in the way she did; why she represented her attempts to claim public authority through the discourses of melodrama and messianism; why she re-created her life within a theatrical scenario. Performing the role of authoritative figure, experimenting with its possibilities and playing it in different ways, was perhaps a response to the absence of recognized role models for the woman leader. After all, one function of theater is to enable a vicarious experience of other lives and other situations for both audience and actor. In performing a series of authoritative characters, then, Tristan explored the dimensions of authority for herself, and revealed the "woman of authority" to outside observers as well.

Even if Flora Tristan's performances did not persuade others to see her as she presented herself, those performances nevertheless provide an insight into both the complexity and dynamism of the historical Flora

Tristan and into the articulation of womanhood during the July monarchy. The discourse of domesticity was asserted powerfully, but focusing on a single life of engagement with its precepts reveals some of the ways such ideas could be contested. Flora Tristan, like other women of her day, created herself in dialogue with contemporary definitions of womanhood, criticizing and challenging their shortcomings but also seizing upon their potential and transforming them for her own ends. Studying this single example therefore reveals the instability of the model of womanhood being offered to women for their emulation, a model that was continually open to challenge and hence in need of continual reaffirmation. In particular, as Flora Tristan illustrates, images of womanhood that emphasized her moral power within the home provided an opening for the creation of an alternative ideal that extended woman's moral authority beyond domestic confines. Tristan provides one example of how such a discursive shift could be achieved.

Nevertheless, discursive challenges are not easily transformed into political victories. This may help explain why Tristan adopted a variety of personae in presenting herself as an authoritative figure, in the hope that one of them might prove more persuasive than others. Beyond that, however, I suggest that there were simply many dimensions to Flora Tristan, only some of which are examined here. When we think we have pinned her down in one guise, she reemerges in another, challenging our judgments and our ability to define and limit her. Flora Tristan seized upon the discursively created feminine forms that populated the contemporary imagination, claiming them as avenues to integrity and power and, above all, claiming the right to be the subject of her own imagining.

NOTES

I wish to thank the Bibiothèque Nationale de France for permission to reproduce the portrait of Flora Tristan in this volume. I also thank my co-contributors to this book, whose stimulating discussion of a range of relevant issues helped shape my thinking about Flora Tristan.

1. Flora Tristan, *Union ouvrière*, 2d ed. (Paris: chez tous les libraires, 1844).

2. Flora Tristan, *Le Tour de France: État actuel de la classe ouvrière sous l'aspect moral, intellectuel et matériel*, 2 vols. (Paris: Maspero, 1980), 2: 217–18.

3. The essential account of Flora Tristan's life remains Jules-L. Puech's, *La Vie et l'Oeuvre de Flora Tristan* (Paris: Marcel Rivière, 1925). More recent studies include Jean Baelen, *La Vie et l'Oeuvre de Flora Tristan: socialisme et féminisme au XIXe siècle* (Paris: Seuil, 1972); Dominique Desanti, *Flora Tristan: Vie et oeuvres mêlées* (Paris: Union générale d'éditions, 1973); S. Joan Moon,

"Feminism and Socialism: The Utopian Synthesis of Flora Tristan," in *Socialist Women: European Socialist Feminism in the Nineteenth and Early Twentieth Centuries,* ed. Marilyn Boxer and Jean Quataert (New York: Elsevier, 1978); Sandra Dijkstra, *Flora Tristan: Pioneer Feminist and Socialist* (Berkeley: Center for Socialist History, 1984); Laura Strumingher, *The Odyssey of Flora Tristan* (New York: Peter Lang, 1988); Máire Cross and Tim Gray, *The Feminism of Flora Tristan* (Oxford: Berg, 1992); Gerhard Leo, *Flora Tristan: La Révolte d'une Paria* (Paris: Editions de l'Atelier, 1994).

4. See Joan Landes, *Women and the Public Sphere in the Age of the French Revolution* (Ithaca: Cornell University Press, 1988).

5. Tristan, *Tour de France,* 2: 36, 146.

6. Flora Tristan, *Pérégrinations d'une Paria, 1833–1834,* 2 vols. (Paris: Arthus Bertrand, 1838), 1: 47.

7. Ibid., xxxvii.

8. See *Union ouvrière,* note 1 above.

9. See Dena Goodman, "Women and the Enlightenment," in *Becoming Visible: Women in European History,* ed. Renate Bridenthal, Susan Mosher Stuard, and Merry E. Weisner. 3d ed. (Boston: Houghton Mifflin, 1998); Sylvana Tomaselli, "The Enlightenment Debate on Women," *History Workshop Journal* 20 (1985): 101–24; Jean H. Bloch, "Women and the Reform of the Nation," in *Woman and Society in Eighteenth-Century France: Essays in Honour of John Stephenson Spink,* ed. Eva Jacobs et al. (London: The Athlone Press, 1979), 3–18.

10. Among the vast literature on Rousseau, see Landes, *Women and the Public Sphere,* chapter 3; Joel Schwartz, *The Sexual Politics of Jean-Jacques Rousseau* (Chicago: University of Chicago Press, 1984); Carol Blum, *Rousseau and the Republic of Virtue. The Language of Politics in the French Revolution* (Ithaca: Cornell University Press, 1986); Paul Hoffmann, *La Femme dans la pensée des lumières* (Paris: Editions Ophrys, 1977).

11. Dorinda Outram, *The Body and the French Revolution. Sex, Class, and Political Culture* (New Haven, Conn.: Yale University Press, 1989), 125–26.

12. Ibid., 72–87; Blum, *Rousseau and the Republic of Virtue,* chapter 11. On women's attempts to challenge such arguments see Dominique Godineau, *The Women of Paris and Their French Revolution,* trans. Katherine Streip (Berkeley and Los Angeles: University of California Press, 1998), chapter 12.

13. For the debate in the Convention that resulted in women's exclusion from political clubs and public meetings, see Darline Gay Levy, Harriet Branson Applewhite, and Mary Durham Johnson, eds. *Women in Revolutionary Paris, 1789–1795: Selected Documents* (Urbana: University of Illinois Press, 1979), 213–20.

14. Erna Olafson Hellerstein, "French Women and the Orderly Household, 1830–1870," *Proceedings of the Annual Meeting of the Western Society for French History* (Denver, 1975), 380, 383; William H. Reddy, *The Invisible Code: Honor and Sentiment in Postrevolutionary France, 1814–1848* (Berkeley and Los Angeles: University of California Press, 1997), 229–30. On the legal position of women under the Civil Code, see Maïté Albistur and Daniel Armogathe, *Histoire du féminisme français* (Paris: Editions des femmes, 1977), 359–64.

15. Michèle Riot-Sarcey, *La Démocratie à l'épreuve des femmes: Trois figures*

critiques du pouvoir, 1830–1848 (Paris: Albin Michel, 1994), 39–40, 99–108; Landes, *Women and the Public Sphere,* 171–73.

16. Laura S. Strumingher, "L'Ange de la Maison. Mothers and Daughters in Nineteenth-Century France," *International Journal of Women's Studies* 2 (1979): 51; Barbara Corrado Pope, "Revolution and Retreat: Upper-Class French Women after 1789," in *Women, War and Revolution,* ed. Carol R. Berkin and Clara M. Lovett (London: Holmes and Meier, 1980), 215–35; Rebecca Rogers, "Boarding Schools, Women Teachers and Domesticity: Reforming Girls' Secondary Education in the First Half of the Nineteenth Century," *French Historical Studies* 19, no. 1 (spring 1995): 153–81. On attempts to transform girls of the popular classes into model mothers, see Laura Strumingher, ed., *What Were Little Girls and Boys Made Of? Primary Education in Rural France, 1830–1880* (Albany: State University of New York Press, 1983).

17. See Marguerite Thibert, *Le Féminisme dans le socialisme français de 1830 à 1850* (Paris: Giard, 1926); Claire Goldberg Moses, *French Feminism in the Nineteenth Century* (Albany: State University of New York Press, 1984); Susan K. Grogan, *French Socialism and Sexual Difference: Women and the New Society, 1803–1844* (Basingstoke: Macmillan, 1992).

18. Bonnie Smith, *Ladies of the Leisure Class: The Bourgeoises of Northern France in the Nineteenth Century* (Princeton: Princeton University Press, 1981); Adeline Daumard, *La Bourgeoisie parisienne de 1815 à 1848* (Paris: S.E.V.P.E.N., 1963); Jean-Pierre Chaline, "Sociabilité féminine et 'maternalisme': les sociétés de charité maternelle au XIXe siècle," in *Femmes dans la cité, 1815–1871,* ed. Alain Corbin, Jacqueline Lalouette, Michèle Riot-Sarcey (Paris: Créaphis, 1993), 69–78; Catherine Duprat, "Le Silence des femmes: Associations féminines du premier XIXe siècle," in ibid., 79–100.

19. Riot-Sarcey, *La Démocratie à l'épreuve des femmes,* 43–46, 57–60, 75, and the works cited in note 17 above.

20. Riot-Sarcey, *La Démocratie à l'épreuve des femmes,* 80.

21. François Guizot, *Histoire de la civilization en Europe,* quoted in Riot-Sarcey, *La Démocratie à l'épreuve des femmes,* 103.

22. Riot-Sarcey, *La Démocratie à l'épreuve des femmes,* 43–49.

23. Outram, *The Body and the French Revolution,* 125, 132.

24. Sharon O'Brien, "Feminist Theory and Literary Biography," in *Contesting the Subject: Essays in the Postmodern Theory and Practice of Biography and Biographical Criticism,* ed. William H. Epstein (West Lafayette, Ind.: Purdue University Press, 1991), 125.

25. See Denise Riley, *Am I That Name?: Feminism and the Category of "Women" in History* (Minneapolis: University of Minnesota Press, 1988).

26. Mary Louise Roberts, "Acting Up: The Feminist Theatrics of Marguerite Durand," *French Historical Studies* 19, no. 4 (fall 1996): 1103–38. See Roberts's essay in this collection.

27. Tristan, *Tour de France,* 2: 188, 213.

28. On the uses of the "pariah" metaphor in this period, see Eleni Varikas, "Paria: une métaphore de l'exclusion des femmes," *Sources: Travaux historiques* 12 (1987): 37–43; Stéphane Michaud, "Se choisir paria: Brève note sur Flora Tristan," *Romantisme* 58 (1987): 39–45.

29. Tristan, *Pérégrinations*, 1: xxxvii.

30. Flora Tristan to Charles-Joseph Traviès, London, July 16, 1839, in *Flora Tristan Lettres*, réunies, présentées, et annotées par Stéphane Michaud (Paris: Seuil, 1980), 102–3.

31. See, for instance, a letter from Tristan to George Sand, February 2, 1842, in *Flora Tristan, La Paria et Son Rêve: Correspondance établie par Stéphane Michaud* (Fontenay/Saint-Cloud: ENS Editions, 1995), 114.

32. Flora Tristan, *Promenades dans Londres, ou l'aristocratie et les prolétaires anglais*, collected and annotated by François Bédarida (Paris: Maspero, 1978), 105–9. The date of this incident is unclear. *Promenades* is an account of Tristan's 1839 visit to London. However, Jean Hawkes notes that the ban on women's admission to the public gallery ended in 1835 and suggests that the incident may have occurred during Tristan's 1831 visit. See Jean Hawkes, ed., *The London Journal of Flora Tristan 1842, or the Aristocracy and the Working Class of England: A Translation of* Promenades dans Londres (London: Virago, 1982).

33. Tristan, *Tour de France*, 2: 216.

34. Ibid., 183–84.

35. Tristan, *Promenades dans Londres*, note 33 above; Tristan, *Méphis*, 2 vols. (Paris: Ladvocat, 1838).

36. Peter Brooks, *The Melodramatic Imagination: Balzac, Henry James, Melodrama, and the Mode of Excess* (New Haven, Conn.: Yale University Press, 1976), 13–17, 27, 81; Martha Vicinus, " 'Helpless and Unfriended': Nineteenth-Century Domestic Melodrama," *New Literary History* 13, no. 1 (autumn 1981): 127–28.

37. See Riot-Sarcey, *La Démocratie à l'épreuve des femmes*, 36–40.

38. On Parisian theater during this period see F. W. J. Hemmings, *Culture and Society in France, 1789–1848* (Leicester: Leicester University Press, 1987) and *The Theatre Industry in Nineteenth-Century France* (Cambridge, Eng.: Cambridge University Press, 1993). For a fuller discussion of the melodramatic elements of Tristan's writings, see Susan Grogan, *Flora Tristan: Life Stories* (London: Routledge, 1998), chapter 10.

39. Tristan, *Tour de France*, 2: 220.

40. Ibid., 212–13, 215.

41. Ibid., 185–86. The *Procureur-Général* of Toulouse, Pierre-Ambroise Plougoulm, had been expelled from the city by a rioting crowd at the time of the 1841 census. See the editor's note, 193.

42. Ibid., 196–97. Tristan noted in concluding her account, "One could create a delightful comedy about this."

43. See Brooks, *The Melodramatic Imagination*, chapter 2; Vicinus, "Helpless and Unfriended," 130, 132.

44. See, for instance, C. L[emonnier], *Religion Saint-Simonienne. Église de Toulouse. Enseignement de l'Athénée. Avenir de la Femme* (Toulouse: A. Hénault, 1831).

45. Brooks, *The Melodramatic Imagination*, 87; Vicinus, "Helpless and Unfriended," 133.

46. Tristan, *Pérégrinations*, 1: xxvii–xxviii.

47. See the account in *Le Droit*, February 2, 1839.

48. Flora Tristan to an unnamed woman, February 7, 1839, in *Lettres*, 96.

49. See Whitney Walton's essay in this collection.

50. Tristan, *Tour de France*, 2: 145.

51. Ibid., 15–16. See also her criticism of the Republicans at Carcassonne and Toulouse, 165–66, 188–89.

52. Riot-Sarcey, *La Démocratie à l'épreuve des femmes*, 78–81, 158. On the gendering of democratic theory in early nineteenth-century France, see also Geneviève Fraisse, *Reason's Muse: Sexual Difference and the Birth of Democracy*, trans. Jane Marie Todd (Chicago: University of Chicago Press, 1995).

53. Tristan, *Tour de France*, 2: 188.

54. Ibid., 143.

55. Ibid., 1: 182.

56. Ibid., 2: 13–14.

57. See her discussion of the role of Señora Gamarra, a leading figure in Peruvian politics in 1833, in Tristan, *Pérégrinations d'une Paria, 1833–1834* (Paris: Maspero, 1980), chapter 18, and Grogan, *Life Stories*, 157–60.

58. Tristan, *Méphis*, 1: 180–83.

59. Tristan, *Tour de France*, 2: 31.

60. On the combination of religious and social radicalism during the July monarchy, see Edward Berenson, "A New Religion of the Left: Christianity and Social Radicalism in France, 1815–1848," in *The French Revolution and the Creation of Modern Political Culture*, ed. François Furet and Mona Ozouf, vol. 3, *The Transformation of Political Culture, 1789–1848* (Oxford: Pergamon Press, 1989), 543–60; Jacques Valette, "Utopie sociale et les utopismes sociaux en France vers 1848," in *1848. Les Utopismes sociaux* (Paris: Editions SEDES: CDU, 1981), 41–52; Frank Paul Bowman, "Religion, Politics, and Utopia in French Romanticism," *Australian Journal of French Studies* 11, no. 3 (1974): 307–24. On Tristan's links with the leading figures in these sects, see Grogan, *Life Stories*, chapter 12.

61. Tristan, *Tour de France*, 2: 140.

62. On the significance of Divine androgyny in the religious movements of the period, see A. J. L. Busst, "The Image of the Androgyne in the Nineteenth Century," in *Romantic Mythologies*, ed. Ian Fletcher (London: Routledge and Kegan Paul, 1967); Frank Paul Bowman, *Eliphas Lévi, visionnaire romantique* (Paris: Presses universitaires de France, 1969).

63. See Kari Weil, *Androgyny and the Denial of Difference* (Charlottesville: University Press of Virginia, 1992), chapter 3.

64. Alphonse-Louis Constant, epilogue to *L'Emancipation de la femme ou le testament de la Paria*, ouvrage posthume de Mme Flora Tristan complété d'après ses notes et publié par A. Constant (Paris: au Bureau de la Direction de *La Vérité*, 1846), 118–19.

65. Tristan, *Tour de France*, 1: 89–91, 176–78; 2: 50, 117–23.

66. Ibid., 2: 119.

67. See Stéphane Michaud, *Muse et Madone. Visages de la femme de la Révolution française aux apparitions de Lourdes* (Paris: Seuil, 1985), chapter 1.

68. Bowman, *Eliphas Lévi*, 13, 25–33; Barbara Corrado Pope, "Immaculate

and Powerful: The Marian Revival in the Nineteenth Century," in *Immaculate and Powerful. The Female in Sacred Image and Social Reality*, ed. Clarissa W. Atkinson, Constance H. Buchanan, and Margaret R. Miles (Boston: Beacon Press, 1985), 173–200; Margaret Talbot, "An Emancipated Voice: Flora Tristan and Utopian Allegory," *Feminist Studies* 17, no. 2 (1991): 219–39.

69. Tristan, *Tour de France*, 2: 19–20.

70. Ibid., 1: 231.

71. Michaud, *Muse et Madone*, 9–10.

72. Riot-Sarcey, *La Démocratie à l'épreuve des femmes*, 48.

73. Landes, *Women and the Public Sphere*, 202–5; Outram, *The Body and the French Revolution*, 84–85, 125.

74. Outram, *The Body and the French Revolution*, 132.

75. Diane Wood Middlebrook, "Postmodernism and the Biographer," in *Revealing Lives: Autobiography, Biography and Gender*, ed. Susan Groag Bell and Marilyn Yalom (New York: State University of New York Press, 1990), 159.

76. Mme M., "Les Pérégrinations d'une paria, par Mme FT," *Revue de Paris*, nouvelle série, 49, no. 1 (Jan. 1838): 50–59; Jules Janin, "Madame Flora Tristan," *La Sylphide*, 2e série, 1 (Jan. 1845): 3–8, 17–20.

77. Eugène Stourm, "Madame Flora Tristan," *L'Union*, 2e année, 12 (1844).

78. George Sand to Charles Poncy, January 26, 1844, in her *Correspondance*, ed. Georges Lubin (Paris: Éditions Garnier Frères, 1969), 6: 410. Tristan later wrote to Sand describing herself as an "apostle in humanity" and regretting that Sand did not believe in her "martyrdom." See Tristan to Sand, March 7 and mid-March 1844, in *Flora Tristan la paria et son rêve*, 201–3.

79. Constant, epilogue to *L'Émancipation de la femme*, 116.

80. The report of the *procureur-général* at Lyon to his superiors in Paris supports her version of their interview, while attempting to put a different slant on the outcome. See Archives Nationales, BB18 1420: 8133 A9 (May 7, 1844).

Republican Women and Republican Families in the Personal Narratives of George Sand, Marie d'Agoult, and Hortense Allart

WHITNEY WALTON

In her (unfinished) memoirs, Marie d'Agoult, who wrote under the pseudonym of Daniel Stern, reconstructs a favorite house she bought in Paris in 1851 near the Champs Élysées. She describes in detail its setting and design, and her own decoration of the interior. D'Agoult appears to have been particularly fond of a small, octagonal-shaped salon the doors of which were ornamented with medallions representing great Renaissance artists — "Dante, Giotto, Guido d'Arezzo, Leonardo, Raphael, etc." She writes, "Above the portrait of Michelangelo I put the adage of Sallust: *Pulchrum est bene facere reipublicae [sic]* [It is beautiful to do well by the republic], as if to give myself the illusion that we lived, like these Florentines, in the heart of a proud and beautiful republic."[1] The passage from Sallust, historian and supporter of the late Roman Republic, was certainly an appropriate maxim for d'Agoult, who spent much of her life furthering the republican cause in France.

But the rest of the passage that these lines introduce is also highly significant in terms of d'Agoult's self-conception as a republican woman. The remainder of the passage reads: "It is beautiful to do well by the republic, and not at all worthless to speak well on its behalf, for renown can be attained through military or peaceful means."[2] Sallust is making a distinction between serving the republic as a statesman or soldier and as a writer, himself having been forced to leave public office, after which he became a historian. Similarly, d'Agoult, barred by her sex from a military or legislative career, believed her contributions to republicanism as a writer were by no means unworthy. Indeed, in the preface to the first volume of her autobiography, d'Agoult asserts that women can influence public life as much as men. The implication is that women's modes of influence are conversation and especially writing. According to d'Agoult, an exceptional woman "by conquering the imagination, exciting the mind, and stimulating the brain to reexamine received opinions, will make an impact on her century by other means than, but perhaps just as effectively as, a legislative assembly or an army captain."[3] D'Agoult, like Sallust, served the republic as a historian and writer, but unlike Sallust, she did not have the option or opportunity of becoming a statesman or soldier. D'Agoult, along with other female supporters of republicanism in the nineteenth century, articulated for themselves a political and public identity despite republicanism's exclusion of women from political rights and even from public life.

George Sand (1804–1876) and Hortense Allart (1801–1879), like Marie d'Agoult (1805–1876), were committed to republicanism, and they formed a cohort of successful women authors who were contemporaries and knew one another and who transformed republicanism in a similar fashion through their writing and their lives. Republicanism appealed to them because it held the possibility of disinterested and representative government, guarantees of personal and civil liberties, and improvements in the condition of the laboring poor. They also saw in it the potential for egalitarian relations between the sexes through changes in laws and cultural practices regarding women and the family. Sand, d'Agoult, and Allart promoted such changes in their autobiographies and other writings and so undermined the republican exclusion of women from politics. They wrote themselves as republican women, creating a new model for women within republicanism between the two poles of republican motherhood and equal rights.

This essay analyzes three different phases in the lives of Sand, d'Agoult, and Allart — as represented in the authors' autobiographies — as feminist challenges to the masculine exclusivity of republicanism. It argues that women writers' life stories presented an alternative to the authoritarian family on which male republicanism was based. Moreover, by dissolving the boundary between private life and public involvement, the three authors' self-narratives authorized a political role for women, much in contrast to the strictly domestic feminine function articulated by revolutionaries in 1793 and codified into law in 1804. This model for women was republican motherhood, the notion that women best served the republic as wives and mothers who imparted republican ideals and virtues to their children in the family setting.[4] By confining women to the private sphere on the grounds that they were naturally suited for house-keeping and childrearing, republican motherhood justified exclusive male participation in the public sphere.

The problem of the masculine gendering of republicanism, starting with the writings of Rousseau and played out initially in the French Revolution, has generated several provocative studies recently. There is no disputing that the majority of revolutionary and republican men denied that women had the capacity for or the right to political participation, but there is significant disagreement among scholars regarding the basis and implications of this position.[5] Lynn Hunt maintains that in the process of eliminating one form of government (absolute monarchy) and erecting another (constitutional republicanism), revolutionaries con-structed these radical political developments in images and language that were familiar to them — namely those of family relations. In Hunt's account the prevailing family romance that defined the French Revolution was that of educated, white, mostly professional men who repre-sented themselves as having destroyed a tyrannical father (Louis XVI) and a corrupt mother (Marie-Antoinette) in order to establish a new government of equal and virtuous brothers (republicanism). After Hunt persuasively layers the visual and textual evidence for this interpretation, she admits that other family romances might also have structured the revolutionary republic and that the exclusively masculine, fraternal republic was by no means inevitable.[6]

By contrast, Carole Pateman and Joan Scott argue that republicanism was inherently patriarchal and masculine, consciously based on a theory of male authority — patriarchy being simply redefined to paternal author-ity in the home and fraternal authority in the state — and female depen-dence — predicated on "natural" sexual difference. According to them, the foundation of republicanism (and contract theory or rights theory) in sexual difference causes enormous difficulties for feminists who, in their quest for a meaningful political egalitarianism, must either deny palpable physical differences between women and men or get entangled in a para-dox of arguing for equality on behalf of all women, which necessarily rein-forces the very difference that is the basis for their disenfranchisement.[7]

Although republican notions of sexual difference were often presented as "natural" and empirically provable, inconsistencies and contradic-tions remained. Feminists have carefully and imaginatively exposed them ever since their articulation in the eighteenth century. Indeed, Geneviève Fraisse posits that no real theory lay behind the exclusion of women

from politics but rather male "phantasms" that complicated the theorizing and counter-theorizing of the practice of excluding women. Here,
then, was a wedge with which to prize open the shutter against women
in republican politics. Women who could undermine the masculine gendering of specific republican and political attributes, notably the capacity for sustained rational endeavor and its public presentation, thus
initiated the process of challenging the exclusion of women from politics
without a confrontational demand for political equality between the
sexes. Fraisse asserts that the French Revolution, by uncoupling knowledge and power, allowed some women to seek knowledge without power
and thereby to establish themselves as independent individuals, an
accomplishment that would ultimately serve as a precondition or as a
sort of bridge to organized feminist demands for equal rights.[8] Sand,
d'Agoult, and Allart used their intellect to create independent existences
for themselves and, in the process, elided the boundary between private
and public. They constructed a female republican identity that was different from republican motherhood, but that did not claim political
equality for women.

Numerous women contemporaries of these three authors did, in fact,
assert political equality for the sexes. Socialist feminists, like Jeanne
Deroin, Désirée Veret, and Eugénie Niboyet, to name only a few, were
articulate and courageous proponents of equal rights, and they have been
the subject of several perceptive analyses of their feminist republicanism.[9]
These works, however, tend to dismiss the contributions of Sand,
d'Agoult, and Allart because the three authors rejected socialist feminists
and their claim for political equality. But this is only part of the story.
Sand, d'Agoult, and Allart engaged in a separate struggle to bring feminist issues to the forefront of republican concerns, a mostly genteel struggle waged in salons and in the pages of novels, essays, and periodicals that
circulated among a predominantly, though not entirely, elite audience.
Their common enterprise was to transform cultural attitudes toward
women and to improve women's civil status as necessary precursors to
equal rights. Although their ideas about republican strategies and state
forms varied, their suggestions regarding women and the family formed
a coherent alternative to republican motherhood and to complete sexual
equality. Their life stories, then, might be considered alternative family
romances about the creation and transformation of republicanism.

Individual biographies of Sand, d'Agoult, and Allart present their
political ideologies and activities, but none I know of considers their
shared constructions of republican womanhood.[10] In the twenty to

ninety years since most biographies of these authors were written, feminist literary scholarship has argued cogently for a gendered reading of female autobiography — one that casts the understanding of a woman's self-narrative in a new light. These works maintain that women writing their own life stories had to write against the masculine premise behind the autobiographical genre and against the social construction of femininity as private and relative and the passive object of a (male) category, rather than public and independent and the individual subject of self-assertion and creation.[11] In addition to reading for difference, that is, accounting for the construction of a gendered identity in a female personal narrative, it is also essential to historicize this process, to attend to the power relations, language, and meanings with which a female author is engaged in her self-representation.[12] In the cases of Sand, d'Agoult, and Allart, a range of republican principles and movements prominent during the July monarchy provided the foundation for their self-narrations and reworkings of republicanism.

I analyze the autobiographies of Sand, d'Agoult, and Allart for their textual constructions of republican self-identities. This interpretation is based also upon my reading of their fiction, essays, letters, and diaries. But I am principally interested in the way these authors rendered themselves for public consumption in engagement with other discourses on republicanism, the family, and women. I wish to show the three women writers' self-narratives as a political strategy both to support and to transform republicanism for feminist purposes.[13] Central to this analysis and to the main argument of this essay is the position of the three authors as transgressive women. As professional writers and women who left their husbands, had extramarital love affairs, bore children out of wedlock (in the cases of d'Agoult and Allart), headed families without men, and wrote about such matters to a large, mainly middle-class audience, these women writers invoked private and public criticism of their family roles and individual identities. It is not surprising, therefore, that their representations of families and of themselves would implicitly or explicitly respond to such criticism. Indeed, they portray the family life they experienced as children and as adults in such a way as to legitimize their eschewing of domestic, dependent femininity and their adoption of certain "masculine" behaviors. Additionally, in order to narrate themselves as republican women, Sand, d'Agoult, and Allart recast republican conceptions of the family and of gender and undercut the republican ideal of separate, masculine and feminine, public and private spheres.

I begin with brief biographies of the three authors to establish a "factual". and chronological framework. I then analyze representations of their birth families as alternative republican family romances in which fathers are constructed as republican liberators rather than absolutist or patriarchal tyrants. Next, I study the women writers' accounts of how they became republicans, their resistance to particular male republicans' attempted domination, and their assertion of an independent female republicanism. Finally, I examine their representations of the families they established as adults as examples of how the three women lived as autonomous individuals in a manner both to fulfill and transform republicanism.

WOMEN WRITERS' FAMILIES AND POLITICS

Aurore Dupin (the future George Sand) was the legitimate daughter of an army officer and a camp follower, but she grew up in female-headed households after her father's death when she was four years old. Her paternal grandmother and her mother competed for her affection throughout her childhood, and even though Aurore spent her adolescence largely under the control of her grandmother, the conflict between the two women ended only with the grandmother's death in 1821. In 1822 Aurore married an illegitimate son of a minor aristocrat, Casimir Dudevant, and had two children. In 1830 she arranged with her husband to divide her time between their country home at Nohant and apartments in Paris. At this time the young matron began a series of love affairs and a writing career that was assured with the overnight success of her first novel, *Indiana,* published in 1832 under the name of Georges Sand (later changed to George).[14] Sand effectively became a single parent with her separation from Dudevant in 1836 when she also gained control over Nohant, the estate she inherited from her grandmother. At the same time Sand became an adherent of democratic socialism, and in 1848 she hurried to Paris to write propaganda for the new republic under the Interior Minister Alexandre-Auguste Ledru-Rollin. Disillusioned with the machinations of male political power holders and power seekers, Sand returned to Nohant after two months and devoted herself to running her household, providing for her family, tending the local community, and writing fiction in the hope that literature might disseminate republican values more effectively than politics.[15]

Like Sand, Marie de Flavigny lost her father when she was young — not quite fourteen years old. He was a French aristocrat and her mother was a rich German bourgeoise. As a child Marie divided her time among French and German family homes, and after her father's death her older brother became the household head. On the marriage market Mademoiselle de Flavigny was a most attractive prize, due to her wealth, status, and beauty. The winner was Comte Charles d'Agoult, who wed her in 1827. D'Agoult had two children by her husband before she left him in 1835 to fulfill her passion for the young pianist Franz Liszt. After several years of wandering and giving birth to three children with Liszt, d'Agoult returned to Paris in 1839 and started her own homes in various Parisian apartments and houses. She also launched her career as a republican salonnière and as a writer under the pseudonym of Daniel Stern beginning in 1841. Like Sand, d'Agoult welcomed the 1848 Revolution and the Second Republic, which inspired her to write what would become her most famous work, the *History of the 1848 Revolution* (1853). For the rest of her life d'Agoult experienced turbulent relations with Liszt and with the surviving children of her two liaisons, but she continued to uphold a liberal republicanism through her writing and salon.[16]

Hortense Allart's birth family was from the upper bourgeoisie. Her father had an administrative post under Napoleon, and after his premature death in 1817, Allart's mother turned to writing to support herself and two daughters until she, too, died in 1821. At an early age Allart aspired to a career in letters, and she published her first work of historical fiction in 1822. Allart lived with a family friend and with a family whose children she tutored until she found herself pregnant by a young Portuguese aristocrat. She went to Italy to give birth to her first son in 1826. For the next several years she lived variously in Italy, France, and England, sometimes with different lovers, and she bore a second son. During the 1830s Allart associated with socialist feminists, and, almost to her own surprise, in 1843 she married a provincial aristocrat from whom she fled after one year. Being a single parent never diminished Allart's abiding interest in politics, which was reflected in the many novels, essays, and histories she wrote throughout her life. A supporter of strong, even authoritarian leadership, and skeptical, even disdainful, of the capacity of the masses for self-government, Allart was hardly as committed to a liberal, much less democratic republicanism, as were Sand or d'Agoult. However, in March and April of 1848 she supported the Second Republic, and her writings reflect a constant, if critical, fascination with republicanism both theoretical and historical.[17]

Since both Sand and d'Agoult became authors after they were married, they adopted pseudonyms because their married names were not their own; they had no desire to put their husbands' names to works written by themselves. Additionally, they chose male pseudonyms in order to be taken seriously as writers, though the public learned of their female identities shortly after their first publications. But pseudonyms also served a more positive function. They were declarations of independence from the subordinated and silent status of wives, and creations of new, authorial identities. Sand even considered her pseudonym as indicating a new marriage between herself and literature. Unlike d'Agoult, who used the name Daniel Stern only on published works, Sand embraced her new name so thoroughly that she signed her personal letters George, was addressed as George by friends and as Madame Sand by acquaintances, often used masculine endings when referring to herself in correspondence, and assumed a masculine narrative voice in some of her published works. By contrast Hortense Allart started publishing as an unmarried woman, signing her first book Mlle H. A., and subsequent works with her full name, or with the addition of de Thérase, that might have been a means of asserting her status as a mature woman, rather than a "mademoiselle." Moreover, after her brief and unhappy marriage to Napoléon de Méritens, she did the opposite of Sand and d'Agoult by adopting the name Hortense Allart de Méritens. And in her final, autobiographical works she used the pseudonym Madame P[rudence] de Saman [L'Esbatx], the surnames also from her husband's family. By assuming the names of her former husband Allart was perhaps advertising her once-married status to enhance her respectability. But given her unconventional behavior and beliefs, she might also have been deliberately flouting the legal rights husbands had over their wives' lives and works.[18]

     These brief sketches of the three authors' family experiences and politics offer the merest backdrop to their own crafted accounts. But two common features are the early death of the father in their birth families and the absence of fathers in the families they established as adults. Sand experienced virtually no paternal or masculine power until her marriage. D'Agoult had an older brother who replaced her father as head of the household, and Allart's father died when she was almost of marriageable age, but for all three, the nuclear family lost its "natural" and certainly legal head. The way the authors represent their fathers, and their broader representations of their birth families, suggests that the absence of paternal authority might have enabled these women to construct independent identities that departed from the common expectation for elite females that they devote themselves to domestic concerns and private life. Moreover, the fathers they represent appear to sanction their daughters' involvement in politics and their support for republicanism.

"FATHERS" AND REPUBLICAN DAUGHTERS

According to conservative and liberal theorists of the family, and implemented in the Civil Code of 1804, men dominated wives and children by a natural right, similar to the natural authority of a king or state. As head of the family that mediated between the individual and the state, the father's function was to control individuals on behalf of the state, which, in practical terms meant preparing children for citizenship roles sharply divided by gender. A girl's future was to be a wife and mother devoted to domestic concerns, while boys would become men who represented families in the public realm, as well as dominating the private life of the home. With the exception of a few utopian socialists, namely Charles Fourier and the Saint-Simonian feminists, this was effectively the position of male republicans on the issue of the family as well.[19] To be sure, a major innovation of the first French Republic that the Civil Code upheld was the principle of equal inheritance. All legitimate children, regardless of sex, were entitled to an equitable share of the family inheritance. Revolutionary proponents of this principle argued that its merit was to reproduce in the family the equality enshrined in the new republican state.[20] But the limits of this vaunted equality were evident in the Civil Code and in published theories of the family in which the authority of husbands and fathers over wives and children was asserted unambiguously.

The three women writers' portrayals of their birth families suggest an idealized republican egalitarianism that probably did not exist, but for which the three authors were ever hopeful. Their remembered, or in some cases, imagined fathers appear as liberators of the authors' independent identities, rather than as authority figures molding their daughters for a domestic career. Sand, d'Agoult, and Allart honored their parents, and especially their fathers, in autobiographical narrative. In this way they diminished the transgressive nature of their own characters and life choices, and legitimized themselves as daughters and as family members. However, Sand and d'Agoult constructed fathers who, in a sense, authorized their daughters to be independent individuals, who even constituted models of values and behaviors for their daughters to emulate. Indeed, Sand and d'Agoult attribute their own republican politics to the direct influence of their fathers. And Allart constructed an alternative "father" in the person of a female friend who influenced Allart's interest in politics, if not in explicitly republican politics.

Almost the first third of Sand's autobiography is devoted to her family history, the life stories of her grandmother, her mother, and especially

Lth.de Thierry Frères.

Jules Boilly. *Mme G. Sand* (1837). Bibliothèque Nationale de France, Cabinet des Estampes. Photo Bibliothèque Nationale de France, Paris

her father. Sand repeatedly justified this lengthy narrative of her family background by asserting that individual life stories were the primary substance of history. In the context of recounting her father's brief life as a boy during the French Revolution and as a soldier in the republican and later imperial army, Sand wrote: "In order to understand the Revolution and the Empire, you will still have to know the whole history of humanity. Here, I am relating a personal history. Humanity has a personal history in every person."[21] Sand suggests here that there is no distinction between the political and the personal, between history and the family, between the public and the private.

Sand was explicit that her father's early death contributed to his being "a shining apparition" in her memory, that he was more an object of Sand's fantasy than a remembered individual, precisely because Sand hardly knew him. In a remarkable passage Sand suggested that her own self-creation was inseparable from her imagined memory of her father: "My being is a reflection — weakened no doubt, but rather complete — of his. . . . had I been a boy and had I lived twenty-five years earlier, I know and I sense that I would have acted and felt in all things like my father."[22] Thus, Sand's story of her father's life was essential to the story of her own life.[23] The thoughts, choices, and character strengths and weaknesses revealed in his many letters that Sand reproduced (and sometimes altered) in her autobiography were, for Sand, her own. Sand's re-creation of her father was essentially her own self-creation. She presented her father as a staunch republican who lived his private life according to his political principles and who therefore transmitted these ideas to his daughter. Implicitly, Sand's republican politics, egalitarian values, and quest for love were sanctioned by her father. Maurice Dupin, according to Sand, supported the republic, despite the fact that his own mother was imprisoned for some nine months under the Terror.[24] Sand writes of her father: "Suffering because of the Revolution to the depths of his being, knowing that his adored mother was threatened by the guillotine, I never see him curse those ideas which gave birth to the Revolution; on the contrary, I see him approve and give his blessing to the downfall of the privileged classes."[25]

Sand asserts that Dupin believed in a meritocracy, and, as further evidence of his egalitarianism, that he married a woman for love, despite her low social origins and the bitter opposition of his mother. Sand writes of her father: "He will marry a daughter of the people, which means he will carry on and apply the egalitarian ideas of the Revolution in the intimacy of his own life. He will struggle in the bosom of his own family against aristocratic principles and the world of the past. He will break his heart, but he will have fulfilled his dream of equality."[26] Here Sand makes explicit the link between the family and politics; she asserts that by marrying a poor woman of the working class Dupin implements his revolutionary, republican politics. And as a being self-created in her father's own (created) image, Sand, by implication, will reproduce Dupin's principles and actions. Sand is the product of this egalitarian union, and she claims that she is practically identical to her father. In the same chapter that begins with her assertion that she would have been just like her father had she been born male and twenty-five years earlier, Sand also says that "assuredly" she would have been a Jacobin had she lived during the Revolution.[27] Sand is constructing simultaneously a political identity for her father and for herself. By doing this she does not appear to be presumptive in asserting a political position, nor is she demanding the right to do so either for herself or for all women. Rather, she casts herself as fulfilling her father's desires and ideals. Sand's political allegiance thus becomes a measure of filial piety rather than a violation of patriarchal, and, one could say, republican, law.

D'Agoult did not go so far as Sand in erasing the difference of gender between herself and her father. Instead, she suggested that her parents represented opposite value systems associated with their different class backgrounds and that she adopted those of her father. D'Agoult wrote disdainfully of her mother's crass, bourgeois materialism and asserted that she rejected it totally. She identified with her father's aristocratic background, which for her embodied values of honor, disinterestedness, and reason. Like Sand, d'Agoult also provides a long genealogy of her family, and among the Flavignys of the past she describes in some detail a sixteenth-century royalist with republican sympathies. In a book that Charles de Flavigny published in 1594 on the kings of France, d'Agoult detects a note of "heresy" in his devotion to the French monarchy. According to d'Agoult this ancestor of hers admired "the constitution . . . of the Helvetic Republic," and declared that had "I been Swiss, and had a Burgermeister infringed on the sovereignty of my country, I would take a thousand lives, if I had them, to uphold my popular freedom." D'Agoult considers her ancestor's independence of mind a typical trait of a cultivated and true gentleman, and she asserts that this characteristic is evident in other Flavignys imbued with "good taste and the gift for literature."[28] In her representation of the Flavigny family's old, aristocratic, royalist lineage, d'Agoult manages to insert an egalitarian, republican principle as utterly consistent and persistent. This is particularly astonishing in the context of her descriptions of her own father's ultraroyalist devotion. Alexandre de Flavigny spent the time of the French Revolution in Germany with the royalist army, he fought with them again during Napoleon's Hundred Days, and under the Restoration, his home of Mortier "became a meeting place for ultras, Vendeans, malcontents and grumblers."[29] As a child d'Agoult was initiated into politics in this

Henri Lehmann. *Mme la comtesse d'Agoult* (1839). Bibliothèque Nationale de France, Cabinet des Estampes. Photo Bibliothèque Nationale de France, Paris

hotbed of ultraroyalism that was her father's home, yet she insists that her Flavigny family inheritance was republicanism. With the death of Alexandre de Flavigny, d'Agoult suggests that she, the daughter, was better suited than her elder brother to inherit this republican legacy as the new head of the household.

D'Agoult was devastated by her father's death in 1819, and she recalled that she immediately submitted to her brother's authority: "I vowed . . . to transfer to this older brother all the filial piety, all the respect and all the love that I had had for my father."[30] But according to d'Agoult, Maurice de Flavigny, the new household head, did not adequately appreciate his sister's unspoken pledge of obedience; despite his good intentions he failed to live up to d'Agoult's expectations of replacing their father. Indeed, in a footnote d'Agoult asserts that Maurice, in the final years of his life, conceded that had d'Agoult been the elder brother, both of their lives would have been better because she had the bolder mind: "Nature apparently was in error by making him the brother and [d'Agoult] the sister. Had the roles been reversed, he added, all would have been better."[31] D'Agoult suggests here, echoing Maurice, that she, though female, possessed the masculine quality of a good mind; her personal characteristics were more suitable to the position of household head than her brother's. She thus undermines the principle of natural sexual differences, as well as that of male authority in the family.

D'Agoult implied that because her brother failed to fulfill his responsibilities as father substitute, her subsequent acts of insubordination might be excused. As an adult, d'Agoult violated family codes of honor by abandoning her husband and by becoming a republican. But at the same time that she defied aristocratic tradition, she turned other aristocratic qualities — namely disinterestedness and reason — to her advantage. "Rocked in my cradle to stories of the Vendean wars, linked by family ties to the elder branch of the Bourbons, . . . impartial study of ideas, and not personal hatreds, led me to opinions that differed from those of my people."[32] D'Agoult maintained that her father's family was actually less class prejudiced than her mother's, so that, paradoxically, she "inherited" egalitarianism and meritocracy from her aristocratic, French background; and she disinherited herself from her maternal, bourgeois legacy of snobbery and status consciousness. "I would never have thought that, in our country of equality and under our democratic standard, anyone could not have regarded as a matter of total indifference whether someone was born count, viscount, marquis, countess or baroness."[33] D'Agoult constructed her father as a symbol of qualities she admired and adopted, even to the point of linking her republican politics with his aristocratic values.

Allart began her autobiography by describing her relationship with a family friend, Laure Regnault de Saint-Jean d'Angély, rather than with her childhood or family background. She even said that Regnault was her first love, and that her "birth" occurred at Regnault's country home:

Sophie Allart Gabriac. *Hortense Allart* (1829). Bibliothèque Nationale de France, Cabinet des Estampes. Photo Bibliothèque Nationale de France, Paris

"I was truly born, if being born means feeling, loving."[34] Several pages later, Allart expressed the wish that she had been Regnault's daughter.[35] In Allart's narrative Regnault assumed more authority than either parent. Indeed, after Napoleon's death in 1821, when Allart and Regnault were commiserating over the loss of their hero, Allart wrote that "it was she [Regnault] who became my emperor."[36] Although Allart remembered her father fondly, she portrayed his significance in her life and in the development of her character as relatively slight and her mother's influence as even less. Breaking with the pattern of women writers (including Sand and d'Agoult) identifying almost exclusively with the father, even in imagined form, Allart constructed for herself a parental figure in the feminine with whom she very much identified.[37] Regnault, the real authority for Allart, was constructed as a woman almost in Allart's own image whose appeal took the form of both feminine and masculine characteristics. Allart describes Regnault as combining firmness and sentiment and sensitivity and heroism, and she claims that this woman "aroused my affection by the qualities that most seduced me."[38] Regnault was a Bonapartist, a witty and celebrated salonnière, and, as a widow, an independent woman. Similarly, Allart favored strong leaders (though not tyrants), she was a professional writer, and she was almost always independent.

To suggest that Regnault authorized Allart to become a republican requires qualification. Allart claims that as a mature woman she renounced her "youthful enthusiasm" for Bonaparte, but she never lost her affection for strong leaders.[39] Allart never identified herself as a republican, and she often expressed hostile disdain for the masses and their revolutionary efforts at democracy. Nonetheless, her historical studies led her to believe that republics were the best form of government for the cultivation of great leaders, and she welcomed the Second Republic early in 1848, agreeing with Adolphe Thiers, that "the Republic is the government that divides [French people] the least."[40] But another reason Allart supported republicanism was its potential to create a new, "egalitarian" leadership elite of both men and women of exceptional ability. Here, I believe, is the connection between Allart's surrogate "father," Regnault, and Allart's republican politics. Allart regarded the public women of the empire (Regnault, Fortunée Hamelin, and especially Madame de Staël) as similar to the female philosopher-kings of Plato's republic; republicanism, for Allart, offered the possibility of sexual equality among intellectual and leadership elites, among whom, of course, Allart placed herself. In her own life story, Allart was carrying on Regnault's qualities of independence, intelligence, and political commitment that, in an ideal republic, might be cultivated into political leadership on an equal basis with men of similar, exceptional abilities.[41]

These three accounts of birth families suggest little, if any, paternal authority over Sand, d'Agoult, and Allart while they were growing up. Moreover, the historical fathers did not live long enough to defend their daughters' honor from sexual transgression, even if they had been so inclined. In the authors' renditions, fathers (or a surrogate authority) represented possibilities for public life that their daughters eagerly and "dutifully" explored. The fathers that Sand and d'Agoult imagined were as much projections of their own identities as remembered parents, and Allart "chose" her model parent and authority in the person of Regnault. The three women writers constructed their fathers in such a way as to make themselves appear to be loyal daughters, adopting characteristics similar to their fathers'. This is not to say that the three authors were merely seeking paternal approval after the fact; rather, I want to suggest that they were taking charge of their own public identities by constructing fathers in their own images. These autobiographical fathers promoted their daughters' individual development and did not confine them to expectations of strictly domestic careers. They also authorized their daughters' republicanism as a kind of family inheritance that might be perpetuated through women writers' families, as well as through their public activities, like writing and political activism. This family romance of "dutiful" daughters fulfilling their fathers' implicitly androgynous republican ideals differs markedly from that of the sons' elimination of the tyrannical father to create a fraternal republic. It implies a more egalitarian republican family that sanctions women as well as men fulfilling their desires and ideals in both public and private life. There is no intimation that sexual difference should inhibit women's life choices, indeed, that sexual difference even exists beyond the social construction of gender. Later, when Sand and d'Agoult were adults, they rejected patriarchal practices of republicanism, even as they accepted certain republican ideals.

BECOMING REPUBLICAN WOMEN

The authors' narratives of childhood that made republicanism a family inheritance, in the cases of Sand and d'Agoult, or that set forth a model of an independent woman with political ideas, in the case of Allart, foregrounded their conscious adoption of republicanism as adults and their living out of republicanism as both a public ideology and a private practice. Both Sand and d'Agoult came to republicanism almost simultaneously with their breaks from marriage and the establishment of independent households. For Allart, who lived independently for most of her life, republicanism was articulated first in the context of her feminism. Their republicanisms were all distinctive, but the implications of republicanism for their lives were similar. For these three women writers, republicanism entailed not only representative or democratic or socialist government, but also economic independence, public self-expression, the freedom and responsibility of heading a household, and some kind of political role for women. They could configure such a feminist republicanism with relative ease because French republicanism in the nineteenth century was highly contested, with no single, monolithic version predominating.

Like all republicans, Sand, d'Agoult, and Allart had to select or redefine their own version of this ideal from among the many competing possibilities articulated and adhered to under the July monarchy. Although republicans generally agreed on electoral reform and guarantees of civil liberties (for men), there was wide variation among them regarding the power structure of a republican regime and the extent and nature of government intervention on social issues.[42] The ideal republic might be authoritarian or democratic; it might define equality in terms of civil rights, or it might pursue a policy of economic equalization through the guarantee of employment for all men with government subsidies; it might foster the competition of free (male) individuals, or it might be predicated upon mutually supportive communities. Perhaps the most innovative republicans were socialist feminists who called for the enfranchisement of all men and women, a communitarian orientation to love, work, and society, and even separate female communities.[43] The stories of their marginalization — including the three women writers' rejection of their ideas and associations — have been told elsewhere.[44] Although some scholars lump Sand and d'Agoult indiscriminately with male republicans in condemning socialist feminists, it is important to acknowledge that Sand and d'Agoult, along with Allart, also set themselves apart from even the republican men they most admired, largely over substantive issues, like divorce, but also over patriarchal behavior.

Sand describes her conscious adoption of republicanism as a conversion that started in 1830 and solidified in 1835 when she met Michel de Bourges, the first among many republicans of different stripes whom Sand befriended. Michel de Bourges, who was Sand's lover and to whom she refers as Everard, expressed his republican ideas to Sand with great eloquence during the protracted Paris "monster trial" of 164 defendants from the uprising in Lyon of 1834.[45] Numerous lawyers, among them a pantheon of prominent republicans, argued for the defense and, according to Sand, their initial unity against the July monarchy fissured into competing republicanisms, ranging from moderately liberal to radically socialist. Sand writes that by this time she "had already been converted to republican sympathy and progressive ideas," and that it was Everard who inspired in her "the ability to feel the vivid emotions that politics had never before awakened in me."[46]

In her letters from this period Sand reveals a fondness for Robespierre, admiring his total commitment to the revolutionary cause and his extension of political rights to even the poorest of men.[47] Although she writes during this same period of her desire to champion improvements in the social condition of women through her fiction, the best hint of her view on the political status of women comes from her letter to Everard published in 1835 as part of the *Letters of a Traveler*.[48] The letter to Everard is more immediate than the account of that period in the autobiography, as well as more suggestive of Sand's self-positioning as a political being during her first embrace of republicanism. Like all of the letters in this volume, this one is written from the perspective of a masculine narrator. Sand describes herself several times as a boy and as a male disciple to Everard, a political mentor. Sand is ardent in her admiration for the republic: "Hail, republic, dawn of justice and of equality, divine utopia" — though she is uncertain about the timing of its arrival on French soil.[49] She relies on great men, like Everard, actually to lead a republic for she believes that they possess the republican virtue of lifelong commitment to this state of equality and democracy. By contrast Sand considers herself a backslider, a person who has led a soft life, indulging in various pleasures, notably love, instead of sacrificing for the future utopia. She explains, however, a different kind of republican virtue for folks like herself, in contrast to exceptional men, like Everard: "The governed must be honest, temperate, faithful, in short *moral,* so that the governors can erect a durable edifice upon their strong and submissive shoulders."[50]

Sand modestly includes her masculine self among the equal and honest but decidedly governed citizenry. But she also articulates a more active role for herself (himself) in service to the republic. Sand's narrator defines "his" role as an artist and not a lawmaker: "I am by nature poetic and not legislative, warlike if need be, but never parliamentary. . . . Will it not be permitted for minstrels to sing romances to women, while you make laws for men?"[51] Although Sand calls herself something of a plow boy, she also claims to be a poet and as such effeminate: "I am a poet, that is a weak man *[une femmelette]*."[52] She thus claims for herself a more passive but no less committed role in the republic than that of the assertive leader, Everard: "In a revolution your goal will be the freedom of the human race; as for me, I will have none other but to get myself killed, in order to put an end to myself and to have, for the first time in my life, served some purpose, if only to raise the barricade by the height of one corpse."[53]

Thus, during the time of her romance with Michel de Bourges and her first enthusiasm for republicanism, Sand delineates for herself and for the majority a role of follower behind the dedicated male leaders governing on behalf of a free and equal people. This might be interpreted as suggesting that Sand believes in civil equality for women and men, but not civic equality. She excuses herself from lawmaking by pleading ignorance — "I can act but not deliberate, for I know nothing and I am sure of nothing"[54] — a statement that might refer to herself as a woman. And although Sand narrates as a male, she calls herself an effeminate male. Still, Sand never suggests that she or women in general have a naturally domestic and private role in society. The effeminacy, she claims, is due to her being a poet, not to any sex-specific, natural trait. Sand plays with gender here, constructing a figure of dreamy, sensitive, idealistic youth being introduced simultaneously and by the same person to both the sensuous pleasure of love and the abstract stimulation of politics. This youthful poet is an indeterminate creature, neither masculine nor feminine, but rather a combination of the characteristics of both.[55]

Yet in the autobiography, written more than a decade after her infatuation with Michel de Bourges had cooled and two or three years after her experience of the 1848 Revolution, Sand totally recasts the boyish apprentice trope. She presents herself as a woman and as disabusing Everard of precisely the illusion of her masculine identity; she has Everard saying, "I saw you in my mind's eye as a young boy, a child poet, whom I made my son."[56] Sand indicates in this section of the autobiography that she seriously questioned Everard's apocalyptic and dictatorial republicanism. Indeed, she invokes the image of the traveler *(le voyageur)* again to tell Everard that she is leaving and rejecting his presumed authority over her, though she is grateful to him for introducing her to a democratic political ideal. In re-created (or fabricated) dialogue, Sand first acknowledges the benefits she gained from Everard's tutelage: "You made me foresee an ideal of fraternity which warmed my glacial heart. In that, you were truly Christian, and you converted me through my feelings."[57] But Sand goes on to say that while Everard posed as one with a clear solution to the social and political ills of the day, he really was still seeking it, and Sand claimed for herself the right to search on her own for an appropriate political philosophy or ideology: "Let me go now to med-

itate on the things you are seeking here, on the principles which may perhaps be formulated and applied to the needs of the hearts and minds of
mankind. . . . You are no wiser than I, although you're a better person."[58] Sand says that she resents and rejects Everard's attempt to control
her and others through his eloquence and false promises: "Your mind
needs to dominate those who listen to the enraptured beliefs that reason
has not yet ripened. It is at that point that reality seizes me and distances
me from you."[59] Significantly, Sand upbraids Everard for behaving as if
he were her father and she his son. Unlike Sand's own (created) father,
who liberated Sand's thoughts, feelings, and desires, Everard was trying
to control Sand, according to her autobiographical version. Moreover,
Sand claims for herself *as a woman* the ability to reason for herself a
political framework for the correction of social problems.

Sand then presumes to re-create Everard's response to her accusations
of his tyranny, and Everard's words are explicit about his belief in natural
sexual differences and their implications for politics. Everard expresses
disappointment in discovering that Sand is not what he had imagined her
to be — a boy, his son. "I see well . . . that you have the ambition and the
imperiousness of undeveloped minds, of beings of pure feeling and imagination — of women, in short."[60] Everard goes on to say that pure feeling
is not adequate for politics, and he asserts a robespierrist position that
action and especially duty often must take precedence over feelings in
politics. He accuses Sand of misguided idealism in a belief that feelings
and actions can be harmonious in politics. The nub of their disagreement, in Sand's representation, is over the issue of individual freedom. In
this rendition Everard elevates some abstract commitment — duty — to a
cause or a state above human liberty, and Sand, apparently, espouses
freedom above duty. Everard's chastisement of Sand's position uses language highly suggestive of his or Sand's awareness of the struggle of
women in the midst of a masculinist republicanism: "Your dream is of an
individual freedom that does not fit in with the concept of duty in general. You worked hard to win this freedom for yourself. . . . You tell
yourself that your body belongs to you and that the same is true for your
soul."[61] Everard accuses Sand of abandoning a worthy cause — the cause
of truth as he defines it — in order to contemplate freely and in solitude
other possibilities, that, from his perspective, can only be chimeras.
Significantly, Sand links her femaleness with individual freedom and
independence, strikingly in contrast to Everard's male, tyrannical author-
itarianism. Sand leaves it to the reader to decide who is right, and she
asserts that she included this long dialogue in the autobiography as an

example of a conflict that was very common among republicans at this time. Sand is by no means launching a frontal, feminist attack against the republican exclusion of women from politics. However, her allusive play and probing of gender in relation to republican politics suggests a tempered, skeptical approach to masculinist republicanism and its adherents. Indeed, she challenges the authority of men to define the meaning of republicanism and to bend women to their political will. She asserts the strength of female intellect and independence that might imply a public, if not political, role for women in republicanism.[62]

Sand spread her new-found republicanism to her friends, including Marie d'Agoult. D'Agoult writes of Sand, whom she first met in 1835 and with whom she maintained close relations for the next three years: "She introduced me to her republican friends."[63] By her own account d'Agoult had long found tedious the traditional, monarchist society of the Faubourg Saint-Germain, and had prided herself on introducing new artistic talent if not new political ideas into her own successful salon. The first hint of any serious consideration of republicanism on her part comes with her meeting with Liszt, who favored republicanism and who was also a follower of Félicité de Lamennais, the Catholic priest who defied the Church with his radical, socialistic faith. Like Sand, d'Agoult professes to have been greatly influenced by individual republicans, including Lamennais and Sand herself. Also like Sand, d'Agoult finds herself resisting the powerful influences around her and charting her own way to a republicanism that includes her feminist concerns. An important episode in this progress was d'Agoult's initial resistance to Lamennais when he tried to talk her out of abandoning her family and fleeing with Liszt.

D'Agoult had heard about Lamennais from Liszt who in fact spent several months at La Chênaie, Lamennais's Breton home, before deciding on the plan of flight with d'Agoult. Just days after Liszt persuaded d'Agoult to run away with him, Lamennais, whom she had never met, showed up on her doorstep. D'Agoult describes in dramatic terms Lamennais's efforts to dissuade her from carrying out the plan with Liszt. D'Agoult suggests that Lamennais, having failed to change Liszt's mind, considered d'Agoult, a woman, to be easy prey to his exhortations. But d'Agoult portrays herself as clever and steadfast in her resistance to Lamennais's indisputable eloquence.

She talks back mentally to Lamennais when he cautions her about the perils that await the revolutionary mind, saying to herself that Lamennais did the same thing she is about to do, that is, follow one's heart even though it entails rebelling against law and authority.[64] D'Agoult is very proud of herself when Lamennais leaves in defeat, muttering that he has "never before encountered such a resistant will in a woman."[65] And this is only the beginning of d'Agoult's resistance to Lamennais. Acknowledging his many merits, including his friendship with d'Agoult after she left Liszt and returned to Paris, and his encouragement of her writing, she also delineates their sharp disagreements over feminist issues, notably her argument in favor of divorce and her critical perspective on maternity that she published in 1847 in her *Essay on Liberty*. D'Agoult asserts that Lamennais is too old to be a good republican, too mired in priestly prejudices.[66] He was never able to dominate d'Agoult — "He did not exercise the absolute influence [over me] that he sought."[67] Resisting the patriarchal domination of male republicans was an important part of d'Agoult's republicanism. In her autobiography, as well as in her other texts, d'Agoult, like Sand, exercised her reason to articulate for herself a republican vision that prominently included various improvements in the social condition of women and civil rights for women.

D'Agoult indicates that during her self-imposed exile with Liszt in Switzerland and Italy she studied philosophers and historians and talked with educated men, all of which assisted in the development of her own, independent thought on republicanism: "I led a very retired life in the intimate society of a few eminent men whose conversation, for example, and compatibility enlivened me and encouraged me in serious study. The Protestant and republican atmosphere of Geneva, interaction with minds such as that of Sismondi . . . rapidly cultivated in me a critical faculty and independence of judgment."[68] By the time d'Agoult broke with Liszt and returned to Paris she was committed to establishing a republican salon, and she aspired to a career in writing. The two goals ultimately were realized, and they coalesced, perhaps most notably, in d'Agoult's *History of the Revolution of 1848*.

In contrast to Sand and d'Agoult, Allart does not focus on republicanism or republican men as particularly influential on her political thought. By listing periodically the names of the historians, philosophers, and novelists she read throughout her lifetime Allart suggests that she derived her political ideas primarily from reading the works of a wide range of authors, though she also indicates her ideas were developed through conversations with a few women and many men — Laure Regnault de Saint-Jean d'Angély, Antony de Sampayo, René de Chateaubriand, Guglielmo Libri, Gino Capponi, Henry Bulwer-Lytton, Pierre-Jean Béranger, Pauline Roland — representing a broad spectrum of political allegiances. Allart was troubled by both revolutions of 1830 and 1848 because they raised for her a problem that she often associated with republicanism—the issue of democracy. Allart found popular revolutions dangerous; in her mind, they presumed to overthrow leadership by educated, intelligent, and capable beings in order to replace it with mob rule: "According to the teachings of God himself, men of talent and of enlightened society must lead the world; but the word *democracy* opens this career to the lower classes, or rather to those ambitious men who fool them."[69] Allart especially condemned democracy in what she considered to be great states, including France.[70] She granted its successful operation in the late medieval and Renaissance republic of Florence because the city-state was small and because the people were notably civic minded.[71] And although she found democratic republicanism extremely problematic for nineteenth-century France, she was by no means a monarchist and assuredly not an imperialist. In her private correspondence Allart expressed approval for republicanism more often than in her published works, probably because the popular connotation of republicanism in her time was often democratic and because she operated mostly in a theoretical language that she constituted for herself from her own, sometimes quirky readings of history and philosophy.[72] But in her autobiography Allart's assertion about the best form of government, led by an elite of the educated and the intelligent, most closely resembles the republican ideal of Plato, including the participation of exceptional women: "The world must be led by an intellectual aristocracy of men and of *women*."[73] Allart's understanding of "aristocracy" was distinctive; she meant a meritocracy, a select group distinguished by intelligence and knowledge in which sexual difference was irrelevant.[74] For her a republic was the most likely form in which this ideal could be realized— elitist while at the same time preserving liberty.

Sand, d'Agoult, and Allart articulated their republicanisms in the midst of a substantial outpouring of printed matter relating to republicanism, notably histories of and documentation from the French Revolution.[75] All three read at least some of the many histories of the French Revolution that appeared from the 1820s through the 1850s.[76] They were all taken by the mystical and socialistic Saint-Simonianism, if only briefly and selectively, and they maintained personal associations with republican figures like Adolphe Thiers, Pierre Leroux, Louis Blanc, and Alphonse de Lamartine, among others. They were engaged in the same controversies as their male peers, namely the effectiveness of popular revolution, the function of the state in social regulation, the extent of guarantees of personal freedom.[77] Allart and d'Agoult wrote essays on these issues, and their histories of republics (Florentine, Athenian, Dutch, and the Second French) outline their own views on democracy, social hierarchy, leadership, and revolution in republicanism.[78] Sand, too, wrote on republican and socialist principles in both her fiction and several articles of nonfiction.[79] But in all their works, Sand, d'Agoult, and Allart assumed or demanded a public role for women and legal reforms to make this possible for more than just elite women. Equally important for their advocacy and transformation of republicanism were their autobiographies with their legitimation and description of female republicanism. The three authors represented themselves as women who contributed to the cause through their intellect, writing, and sociability, rather than by being dependent and domestic wives, focused solely on motherhood. The autobiographies describe their own, female-headed families as consistent with republican ideals. In these families women writers eliminated the division between private and public existence and established the mother as head of household, rational thinker, and income provider — all attributes of a male republican individual, and not of a republican mother.

WRITING REPUBLICAN FAMILIES

Throughout their autobiographies, as well as in other works of nonfiction and fiction, Sand, d'Agoult, and Allart suggest alternative family relations and configurations to the model of patriarchal authority.[80] They present arguments in favor of the legalization of divorce, improved education and civil status for women, and reforms to equalize the powers of husbands and wives, fathers and mothers in the family.[81] In this they were not alone; utopian socialists and even liberal republicans advocated all or some of these changes as well.[82] But their version of a transformed, feminist republic was distinctive. They sought a new synthesis of female intellect, sociability, and motherhood in a family setting that was egalitarian and not rigidly separated from public life. They eschewed both the communitarianism of the socialist feminists and the republican motherhood ideal of liberals and some socialists that regarded women as primarily, even solely, mothers and always in relation to male family members. They operated within the limits of the heterosexual marriage and the nuclear family, reconfiguring the power relationships and division of labor within these units.[83] While awaiting the republican state and the legal transformation of the family, the three women writers created families of their own that, both by circumstance and by choice, carried out many of their republican ideals. As single mothers for much of their lives, Sand, d'Agoult, and Allart combined domestic, private functions with professional, public activity and made a virtue out of doing so. The fact that none of the three ever established enduring relationships with one man as a husband figure does not mean that they rejected the possibility. They implicitly attributed their single state to the failings of the existing legal system and social practices. Sand and d'Agoult, more than Allart, upheld the ideal of egalitarian marriage with mothers and fathers sharing the responsibilities of child rearing. But by portraying in their autobiographies the satisfactions of their own, female-headed families, all offered proof that women could succeed as intellectual professionals and heads of households. By their own examples, Sand, as poet and caregiver; Allart, as scholar and mother; and d'Agoult as republican salonnière represented models of republican womanhood.

After her separation from Dudevant, Sand returned to Nohant and experienced the fulfillment of the dream of her own house where she could truly be a writer. As the new head of her household, Sand appropriated space that she felt had not been hers before, and she relished this unprecedented freedom. "I had a large room on the ground floor, furnished with a small iron bed, a chair, and a table. After friends had left and the doors were closed, I could, without disturbing anyone's sleep, walk in the garden shielded like a citadel, work for an hour, go out and return, count the stars as they were disappearing, greet the sun when it rose, believing myself finally to be in the deserted house of my dreams. . . . That was perhaps the place where, right or wrong, I most thought myself a poet."[84] Soon thereafter Sand's children returned from boarding school and family friends from where they had stayed during the separation trial, and Sand began the arduous task of "sailing the fragile bark of family security" as a single parent and working mother.[85] In her own home and in the family of her own design, Sand freely cultivated her multiple identities as writer, mother, lover, and friend, though not without difficulty. "Respect for art; obligations of honor; moral and physical care of children, which always comes before all else; details of the house; duties of friendship, charity, and kindness! How short are most days for keeping disorder from taking over the family, the house, business affairs, or the brain!"[86] Sand's experiences of marriage, love, and separation suggested to her that the legal and social conditions of her time prevented the loving and egalitarian relationship between spouses that she considered the foundation of ideal, republican family life. Sand's stories about her own families were inseparable from her ideas about gender relations and families in general. "I conclude that marriage must be made as indissoluble as possible. . . . But the indissolubility of marriage is possible only on the condition that it is voluntary, and to make it voluntary, it must be made possible. So, if to get us out of this vicious circle, you find something besides the insistence on equal rights between man and woman, you will have made a still better discovery."[87]

In contrast to Sand, as well as to d'Agoult, Allart hardly spoke of a family as such in her autobiography. She asserted that bearing, nurturing, and rearing her first illegitimate child were her conscious choices, made to conform to her love of openness and truth.[88] She made a home for herself and her seven-year-old son in a small village just outside of Paris that she described primarily in terms of its conduciveness to her writing: "Here in the country . . . I begin a new life, studious as before but also happily calm, surrounded with books . . . "[89] Allart's country homes with her two sons were always presented in similar terms, first as promoting her individual development as a writer and second as providing an affordable setting for rearing her children. In an intriguing passage from a letter to Sainte-Beuve, Allart compared her satisfaction with an independent life and motherhood to the joys of a male head of household. Describing her return from Paris, after walking alone from the coach station to her home in the country on a beautiful winter night, Allart wrote: "Everything was quiet, everything gently recalled the man in his own home *[l'homme à son foyer domestique]*. And finding myself here, all alone, I feel a charm that I cannot express. I hear only the tender breathing of my sleeping child; everyone in the village is asleep except I who write to you." Allart then indicates that she would like to share this quiet life with Sainte-Beuve and that she would love to have them read books together. She tells Sainte-Beuve that one can live very well alone with books; indeed, she writes that she lives surrounded by books written by wise men that are her "true lovers."[90] For Allart a family, even with a man, would exist fundamentally for female intellectual endeavor, and she would never give up her own sense of being the "man" of the house.

Allart considered her situation as a single mother and professional writer to be perfectly adequate, and she frequently extolled the lives of amazons who lived proudly and freely without men. As she demonstrated in stories like *Settimia* and "Marpé," strong and intelligent women needed neither husbands nor homes for their happiness and fulfillment.[91] Indeed, while both heroines revel in their love relationships

with men, they find their greatest satisfaction in independence, the cultivation of their minds, or single motherhood. Allart believed that a well-
ordered state should be run by men *and women* of superior ability, and
that the family must in no way inhibit the development of these exceptional individuals. Since women suffered most from the patriarchal,
nuclear family, she favored reforms that would promote female development whether in the context of the two-parent family or not.

D'Agoult was the most explicit about her determination to create a
miniature republic out of her home and family, presenting in her autobiography a household that might serve as a model of a woman's own
republicanism. She pointedly included among her portraits of great
artists from the Florentine republic and the quote from Sallust, a replica
of the *Mona Lisa* "to remind [viewers] of the feminine influence in these
glorious lives."[92] A feminine influence on republicanism is something
that d'Agoult sought to cultivate in her own life as well by gathering in
her home "prominent men of the republican party" who "formed a salon
around us, a real salon, enlivened by a liberal spirit, but varied in its
nuances."[93] The center of this salon was, however, Marie d'Agoult and
her offspring. D'Agoult describes her house as filled with beautiful children and grandchildren, playing the piano, drawing, doing lessons — all
under the leadership of the female head of the household — d'Agoult herself. "In our pleasant existence we had a penchant for work. The mother
set the example; all, including the smallest child, followed suit."[94]
D'Agoult goes on to describe the elevated and genial atmosphere of her
house that smoothly combined private, family life with public, political
sociability: "A charming intimacy formed in my house that was like a
sweet and gentle little republic."[95] In her written family and home
d'Agoult constructed a republic that differed significantly from the fraternal brotherhood that excluded women from public activity and designated them solely to domestic obedience. While acknowledging women's
identities as daughters, lovers, and mothers, d'Agoult, Sand, and Allart
indicated that women also existed independently of their relations with
men and with other family members. Their own stories revealed that
women could promote republicanism through public life, as well as
through the family.

Sand, d'Agoult, and Allart wrote themselves as women into the narrative of republicanism. Unlike other feminists — for example, Olympe de
Gouges in 1791 or socialist feminists in 1848 — they avoided engaging
directly in a theoretical debate with male republicans about whether
equality for all included women.[96] They shifted the ground of discussion

from the political rights of the individual to the implementation of republican principles in a truly egalitarian family. They proposed a transformation of the family that eliminated the barrier between private and public life and that denied the exclusion of women from republican politics. Sand, d'Agoult, and Allart were patient, in the sense that they believed improvements in the female condition and in attitudes toward women must necessarily precede political equality. Indeed, early in 1848 they appeared to trust their fellow male republicans to implement the legal changes that would eventually equalize the civil status of women and men. But in the face of the disappointing outcome of the Second Republic, the three authors were fortunate enough in their education, talent, and financial condition to act on their ideals about female capability and present them to the reading public. The female-headed families of Sand, d'Agoult, and Allart were perhaps truer to republican ideals of liberty, equality, and fraternity (broadly defined to include both sexes) than anything imagined by most male republicans. According to these family romances, republicanism starts in the family, and the women and men in families have the power to determine the gendering, or ungendering, of republicanism.

NOTES

I wish to thank Rachel Fuchs, Jo Burr Margadant, Michael Smith, and the members of the New York Area Seminar in French History for their helpful comments on earlier versions of this essay. I am also very grateful to the other contributors to this book and to all the participants in the student-author conference for their insights, suggestions, and collegiality.

1. Marie d'Agoult, *Mémoires, souvenirs et journaux de la comtesse d'Agoult (Daniel Stern)*, ed. Charles F. Dupêchez (Paris: Mercure de France, 1990), 2: 40.

2. I am very grateful to Nicholas Rauh for identifying the larger passage in Sallust and for his translation and interpretation. The passage in Latin is "Pulchrum est bene facere rei publicae etiam bene dicere haud absurdum est; vel pace vel bello clarum fieri licet." Sallust, *Bellum Catilinae*, with English translation by J. C. Rolfe (Cambridge, Mass.: Harvard University Press with W. Heinemann, Ltd., 1965), chap. 3, p. 7, l. 1 of original text.

3. D'Agoult, *Mémoires, souvenirs et journaux*, 1: 30.

4. A key text in the formulation of the ideal of republican motherhood is the speech by André Amar at the meeting of the National Convention on 9 Brumaire (1793) justifying the abolition of women's political clubs. Amar enumerates the capabilities required to govern as including "extensive knowledge, unlimited attention and devotion, a strict immovability, and self-abnegation," and he asserts that women in general are incapable "of these cares and of the qualities

they call for." He goes on to say that, "The private functions for which women are destined by their very nature are related to the general order of society; this social order results from the differences between man and woman. Each sex is called to the kind of occupation which is fitting for it." Amar contends that men are suited for "everything that calls for force, intelligence, capability, . . . he alone seems to be equipped for profound and serious thinking which calls for great intellectual effort and long studies which it is not granted to women to pursue." Female character, according to Amar, suits women for educating children and imbuing them with republican virtue: ". . . such are their functions, after household cares." "We believe, therefore, that a woman should not leave her family to meddle in affairs of government," and "We believe, therefore, . . . that it is not possible for women to exercise political rights." "The National Convention Outlaws Clubs and Popular Societies of Women," in *Women in Revolutionary Paris, 1789–1795*, ed. Darline Gay Levy, Harriet Branson Applewhite, and Mary Durham Johnson (Urbana: University of Illinois Press, 1979), 215–17. See also Joan B. Landes, *Women in the Public Sphere in the Age of the French Revolution* (Ithaca: Cornell University Press, 1988), 129–38.

5. Siân Reynolds, "Marianne's Citizens? Women, the Republic and Universal Suffrage in France," in *Women, State and Revolution: Essays on Power and Gender in Europe since 1789* (Amherst: University of Massachusetts Press, 1987), 102–22; Michèle Riot-Sarcey, *La Démocratie à l'épreuve des femmes: Trois figures critiques du pouvoir, 1830–1848* (Paris: Albin Michel, 1994), 78–81, 124–25; Ronald Aminzade, "Class Analysis, Politics, and French Labor History," in *Rethinking Labor History: Essays on Discourse and Class Analysis*, ed. Lenard R. Berlanstein (Urbana: University of Illinois Press, 1993), 103–4. See also Pamela M. Pilbeam, *Republicanism in Nineteenth-Century France, 1814–1871* (New York: St. Martin's Press, 1995), 172–74.

6. Lynn Hunt, *The Family Romance of the French Revolution* (Berkeley and Los Angeles: University of California Press, 1992), 203, and "Reading the French Revolution: A Reply," *French Historical Studies* 19 (fall 1995): 289–98. See also Olwen H. Hufton, *Women and the Limits of Citizenship in the French Revolution* (Toronto: University of Toronto Press, 1992).

7. Carole Pateman, *The Sexual Contract* (Stanford: Stanford University Press, 1988); Joan Wallach Scott, *Only Paradoxes to Offer: French Feminists and the Rights of Man* (Cambridge, Mass.: Harvard University Press, 1996). See also Landes, *Women and the Public Sphere;* Karen Offen, "Defining Feminism: A Comparative Historical Approach," *Signs* 14 (autumn 1988): 119–57; Claire Goldberg Moses and Leslie Wahl Rabine, *Feminism, Socialism, and French Romanticism* (Bloomington: Indiana University Press, 1993).

8. Geneviève Fraisse, *Reason's Muse: Sexual Difference and the Birth of Democracy*, trans. Jane Marie Todd (Chicago: University of Chicago Press, 1994). In contrast to Fraisse and Scott, Mona Ozouf characterizes French women writers, including George Sand and the self-proclaimed feminist Hubertine Auclert, as fairly passive in their acceptance of legal and political discrimination against women. Ozouf maintains that educated French women got along well with men and enjoyed male gallantry; therefore, they saw no reason directly to confront men with arguments in favor of equality for the sexes. Although Sand,

d'Agoult, and Allart chose writing rather than social movements as a means to combat inequality between the sexes, I interpret their writings as very deliberately challenging patriarchy in the home and the exclusion of women from politics. Mona Ozouf, *Women's Words: Essay on French Singularity*, trans. Jane Marie Todd (Chicago: University of Chicago Press, 1997). For an analysis of the British case of the exclusion of women from politics and its implications for feminism, see Leonore Davidoff, "Regarding Some 'Old Husbands' Tales': Public and Private in Feminist History," in *Worlds Between: Historical Perspectives on Gender and Class* (New York: Routledge, 1995), 227–76.

9. Riot-Sarcey, *La Démocratie à l'épreuve des femmes;* Moses and Rabine, *Feminism, Socialism, and French Romanticism;* Scott, *Only Paradoxes to Offer;* Claire Goldberg Moses, *French Feminism in the Nineteenth Century* (Albany: State University Press of New York, 1984). See also Laura S. Struminger, "Looking Back: Women of 1848 and the Revolutionary Heritage of 1789," in *Women and Politics in the Age of the Democratic Revolution*, ed. Harriet B. Applewhite and Darline G. Levy (Ann Arbor: University of Michigan, 1990), 259–85; Felicia Gordon and Máire Cross, *Early French Feminisms, 1830–1940: A Passion for Liberty* (Cheltenham: Edward Elgar, 1996), chapters on Deroin, Flora Tristan, and Pauline Roland.

10. Early in the twentieth century a popular biographical mode for French women of letters was to relate the personality to the literature and the life to literary relationships. Wladimir Karenine, *George Sand: Sa vie et ses oeuvres*, 4 vols. (Paris: Plon, 1926); Léon Séché, *Hortense Allart de Méritens* (Paris: Société de Mercure de France, 1908). During the 1950s and 1960s some biographers of Sand and Allart focused on their active sexual lives, namely, André Maurois, *Lélia: The Life of George Sand*, trans. Gerard Hopkins (New York: Harper & Row, 1953) and André Billy, *Hortense et ses amants* (Paris: Flammarion, 1961). The argument of both these works is that Sand and Allart are interesting only because of the famous men with whom they had love affairs. By contrast, a carefully researched work that avoids sensationalizing is Lorin A. Uffenbeck, *The Life and Writings of Hortense Allart, (1801–79)*, Ph.D. dissertation, University of Wisconsin-Madison, 1957. In the 1970s, biographies of Sand especially but also of d'Agoult were primarily concerned to represent them as feminists, or occasionally as antifeminists. The following titles are only a sample of the deluge of biographies of Sand in the United States. Curtis Cate, *George Sand: A Biography* (Boston: Houghton Mifflin, 1975), seeks to protect Sand from association with feminists from her own time and especially from feminists of the 1970s who, according to Cate, espoused a sexual promiscuity and licentiousness that Sand would have condemned. Ruth Jordan, *George Sand. A Biographical Portrait* (New York: Taplinger Publishing Company, 1976), denies that Sand was a feminist comparable to the Pankhursts and instead asserts that she was a "self-centered woman who wanted to have her own way" (xiii). Joseph Barry, *Infamous Woman: The Life of George Sand* (Garden City, N.Y.: Doubleday, 1977), maintains that Sand possessed an "androgynous mind" and that her life is best understood as her effort to combine the different halves of her being. Tamara Hovey, *A Mind of Her Own. A Life of the Writer George Sand* (New York: Harper & Row, 1977), regards Sand as a feminist who escaped from the

imprisonment of the feminine domestic ideal and succeeded in the larger world beyond the home. Renée Winegarten, *The Double Life of George Sand. Woman and Writer. A Critical Biography* (New York: Basic Books, 1978), also presents Sand as a pioneering feminist, the first woman to tell "what none had told hitherto about woman and the inner life of her sex" (vii). A presentist-oriented feminist biography of d'Agoult is Dominique Desanti's, *Daniel, ou le visage secret d'une comtesse romantique, Marie d'Agoult* (Paris: Stock, 1980). A recent biography that defends d'Agoult from the accusation that she was a bad mother is Charles Dupêchez's, *Marie d'Agoult, 1805–1876* (Paris: Perrin, 1989). Jacques Vier's *La Comtesse d'Agoult et son temps*, 6 vols. (Paris: Albin Michel, 1955–63) is in general a superb, thoroughly researched study that places d'Agoult firmly in her historical context and takes pride in asserting that d'Agoult maintained her rationality and femininity by eschewing association with and behavior resembling nineteenth-century French feminists.

11. The Personal Narratives Group, Joy Webster Barbre, *Interpreting Women's Lives: Feminist Theory and Personal Narratives* (Bloomington: Indiana University Press, 1989); Susan Stanford Friedman, "Women's Autobiographical Selves: Theory and Practice," in *The Private Self: Theory and Practice of Women's Autobiographical Writing,* ed. Shari Benstock (Chapel Hill: University of North Carolina Press, 1988), 34–62; Nancy K. Miller, "Writing Fictions: Women's Autobiography in France," in *Life/Lines: Theorizing Women's Autobiography,* ed. Bella Brodzki and Celeste Schenck (Ithaca: Cornell University Press, 1988), 45–61; Sidonie Smith, *A Poetics of Women's Autobiography: Marginality and the Fictions of Self-Representation* (Bloomington: Indiana University Press, 1987).

12. Scott, *Only Paradoxes to Offer,* 13; Carolyn Steedman, "La théorie qui n'en est pas une; or, Why Clio Doesn't Care," in *Feminists Revision History,* ed. Ann-Louise Shapiro (New Brunswick, N.J.: Rutgers University Press, 1994), 73–94; Kathleen Canning, "Feminist History after the Linguistic Turn: Historicizing Discourse and Experience," *Signs* 19 (1994): 368–404.

13. Jo Burr Margadant, "Introduction: The New Biography in Historical Practice," *French Historical Studies* 19 (fall 1996): 1045–58; Carolyn Steedman, *Childhood, Culture and Class in Britain: Margaret McMillan, 1860–1931* (New Brunswick, N.J.: Rutgers University Press, 1990).

14. By 1833 Sand had dropped the *s* from Georges. Isabelle Hoog Naginski, *George Sand: Writing for Her Life* (New Brunswick: Rutgers University Press, 1991), 3.

15. George Sand, *Story of My Life: The Autobiography of George Sand,* a group translation edited by Thelma Jurgrau (Albany, N.Y.: State University of New York Press, 1991). *Story of My Life* is a complete translation of George Sand, *Histoire de ma vie,* in *Oeuvres autobiographiques,* ed. Georges Lubin, 2 vols. (Paris: Gallimard, 1970–1971); George Sand, *Correspondance,* ed. Georges Lubin (Paris: Garnier frères, 1964–), esp. vols. 1–8.

16. D'Agoult, *Mémoires, souvenirs et journaux. Mémoires, souvenirs et journaux* includes, along with additional, explanatory footnotes, Daniel Stern [Madame d'Agoult], *Mes Souvenirs, 1806–1833* (Paris: Calmann Lévy, 1877); Comtesse d'Agoult (Daniel Stern), *Mémoires, 1833–1854,* intr. Daniel Ollivier

(Paris: Calmann-Lévy, 1927). Much of d'Agoult's correspondence with Hortense Allart is located in the Bibliothèque Nationale de France, Manuscrits, Fonds Daniel Ollivier, N.A.F. 25181, 25185. Her correspondence with Liszt is published as Franz Liszt, *Correspondance de Liszt et de la Comtesse d'Agoult, 1833–1864,* ed. Daniel Ollivier, 2 vols. (Paris: Editions Bernard Grasset, 1934).

17. Mme P. de Saman, *Les Enchantements de Prudence,* 2d ed. (Paris: Michel Lévy frères, 1873); Hortense Allart de Méritens, *Lettres inédites à Sainte-Beuve (1841–1848),* ed. Léon Séché, 2d ed. (Paris: Société du Mercure de France, 1908); Hortense Allart, *Nouvelles Lettres à Sainte-Beuve (1832–1864),* ed. Lorin A. Uffenbeck (Geneva: Librarie Droz S.A., 1965). Uffenbeck cites Jean Bonnerot as asserting that Allart burned letters in her own possession before she died. Uffenbeck, *The Life and Writings of Hortense Allart,* 311.

18. Christine Planté, *La petite soeur de Balzac: Essai sur la femme auteur* (Paris: Seuil, 1989), 32–33; Roger Bellet, "Masculin et féminin dans les pseudonyms des femmes de lettres au XIXe siècle," in *Femmes des lettres au XIXe siècle. Autour de Louise Colet,* ed. Roger Bellet (Lyon: Presses universitaires de Lyon, 1982), 249–81; Annie Prassoloff, "Le Statut juridique de la femme auteur," *Romantisme* 77 (1992): 9–14; Carla Hesse, "Reading Signatures: Female Authorship and Revolutionary Law in France, 1750–1850," *Eighteenth-Century Studies* 22 (spring 1989): 469–87; Sand, *Story of My Life,* 908; d'Agoult, *Mémoires, souvenirs et journaux,* 2: 32.

19. Geneviève Fraisse, "A Philosophical History of Sexual Difference," in *A History of Women in the West,* ed. Geneviève Fraisse and Michelle Perrot, vol. 4, *Emerging Feminism from Revolution to World War* (Cambridge, Mass.: The Belknap Press of Harvard University Press, 1993), 48–79; Michelle Perrot, "The Family Triumphant," in *A History of Private Life,* ed. Philippe Ariès and Georges Duby, vol. 4, *From the Fires of the Revolution to the Great War,* ed. Michelle Perrot (Cambridge, Mass.: The Belknap Press of Harvard University Press, 1990), 99–111; Susan Groag Bell and Karen M. Offen, eds., *Women, the Family, and Freedom: The Debate in Documents* (Stanford: Stanford University Press, 1983), 1: 39–41, 112–15, 169–70; Louis Devance, "Femme, famille, travail et morale sexuelle dans l'idéologie de 1848," *Romantisme* 13–14 (1976): 79–103. Yet another discourse on the family involved the regulation and moralization of working-class and poor families; see Rachel G. Fuchs, *Poor and Pregnant in Paris: Strategies for Survival in the Nineteenth Century* (New Brunswick, N.J.: Rutgers University Press, 1992), chap. 2; Katherine A. Lynch, *Family, Class, and Ideology in Early Industrial France: Social Policy and the Working-Class Family, 1825–1848* (Madison: University of Wisconsin Press, 1988), chap. 2; Jacques Donzelot, *The Policing of Families,* trans. Robert Hurley (New York: Pantheon, 1979).

20. Margaret H. Darrow, *Revolution in the House: Family, Class, and Inheritance in Southern France, 1775–1825* (Princeton: Princeton University Press, 1989).

21. Sand, *Story of My Life,* 272.

22. Ibid., 169.

23. For a psychoanalytic interpretation of Sand's representation of her father, see Naomi Schor, *George Sand and Idealism* (New York: Columbia University

Press, 1993), chap. 5. See also Kathryn J. Crecelius, *Family Romances: George Sand's Early Novels* (Bloomington: Indiana University Press, 1987), 7–9.

24. Madame Dupin was arrested for hoarding silver and jewels, but the papers that were never discovered and that would have sealed her fate were testaments that she had loaned money to the comte d'Artois for his counterrevolutionary activities. Sand, *Story of My Life*, 106–7. Sand quotes letters from her father to her grandmother in prison, indicating that he supported the revolutionary war effort; however, she does not mention the likelihood that these letters were self-censored in order to reach the imprisoned Madame Dupin: "If the Austrian, English, Spanish, and all the other nations that wage war with us could be eliminated, we would have peace and, consequently, liberty." Ibid., 138. Again, "We owe our salvation to the Convention. Without it, they say, all patriots might have become victims of Robespierre's tyranny." Ibid., 141. Sand also writes, "My father was not a Royalist and never had been. . . . this youth condemned and renounced the past without reservation or regret. . . . yearning for the independence of the homeland and the magnanimous reign foretold in the theories of eighteenth-century writers. Soon he would go and seek the last breath of this democratic life in the army . . ." Ibid., 150.

25. Ibid., 346.

26. Ibid., 317.

27. Ibid., 177.

28. D'Agoult, *Mémoires, souvenirs et journaux*, 1: 39.

29. Ibid., 43, 63–64, 82–85.

30. Ibid., 122.

31. Ibid., 123.

32. Daniel Stern, *Histoire de la Révolution de 1848*, 2d ed. (Paris: Charpentier, 1868), 1: ix.

33. D'Agoult, *Mémoires, souvenirs et journaux*, 1: 73.

34. Saman, *Les Enchantements*, 2.

35. Ibid., 9.

36. Ibid., 14.

37. Leslie Wahl Rabine, "Feminist Texts and Feminine Subjects," in Moses and Rabine, *Feminism, Socialism, and French Romanticism*, 85–86, 125.

38. Saman, *Les Enchantements*, 6.

39. Ibid., 5.

40. Undated letter, probably late March 1848, in Allart de Méritens, *Lettres inédites à Sainte-Beuve*, 300; Hortense Allart de Méritens, *Second petit livre. Études diverses* (Paris: Renault, 1850), 47.

41. Hortense Allart, *Lettres sur les ouvrages de Madame de Staël* (Paris: Bossange père, 1824), 136–137; Hortense Allart de Méritens, *La Femme et la démocratie de nos temps* (Paris: Delaunay, 1836), 6, 8, 10–12, 122–123; Hortense A. de Méritens, *Histoire de la République d'Athènes* (Paris: n.p., 1866), 367; Mme P. de Saman, *Les Nouveaux Enchantements* (Paris: Michel Lévy frères, 1873), 158.

42. Claude Nicolet, *L'Idée républicaine en France, (1789–1924): Essai d'histoire critique* (Paris: Gallimard, 1982), 136–37.

43. Moses and Rabine, *Feminism, Socialism, and French Romanticism;* Riot-Sarcey, *La Démocratie à l'épreuve des femmes.*

44. Riot-Sarcey, *La Démocratie à l'épreuve des femmes;* Aminzade, "Class Analysis, Politics, and French Labor History," 103–4; Pilbeam, *Republicanism in Nineteenth-Century France,* 172–74. See also Moses, *French Feminism,* 140–41. For an analysis of women writers' rejection of socialist feminists in 1848, see Whitney Walton, "Writing the 1848 Revolution: Politics, Gender, and Feminism in the Works of French Women of Letters," *French Historical Studies* 18 (fall 1994): 1001–24.

45. Robert J. Bezucha, *The Lyon Uprising of 1834: Social and Political Conflict in the Early July Monarchy* (Cambridge, Mass.: Harvard University Press, 1974), chap. 8.

46. Sand, *Story of My Life,* 1031–32.

47. Letter from Sand to Luc Desage, date estimated to be 1837, in Sand, *Correspondance,* 4: 9–16

48. In a letter to Frédéric Girerd from the end of April or the beginning of May 1837, Sand asserts that she will be the Spartacus to liberate women from enslavement. She was creating the character of Edmée in *Mauprat* at this time. Sand, *Correspondance,* 4: 19. Sand asserts in her autobiography that her most autobiographical work prior to the *Story of My Life* was the *Lettres d'un voyageur.* Sand, *Story of My Life,* 72, 1012–15. These letters are fascinating experiments in romantic writing, articulating dreamlike fantasies, suicidal self-doubt, and diverse reflections on nature, love, relationships, and Sand's own identity.

49. George Sand, *Lettres d'un voyageur,* new ed. (Paris: Calmann-Lévy, 1927), 167.

50. Ibid., 165.

51. Ibid.

52. Ibid., 167, 182.

53. Ibid., 182.

54. Ibid., 183.

55. On the fluidity of sexual and gender boundaries during the July monarchy, see Victoria Thompson, "Creating Boundaries: Homosexuality and the Changing Social Order in France, 1830–1870," in *Homosexuality in Modern France,* eds. Jeffrey Merrick and Bryant T. Ragan Jr. (New York: Oxford University Press, 1996), 102–27. On the ambiguity of androgyny and the influence of Sand's cross-dressed image in French literature during the July monarchy, see Isabelle de Courtivron, "Weak Men and Fatal Women: The Sand Image," in *Homosexualities and French Literature: Cultural Contexts/Critical Texts,* ed. George Stambolian and Elaine Marks (Ithaca: Cornell University Press, 1979), 210–27.

56. Sand, *Story of My Life,* 1036.

57. Ibid., 1034.

58. Ibid., 1034–35.

59. Ibid., 1035.

60. Ibid., 1036.

61. Ibid., 1036–37.

62. For more on Sand's political ideas and writings, see George Sand, *Politique et polémiques, 1843–1850,* intro. Michelle Perrot (Paris: Imprimerie Nationale, 1997).

63. D'Agoult, *Mémoires, souvenirs et journaux,* 2: 30.

64. Ibid., 22.

65. Ibid., 24.

66. Ibid., 26. In her journal d'Agoult went further in her analysis of Lamennais's limitations as a republican ("He is condemned to be an amateur republican"), in particular of his failure to exploit Sand's willingness to work in partnership with him on the dissemination of his ideas. D'Agoult believed that Lamennais missed a golden opportunity to benefit from Sand's literary talent, from her offer to put her writing skills at his disposal, "to make herself in a sense the handtool *[le manoeuvre]* of his thought. He did not realize that he could have given his impetus to the writer most capable of popularizing his ideas and presenting them in a form that was less austere and more lively." D'Agoult maintains that Lamennais mishandled Sand, that he contradicted her beliefs (notably about the need to legalize divorce), and that he failed to convince her of his own position. But d'Agoult suggests that had their partnership actually worked out, Sand would have contributed more than just "translation" skills to this joint enterprise. "These two intelligences that, in modifying one another, would have approached the truth, perhaps as much as is humanly possible, will remain incomplete." Ibid., 120–21.

67. According to d'Agoult, Lamennais was also unable to sustain a leading role among male republicans. In 1848 d'Agoult claims that she brought together Lamennais and Lamartine, at Lamartine's request, in her home to discuss the constitution of the Second Republic. After Lamennais's proposed constitution met with indifference on the part of Lamartine, Lamennais resigned from the Constitutional Committee. Ibid., 25–27.

68. Ibid., 17.

69. Saman, *Les Enchantements,* 193.

70. Ibid., 256.

71. Hortense Allart, *Histoire de la république de Florence,* part 1 (Paris: Moutardier, 1837).

72. In a letter to Sainte-Beuve of July 30, 1848 Allart argued that Thiers should pay attention to the work of Pierre Leroux and adopt some, though not all, of his ideas. Allart, *Nouvelles lettres à Sainte-Beuve,* 63.

73. Saman, *Les Enchantements,* 251. In a letter to Marie d'Agoult of 1847 (no other date), Allart wrote: "Plato will save us, he who said *political man* and *political woman.*" The emphasis is in the original. BN, Manuscrits, Fonds Daniel Ollivier, N.A.F. 25185.

74. Allart, *La Femme et la démocratie.* Allart's meritocracy is reminiscent of Napoleon, but I hesitate to label her a bonapartist since she objected strenuously to misogyny, militarism, and imperialism.

75. Pilbeam, *Republicanism in Nineteenth-Century France,* 25–26; Pierre Rosanvallon, *L'Etat en France de 1789 à nos jours* (Paris: Editions du Seuil, 1990), 100–10; Ceri Crossley, *French Historians and Romanticism: Thierry, Guizot, the Saint-Simonians, Quinet, Michelet* (London: Routledge, 1993).

76. Sand and Allart frequently praise and criticize histories by Adolphe Thiers, François Mignet, Alphonse de Lamartine, and Louis Blanc. See, for example, Sand, *Story of My Life,* 338; Sand, *Correspondance,* 8: 107–8; Allart, *Lettres inédites,* 116–17, 269, 276, 290; Allart, *Nouvelles lettres,* 20–21, 26, 66.

D'Agoult mentions in *Mémoires, souvenirs et journaux* that she read histories by Thierry, Thiers, Guizot, and Mignet, 2: 18; Phyllis Stock-Morton, "Daniel Stern, Historian," *History of European Ideas* 8 (1987): 489–501.

77. Nicolet, *L'Idée républicaine,* 343–44, 347; Aminzade, "Class Analysis, Politics, and French Labor History."

78. Daniel Stern, *Essai sur la liberté considérée comme principe et fin de l'activité humaine* (Paris: Aymot, 1847); *Histoire de la Révolution de 1848; Histoire des commencements de la république aux Pays-bas, 1581–1625* (Paris: Michel Lévy frères, 1872); *Lettres républicaines* (Paris: Edouard Proux, 1848); Allart, *La Femme et la démocratie;* A. de Méritens, *Histoire de la République d'Athènes;* Allart, *Histoire de la République de Florence.*

79. Sand, *Politique et polémiques.*

80. Whitney Walton, "Literary Production and the Rearticulation of Home Space in the Works of George Sand, Marie d'Agoult, and Hortense Allart," *Women's History Review,* 6 (1997): 115–32.

81. Whitney Walton, "Sailing a Fragile Bark: Rewriting the Family and the Individual in Nineteenth-Century France," *Journal of Family History* 22 (April 1997): 150–75.

82. Ernest Legouvé, *Histoire morale des femmes,* 10th ed. (Paris: J. Hetzel et Cie, 1896); Karen Offen, "Ernest Legouvé and the Doctrine of 'Equality in Difference' for Women: A Case Study of Male Feminism in Nineteenth-Century French Thought," *Journal of Modern History* 58 (June 1986): 452–48; Riot-Sarcey, *La Démocratie à l'épreuve des femmes,* 78–81, 124–25; Moses and Rabine, *Feminism, Socialism, and French Romanticism,* 35–40, 59, 82, 93, 289–92; William Fortescue, "Divorce Debated and Deferred: The French Debate on Divorce and the Failure of the Crémieux Divorce Bill in 1848," *French History* 7 (1993): 137–62.

83. Sociologist Jesse Pitts posits two fundamental value systems underlying the French family of the upper classes — the aesthetic-individualistic values of the aristocracy and the doctrinaire-hierarchical values of the bourgeoisie — that combined in creative ways during the nineteenth century. The main focus of his essay, however, is on the twentieth century, and he hardly accounts for gender relations in the models. Jesse R. Pitts, "Continuity and Change in Bourgeois France," in *In Search of France: The Economy, Society, and Political System in the Twentieth Century,* ed. Stanley Hoffmann et al. (New York: Harper & Row 1963), 235–304.

84. Sand, *Story of My Life,* 1068–69.

85. Ibid., 1083.

86. Ibid.

87. Ibid.

88. Allart, *Les Enchantements,* 103.

89. Ibid., 234.

90. Letter of December 21, 1841, in Méritens, *Lettres inédites à Sainte-Beuve,* 34. Just two years later Allart's desire to share her life with a man led her into a brief marriage of one year. Thereafter, she was scathing in her critique of the institution of marriage in terms of how it subordinated women. See, for example, Saman, *Les Enchantements,* 311–12.

91. Mme Hortense Allart, *Settimia,* 2 vols. (Bruxelles: Ad. Wahlen et Cie,

1836). "Marpé" first appeared in Hortense Allart de Méritens, *Troisième petit livre. Études diverses* (Paris: Renault, 1851). It is also integrated into her autobiography, *Les Enchantements.*

92. D'Agoult, *Mémoires, souvenirs et journaux,* 2: 40.

93. Ibid., 41.

94. Ibid., 40.

95. Ibid., 1: 202.

96. Scott, *Only Paradoxes to Offer;* Riot-Sarcey, *La Démocratie à l'épreuve des femmes,* 190–93, 202–3; Moses, *French Feminism.*

Clotilde de Vaux
and the Search for Identity

MARY PICKERING

A woman always inspires more or less the sentiments that
she wants.

Clotilde de Vaux, July 1845

Clotilde de Vaux died of tuberculosis in April 1846 at the age of thirty-
two. Auguste Comte, the founder of sociology and positivism, had fallen
in love with her the year before and promised to immortalize her by associating her name with his.[1] To make her worthy of such an honor, he
claimed that she was "the most eminent woman in terms of [her] heart,
mind, and even character that universal history has ever presented."[2]
Ironically, however, close affiliation with Comte proved disadvantageous. Inasmuch as Comte's campaign to integrate worship of de Vaux
into his Religion of Humanity seemed demented, scholars who studied
his intellectual development considered his relationship with her an
embarrassment. John Stuart Mill, among others, accused her of being
responsible for Comte's decline.[3] Because Comte appeared mad or, at the
very least, deluded by his love for her, de Vaux was deemed unworthy of
serious attention. In 1928, Dr. Georges Morin called her a proud "little
woman" with "literary pretensions" and a "surly," "neurotic," and
"vain" character.[4] While Comte exploited her image to appeal to women
and to show the importance of regenerating society by infusing it with
feminine affection, Morin represented her in such a manner as to keep
the medical profession closed to intelligent women. Thus even when
attention was focused on her, de Vaux served only as a useful instrument
of a male-dominated culture. Yet feminist scholars have also neglected
her, ignoring her voluminous correspondence with Comte, which was
first published in 1884.[5] To challenge the assumption that de Vaux was

Portrait of Clotilde de Vaux by Antoine Etex. Association Internationale de la
Maison d'Auguste Comte.

a dull target of a man undergoing a midlife crisis, this essay charts her
attempt to establish her identity as a respectable woman of ideas free
from the control of others. By resurrecting another nineteenth-century
woman's voice, it sheds light on what Karen Offen has aptly termed the
"sexual politics of the July monarchy," an era that looked dimly on independent women.[6]

Clotilde Marie was born in 1815 in Paris.[7] Her mother, Henriette-Joséphine de Ficquelmont, came from an impoverished aristocratic family; her father was Joseph-Simon Marie, a retired captain and a tax collector. After Clotilde's brothers Maximilien and Léon were born, respectively in 1819 and 1820, the family moved to Méru, a small town near Beauvais. A quick-witted but sickly child, Clotilde was sent at age nine to a Parisian boarding school, where she disobeyed the strict nuns and refused to study. After nine years, she returned home, eager to be with her mother again, but she soon grew lonely and weary of her father's avaricious, tyrannical ways.

In September 1835 she gladly married one of her father's employees, Amédée de Vaux, a shady character of dubious aristocratic lineage. Captain Marie compensated for his inability to provide a dowry by arranging for his son-in-law to take over his job. As a spouse, Clotilde upheld the bourgeois ideal of the separation of spheres, which was being strongly promoted in the late 1830s after having been questioned by the Saint-Simonians earlier in the decade.[8] Her uncle, who was the count of Ficquelmont and an ambassador, reviewed the typical duties of a wife: "The condition of the woman is different from that of the man. The house . . . is her empire and her existence; it is there that all the duties of daughter, wife, and mother are placed. It is thus only there that she can find happiness."[9] Complaining that she felt "alone" and "exiled," Clotilde, however, found marriage disappointing.[10] She feared pregnancy because she was chronically ill, and she was irked by her husband's increasing indifference. The reason for his preoccupation became clear in June 1839, when he suddenly fled to Belgium to escape prosecution for having stolen taxpayers' money to pay his secret gambling debts. Clotilde was disgraced. Unable to forgive her husband, who subsequently disappeared in the Dutch East Indies, she was forced to reside again with her parents, who now lived in Paris.

At age twenty-four, de Vaux found herself in an impossible situation. She was married to a man she would never see again, but she could not remarry due to the illegality of divorce. She was penniless, yet she could not work because she had no skills, suffered from poor health, and risked losing her status as a middle-class woman—a status that was already endangered by the widely reported scandal that marginalized her. She was a complete burden on her parents, who were already struggling to survive on Captain Marie's small pension.

Feeling as confined as she had in her boarding school and at home in Méru, she decided after several trying years to realize her goal of independence by writing — an occupation that offered many nineteenth-century women a way to earn money in a respectable fashion. Due to the revival of the women's emancipation movement and the rise of the popular press, the "woman of ideas" became an increasingly visible figure in the 1830s and 1840s. George Sand, Delphine Gay de Girardin, the Countess Marie d'Agoult, and Flora Tristan were among the prominent French women writers and activists who sought to use the printed word to influence public opinion.[11] De Vaux's own mother also served as a role model. Henriette Marie wrote essays on poverty that offered remedies for the "social question." Whereas her mother chose to speak out against social injustice on an abstract plane, de Vaux was attracted to writing as a means of personal catharsis; her stories allowed her to vent her feelings of frustration and anger at social codes that circumscribed her behavior. Writing helped her secure a new identity and gave her life meaning and purpose. Yet she found concentrating in her parents' apartment difficult, especially after her brother Max and his wife moved in while he tried to launch an academic career. The commotion of a full house forced even Captain Marie to leave. With the help of a small allowance from her uncle, de Vaux was finally able in February 1844 to set up her own small apartment at 7, rue Payenne, a block from her parents' place at 24, rue Pavée in the Marais.

At her mother's insistence, de Vaux continued to take her meals at rue Pavée. At dinner one evening in April 1844, Max introduced her to Auguste Comte, who had been Max's tutor at the École Polytechnique. Comte was the author of the *Cours de philosophie positive* (1830–1842), a work regarded by John Stuart Mill as the "one of the most profound books ever written on the philosophy of the sciences."[12] Forty-six years old, Comte was dressed in his habitual black suit. He was short, pot-bellied, and balding. De Vaux giggled and whispered to her sister-in-law, "He is so ugly!"[13] Having separated from his wife in August 1842, Comte found de Vaux's pale delicate face, light brown ringlets, and large blue eyes alluring. Yet, despite the fact that he was a frequent guest of the Maries, he did not write to her until April 1845, when they discovered they had a common interest in literature. Comte sent her a translation of *Tom Jones*, which he found superior to the one she was reading. Hoping to benefit from Comte's "fine and noble lessons," de Vaux thanked him and put herself in a subordinate position as his student.[14] Pleased that she did not appear to be domineering and aggressive like his estranged wife, Comte eagerly accepted the role of teacher. He even signed his letters, "Your philosopher."[15] He began to write her more often in order to go beyond the conventional conversation of her mother's salon. De Vaux likewise felt the need to express herself more fully than she could in that environment. Determined to construct a new self, she sought to transcend the traditional familial context that had fashioned her previous identity.[16]

Comte and the positivists portrayed his relationship with de Vaux as one of great purity and harmony. But, in truth, it was an intense battle between the sexes. The fighting started early. One day in early May 1845, Comte begged de Vaux to let him see her alone in her apartment. Insisting that she was only an "old friend," she made it clear that she "rarely" received men in private and liked Comte's company simply because he gave her the opportunity to discuss ideas. But all he could talk about was her beauty and the "ravishing insomnias" caused by his feelings for her. Worried about being seventeen years older than de Vaux, he boasted that he had preserved "in full physical maturity all the vitality and impetuosity of youth, with all the advantages of its spontaneity."[17] There was little doubt that he wanted an affair with her.

Comte was acting aggressively in accordance with a set plan, not according to her cues. He assumed that because they were both marginal figures, separated from unsuitable spouses who had not understood them, she was as much in need of love and affection as he was. Working on his philosophical system offered only a "painfully" incomplete compensation for the emptiness and loneliness he felt within. Moreover, he needed her to satisfy an intellectual objective. He had been suffering for months from poor physical and mental health because he did not know how to make his next book, the *Système de politique positive*, "sufficiently distinct" from his first work. The *Cours* had reorganized ideas and established the new discipline of sociology to eliminate social discord. The *Système* was supposed to restructure feelings, thereby completing the preparation for the new positive age of science and industry. To write effectively about the complex social and moral issues involved in this work, Comte believed he needed more than an intellectual understanding of emotions; it was essential to have a personal experience of them. He counted on an emotionally intense relationship with de Vaux to develop his affections, which he believed had been stunted due to his poor family and marital relations. In this way, she would provide him with the requisite material for his second great work. Finally, he wanted her for his own sexual gratification. Perhaps due to impotence, Comte had enjoyed no sexual relations since 1834. He now discovered a "charming" reawakening of his strong sexual urges. To justify an extramarital relationship, he explained to de Vaux that because it was not their fault that they could not find love in the "regular" social order, they were "morally authorized" to seek satisfaction in an unconventional manner.[18]

Young and relatively new to Paris, de Vaux was flattered to be wooed by an important individual, who called her one of the few women whose "heads had not spoiled their hearts." Yet her agenda was different from the one he was trying to impose on her. Comte, the man of ideas, was suffering from intellectual fatigue and wanted stimulation from newly discovered emotions. De Vaux, whom he erroneously considered typical of the "affective sex," demanded to be "spared" emotional burdens. For the past two years she had been infatuated with a married man, an experience that taught her that "love without hope kills the body and soul." Now she sought to achieve something on her own and become a woman of ideas. Just as Comte liked to say to his critics that the age of discussion was over for him, she announced that she was through with the "deadly" business of dabbling in emotions. There was almost a reversal of gender roles in the way she exerted authority and ordered him to be reasonable, to avoid "strong emotions," and to use his "manly powers" of self-control.[19] Her sole desire was for the peaceful solitude that she needed in order to write. She had no intention of pursuing another fruitless relationship that would distract her from her new career — a career that she hoped would satisfy her quest for success and self-fulfillment. In short, she wanted a relationship with Comte only to stimulate her mind, not her emotions, which were the source of great pain to her.

In effect, both de Vaux and Comte were in the process of changing their self-representations. Each hoped to use an image they had of the other to achieve this transformation. However, Comte's image of de Vaux and her picture of him proved to be static, incomplete, and somewhat outdated in view of the fact that each of them sought to move beyond their previous selves.

The situation required great delicacy on de Vaux's part. It was not politic for her to tell Comte that she would not sleep with him because she found him unattractive. Instead, to maintain her distance and to escape the sexual anonymity that threatened her individuality, she used the nineteenth-century assumption that women were devoid of sexual desire. Forced to abandon the passive, vulnerable role that she had first adopted as part of her performance as his student, she made him aware that he must make his affection as "innocent" as hers.[20]

Comte found her rules of chastity "more painful" than de Vaux could ever imagine. Rejected as a lover, he feared he would go mad as he had in 1826, when he spent eight months in an asylum. Yet true to his bourgeois upbringing, he imagined that exercising self-control improved moral character. As a result, de Vaux began to assume a new preeminence in his eyes. A devotee of the theater and opera, Comte immediately dramatized her influence on him, making her solely responsible for his "moral resurrection" and "second career." He claimed that by her moral superiority, she had rid him of the "crudeness" of the male sex and transformed him into the virtuous champion of humanity. She had also made him recognize the importance of the emotions, which he now could express more fully. He was certain that his increased openness and benevolence would enrich the *Système,* which he decided to dedicate to her. Attributing both his moral and intellectual improvement to her influence on him, he wrote that she would join other women who became "immortal by exercising a similar authority over men born for posterity."[21]

Comte's attitude was typical of his age. Reflecting the impact of the bourgeois cult of domesticity and model of the "perfect lady," most nineteenth-century men believed that women were "naturally" virtuous and morally superior, chiefly because they had no sexual desire.[22] De Vaux exploited this assumption and performed her femininity to her advantage to get what she wanted from Comte. Like him, she was an enthusiast of literature and the opera; she understood his melodramatic, moral universe. Yet she refused to allow him to adore her. She found such worship not only disingenuous but constricting. It was further proof that he wanted to know only the side of her that fit his ideal of the perfect woman. Standing up to the great philosopher of positivism, de Vaux told Comte, "I place you . . . on the pedestal that you are erecting for me; it suits you better by far than it does me." She certainly did not see herself as morally superior: "I have not yet found perfection in others or in myself. There are large ulcers deep down in every human stomach; the key is to know how to hide them." To avoid "embarrassing talks," Comte was to confine his discussion to matters pertaining to their "heads," not their hearts.[23] She hoped that if they selected roles that privileged the pursuit of knowledge and to that end required emotional concealment, they could create a relationship that would not be based on gender stereotypes, tensions, and inequalities. In seeking independence through knowledge, de Vaux held onto this gender-free vision, despite the fact that she acknowledged artfully hiding her faults to reinforce her virtuous appearance and thereby increase the moral authority associated with being feminine.

Censored by de Vaux, Comte reconfigured his positivist philosophy to seduce her, catering to her original self-representation as a student eager for instruction. On June 2, he wrote a short essay, "Lettre philosophique sur la commémoration sociale," in honor of the feast day of her patron saint, Sainte-Clotilde. In reply to de Vaux's dismissal of his attempt to put her on a pedestal, he declared that the need to imitate models was "inherent in the laws of human nature." Condemning "the foolish distinction between the public order and the private order," Comte insisted that in the new positive age, women anonymously working in the domestic sphere would be honored for their contributions to civilization. Women would also be the "intimate auxiliaries" of positivist philosophers. Because women represented feelings and philosophers thoughts, there was a "natural affinity" between them. Together they would disseminate moral principles throughout society. Modifying the stance he had taken in the *Cours,* where he had said women remained throughout their lives in a "state of continued infancy," he now devoted positivism to the "adoration of women."[24] Such changes were necessary to convince de Vaux that she had a historically dictated role to work closely with him.

De Vaux suspected that his philosophy was not really addressed to women. She stated, "If I were a man, you would have me as an enthusiastic disciple; I offer you in recompense a sincere admirer." With some bitterness, she pointed out that it was the "lot of a woman" to use arguments based on feelings, not reason, and to walk modestly behind a great man even if she had to "lose some of her élan."[25] De Vaux recognized that women ultimately lacked the kind of power men possessed.

Nevertheless, de Vaux was pleased with the "Sainte-Clotilde" as Comte called his essay. His depiction of the future strong role of women echoed in more conservative tones the demands of the women's rights activists of the 1840s. As an aspiring writer who was not ensconced in the radical camp, de Vaux was flattered by his suggestion that she could make an important contribution to society even though the traditional roles of wife and mother were closed to her. She was to achieve some measure of success, but not in the way Comte desired.

On June 20 and 21, 1845, *Le National,* the prominent republican newspaper run by the leftist Armand Marrast, published her short story, "Lucie" as a front-page serial. Inspired by the epistolary approach of *Tom Jones,* the book that Comte had lent her, the narrative consisted chiefly of a series of letters. De Vaux was a gifted letter writer, but unlike her personal letters, her fictional ones were unnatural and melodramatic.

The story expressed de Vaux's anguish. Lucie, a twenty-year-old girl living in the provinces, is abandoned "without hope" in poverty and "isolation" by her husband, a murderer and gambler. Very talented, the fictional character fulfills her desire for independence by becoming a teacher in Paris. Resolved to remain single, she does not object to the unjust laws against remarriage, for she considers "her chain" to her husband an important "barrier that she had voluntarily placed between men and herself."[26] She prefers to read, listen to music, and study philosophy than to associate with men. Yet after describing Lucie as a courageous intellectual, de Vaux had her retreat from her position. Lucie claims that she would give up the pleasures of the mind and all success for the superior, regenerating joys of motherhood. It is evident that she is an untraditional woman chiefly because of force of circumstance. Her yearning to assume women's conventional roles was de Vaux's as well.

Lucie's neighbor, Maurice, eventually falls in love with her. De Vaux used him to vent her anger. Lashing out at the law that binds her to her hateful husband, Maurice calls Lucie a "beautiful martyr of social injustices" and "oppression." Maurice then asks, "Why does one see common women fascinate superior intellects and become the object of a true cult? How does it also happen that the generosity and nobility of certain women are so often seen battling egoism and coarseness"? Not flowing naturally from the text, these questions reflect the extent to which de Vaux was disturbed by Comte's worship of her. Nevertheless, she used the image of women's moral superiority to advance the story. Dressed in white, which highlights her moral purity, Lucie is an "angelic woman," who inspires "generous and elevated sentiments."[27] To de Vaux and to many of her female contemporaries, women's supposed generosity and elevation were sources of empowerment. Lucie's moral superiority, for example, drives Maurice to rebel against social norms and to petition the government to change the unjust law prohibiting divorce.

Maurice and Lucie soon become lovers. But Maurice, like Comte, gradually wants to imprison Lucie in his view of what a woman should be. He objects to her copying music to earn money: "Is not woman's true role to give to man the care and pleasures of the domestic sphere, and to receive from him in exchange all the means of existence procured by this work? I prefer to see a poor mother . . . wash the laundry of her children than to see her fritter away her life in spreading the products of her intelligence outside." Maurice defends the traditional separation of spheres, which denied women any economic rights, reinforced their dependence on men, and belittled their minds. Yet at the same time he claims it is acceptable for an eminent woman to be "pushed outside the family sphere by her genius" in order to be able to find fulfillment in society.[28] His inconsistency on the matter of woman's proper behavior suggests that de Vaux was searching for a loophole in the ideology of the separation of spheres to allow exceptionally intelligent women to excel. With the model of George Sand in her mind, she was ruminating over the possibility of including herself among the women geniuses so that she would not feel obliged to repress her spirit and defer modestly to great men like Comte.

Yet projecting her own ambivalence onto her protagonist, de Vaux made Lucie hesitant to question society and flout bourgeois conventions. The fear of challenging "respectable" social institutions prevents Lucie from yielding at first to Maurice's advances. Moreover, Lucie seeks to keep her distance from the movement in favor of women's political and economic rights, which she considers ridiculous. However, she admits, almost in spite of herself, that she is proud to play the part of a "true heroine," fighting "against oppression where it is real." To justify her rebellious feelings, she writes, "Laws undermine the . . . happiness of the woman by pushing her out of her sphere and making her sometimes ignore her sublime destiny [of marriage and motherhood]."[29] It is not her fault but society's that she is unable to assume the role of wife and mother. In the end Lucie dies abruptly after her husband is captured and she realizes she must put an end to her affair. Maurice, in a theatrical move, then shoots himself.

De Vaux's story reflects the complexity of the "woman question" of the day. The main problem, which had been at the center of public discussion since the Saint-Simonians and Charles Fourier helped revive feminist demands in the 1830s, was the nature of woman's proper role in society. Vaux shared Lucie's desire to be an intellectual, self-sufficient, accomplished woman. Like George Sand, she wanted the freedom to wander unescorted through Paris and enjoy the sense of being "an abandoned woman."[30] But she also shared Lucie's second desire, her longing to be a wife and mother. The tragedy was that society would not let her construct multiple selves along these diverse lines. It was not possible for a woman to achieve intellectual and emotional satisfaction simultaneously. Denouncing the "disorder" in society, de Vaux expressed her frustration through her various characters but was loath to challenge society and lose men's respect. Above all, she did not want to resemble her feminist contemporaries, who foolishly "stamp their feet at the idea of never being a deputy and ride a horse to demonstrate that they would be . . . excellent colonels." Unable to offer a solution to the oppression of women, de Vaux ended the story on a tragic, pessimistic note, pointing out that man has little power "to repair the evil he produces." Here there is a telling silence on the issue of women's response to mistreatment; what de Vaux would have liked to have said but felt she could not is that woman has no power to eliminate the injustice created by man. After witnessing Lucie's death, a doctor in the story comments, "No woman felt more profoundly than she the grandeur of her role." Lucie displays "grandeur" in courageously playing the "victim" of social injustice in this melodrama. However, dying from weakness caused by depression, she could not be considered heroic because she did not overcome or even alter her situation.[31] De Vaux was too conventional to allow her heroine to defy social norms completely. Perhaps de Vaux also feared that if she took a more radical stance, Marrast would refuse to give her story a prominent front-page position. As a result, she did not allow her heroine any alternative but death. It is indeed ironic that de Vaux sought to profit from this tragic tale to become a recognized writer and avoid the same fate.

Comte read "Lucie" in tears, certain that de Vaux was surreptitiously expressing her love for him through the protagonist's affair with Maurice. De Vaux rejected his reading of her text. Emboldened by her success, she demanded that Comte respect her work and angrily retorted, "It is absolutely impossible for me to understand you. . . . Nothing is mysterious in my situation, and I have nothing more to confide [to you] than what I have told you." Despite this rejection, Comte increased his visits to the Marie household until de Vaux told him to come to rue Pavée only on Mondays and Fridays. She promised to *try* to go to his apartment on the Left Bank once a week. She warned him not to visit her. Unknowingly challenging the separation of spheres, which had emerged when work was no longer done in the house, she wrote, "I reserve my home for my workshop." She sought to empower herself by transforming her private life into her public life. By calling what she did at home her work, she gave value and meaning to her existence. But Comte made light of her demand for independence; he insisted that he be allowed to see her "sanctuary," a metaphor he used for her body.[32]

Trying to maintain their relationship on a different plane, de Vaux soon surprised Comte by telling him that Marrast offered her the opportunity to write a weekly column for *Le National*. She was to discuss issues relating to education, particularly women's education, which was an important topic in the midnineteenth century, when many women were demanding the right to better instruction as the first step to improv-

ing their condition and creating sexual equality.[33] De Vaux decided to
devote her first article to the "silliness and vices of religious education" —
an article motivated by her own memory of the "abuses" she suffered as
a student. Reflecting the growing importance of women writers, she was
also assigned the task of reviewing their novels. She was delighted to have
the chance not only to earn her living but to do meaningful work that
allowed her to display her abilities. She yearned for fame, which would
allow her to escape the "rut" in which she was stuck.[34]

De Vaux's success did not, however, please Comte. The battle between
them now extended from their bodies to their minds, or psyches. De
Vaux shared contemporary males' unease with accomplished women.
On one hand, she boasted about not having a grain of feminine coquet-
terie or fickleness within her, but on the other she took pride in the fact
that she had never been initiated into the "marvels of the square of the
hypotenuse." She deeply feared being called a pedant. Comte decided to
reinforce her insecurities to dissuade her from working at Le National.
He warned her that the profession of journalism exerted a "disastrous
influence," for it would make her even more skeptical and critical than
she already was.[35] She risked turning into a *femme auteur,* who was
linked in his mind to feminist demands for freedom and equality, domestic chaos, and political and social upheaval.[36] Emancipated women, such
as the bluestockings, seemed to him unemotional and thus unfeminine.
The unspoken evil in his discourse was George Sand. If de Vaux became
the reviewer of books written by Sand and other women, she risked
becoming "exposed to the cajoleries and animosities of the blue race
[bluestockings]" and might pattern her own life after theirs. Due to "the
deplorable fecundity of our women writers," she would also have too
much work to do. To him, a woman's ability to speak about a novel was
insignificant, for she should cater above all to a man's needs. Comte cautioned, "Be careful . . . of developing your talent at the expense of the
correctness of your ideas and the purity of your sentiments," both of
which "distinguish you . . . from this blue race."[37]

Comte was jealous. He resented the fact that Le National had refused
to publish his own work. Railing against her being appointed a "quasi
minister of education," a job that "does not at all suit a woman," Comte
also worried that if de Vaux wrote on the school system, which was a
major, politically divisive issue, she would take on a public persona. She
would have greater success and wield more power through her pen than
he did. Moreover, his considerable displeasure at de Vaux's being given
the "entire feminine critique of Le National" betrays his fear that she

might convert to the women's movement, which posed a danger to positivism by taking away potential supporters.[38]

Another source of irritation was Marrast's power over de Vaux. Once close friends, Marrast and Comte had become increasingly estranged. Marrast was more to the left politically, and he supported liberal professors at the École Polytechnique whom Comte accused of persecuting him. Moreover, Comte suspected Marrast of having made advances to his wife. Indeed, once again he and Marrast were sexual rivals. A handsome man with a dashing mustache and dandy-style clothes, Marrast was the man with whom de Vaux had been in love for the past two years. She had met him through her brother Max, who was active in the circle of left-wing journalists. But Marrast did not pay her much heed until he learned of Comte's interest in her and decided to spite him. De Vaux was in a quandary as to what she should do; she opposed adultery and his unchivalrous maneuvers, yet she needed him to help her achieve literary success. Her case was typical of many women of the time. Once they began to seek freedom in the public sphere, men assumed they wanted sexual freedom as well. Some men wanted them to prostitute themselves, in effect, to degrade themselves, to achieve their goal. De Vaux's refusal to go to bed with Marrast when he came to her apartment to discuss "Lucie" led him to deny her request that he publish Comte's "Sainte-Clotilde." Having punished both de Vaux and Comte on that score, he now offered her the job of covering women's issues for *Le National* in another attempt to possess her. Comte tried to discredit him by calling him superficial. De Vaux dismissed Comte's derogatory remarks and immediately set to work on her first article.

Comte was soon pleased to discover that de Vaux wanted his assistance, though it was for the same reason she had sought Marrast's support: her need for money. Plagued by mounting medical bills and anxious about the state of her wardrobe, de Vaux asked Comte on August 11 for a fifty-franc loan. Catering to his penchant for representing himself as her protector and spiritual director, she acknowledged that she was probably making him play "the role of God" with her, but he was "so sensitive and so good" that he might not mind doing her "a little favor as an intimate friend."[39] Such flattery went a long way with Comte. Although he had recently lost his main position at the École Polytechnique and was in severe financial straits himself, he obligingly told her to regard his purse as hers. He assumed he could resume teaching in another capacity or find wealthy, powerful supporters if he began to have problems. Questions of money were beneath his dignity. This insouciance was not shared by de Vaux, who depended entirely on family members for her daily existence and had not developed a network of friends or skills that she could fall back on in case of need. Her request for money from Comte proved compromising. Comte recognized that his economic power gave him more control over her than his intellectual superiority. At least if she was financially indebted to him, he had the right to see her. He demanded that she not tell her parents about his loans so they would not come up with the money. He wanted her all to himself. She was outraged but could do nothing.

De Vaux desired to be loyal to her mother, whom she sincerely loved. However, de Vaux was unhappy, for she "glimpsed what was bitter and implacable in feminine rivalries." Madame Marie had once been very close to Comte, with whom she had enjoyed discussing her articles on the problems of the working class. Now she was jealous that he found her young daughter more appealing and interesting. She also deeply feared losing de Vaux to him. To increase her domination over de Vaux and thereby win her back, she decided to control more tightly her brother's allowance to her. Comte derided Madame Marie's "maternal despotism," but he was as possessive as she was.[40] He demanded that de Vaux visit him more often at his place. She had gone there only twice, and the purpose of one of those visits was to collect her fifty-franc loan.

On September 3, both he and de Vaux became the godparents of Max and Félicie's son. Setting out his theories in an essay that greatly alarmed the Maries, he asserted that the baptismal ceremony represented the "spiritual wedding" that he and de Vaux could never have. She would be his "spiritual wife," and the baby would represent their child. Comte held de Vaux's hand throughout the ceremony and at one point kissed her cheek. She returned the kiss. Comte took her "holy kiss" to be a sign of his triumph over her family and over her own scruples.[41] At the end of the festive champagne dinner afterward, he gave her yet another kiss. De Vaux could not object because of her desperate need for money. She understood that she was a pawn in a war between her family and Comte, all of whom she found egotistical in wanting her for themselves.

The ceremony aggravated her distress, for it made her acutely aware of the fact that she herself would never have a child. Desperate, de Vaux asked Comte for his help: "Since my bad fortune, my only dream has been maternity, and I have always promised myself to give a share in this role only to a distinguished man, one who was worthy enough to understand it. If you believe you can accept all the responsibilities attached to family life, tell me, and I will decide my fate."[42] Just as he was using her, she decided to exploit him. She needed his money and his procreative capacity. Perhaps she wanted a sexual relationship as well. All this talk about maternity was a way to make her own sexual urges more ennobling and ladylike.[43] Stupefied, Comte read her "divine letter" on his knees before his "altar" to her, that is, the chair she sat on when she visited him.[44]

A close reading of their correspondence reveals that neither de Vaux nor Comte felt comfortable about adultery. Although he rationalized that marriage ceremonies were "really indispensable" only for the masses, he ordered de Vaux never to discuss their affair in public. De Vaux clearly had second thoughts. The impropriety of an affair might estrange her from her family, upon whom she depended for financial support. She was not at all attracted to Comte, who was old, poor, and sick. While Comte in his letters was calling her "my adorable wife," she could bring herself to write only "my tender old man [père]."[45]

De Vaux arrived at Comte's apartment on September 7, still perplexed as to the best course of action. Comte made every effort not to throw himself upon her. After a few minutes, she recognized her imprudence; she knew she was "incapable of giving" herself "without love." Her desire for freedom suddenly eliminated her yearning for children. Telling Comte she would see him only at her mother's apartment, she walked out. She warned him not "to abuse the power" that she had given him. Furious and in a state of collapse, Comte felt victimized by *her* power, the power she had over her body: "What! Friday you spontaneously made me the unforeseen promise of imminent happiness, Saturday you confirmed it, Sunday, you avoided it, and Monday, you took it back! Aren't you abusing a little the feminine privilege?" He had paid for this pleasure by lending her money. He renewed his demands for sex, the "indispensable" and "irrevocable" sign of her commitment to him. De Vaux accused him of planning to rape her: "If you constrained me, by whatever means possible, to yield to you on this point in question, I would never see you again. You do not know to what degree of exasperation violence of this genre would push me; a woman who has been continent for a long time can give herself [to a man] only with enthusiasm or the resolution to become a mother." Reminding him to treat her as a mature woman instead of a "little girl," she added, sarcastically, "I know myself better than the leading scholar of the world [does]."[46]

De Vaux could not cut off ties with Comte completely. He was a necessary financial resource. In fact, she borrowed another fifty francs from him around the time of this episode. Moreover, in intellectual matters,

which were important to her, she felt "privileged" to know him: "I experience pleasure in being able to be myself from time to time, and I feel
that when I am near you I can think on a more elevated plane." He gave
her the impression that her work, which focused on the emotions of the
domestic sphere, complemented his own, which concentrated on the
public sphere. De Vaux also needed his moral support and advice. She
had no other friends and resented her family for trying to limit her success. As he became her confidant, de Vaux did begin to feel some genuine
affection for him. She said repeatedly that she found him "the best of
men and the most just." He made her "very happy." In late September,
she even boldly cut off a lock of her hair at one of her visits to prove her
gratitude for his attachment. It became part of his worship of her, for he
placed it on the "altar" in front of which he prostrated himself every
morning. Playing with his emotions, she must have known such an act
would raise his hopes once again for some bigger prize. On September
30, she flattered him by calling him a "perfect man" and asked him for
another hundred francs.[47] This large sum was, in a sense, his payment for
her hair, which was in turn a substitute for her body. Although initially
she had sought to keep gender out of their relationship, she now
reminded him of her gendered self, engaging in an intangible game of
prostitution so that she could continue to work.

De Vaux hated this game, but she was driven by her "need and love
of independence." Using the rhetoric of women's rights activists, she
astutely realized that she needed to write to gain financial independence,
which represented the key to her personal "emancipation." She yearned
for freedom from her relatives and others like Marrast and Comte, who
gave her favors in return for her dependence. Money would give her the
power "to be able to say '*I want.*' "[48]

Her hopes were partly dashed in early October. Marrast rescinded his
offer to make her a columnist for *Le National,* after having read her trial
articles and received her refusal to engage in a more intimate collabora-
tion. Not a leftist like her publisher, she confronted the difficult task
faced by all French journalists at the time, that of matching her style and
outlook to the newspaper for which she worked while remaining true to
her own opinions and thus maintaining her integrity.[49] As a woman, she
also had to struggle to preserve her honor in the complex world of sexual politics. Though incensed by Marrast's decision to dismiss her, she
still hoped he would print excerpts of the new novel that she was writing, *Willelmine.*

De Vaux was bolder in *Willelmine* than in her previous work. She adopted a public authorial voice, dropping the epistolary form used in "Lucie." Willelmine is the principal narrative voice and tells the tale in the first person. During the midnineteenth century, it was still relatively rare for a woman writer to displace the traditional male subject, to make her female character the center of the narrative, and to write an autobiographical novel.[50] Yet de Vaux had a desperate drive to succeed and tell her story. She knew that her perennial problems with poor health might cut short the time she had to achieve her goal.

The book originated in de Vaux's desire to challenge George Sand. Comte had lent de Vaux Sand's *Lettres à Marcie,* which charted the troubled life of Marcie, a so-called exceptional woman, who was intent on cultivating her own career but uncertain whether she should pursue marriage. The book is puzzling, especially because Sand did not complete it.[51] She seemed to be arguing that women should have the freedom to pursue a creative, rewarding career to realize their potential and become equal to men. Yet as one critic put it, Sand was a "feminine reactionary," for she severely condemned adherents of the women's rights movement for being too aggressive in the public sphere and for disregarding the sanctity of marriage and motherhood. Women, Sand suggested, should patiently practice moderation and kindness, instead of militantly claiming their right to vote or to have a profession.[52] Comte gave de Vaux the book as part of his campaign to undermine her. Knowing she would identify with Marcie, he wanted to show her the dangers of devoting herself to a career. "True social principles" had to be defended against the "vulgar anarchical utopias" portrayed by Sand.[53] De Vaux, he proclaimed, was indeed "the woman destined to repair . . . the moral ravages resulting today from the deplorable use of a fine feminine talent."[54] Considering Sand a sexual libertine and opponent of marriage, de Vaux enjoyed reading Sand's "eloquent refutation of herself." She took up Comte's challenge and devoted herself to a story discrediting the idea of the independent, creative woman, toward which Sand had shown such "strange" ambivalence.[55]

Willelmine is a *roman d'education.* Willelmine, a repentant feminist, explains that she was originally taught to seek independence by her widowed mother, who was reacting against the poor treatment she received from Willelmine's father. "As I grew up, . . . [my mother] spoke to me about the happiness that a woman can find in an exceptional destiny. She showed me the glory that I would enjoy in obtaining the instruction and insights that are prohibited to my sex. Soon she depicted men and marriage to me in an odious light." Whereas Sand criticized the limited education that men permitted women to receive, de Vaux suggested that Willelmine's extensive range of studies, including the sciences, had repressed her emotions and turned her against the "true role" of women. Continuing to relate her life's story, Willelmine reveals that she eventually became a celebrated writer devoted to the cause of women's independence — "the only truly noble and grand sentiment that there is in us." Her works also displayed a sincere interest in the downtrodden, a reflection of Madame Marie's influence. When she was not involved in social crusades, Willelmine led a self-indulgent, decadent life, causing a scandal wherever she went. By rebelling against society and adopting the roles of novelist and poet, Willelmine was, in effect, George Sand herself — the kind of woman Marcie was considering becoming. De Vaux had Sand's affair with Alfred de Musset in mind when she depicted Willelmine's romantic involvement with another famous writer. However, Raoul, Willelmine's lover, turned out to be a shallow opportunist. When he completely abandoned her one day, she went mad. She was rescued from her asylum by a wealthy, conservative man who inexplicably brought her to live with his widowed sister and niece in the country. De Vaux never finished the book, but she intended to make Willelmine realize her errors. In the end, Willelmine would return to "the tranquility and full life of the family" and recognize the importance of the roles of wife and mother. Stressing women's dependence on men, their emotional nature, and their intrinsic "need for protection," *Willelmine* thus represented a diatribe against the liberated woman and the concept of free love. It was, as de Vaux put it, a "useful" critique of Sand.[56]

What is most interesting about the book is that de Vaux unconsciously refuted herself in the same fashion Sand had. She made Willelmine a kind, intelligent woman and ridiculed those who equated "a bluestocking" with "a lioness or poisoner." Willelmine herself was full of contradictions, condemning marriage at one moment but seeking to wed Raoul the next. Her confusion regarding the ideal of domesticity seemed to mirror de Vaux's. Perhaps reflecting her own sympathy for Sand, whose life was constantly observed and deemed scandalous, de Vaux made fun of biographers who represented Willelmine as "a bizarre being, inclined since . . . youth to odious penchants" and to passionate romances with "young mountain shepherds." One "generally esteemed" male character finally announced at one point in the novel that "liberty of thought" should "exist for women as [it does] for men" and that "we all push too far the love of privileges that excludes any rivalry between us and women."[57] There was in both Sand's and de Vaux's stories a tension between their yearning to create independent women and their concept of women's proper role in the social order.[58]

Moreover, most of the men in de Vaux's work appeared superficial or cruel; they tended to victimize women in some way. The main male character, Raoul, used Willelmine's works to make money for himself while having affairs on the side. What happened to Willelmine reflected de Vaux's fears that Marrast, like Raoul, would regard her as an "instrument" and take advantage of her sexually, intellectually, and financially. Charting Willelmine's breakdown, de Vaux knew that she would not be able to cope psychologically with another disappointment in her own life. Another male character in de Vaux's story was Stéphane Sax, a philosopher, who rescued Willelmine after a suicide attempt in the beginning of the novel and watched her recover. Obviously modeled on Comte, he looked forward to the day when he would acquire "full control" over her. Léonce Montgolfier, Willelmine's supposed savior at the end of the story, tried to dominate her as well.[59] All three men were intent on destroying one of Willelmine's — and by extension de Vaux's — defining characteristics, her desire for independence. The faults of these men lent support to Willelmine's original argument in favor of women's liberation.

De Vaux's ambivalence toward conventional gender roles is also evident in the fact that the strongest, most admirable woman in the story was Montgolfier's sister, Madame Rolland. Having lost her husband, Madame Rolland learned to rely chiefly on herself and promoted the importance of "independence" and "solitude" — the same values that de Vaux extolled in her letters to Comte. Unlike Willelmine, who feared the study of the sciences, Madame Rolland relied on them to make the lands on her estate more fertile and profitable. Indeed, Willelmine was surprised that this "positive woman" was not "dry and austere" but the "sweetest" woman she had ever met.[60] Here de Vaux was defending women's study of the sciences, although earlier in the novel she had mocked Willelmine's pursuit of this subject and in a letter to Comte written several months before, she had derided her own knowledge of mathematics. Through her kind heart and keen mind, Rolland, according to de Vaux, had also succeeded in giving her daughter an excellent education, for she believed that the "most imposing task that a woman could embrace" was "that of bringing up another [woman]." Education taught women to exert an "empire over themselves," that is, to subordinate their penchants to their reason. Madame Rolland's discourse on the importance of "the education of women," which sounds strangely similar to that of Willelmine's mother, encapsulated material that de Vaux had undoubtedly planned to use for her column for *Le National*.[61]

Years before tackling *Willelmine,* de Vaux explained to her brother Max, "There is often a lack of harmony between my heart and my character. One goes to the right, the other to the left."[62] This disjuncture is evident here. De Vaux wrote the book to condemn incipient feminism but ended by defending many of its precepts. The central problem faced by Sand and the protagonist of her work, Marcie, and by de Vaux and the female characters in her story, Willelmine and Rolland, was that of finding a worthy role in society for the intelligent woman. Sand's and Vaux's inability to resolve this problem and their ambivalence toward the women's rights movement may have contributed to the unfinished state of both of their works.

There was a touch of irony in de Vaux's ambition. She believed that by challenging Sand, one of the most compelling literary figures of the age, and by debating the controversial subject of marriage — a "gold mine" — the book would bring her success and wealth.[63] To achieve celebrity as a woman writer, de Vaux ironically took advantage of the liberty that the women's movement was demanding only to use it against that movement. In effect, she sought independence through her writing to emphasize women's need for a protector, and she yearned to be heard as a woman only to defend the silencing of women. However, the status quo that she hoped to maintain seemed tarnished and inadequate. *Willelmine* is telling in what it leaves out: any allusion to a happy marriage.

As de Vaux labored on her book, she had to face myriad problems that would have proved daunting to any writer. Her continual struggle against poor health, Comte's constant pressure to become more than a friend, and her financial difficulties wearied her. Moreover, she and her mother were engaged in their "first serious war."[64] As an aspiring writer herself, Madame Marie felt threatened by her daughter's potential literary success.[65] She also feared that de Vaux's depiction of Willelmine's mother as a controlling, man-hating figure would reflect poorly on herself.

Her efforts to tie de Vaux more closely to her failed, especially after her daughter became extremely ill. On October 11, 1845, after a night at the opera with Comte, de Vaux began coughing up blood, a sign of her consumptive state. In the following weeks, she suffered from lung congestion, migraines, insomnia, and high fever. The Marie family doctor, Chérest, misdiagnosed her and gave her the drug digitalis, believing she had a heart condition. The medication made her agitated and further depleted her energy. She had almost no energy, and her work on *Willelmine* diminished. Without telling her mother the full extent of her illness for fear she would further intrude on her life, de Vaux asked her for her entire allowance from her uncle so that she would not have to eat at rue Pavée and could conserve her strength for her work. But Madame Marie gave her only fifty francs, sarcastically telling her to wait for her writings to bring her wealth and liberation.

Exasperated and desperate for freedom from her family, de Vaux leaned more on Comte, who gave her his maid, his money, in fact anything she wanted. In late November, to gain more control of her, Comte persuaded her to stop seeing Chérest, who was in love with her, and to go secretly instead to his own physician, Félix Pinel-Grandchamp. Relishing his "noble office of protector" and calling her his "only real wife," Comte never felt so generous, virtuous, and happy as when he helped her.[66]

She finally allowed Comte to visit her at her apartment once a week. Pleased at having access to her "sanctuary," he nervously reminded her that he hoped for a more "complete union." His increasingly frequent use of the informal pronoun "*tu* [you]" indicated his desire for greater intimacy. Infuriated, de Vaux demanded that he understand that she was weak, in fact "destroyed" by her illness. She did not welcome "new pains" that would add more turmoil to her already fragile existence. Yearning "to die without ties," she cherished her independence and work above all else. She told him, "I made a marriage of convenience, and I admit that I like celibacy almost as much."[67] But his demands for her body were not altogether unwelcome, for they made her feel at least alive and desirable.[68] Comte's constant harassment, combined with her own depression, drove her at one point to consent to sleep with him. However, presenting herself as an "honest and pure woman," she explained that she agreed to do so only because she was "tired of suffering or of making others suffer." She made it clear that she still considered Comte a very close friend or relative, nothing more: "I like you a great deal; it is, unfortunately, not love any more for me than it is for you."[69] His adoration of her was not real love, that is, a love based upon knowledge of what she was really like. She knew that he loved only a certain image of woman that made him feel better about himself, that is, more tender and generous than other people saw him. Ashamed and intimidated, Comte quickly retreated, boasting about his enormous self-discipline. He wished that outsiders knew of their sacrifices so they could see the high level of purity that humans could attain. Yet the struggle to overcome his sexual urges was not over. His letters were peppered with crude allusions to the "physical inconveniences" caused by his continence: "You alone really know where . . . [my insomnia] comes from, and how I am unable to cure myself of it by myself."[70] Even while she was dying, he gave her forbidden kisses and lusted after her body whenever she fainted in his presence. Until the end, his sexual appetites were at war with his self-representation as the virtuous regenerator of humanity.

To complicate matters further, Comte could not fulfill his sexual desires without eliminating the divine status that de Vaux had assumed in his eyes. No other woman combined to the same degree "moral purity with mental superiority." To encourage others to emulate her, he planned to make the "cult of woman" part of the secular Religion of Humanity that he was creating for the imminent positive stage of history. Preparing the ceremonies for her "glorification," he knelt down every morning in front of his "altar" and recited a "love prayer" that consisted of passages from her letters "charting the course" of their "holy affection." Part of this "morning prayer" was based on the Our Father. It affirmed that she was his "only real wife, not only in the future, but now and forever." De Vaux played along with this farce. At one point, she sent him a short banal poem, "Thoughts of a Flower," which expressed her sadness at never having experienced love. He placed the poem as well as "Lucie" with the other "dear relics" of her existence.[71]

Because he could not establish her tie to him in the "natural" way, that is, by means of an "ineffable voluptuous pleasure," Comte was very insecure. Weary of his entreaties and encouraged in mid-December by news that *Le National* was eagerly awaiting new material from her, de Vaux wanted more time to herself to finish her novel so that she could make a name for herself and not die like the small light of a "candle-end." To belittle her achievement, Comte bluntly told her that Marrast had offered her work at *Le National* in exchange for physical intimacy. Revealing a singular lack of self-knowledge, Comte denied his jealousy. It perhaps never occurred to him that both he and the "odious" Marrast were yearning for the same pleasure with the same convenient argument that, as an abandoned wife, she was justified in seeking socially unacceptable pleasures. De Vaux sprang to Marrast's defense. In his place, "many men might have done the same or worse than he had done." It was the risk that ambitious women knew they had to take. She was confident she could use her charms to get what she wanted from Marrast: "I have always had intimate relationships with men; I know them better than I know women."[72]

Marrast invited her to a soirée on February 18. Desirous to conserve her energy to complete her novel so that she could deliver it to him, she decided not to attend. She resorted to the pretext that she would be out of town, explaining to Comte that if she simply turned Marrast down without offering an excuse, she would appear to be a boor, "prude," or "morose person," all of whom were associated in her mind with "women who lack self-confidence." De Vaux's insistence on fabricating an alibi angered Comte. She had recently refused to dine alone with him after her Wednesday visits on the grounds that "a woman who goes to dine at a man's makes a little *tour de force*." Appealing to her supposed fear of causing a scandal, Comte said tauntingly that Marrast must "know very well that a young woman cannot go alone to such parties" without suggesting that she could be taken home by "any available man." Comte wanted her to feel insulted in the hope that she would break off her relationship with Marrast. Paying no attention at all to Comte's orders, de Vaux sharply retorted that she would gladly attend Marrast's party alone: "My look of the independent woman gives me my right of solitary entrance into the most decent houses."[73] After all, she was sure of herself in ways he was not. De Vaux was frustrated; she was adored by Comte, whom she did not desire, and she loved Marrast, who had no genuine passion for her. Nevertheless, she resisted both men, despite their financial and professional aid.[74] She empowered herself by using conventional rules of gender behavior to her best advantage when she wanted and then making exceptions when it suited her.

In late February, de Vaux's health began to deteriorate rapidly, especially after Dr. Pinel-Grandchamp prescribed cod liver oil, which further weakened her. Comte became even further unbalanced. He wrote de Vaux one love letter after another, proclaiming repeatedly the "perfect purity" of his affection. Frustrated that she did not fit into a clear category, he gave her myriad roles, calling her his wife, sister, and daughter. He even dreamt about legally adopting her so that she could at least take his name and reside in his house. Depressed at not receiving more support from others, de Vaux was "very touched" by his "constant solicitude" but complained, as she had many months before, that "so many people have loved me on condition that I love them exclusively." As the weeks passed, her insomnia, loss of appetite, and fever made it increasingly difficult for her to give to Comte and her family the attention they demanded. She began to retreat from the world, restricting their entry into her apartment, where she now was confined, and insisting on her "rights" as an invalid to do what she wanted. She would not give up the "bit of independence" that she had worked hard to attain and that made her "so happy."[75] Indeed, she tried to use her illness to create more space for herself. Yet by incapacitating her, her illness reinforced her passivity and dependence, two key components of the traditional representation of womanhood that she had resisted.

As Comte and the Marie family became greater rivals for her limited time, the animosity between them increased dramatically. Comte claimed he alone knew de Vaux and could take care of her, for she had shared with him her ambitions, her frustrations with her family, and the secret, intimate details of her illness and financial situation.[76] Having loaned her five hundred to six hundred francs, he fancied himself the master of the household and tried to prevent others, especially Madame Marie, his biggest adversary, from seeing her. Jealous of his relationship with de Vaux, the Maries blamed him for hiring the quack whose treatment had aggravated her illness. Fights broke out in front of de Vaux over money matters and even the manuscript of *Willelmine,* which Comte wanted her to leave to him. Tired of such scenes, de Vaux said to her sister-in-law, "Do you see, it is better that I die."[77]

Finally, she agreed with her family that she would have been cured if the incompetent Pinel-Grandchamp had not added severe intestinal problems to her bronchial ailment. She returned to Dr. Chérest, who said nothing now could be done for her. On April 5, when Comte heard that de Vaux would die that very day, he went straight into her room, bolted the door, and refused for hours to heed the pleas of desperate family members to let them enter. Around three o'clock, de Vaux suddenly uttered, as though as she were playing the death scene in the last act of an opera, "Comte! remember that I suffer without having merited it."[78] Only after she died did he open the door. Madame Marie told her daughter-in-law, "No, never will I pardon Auguste Comte for having stolen from me the last sigh of my daughter."[79] In her eyes, Comte took on villainous proportions.

Manipulated in various degrees by those around her, de Vaux was a suitable figure for the drama concerning her role in his development that Comte replayed both in his mind and works until his own death. Yet she was not a completely passive, weak figure. After her failed marriage, she realized that by force of circumstance and the law, she had no identity; she had no family of her own, no status as a citizen in France, and no property. She decided to use the few means available to nineteenth-century women to construct an autonomous life and create her own story. An avid letter-writer, she chose to find respect and a public voice as an author. Yet her gender, her body (both in terms of her illness and her beauty), her peculiar status as a single married woman, her class, and even her talent conspired against her. Her difficulties shed light on problems faced by nineteenth-century women of ideas, especially "ordinary" women who sought prominence in the nineteenth-century literary world despite their traditional views and limited skills. Their quest for celebrity was difficult to achieve in an age when women's rights activism was waning after the initial experiment with the Saint-Simonian variant of feminism had proven risky.[80] The new identity that literary women were carving out for themselves in the public sphere threatened both men and women. Everywhere they turned they found themselves involved in power struggles and cultural contests.

In her fight to invent herself, de Vaux encountered conflicts with men who sought to monopolize their position as leading intellectuals. Her brother Max, an aspiring writer on politics and science, resented the fact that his mentor preferred her work to his. Marrast undermined de Vaux's self-confidence by suggesting that the value of her articles depended on her conduct in bed. He wanted her body as a way of achieving victory over Comte. Comte too desired her body but also wanted her mind and heart.

De Vaux's aspirations involved competition with women. Her mother refused to give her money because she wanted her to feel the "stumbling blocks of emancipation." She did not wish de Vaux to succeed where she had failed. After de Vaux's death, Madame Marie told Comte, that she would not allow *Willelmine* to be published: "Our feelings do not need the joys of pride."[81] At the same time, de Vaux was involved in a rivalry of sorts with George Sand, which came to involve Marrast and Comte. De Vaux was one of many woman writers who, according to Janice Bergman-Carton, tended to "identify themselves with and capitalize on Sand's eminence and visibility."[82] To become famous, de Vaux decided to challenge the most important woman writer in France. Marrast approved of her objective because it would sell more newspapers. Comte set de Vaux against Sand in the first place to buttress the social order. But in developing a more emotional strain of positivism to attract women supporters like de Vaux, Comte began to seek help from a "worthy feminine pen." In January 1846, he tried to persuade Sand to use her literary talents to propagate positivism. At the same time, he offered to make de Vaux a "regular collaborator" in his periodical, the *Revue Positive,* once it was established.[83] His aim was to exploit the *femme auteur,* whom he had at least initially disliked, to further his own agenda.

Overshadowed by Sand and controlled by Comte, de Vaux would have been at a severe disadvantage if his plan had been implemented.

With only one published short story, de Vaux did not succeed in establishing a public image for herself. Ultimately Comte had the victory as the man of ideas because it is due to his fame that she is remembered at all. Reflecting the essentialism and binary thinking of the day, he had offered her the two stock roles for women at this time, that of the fallen woman and that of the angel in the household. After she had rejected the first option, his male gaze fixed her as the perfect woman — docile, emotional, capricious, and dependent. He and her mother used this stereotypical image of woman to deter her from a full-time writing career. After she died, Comte represented her as his collaborator and muse, typical "feminine" roles contributing to someone else's self-definition. As such, she was a "real model" for all women.[84]

De Vaux theoretically supported the conventional image of the woman that dominated early nineteenth-century society. Like other women trying to define themselves in the face of a hostile society, she worried that her success might jeopardize her desirability as a woman and her social status as a bourgeois lady. At a time when essentialism dictated that every woman was similar, the distinctiveness of women writers made them seem unfeminine.[85] This danger was even more acute for de Vaux, who wished very much to remain feminine and already felt uncertain about her role as a woman because of her inability to have children in an age that exalted motherhood.[86] Pressured to conform to the norms of female identity dictated by the culture at large and held by Comte, Marrast, her mother, and others in her entourage, she performed the role of the traditional woman when appropriate. She proclaimed her lack of sexual desire, her deficient education, her financial dependence, her physical weakness, and her opposition to George Sand and Sand's protagonist, Marcie. In "Lucie," she projected an image of woman as innocent victim of society. In *Willelmine,* she played the fallen woman, who is saved by a man and revealed to be ultimately virtuous. In both works, she celebrated motherhood, which eluded her protagonists.

Though de Vaux performed these conventional gender roles to survive, she played other parts as well in order to give herself the sense that she had some agency and control.[87] In her writings and behavior, she presented herself as a savvy manipulator of men and came to challenge the traditional representation of women. Without a family, she felt she could not use the argument employed by other contemporary women, such as Jeanne Deroin, who claimed that women had a right to intervene in the public sphere on the basis of their maternal role.[88] De Vaux wanted to construct a new female identity without reference to its traditional maternal and domestic grounding and without male control. Independence was her "*idée fixe,*" as she put it herself. [89] This ambition to achieve individuality appeared masculinist because it was materialistic and self-serving, not spiritual and altruistic. It also threatened men.[90] Although de Vaux derided women's rights activists who demanded gender equality, she sought in effect to realize their objective by claiming the male privilege not only to earn the economic wherewithal to live independently but also to affect public discourse through her writing.[91] Through Lucie and Willelmine, de Vaux became a spokesperson for social justice, imitating to a certain degree Sand and Madame Marie. This role of social non-conformist suited de Vaux as well as her traditional ones.

In sum, Clotilde de Vaux was a collection of different selves, partaking of aspects of the many rich and diverse images made available by the culture at large. To conform to bourgeois convention, she played the abandoned wife, innocent victim, household angel, inspiring muse, and dependent invalid. To resist traditional representations of women, she performed the parts of enthusiastic student, rebellious daughter, prostitute, independent woman of ideas, writer, and social reformer. These varied selves originated in, evolved within, or represented a reaction to the texts that surrounded her. These texts include her stories and letters, which portrayed women as victims of evil men, an unjust society, bad mothers, and a poor education; George Sand's novels, which depicted transgressive female protagonists; Comte's philosophical works and correspondence, which celebrated the role of women, especially de Vaux; and her mother's articles, which directed her attention to broad issues of social reform.[92] Having found satisfaction in performing her many parts, de Vaux did not want Comte to bolster his latest self-representation as the forlorn, emotional, virtuous lover by immortalizing her in a single, selfless image of what every woman should be. She resisted Comte's making her forever into an exemplary moral agent, the role that many women of her day used to empower themselves and a role that she resorted to from time to time to her own benefit.

At the end of their relationship, in her last letter to Comte, de Vaux announced with great bitterness, "I have never dared to be myself with you."[93] In a sense, she informed him that she had been acting throughout their relationship and that there was a real, fixed self behind her performances, one that did not meet his expectations and opposed his corrupt representation of her. Whether such an essential, coherent self truly existed in de Vaux, or resides in anyone for that matter, poses an enigma that continues to be discussed at great length. If we grant that the concept of an essential self has validity, other vexing problems emerge: it is not clear whether de Vaux herself understood this self and whether scholars 150 years later can escape the preconceptions of their own age and use her correspondence, writings, and the cultural resources of the period to reconstruct that self. But perhaps all of these difficulties are ultimately immaterial because de Vaux was not attempting to unveil her authentic self but to exploit the notion of it. By telling Comte that he did not know her "real" self, she sought to assure her final victory over him and take her revenge. Angry that he had made no effort to inhabit her world or allow their relationship to develop on a more cerebral plane as she had desired, she insisted at the end on remaining mysterious and inaccessible to him. She resisted his project of transparency, which he had adopted from the French revolutionaries and realized in his major philosophical works, where he openly discussed his personal life.[94] This project was important to reform-minded men like Comte, who felt obligated to prove their virtue and honesty, especially in midnineteenth-century France, when codes of honor were still followed.[95] But because she was a bourgeois woman who had not had the pleasure of great public acclaim, de Vaux did not feel as privileged and secure as these men to allow herself to revel in a public display of a fragmentary self.[96] She reacted by resorting to women's traditional sphere — the private — and making the very private — her perceived sense of inner identity — even more private. Just as Dora would later mystify Sigmund Freud, de Vaux delighted in this way of baffling the self-satisfied social scientist. Despite the pride that Comte took in his intellectual superiority, she informed him that he could not grasp her essence, which was hers to reveal or conceal. In this way, she subtly mocked his faith in reason and his other self-representation as a genius. She demonstrated that his image of her, which he was going to use to encourage women's "innate sociability," was a fraud; there was a limit to her sociability.

In effect, de Vaux's assertion that there was another self, a secret layer that lay beneath all the other performed ones, was a subversive performative act. As Judith Butler has pointed out, "gender performance always and variously occurs" in a "situation of duress."[97] De Vaux was working out her last survival strategy, which she felt was required to preserve the dramatic, transformative potential of her character. Her claim to possess an inaccessible, authentic self, around which circulated multiple constructed selves, was ultimately a ploy of self-identification, contributing to her sense of individuality, agency, and freedom. De Vaux's battle with Comte demonstrates that nineteenth-century women were playing with complex issues of identity to resist their male contemporaries' urge to create stable female allegories, which were used by these men to project a vision of a better society, but a society that inevitably continued to subordinate women.[98]

NOTES

I would like to express my appreciation to Isabel Pratas-Frescata and Gilda Anderson for greatly facilitating my research at the Maison d'Auguste Comte and to Trajano Bruno de Berrêdo Carneiro, the president of the International Association of the Maison d'Auguste Comte. I thank this association for graciously allowing the University of California Press to use a photo of its famous portrait of Clotilde de Vaux by Antoine Etex. I am also very grateful to my graduate students at San Jose State University for their advice. Michele Quinnette was particularly helpful. Finally, I would like to thank Jo Burr Margadant, Bonnie Smith, and the other authors in this collection for their encouragement, assistance, and good humor.

1. For information about Comte's establishment of positivism and sociology, see Mary Pickering, *Auguste Comte: An Intellectual Biography*, vol. 1 (Cambridge, Eng.: Cambridge University Press, 1993).

2. Auguste Comte, *Testament d'Auguste Comte avec les documents qui s'y rapportent: Pièces justificatives, prières quotidiennes, confessions annuelles, correspondance avec Mme de Vaux*, 2d ed. (Paris, 1896), 239. The translations of all the passages in French are my own.

3. John Stuart Mill, *Auguste Comte and Positivism* (Ann Arbor: University of Michigan Press, Ann Arbor Paperback, 1961), 125.

4. Georges Morin, "Auguste Comte, Médecin de Clotilde de Vaux," *Paris Médicale* 4 (October 1928): 239, 243.

5. Comte published their correspondence in his *Testament*, the first edition of which was published in 1884.

6. Karen Offen, "Women's History as French History," *Journal of Women's History* 8 (spring 1996): 153.

7. Most of the information in this introductory section is based on Charles de Rouvre, *L'Amoureuse Histoire d'Auguste Comte et de Clotilde de Vaux* (Paris: Calmann-Lévy, 1917), 2–94; André Thérive, *Clotilde de Vaux ou la déesse morte* (Paris: Albin Michel, 1957), 7–37. Rouvre's book is the standard work. The grandson of Maximilien Marie and the grandnephew of Clotilde de Vaux, he based his research on family archives and oral history.

8. Michèle Riot-Sarcey, *La Démocratie à l'épreuve des femmes: Trois figures critiques du pouvoir, 1830–1848* (Paris: Albin Michel, 1994), 121–28.

9. Comte de Ficquelmont, quoted in Thérive, *Clotilde de Vaux*, 28.

10. Clotilde de Vaux to her parents, n.d., archives of the Maison d'Auguste Comte in Paris (hereafter MAC).

11. Janis Bergman-Carton, *The Woman of Ideas in French Art, 1830–1848* (New Haven, Conn.: Yale University Press, 1995), 1. On Sand's influence, see Carolyn G. Heilbrun, *Writing a Woman's Life* (New York: Ballantine Books, 1988), 37.

12. Mill to John Pringle Nichol, December 21, 1837, in *The Earlier Letters of John Stuart Mill, 1812–1848,* ed. Francis E. Mineka, 2 vols. (vols. 12 and 13 of *The Collected Works*) (Toronto: University of Toronto Press and Routledge & Kegan Paul, 1963), 12: 363.

13. Clotilde de Vaux, quoted in Rouvre, *L'Amoureuse Histoire,* 110.

14. Clotilde de Vaux to Comte, May 1, 1845, in Auguste Comte, *Correspondance générale et confessions,* ed. Paulo E. de Berrêdo Carneiro, Pierre Arnaud, Paul Arbousse-Bastide, and Angèle Kremer-Marietti, 8 vols. (Paris: Écoles des Hautes Études en Sciences Sociales, 1973–1990), 3: 4. Hereafter, this work will be cited as *CG.*

15. Comte to de Vaux, October 14, 1845, *CG,* 3: 152.

16. From April 1845 to April 1846, Comte wrote de Vaux ninety-five letters, while she composed eighty-six.

17. De Vaux to Comte, May 15, 1845, *CG,* 3: 12; Comte to de Vaux, May 17, 28, 1845, *CG,* 3: 14, 21.

18. Comte to John Stuart Mill, October 21, 1844, *CG,* 2: 287, 288; Comte to de Vaux, May 17, 24, 1845, *CG,* 3: 13, 20.

19. Comte to de Vaux, December 30, 1845, *CG,* 3: 258; de Vaux to Comte, June 5, September 5, 9, 1845, *CG,* 3: 34, 108, 120.

20. Comte to de Vaux, May 24, 1845, *CG,* 3: 20.

21. Comte to de Vaux, May 17, 24, 1845; February 22, 1846; *CG,* 3: 14, 20, 327. See also Peter T. Cominos, "Innocent Femina Sensualis in Unconscious Conflict," in *Suffer and Be Still: Women in the Victorian Age,* ed. Martha Vicinus (Bloomington: Indiana University Press, 1972), 155.

22. Comte to de Vaux, May 24, 1845, *CG,* 3:20. See also Martha Vicinus, introduction to *Suffer and Be Still,* vii–xv.

23. De Vaux to Comte, May 29, December 10, 1845, *CG,* 3: 23, 24, 228.

24. "Lettre philosophique sur la commemoration social," June 2, 1845, *CG,* 3: 28, 31–33; Auguste Comte, *Physique sociale: Cours de philosophie positive, leçons 46 à 60,* ed. Jean-Paul Enthoven (Paris: Hermann, 1975), 186.

25. De Vaux to Comte, January 15, 1846, *CG,* 3: 288.

26. De Vaux, "Lucie," *CG,* 3: 427, 428.

27. Ibid., 428–31.

28. Ibid., 435.

29. Ibid., 432, 433.

30. De Vaux to Comte, October 30, 1845, *CG,* 3: 169.

31. De Vaux, "Lucie," *CG,* 3: 433, 437, 438.

32. De Vaux to Comte, July 3, 19, 1845, *CG,* 3: 55, 68; Comte to de Vaux, July 20, 1845, *CG,* 3: 69.

33. James F. McMillan, *Housewife or Harlot: The Place of Women in French Society, 1870–1940* (New York: St. Martin's Press, 1981), 46.

34. De Vaux to Comte, July 20, October 16, 1845, *CG,* 3: 69, 154.

35. De Vaux to Comte, October 30, 1845, *CG,* 3: 169; Comte to de Vaux, July 22, 1845, *CG,* 3: 70.

36. Bergman-Carton, *The Woman of Ideas*, 53, 87; Geneviève Fraisse, *Reason's Muse: Sexual Difference and the Birth of Democracy*, trans. Jane Marie Todd (Chicago: University of Chicago Press, 1994), 38n1.

37. Comte to de Vaux, June 6, July 22, 1845, CG 3:37, 72, 74.

38. Comte to de Vaux, July 22, 1845, CG 3: 72, 74. On the growing popularity of journalism among women writers, see Bonnie G. Smith, *Changing Lives: Women in European History since 1700* (Lexington: D. C. Heath, 1989), 210. On the association between the private and the feminine, see Gary Kelly, *Women, Writing, and Revolution, 1790–1827* (Oxford: Clarendon Press, 1993), 10. On Comte's attitude toward the women's movement, see Mary Pickering, "Angels and Demons in the Moral Vision of Auguste Comte," *Journal of Women's History* 8 (summer 1996): 10–40.

39. De Vaux to Comte, August 11, 1845, CG, 3: 91

40. De Vaux, "Lucie," 430; Comte to de Vaux, November 10, 1845, CG, 3: 186.

41. Comte to de Vaux, September 2, 5, 1845, CG, 3: 102, 106. The essay was called "Lettre philosophique sur l'appréciation sociale du baptême chrétien," CG, 3: 97–100.

42. De Vaux to Comte, September 5, 1845, CG, 3: 108.

43. Rouvre, *L'Amoureuse Histoire*, 216.

44. Comte to de Vaux, September 6, 1845, CG, 3: 109.

45. Comte to de Vaux, September 6, 1845, *CG*, 3: 109–10; de Vaux to Comte, September 6, 1845, *CG*, 3: 112.

46. De Vaux to Comte, September 8, 9, 1845, CG, 3: 114, 119, 120; Comte to de Vaux, September 9, 1845, CG, 3: 115, 116.

47. De Vaux to Comte, September 30, November 2, December 8, 1845, and February 12, March 8, 1846, CG, 3: 139, 172, 318, 352; Comte to de Vaux, October 25, 1845, CG 3: 163.

48. De Vaux to Comte, July 3, October 7, November 11, 1845, CG, 3: 55, 145, 186.

49. William M. Reddy, "Condottieri of the Pen: Journalists and the Public Sphere in Postrevolutionary France (1815–1850)," *American Historical Review* 99 (1994): 1556.

50. Susan Sniader Lanser, "Toward a Feminist Poetics of Narrative Voice," in *Fictions of Authority: Women Writers and Narrative Voice*, ed. Susan Sniader Lanser (Ithaca: Cornell University Press, 1992), 175, 177.

51. The book is a compilation of the six articles on the "woman question" that Sand had contributed in 1837 to the journal *Le Monde*. When Lamennais refused to allow her to address the issues of divorce and separation, she stopped the series after the sixth letter. In the story, the main character, Marcie, is an intelligent, beautiful, loving young woman, who fears that her poverty makes it impossible for her to find a suitable spouse. Influenced by Saint-Simonianism, she yearns for a male career and lashes out at society for unjustly quashing her ambition. In response to her request for advice on how to deal with her loneliness and probable spinsterhood, a male friend addresses these letters to her, giving her contradictory advice. At times, he tells her that it is better to stay celibate than to enter a loveless marriage to a mediocre man who would have the right to control her. She should rise "above" her "sex" and become a writer, despite the risk that

such independence might lead to "isolation." At other times, he advises her to wait for a suitable man to marry, despite the remoteness of the possibility of such a man emerging. Because of these contradictions and the fact that the work is incomplete, Sand's position on the "woman question" in the *Lettres à Marcie* is difficult to ascertain. George Sand, *Lettres à Marcie*, in Sand, *Les Sept Cordes de la Lyre* (Paris: Michel Lévy Frères, 1869), 173–74; George Sand to Lamennais, February 28, 1837, in George Sand, *Correspondance*, vol. 3 (Paris: Garnier Frères, 1967), 711–14. For information on the discord between Sand and Lamennais, see Kristina Wingård Vareille, *Socialité, sexualité et les impasses de l'histoire: l'évolution de la thématique sandienne d'Indiana (1832) à Mauprat (1837)* (Stockholm: Uppsala, 1987), 493–97.

52. Curtis Cate, *George Sand: A Biography* (Boston: Houghton Mifflin, 1975), 419. See also Sand, *Lettres à Marcie*, 230.

53. Comte to de Vaux, January 9, 1846, CG, 3: 272.

54. Comte to de Vaux, August 11, 1845, CG, 3: 92

55. De Vaux to Comte, August 7, 1845, CG, 3: 86. The last name of one character in the story, Stéphane Sax, is a veiled reference to Sand's famous ancestor, the field marshall Maurice de Saxe.

56. Clotilde de Vaux, *Willelmine* (Paris: Edition Positiviste, 1929), 2, 4, 25; de Vaux to Comte, August 11, 1845, CG, 3: 91.

57. De Vaux, *Willelmine*, 14, 15, 19.

58. Claude Holland, "Mademoiselle Merquem: De-Mythifying Woman by Rejecting the Law of the Father," in *The World of George Sand*, ed. Natalie Datlof, Jeanne Fuchs, and David A. Powell (New York: Greenwood Press, 1991), 178.

59. De Vaux, *Willelmine*, 3, 19.

60. Ibid., 27, 28.

61. Ibid., 30, 32.

62. Clotilde de Vaux to Maximilien Marie, August 2, 1840, MAC.

63. De Vaux, *Willelmine*, 17.

64. De Vaux to Comte, October 9, 1845, CG, 3: 148.

65. Mémoire of Madame Marie, no date, MAC.

66. Comte to de Vaux, October 19, 1845, CG, 3: 156.

67. Comte to de Vaux, November 20, 24, 1845, CG, 3: 200, 207; de Vaux to Comte, December 5, 8, 11, 1845, CG, 3: 221, 224, 231.

68. Thérive, *Clotilde de Vaux*, 150.

69. De Vaux to Comte, November 23, 1845, February 13, 1846, CG, 3: 205, 320.

70. Comte to de Vaux, December 2, 1845, CG, 3: 212. See also, Comte to de Vaux, February 12, 1846, CG, 3: 316. In *Willelmine*, Maurice refers to Lucie as the "ideal of Galatea." Galatea was the statue created and adored by Pygmalion, who prevailed upon Aphrodite to bring her to life. This reference reflects de Vaux's awareness of men's propensity to worship their idealized image of women.

71. Comte to de Vaux, September 6, October 25, November 30, December 4, 1845; February 15, 1846, CG, 3: 109, 163, 210, 216, 323. "Thoughts of a Flower" may be found in CG, 210–11.

72. Comte to de Vaux, December 10, 12, 26, 1845, *CG*, 3: 230, 232, 252; de Vaux to Comte, December 14, 26, 1845, *CG*, 3: 236, 253, 254.

73. De Vaux to Comte, January 27, February 12, 1846, *CG*, 3: 306, 319; Comte to de Vaux, February 10, 1846, *CG*, 3:315.

74. Rouvre, *L'Amoureuse Histoire*, 317, 375.

75. Comte to de Vaux, March 1, 1846, *CG*, 3: 341; de Vaux to Comte, February 27, 28, 1846, *CG*, 3: 336, 337.

76. Rouvre, *L'Amoureuse Histoire*, 165.

77. Clotilde de Vaux, quoted in Rouvre, *L'Amoureuse Histoire*, 364.

78. Ibid., 374.

79. Madame Marie, quoted in Rouvre, *L'Amoureuse Histoire*, 381.

80. Offen, *Women's History*, 148.

81. De Vaux to Comte, January 4, 1846, *CG*, 3: 268; Madame Marie, Réponse à Monsieur Comte, n.d., MAC. See excerpt in Rouvre, *L'Amoureuse Histoire*, 398. Comte never received from the family the manuscript of *Willelmine* or his last letters to de Vaux.

82. Bergman-Carton, *The Woman of Ideas*, 199.

83. Comte, *Testament*, 239; Comte to de Vaux, October 29, 1845, *CG*, 3: 168.

84. Comte to de Vaux, February 15, 1846, *CG*, 3: 323.

85. Sidonie Smith, "Autobiography Criticism and the Problematics of Gender," in *A Poetics of Women's Autobiography: Marginality and the Fictions of Self-Representation* (Bloomington: Indiana University Press, 1987), 9–10.

86. Jo Burr Margadant, "The Duchesse de Berry and Royalist Political Culture in Postrevolutionary France," *History Workshop Journal*, 43 (1997): 24–26. See Margadant's essay in this collection.

87. On the importance of agency, see Sherry B. Ortner, *Making Gender: The Politics and Erotics of Culture* (Boston: Beacon Press, 1996), 2. On strategies of survival, see Judith Butler, "Performative Acts and Gender Constitution: An Essay in Phenomenology and Feminist Theory," in *Performing Feminisms: Feminist Critical Theory and Theatre*, ed. Sue-Ellen Case (Baltimore: Johns Hopkins University Press, 1990), 273.

88. Bergman-Carton, *The Woman of Ideas*, 95.

89. De Vaux to Comte, December 28, 1845, *CG*, 3: 257.

90. Joan Scott, *Only Paradoxes to Offer* (Cambridge, Mass.: Harvard University Press, 1996), 69.

91. For insights regarding the threat of the independent woman in the interwar period, see Mary Louise Roberts, *Civilization without Sexes: Reconstructing Gender in Postwar France, 1917–1927* (Chicago: University of Chicago Press, 1994).

92. On this idea of a woman's life caught up in texts, see Kali A. K. Israel, "Writing Inside the Kaleidoscope: Re-Representing Victorian Women Public Figures," *Gender and History* 2 (spring 1990): 40–48; Israel, "Drawing from Life: Art, Work, and Feminism in the Life of Emilia Dilke (1840–1940)" (Ph.D. diss., Graduate School-New Brunswick, Rutgers, the State University of New Jersey, 1992), 1–52.

93. De Vaux to Comte, March 8, 1846, *CG*, 3: 352.

94. Mary Pickering, "Rhetorical Strategies in the Works of Auguste Comte, "*Historical Reflections/Réflexions Historiques* 23 (spring 1997): 160.

95. Robert A. Nye, *Masculinity and Male Codes of Honor in Modern France* (Oxford: Oxford University Press, 1993), 32.

96. On the provocative question of whether socially disadvantaged people can find liberation in a completely diffused self, see Laura Lee Downs, "Reply to Joan Scott," *Society for Comparative Study of Society and History* 35 (April 1993): 450.

97. Judith Butler, *Gender Trouble: Feminism and the Subversion of Identity* (New York: Routledge, 1990), 139. On the construction of selves, see Butler, "Performative Acts," 279.

98. On the male search for female allegories to replace the iconic imagery of the kings, see Bergman-Carton, *The Woman of Ideas*, 211.

Acting Up

*The Feminist Theatrics
of Marguerite Durand*

MARY LOUISE ROBERTS

"Feminism owes a great deal to my blond hair," Marguerite Durand once declared in a prickly response to her critics. "I know it thinks the contrary, but it is wrong."[1] Durand was best known as the (blond and) beautiful editor-in-chief of *La Fronde,* the women's daily paper of the fin de siècle. She began her career as an actress, debuting at the Comédie-Française in 1882 at the age of seventeen and enjoying success there until her marriage to the young deputy Georges Laguerre three years later. When Laguerre became deeply involved in the Boulangist movement, Durand emerged as the driving force behind its primary propaganda organ, *La Presse*. After the collapse of the Boulanger campaign, Durand divorced Laguerre and continued her career as a journalist at *Le Figaro* in 1891. In 1896, she became a self-avowed feminist, and the following year she founded *La Fronde,* written and produced exclusively by women. Always cagey about calling *La Fronde* a feminist paper, Durand nevertheless affirmed the importance of feminism to all French women and gave feminist leaders a voice in her paper.[2]

Marguerite Durand's comment concerning blond hair, which earned her some notoriety in her later years, could serve as a saucy epigram for her feminism — a political enterprise that, she believed, could be advanced by conventional feminine wiles.[3] By posing herself in opposition to the movement ("it thinks the contrary, but it is wrong"), Durand made reference to her quarrels with other feminists. Although *La Fronde* was an important forum for feminist propaganda in the period, Durand was somewhat of a pariah among her peers. Other feminists perceived her as snobbish and *mondaine,* wobbly on suffrage and scandalous in her relations with men.[4] For many years prior to the war, Durand openly spoke out against the vote for women. Like many of her republican contemporaries, she was afraid that female suffrage would ensure the power of the priest against the Republic. In addition, Durand was and is still thought of as a bourgeoise who took many lovers, flaunted her beauty, and pooh-poohed militant, socialist feminism.[5] The implicit understanding of Durand has often been that she was a dupe of patriarchy who, consciously or unconsciously, embraced a notion of woman as nothing more than a sexual object.[6] Yet Durand also ran a daily paper for five years that was produced by women and that routinely took radical views on feminist issues such as female trade unions and higher education.

My purpose here is not to "explicate" or "justify" Durand's life and contributions. Historians have already explored her biography, her paper, *La Fronde,* and her role in fin-de-siècle feminist debate.[7] Nor is my aim to offer up the "truth" of Durand's life — to do her "justice" or to present her "whole" or "completely" to readers for the first time. Rather, perhaps quite selfishly, I want to use Durand's life in order to answer a set of questions about how change in women's lives occurred during this period. How did women such as Durand, sometimes called "new women," break free of the nineteenth century "real woman" ideal considered "natural" to female identity? How did they extricate themselves from this ideal, which defined woman as nothing more than a decorative creature and a domestic housewife? How did they shape new, unconventional lives? In addition, I want to investigate the nature of Durand's politics. How could blond hair be feminist? What did it mean to serve up conventional wiles as a political enterprise? Why did other fin-de-siècle feminists heap such scorn upon this approach? Was or was not Durand a victim of internalized sexist beliefs? By exploring such questions, I want to widen the margins within which we write the history of feminism in this period. Durand's politics fit uneasily into a narrative preoccupied with the vote and social reform because her approach was structured primarily by aesthetic rather than suffragist or legal preoccupations.[8] In founding *La Fronde,* Durand set out to create what I will call a "feminist aesthetics." She urged women "not to renounce their privileges, elegance of manners and dress, charm, beauty" because these things, too, could be used as political tools.[9] She believed that resistance to the new woman or feminist of the period was as much aesthetic as political in nature.

Attention to aesthetic issues was an appropriate strategy in nine-teenth-century France, where, to recall Debora Silverman's phrase, "the role of woman as an orchestrated objet d'art" fundamentally shaped female identity.[10] But Durand's preoccupation with public image and beauty can also be explained by her early career as an actress. Although she left the stage in her twenties, Durand continued to play roles, enact scripts, assume identities, and perform in the theater of politics. In short, Durand enacted a theatrics of self that was both deliberate and politically successful. Because of the actress' seedy reputation for sex and self-display, she has often been considered, in the words of one critic, "an embarrassment to feminist scholars."[11] But Durand's life suggests that in fact the acting profession served as a crucial site for the transgression of conventional gender identities at the fin de siècle. As we shall see, the links between "acting" and "acting up" lay at the heart of gender trans-formation in this period.

THE BLOND BEAUTY

To grasp the nature of Marguerite Durand's feminism, we would do well to follow the lead of the feminist-activist Georges Lhermitte, who said this of Durand in his 1936 obituary: "In order to understand the phrase she once used to describe her efforts, 'Feminism will never know what it owes to my blond hair,' you had to have known how resplendent with beauty she was during this era. The phrase was true. Marguerite Durand appeared to be a beacon toward which all efforts converged."[12] Lhermitte's obituary is but one example of an idealizing narrative of Marguerite Durand that far predated her death. In 1897 when *La Fronde* was founded, one journalist noted how "the entire press is preoccupied with this innovation, giving the names of the editors, describing the newspaper office . . . and going on at length concerning the beauty of its editor and founder Madame Durand."[13] It was not Durand's consider-able journalistic experience or her editorial skills that most absorbed the attention of her colleagues during the early weeks of *La Fronde*. Rather, it was her blond good looks.[14]

Again and again journalists praised Durand as "very blond," "very beautiful," "deliciously witty and pretty," or "very seductive, passionate even."[15] When asked what he thought of *La Fronde*, Maurice Barrès responded, somewhat incongruously, that "Madame Marguerite Durand is one of the prettiest *parisiennes* of our era."[16] E. Ledrain, of *L'Éclair*, agreed that Durand was "the prettiest woman in Paris" and also "a throwback to the eighteenth century," a Marie Antoinette tending the flocks of Trianon.[17] It was perhaps Edmund Burke's famous image of Marie Antoinette as "glittering like the morning-star, full of life and splendor" that Durand evoked at the fin de siècle.[18] After attending one of Durand's famous parties in 1903, an awestruck Georges Avril of *Éclaireur* described *La Fronde's* editor-in-chief as "the resplendent Marguerite Durand, *directrice diamantée.*"[19] The female journalist Séverine later remembered Durand's face as "haloed by gold," and Lhermitte, of course, exalted her as "resplendent with beauty."[20]

Like Marie Antoinette, Durand was fair-haired, or in the journalist Marie Dutoit's adoring words, "a great blond prophetess."[21] "The gold, frothy halo" of Durand's hair, more than any other element of her beauty, was the object of fetishistic attention.[22] In a discourse that drew upon distinctions of race as well as gender, *Le Journal* admired her as "white and blond as a flake of snow in the wheatfield"; a Marseilles journal used the same image: "She is a woman who is still very pretty, blond as the wheatfield."[23] In a sonnet written for Durand, Paul Bourget called her "a beloved blond muse," and referred to her "delicate and touching beauty."[24] And Maurice Barrès once proclaimed in all serious-ness that Durand's hair, "which is the color of moonlight, alone obliges you to fall in love with her."[25] Journalists also analyzed other parts of Durand's body with the same meticulous, rigorously thorough attention to detail. Durand's skin had "the iridescent whiteness of the ingenue," and her "inexpressibly sweet blue eyes" were like "the mirror of a spring-time sky."[26] "Transparent as an opal," her face was "haloed by gold."[27] Also admired was "the seductiveness" of her hands and her face, her "beautiful set of shoulders," her "sparkling eyes," her "delicate fingers" and last but not least, her "vibrant voice."[28]

How can we account for this obsession with Durand's beauty? Even if we concede that she was a seductive goddess worthy of her admirers, the preoccupation still merits closer analysis. For physical beauty was not usually the first thing one talked about when describing a journalist. Nor was the attention a mere symptom of misogyny, as no other *frondeuse* was described in the same way. How then can we account for this fixa-tion on Durand's appearance? The answer lies in a comment made by *Le Soleil,* which took the appearance of *La Fronde* as an occasion to recall how Durand had "shone like a star at the Comédie-Française . . . Her débuts were cause for sensation."[29] Journalists such as this one inter-preted Durand's debut as a journalist through her much earlier debut as a *comédienne.*[30] They made explicit a connection to Durand's acting career that was implicit but still pivotal elsewhere. By fetishizing the particularities of that beauty — her hair, her eyes, her skin, her hands — the press inscribed Durand in an idealized narrative usually reserved for actresses and courtesans.

Clearly Durand's career as an actress had a profound impact on her self-image and presentation of self. She began acting at the age of seventeen, when she defied her mother's wishes by leaving the respectable convent school where she had spent her childhood and entering the Conservatoire. After she had won the Conservatoire's *premier prix* in comedy, she was asked to join the Comédie-Française, where she enjoyed considerable success for three years.[31] Somewhat abruptly, she then left her career to marry and rarely spoke of it later.[32] But while she was the editor of *La Fronde,* she occasionally appeared on stage. During the years 1901–1902, for example, Durand made a tour with the famous actor Constant Coquelin, playing in such major cities as Geneva and Berlin, and becoming the object of massive public attention. At the time, Durand seriously considered founding a French theater in Berlin, which she would direct herself.[33] And while in Berlin with Coquelin in 1902, Durand gave a controversial but well-attended public lecture on French feminism. Press reports of her visit merged the stage appearances and the lecture as part of the same performance.[34]

In this way, acting and feminism were closely linked for Durand. The feminist Mme. Jules Allix once "applauded" her on *La Fronde,* which she likened to a "theater" of "public events."[35] *Le Soleil* also called the paper "another theater, another scene" for Durand, "one where you can always win success and hear the noise of applause."[36] The journalist Séverine conjectured that her good friend had left the theater because "too many of her own, her very own ideas, buzzed in this pretty head for her to be satisfied with interpreting the ideas of others." Durand wanted "to assert herself . . . on another bigger, better-ventilated stage, on a greater horizon . . . She has always been keen to act for the pure joy of acting, never simply for the result."[37] Durand's 1910 campaign for the Paris municipal council epitomizes her talent for acting in this way. Because she could not vote and was not a legal citizen, public attention lay at the heart of Durand's strategy: she was acting for the pure joy of it.[38] Her campaign speeches were held in theaters packed with famous Parisians, including theater stars, high-society people, politicians, and writers. Hundreds more were turned away at the door.[39] In fact, the lectures were theater of the first order, described as "premieres" and "performances" by the press.[40] Given Madame Durand's "verbal and personal" gifts, argued one journalist, she "was easily able to seduce the constituents," including himself.[41] He and others dwelled on Durand's dramatic entrance on stage, her "charming" costume (blond hair framed in a *panache de plumes,* a pitch-black fur boa "encircling" her neck and arms, a "lavish" dress in velour and lace), her voice ("sweet and nicely resonant," "almost tender," "blond, like her"), her diction ("moving and always spiritual"), her hands ("slender and pink, throwing the light of a ring at the smallest movement of her fingers") and, of course, her "grand, blond, elegant" beauty.[42] When a member of the audience asked Durand what "shade" of republican she was (radical, socialist, radical-socialist), another voice cried out: "What shade, stupid? Can't you see that she is blond?"[43]

NINETEENTH-CENTURY PERCEPTIONS OF THE ACTRESS

Although Durand left her acting career as a young woman, her years as an actress clearly shaped her identity and politics. In considering Durand's feminism, then, it makes sense to map out the cultural meanings attached to the acting profession, particularly for women. Acting was a "pariah" profession in France. The liminal status of the profession resulted in part from the refusal of the *ancien régime* Church to admit actors and actresses into the community of the faithful. Although the Church officially changed its policy in 1830, the old stigma persisted throughout the century.[44] Actors and actresses also had to combat what Jonas Barish has called "the antitheatrical prejudice." Certainly a progressive republican theatrical tradition existed in modern France, as Hugo's "Hernani" (1830) illustrates. But centuries-old antitheatrical prejudices were also given new life in the modern period by Jean-Jacques Rousseau's *Lettre à d'Alembert sur les Spectacles* (1758).[45] Rousseau's ideas about theater and acting were enormously influential and helped to shape the cultural construction of the actress even at the end of the nineteenth century.[46] In fact, antitheatrical prejudices became so prevalent and diffuse by this period that it is difficult to label them as strictly "Rousseauian." But this does not preclude looking to Rousseau for the clearest and most elaborate statement of the assumptions involved. Because Rousseau's ideas on the actress lay at the heart of Marguerite Durand's identity as a woman, they are worth exploring in some detail.

Writing in response to the proposition by the Encyclopedist d'Alembert to establish a theater in Geneva, Rousseau objected on the grounds that the stage trivialized morality by presenting virtue as a the-atrical game.[47] In an indictment that drew on an already venerable antitheatrical tradition, Rousseau condemned actors and actresses for leading disorderly, licentious lives, and for practicing an art of artifice and deceit. The actor, Rousseau argued, was trained in duplicity. Unlike the orator, who "represents only himself," the stage actor "displaying other sentiments than his own, saying only what he is made to say, often representing a chimerical being, obliterates himself."[48] Rousseau's fear lay in what Jean Starobinski has called "*le mensonge de l'apparence*," the actor's desertion of his or her "true" self — the seat of morality for Rousseau — created a gap between "outer countenance" and the "dispo-sitions of the heart" in which evil could enter.[49] To act was a form of prostitution — a selling of the self in the desire to seduce the audience.

Such a "*trafic de soi-même*" especially characterized actresses who, according to Rousseau, were prostitutes *par excellence*. Due to the "moral differences between the sexes," actresses were doubly duplici-tous: like actors, they lived in a dangerous world of artifice; and like all their sex, they were naturally skilled in the deceit of love.[50] Artifice and reality mingled promiscuously in an actress's life: she who "sets herself for sale in performance" does "the same in person." So completely "obliterated" was the actress's self, according to Rousseau, that *any* kind of performance was possible: she is "the first to parody her role" and "would not think herself ridiculous" even in playing the virtuous woman — "even in feigning to take for her own the discourses of pru-dence and honor that she sells to the public."[51] By parodying a virtuous woman, the actress debases herself. But at the same time, by exposing the artifice of female virtue itself — as a set of discourses that even the most unvirtuous can perform — the actress threatens the naturalized notion of the happy, virtuous domestic mother so dear to Rousseau. The actress's "obliteration" of self allows her to stage a performative identity that sub-verts essentialized notions of gender.[52]

Rousseau's brand of antitheatricalism, with its links to misogynism, persisted into the late nineteenth century. "An actress is a deceptive being," and "the theater lives only through illusion," wrote one critic in 1861.[53] In a series of critical writings on the theater in the 1880s, the dramatist Octave Mirbeau charged actors and actresses with a radical falsity that drained all moral value from their lives. An imaginary por-trait of a matinée idol placed him in a nightmare where everything tan-gible in his life was transformed into stage fakery; his savory chicken became a paper mâché prop, and his tears, loudly falling glass balls.[54] In his portrait *Les Vieilles actrices* (1884), J. Barbey d'Aurevilley portrayed the actress as a dissembler, a cocotte, and a mysterious seducer.[55] Léon Bloy's novel *Le désespéré* (1887) condemned the actor as the worst kind of prostitute, as he who "abandons himself, without choice, to the multitude."[56] In 1892, the prominent drama critic Jules Lemaître declared that Rousseau's "gloomy reflections" on the theater "had not lost any of their relevance *[saveur]*." The theater was still nothing but "a frivolous and dangerous diversion that discouraged serious thought."[57] As for actors, Lemaître condemned them in words that echoed those of Rousseau: "To show oneself in public for money with the aim of amusing other men . . . to express ideas and passions that are not your own, to seem to be what one is not — all this is to be missing to oneself, to violate in oneself the dignity of citizenship." Women compromised their dignity on stage less than men because, according to Lemaître, "to a much greater extent, they are naturally actresses in real life. We have become accustomed to not expecting as much sincerity of them, so that they seem less like they are lying when they play a role."[58]

Since Lemaître was arguably one of the most important theater critics of his day, it is clear that the rousseauist construction of the actress still pervaded late nineteenth-century French culture. And one has only to read Zola's *Nana* (1880) to recognize how the actress, the prostitute, and the dissembler remained joined in the French imagination.[59] Another notorious blonde, Nana first appears in the novel on the stage, where as Venus she "take[s] possession of the audience . . . A wave of lust was flowing from her as from a bitch in heat . . . with a twitch of her little finger, she stirred men's flesh." Parodying the role of the actress through her complete lack of talent, Nana erases the line between theater and brothel.[60] Although Nana performed in a popular, low-culture theater very different from the Comédie-Française, her case illustrates how actresses were often known as prostitutes off as well as on the stage. In 1903, a scathingly critical portrait of Marguerite Durand reminded its readers that "at the beginning of her life, she was to be found in the theater," where women were found with children but never husbands.[61] Throughout the century, actresses were forced into prostitution, often using the stage itself as a way to solicit customers. As Durand herself once pointed out, prostitution among actresses resulted from an abusive situation concerning costuming: stage management refused to take responsibility for the costumes actresses needed in contemporary plays, so that they often had to spend up to 15,000 francs a year in order to supply their own wardrobe.[62] Because such sums often represented an entire year's salary, actresses were forced to seek other less respectable sources of income. Although this situation was changing by the fin de siècle, the disguised prostitution of the theater blurred the line of demarcation between the genuine actress and the demimondaine.[63] So did some of the most famous actresses of the era, such as Sarah Bernhardt, who had so many marquis, vicomtes, and maréchals knocking on her bedroom door that she had to hire someone to direct traffic and avoid awkward collisions.[64]

But the example of "*la grande, la divine*" Sarah Bernhardt, who was a friend of Marguerite Durand, reminds us that actresses were idols as well as pariahs.[65] The theater was the most popular of the arts at the fin de siècle, and the stage, according to the actor Frédérick Lemaître, both "a pedestal and a pillory."[66] Actresses were idolized as seducers as much as they were scorned as prostitutes. As Léopold Lacour, a writer and friend of Durand once put it, an actress on the stage served as "the living image of all a woman's seductions, of all the tender, violent, heroic and cowardly feelings that a woman can inspire."[67] Rousseau himself acknowledged the seductive power of the actress when he claimed that plays about love "extend the empire of the fair sex" because "love is the realm of women"; he feared that actresses would gain the same power over their audience that they already had over their lovers.[68] Over a century later, Sarah Bernhardt called the dramatic art "essentially feminine" because "[t]o paint one's face, to hide one's real feelings, to try to please and to endeavour to attract attention — these are all faults for which we blame women, yet for which great indulgence is shown."[69] Like Rousseau, Bernhardt described the actress as a natural dissembler, but also as an object of indulgence — the complex projection of male desire as well as anxiety and frustration. Perhaps as a way to gain control over this vexed and ambiguous mix of feelings, nineteenth-century male drama critics made fervid, elaborate attempts to catalogue as precisely as possible the nature of an actress's seductive power — to inventory the salient details of her beauty.[70] For Marguerite Durand, that detail was her blond hair.

The actress, then, came to bear a heavy symbolic load in nineteenth-century French culture: she represented female seduction, which, in turn, became the ruling metaphor of theater itself.[71] To refer to the "seduction of the theater" was still commonplace at the fin de siècle.[72] Even after the war, a journalist was to write: "It is love that is the element of theater, and hence woman that is its main principle."[73] Such a symbolic role had its ups and downs for actresses. On the one hand, critics condemned the actress as a bad wife and mother, an immoral and indecent woman.[74] But on the other hand, such a judgment also offered her a social advantage, for in the nineteenth century, a career on the stage was one of the few ways that women might earn an income and compete professionally with men. The theater was, as one historian has put it, "a topsy-turvy world" inasmuch as gender roles were often reversed, both on the stage and off.[75] Again instructive is the example of Sarah Bernhardt, who wielded enormous professional and financial power in the world of the theater.[76] Beginning in the 1880s, Bernhardt produced plays, managed a number of theaters, and even gave one her name. Despite her many lovers, she married only briefly and chose to lead an independent — and lavish — life supported by her own earnings. By entering the world of the stage, Bernhardt lost respectability but escaped the strictures of domestic life.[77] Her very pariah status enabled her to enjoy enormous independence.

FEMINISM AND THE FEMININE

At some point in her young life, Marguerite Durand realized that by remaining an object of pleasure, she could become an independent and powerful subject. She took the notion of seduction as power, which she first learned as an actress, and applied it to a new purpose: feminist politics.[78] The enormous tensions involved in such an approach to politics are transcribed in the serpentine trajectory of Durand's life, which at first glance appears to be nothing more than a mass of contradictions, full of strange twists and turns. The desires for personal freedom and social probity tugged equally at her. The social ambiguity of her birth — she was an illegitimate child born into a cultured, well-to-do bourgeois family — would shape both her identity and politics in a fundamental way, as she struggled to lead a free but socially respectable life. Strong maternal guidance landed her in a convent school, but she abandoned that safe and reputable world for the more dangerous and unconstrained one of the theater.[79] After several years, she stopped acting in order to marry Laguerre, a move that, again, can be seen as a strategy to gain bourgeois respectability.[80]

But even after her marriage, far from retreating into a domestic existence, Durand learned the art of politics and the trade of journalism. Dubbed the "Madame Roland of Boulangism," Durand seemed to model her approach to politics after the *salonnières* of the previous century. Like them, she held an important salon on the rue Saint-Honoré and maintained a position at the very center of the Boulangist movement.[81] At the same time, still only twenty years old, Durand directed Boulanger's primary propaganda paper, *La Presse*. Contradictory perceptions of Durand emerge from this period. On the one hand, the prominent republican Ernest Constans used to brag that the struggle against Boulanger was not hard because "there were only two men in this history — Madame Laguerre and myself."[82] At the same time, another contemporary remembered that Durand's "smiling grace" and "sedulous charm" were so alluring that one of her admirers donated 10,000 francs to the charity office in the arrondissement represented by Laguerre "for the sole privilege of walking across the Café de la Paix with Durand on his arm."[83] Durand, then, was perceived both as power player and decorative object, virile and yet seductive.

These sorts of contradictions also characterize Durand's embrace of feminism in 1896, an event which, by her own account, figured as an epochal turning point of her life.[84] Durand eventually divorced Laguerre and continued her journalistic career at *Le Figaro* where, beginning in 1891, she wrote "Le Courrier du Figaro." The column printed surveys or topical questions and answers, supplied gossip about Parliament and made Durand "the woman about town."[85] In 1896, Durand bore a son whose father was a prominent editor at *Le Figaro*, Antonin Périvier. No sooner was the child born than Périvier tried to take him away from Durand after the two quarreled viciously. Aided by Georges Clemenceau, Durand took Périvier to court in order to get the child back.[86] During this same period, an international feminist conference took place in Paris, and Durand attended in the hopes of getting a humorous piece for *Le Figaro*.[87]

Given her need for both personal freedom and social probity, her attraction to feminism was bound to be both strong and ambivalent. As she later put it, she entered the hall "in the frame of mind characteristic of most women of my generation and education, which can be interpreted as 'the power of woman is in her weakness . . . In the daily struggle for life, for which man alone is destined, she loses her charm. But with a smile . . . etc., etc., etc.' "[88] At the time of the conference, then, Durand conceived herself as a woman in classic real-woman terms. Best articulated in Michelet's *La Femme* (1860), the discourse of *la vraie femme* or the real woman exercised enormous influence over the way in which nineteenth-century French men and women imagined the female self. (Durand's decision to trail off her sentence with a few bored et ceteras here reveal her assumption that the discourse was so prevalent as to require little explanation.) The discourse defined woman as an emotional creature whose charm lay in her role as a decorative object and her weakness and in the fulfillment of her domestic role within the home.[89]

But as a former actress, a journalist, a divorcee, and an embattled single mother, Durand was also constituted by the real woman ideal as a failed "other." As a professional woman working outside the home, she resembled more *la nouvelle femme* than *la vraie femme.* The image of the new woman had emerged in the French press some years before, at the same time as educational advances for women, their entry into new professions, and the acceleration of the feminist movement were threatening to disrupt traditional nineteenth-century gender relations. During the decade, the new woman and her so-called threat to the traditional nineteenth-century domestic ideal for women became the subject of heated discussion in the press. Women teachers, journalists, doctors, lawyers, scientists, and feminists were portrayed as *hommesses* who scorned marriage and children in order to pursue a career.[90] As ways of imagining the female self, "*la vraie femme*" and "*la nouvelle femme*" were opposite images that depended upon each other for their own construction. The two "are in conflict and the world is fighting over them," observed the feminist journalist Jane Misme in 1901.[91]

Durand was attracted to feminism as a single, independent woman who, because of her acting career and her divorce, could no longer, or did not want to, define herself as a domestic woman. Because French bourgeois feminism privileged liberal self-determination as a means of agency, it allowed Durand to think ambitiously rather than shamefully about her life as a single, independent woman.[92] One way of understanding Durand in this period, then, is that the Real and the New competed fiercely in the way she imagined herself as a woman. This inner conflict led her, in turn, to a contradictory notion of feminism. In an interview for *Gil blas* two days before *La Fronde* began publication, Durand recalled how she had been "surprised" by the "good ideas" of the feminists present at the 1896 conference. Durand condemned the "false" discourse of the new woman at the same time that she subscribed to it herself by describing feminists as "provocative" and "eccentric." At one point she stated, "I decided that these women (who admittedly do not always defend their ideas with great skill) were not known by the public, which was getting false ideas concerning them. That is to say, until now the promoters of feminism have been only provocative, somewhat eccentric types . . . And I thought that today, the period of ridicule being over for feminism, it was time to give this noble cause a serious, useful news-

paper."[93] If Durand set out to pull feminism into bourgeois convention-
ality, as she claims to do here, it was as a way to make herself more conventional as well—to reconcile her own lifelong need for both personal
freedom and social probity. She was also interested in giving feminism
visibility, again pulling it in from the margins and making it "known by
the public." To do this, Durand would exploit the two major cultural
commodities of her era—the newspaper and the theater—and draw on
an aesthetics of the spectacle finely tuned to her time. Feminism would be
about being *seen*—in the sense of being both visible and attractive.

Durand's efforts can be understood only within the context of contemporary antifeminism, best illustrated here by the views of her male
colleagues at *Le Figaro* also covering the convention. "If it should ever
succeed, the so-called feminist movement soon will have transformed
women and created a third sex," declared Maurice Leudet on the first
day of the conference.[94] Making use of Molière's *Les Femmes savantes* in
his analysis, Leudet drew on the old discourse of the *bas bleu* or bluestocking; he pictured the feminists at the conference with thick eyeglasses
and lorgnettes.[95] So too did "Le Passant," another journalist at *Le
Figaro*: "Unfortunately up until this moment, those women who have
rebelled have worn glasses and been scholars *[savantes]*; they have borne
too close a resemblance to men, the effect of which was to render their
position less interesting."[96] As Durand was quick to notice, these journalists objected to feminism on primarily aesthetic grounds. The most
important fact to note about the feminists was not their ideas or
demands but their unfortunate lack of charm or "interest."

This kind of objection to the new woman was, in fact, widespread. In
1900 E. Ledrain of *L'Éclair*, who had earlier praised Durand as a "white
and blond beauty," described feminists as "abandoning the sweetness of
their sex with their hands on their hips—a very unaesthetic bearing."[97]
A central facet of the new-woman image was her scorn for a conventional feminine aesthetic. In Debora Silverman's words, the new woman
"rejected decorative opulence in appearance, and challenged the role of
woman as an orchestrated objet d'art." Somber in both appearance and
behavior, simple in dress, devoid of all feminine coquettishness, she was
hence perceived as virile, desiccated, and ugly.[98] Art critics complained
that the visual model of the new woman was forcing a redefinition of
female portraiture. Traditionally female portraits had entailed "an exercise in decorative mastery," in which women were painted "as objets
d'art as luxuriant as the decor surrounding them" (in contrast to male
portraits, which were "occasions for exploring character and expressing

inner life.") But the new woman, art critics explained, was sober, simple and austere in her appearance; she had renounced decorative opulence: "The new woman is not beautiful. She looks rather like a boy . . . The [new women] are no longer women of pleasure and leisure but women who study, of very sober comportment."[99]

The visual image of the new woman defied a long-established gendered aesthetic. As Naomi Schor has shown, the "detail," given visual form in ornament and decoration, had characterized a feminine aesthetic for centuries. In relation to "masculine" representational art, the feminine detail was devalorized: it expressed nothing, it was particular, superficial, and insubstantial. In this way, the gendering of the detail was linked to the censure of women as frivolous and thoughtless.[100] At the turn-of-the-century, the decorative and its association with the feminine was at the center of debates concerning art nouveau and the development of a modern style.[101] If feminists chose a manner of dress that scorned decoration and ornament, it was (consciously or unconsciously) to challenge an aesthetic economy that historically had trivialized them. But at the same time, to reject a conventional feminine aesthetic was to risk censure as women who lacked beauty and therefore were not (real) women at all.

Durand set out to correct this putative deficit in feminist aesthetics. As a former actress, she knew that beauty, in the form of seduction, was power. She herself had enjoyed firsthand the pleasures and privileges of being a beautiful woman in French society. Her colleague Leudet put it this way in reporting on the feminist congress: "You don't need to be a major philosopher in order to recognize that women would like to widen the borders of their Empire — that of beauty and grace — and aim to be the rival of the man everywhere they do work and activity."[102] In nineteenth-century France, female beauty gave a woman enormous power, an "Empire" whose borders stretched far and wide. Durand dismissed the idea that "while a woman's intelligence is being carefully and completely developed, her sense of the aesthetic alone will be arrested — that is an absurdity."[103] Beauty, she argued, was a political act: "For a feminist, the extreme care of one's person and a studied sense of elegance are not always a diversion, a pleasure, but rather often excess work, a duty that she nevertheless must impose upon herself, if only to deprive shortsighted men of the argument that feminism is the enemy of beauty and of a feminine aesthetic."[104] Durand was careful here to dismantle the traditional linking of beauty to frivolity. Far from being a "diversion" or a "pleasure," beauty was work, a self-imposed duty. If men were "short*sighted*," then in Durand's view, feminism must have a visual component — it must be about *seeing* and being *seen,* as much as behavior or ideas.

Drawing on a tradition in French culture at least as old as the *salonnières,* Durand politically exploited her beauty and power of seduction. By representing herself as a traditional real woman, Durand managed to fend off the kinds of attacks her colleagues at *Le Figaro* had launched at feminists and new women. At the same time, however, she transgressed conventional gender roles by editing her own newspaper and expressing "radical" political views. In other words, to a certain degree at least, she got what she had always wanted: both freedom and respectability. This is how Durand herself explained the notorious comment concerning blond hair: "I was not much more than thirty when I founded the *Fronde.* The fact of seeing a woman who was still young and not totally out of favor *[disgraciée],* who made her life seem easy, who was interested in the lot of other women and made that her preoccupation and the object of constant effort — all this was at first astonishing and then interesting: it was new. Feminism owes a great deal to my blond hair."[105] Durand's attitude was condescending and possessive. She presented herself as a happy foil to other feminists, a living refutation of the equation of feminism with eccentricity and ugliness. She did nothing to refute antifeminist admirers who favorably compared "her charm . . . allied with grace" or her "desire for elegance" with the "virago wanting to wear the pants" or the "pedantic spirit pickled in science like fruit in a jar of vinegar."[106] Posing for photographs in elaborate dresses and hairstyles, she reveled in descriptions of herself as "truly feminine from the tip of the gold, frothy halo of her hair, to her pensive eyes and smiling mouth, to the tips of her delicate fingers, which seem better designed to manage a fan than brandish a standard."[107] Like any star of the stage, Durand wanted to be not just any feminist, but *the* feminist — *the* one to lead the way. She was convinced that she alone could and should "rescue" feminism from ugliness.

La Fronde was founded with this aim in mind. From her experience at *La Presse,* Durand probably gained a feel for the political power of visual imagery — central to the success of Boulangism.[108] She also became aware of political journalism as a powerful political and cultural force. "Once a vehicle of ideas — particularly political ideas — at the service of only a certain class," she once argued, "the newspaper today has become the indispensable 'thing' for all classes."[109] For feminists, Durand believed, the new mass press could serve as a potent tool to correct "false" images

Portrait of Marguerite Durand by Walery. Reproduced with the permission of the Bibliothèque Marguerite Durand.

of women and produce new ways of imagining the female self. The bourgeois dailies had rendered women's lives invisible. Women journalists
hid behind pseudonyms and did little more than write review articles and
literary chronicles.[110] This lack of visibility reinforced their social marginality. To write copy on politics, the stock market, and the business
world, as she would in *La Fronde,* a woman was forced "to leave her
home, to see, to hear, to observe, to understand and to judge beyond the
limited circle of her family."[111] In this way, Durand nurtured the already-
rich historical links between journalism and feminism.[112] In addition,
Durand saw the press as an effective medium through which to promote
her feminist aesthetics. She once described *La Fronde* as a "personification" of feminism itself, a feminism "which up until that time had been
scattered, inconsistent and off-putting and which [*La Fronde*] made amiable, and *attractive.*"[113]

THE FEMINISM OF *LA FRONDE*

When Durand ran for political office in 1910, the journalist Charles
Vincent argued that "aesthetics would have everything to gain" by her
entry into the municipal council.[114] Was the comment sarcastic? Was
Durand a dupe of patriarchy? She herself did not seem to think so, as she
perceived herself as a rebel often forced to sacrifice the respectability she
so fervently sought. "In all things, one must have the courage of one's
own opinion," she wrote in 1898, "and not demand respect from a
world whose prejudices one wittingly goes against."[115] But many of
Durand's feminist contemporaries saw her differently — as insincere and
even dangerous. When in 1902, Durand argued to a group of Berliners
that the new woman need not renounce her privileges of charm and
beauty, a French journalist remarked that she "on all scores easily convinced the French and German gentlemen" but alienated many of the
feminists.[116] Hardly appreciative of Durand's own self-styled approach,
Hubertine Auclert, for example, wrote her off as an pretentious
"*cocotte.*"[117] The socialist feminist Madeleine Pelletier remembered her
experience at *La Fronde*'s offices in this way: "I had the idea of going
there and naively, I brought an article [to submit]. A woman in a very
low-cut dress received me with haughtiness; she took the article and told
me that I would see it if it appeared; I would have to buy the paper every
day. Evidently I didn't look rich enough in my dress . . . which wasn't
even worth twenty francs, and that was much more important than what
was in my article."[118] Pelletier provides us with a window for under-

standing other feminists' condemnation of Durand. Her perception that her appearance meant "much more" than the content of her article roughly transcribes the aims of Durand's feminist aesthetic. But seen through Pelletier's eyes, the notion that a woman's beauty mattered as much to the cause as her ideas was nothing more than *mondaine* superficiality. At the heart of Durand's project lay a class snobbery that alienated many socialist and working-class feminists.

But such scorn was not without irony because Durand, in fact, staunchly defended the labor interests of working women. *La Fronde* was completely typeset by women and Durand insisted on paying her female typographers the same wage as their male counterparts, a move that earned her the condemnation of the male *syndicat* (from which women were excluded). In response, Durand founded the *Syndicat des femmes typographes* in 1899 and donated 1,000 francs to secure its financial future; the next year saw the legal creation of a cooperative society of female typographers.[119] In *La Fronde* itself, women's strikes were followed closely and given financial support; similarly, union legislation passing through the Senate was vigorously endorsed.[120] Long investigative pieces exposed the low wages and dangerous conditions of women who worked in *ateliers de couture* and factories.[121] Durand's syndicalist efforts were only part of her progressive, often radical approach toward women's issues. Articles in *La Fronde* took courageous stands on several other issues, including single motherhood and equal wages for *institutrices*. Perhaps most importantly, in the pages of their paper, Durand and the *frondeuses* challenged the meaning of female identity itself by condemning the male literary construction of the "eternal feminine."[122] And even after *La Fronde* ceased publication, Durand continued to fight for the rights of women workers. She established an *Office du Travail et des Intérêts féminins* (1907) that held conferences, conducted surveys, and collected information on women's work, including salary, health, and safety issues.[123]

Given Durand's impressive record of feminist radicalism, then, it seems fair to ask: why did she alienate so many other feminists? Her Office du Travail and other labor projects were scathingly criticized by the C.G.T. (*Confédération Général du Travail,* the primary trade union in France) and socialist feminists, who accused her of being financed by her "good friends" Georges Clemenceau and René Viviani.[124] Although Durand's relations with the socialist left were complex, in general much of the scorn heaped upon her sprang from the politically ambiguous nature of her feminist aesthetics. The wealth of erotic associations in

Durand's public image — to the actress, to the demimondaine — rendered her vulnerable to trivialization as a decorative object and defamation as a prostitute. To carry the banner of feminism onto this slippery terrain was, for many feminists, not worth the risk: if Durand could exploit beauty as political, she could just as often be reduced to a powerless object of pleasure.[125] She incurred the wrath of her peers for provoking this chancy situation and dragging the discourse of feminism with her. That the risk was very real is proven by a sarcastic article, dated 1900, that recreated, in the form of a one-act play, a mock meeting of the editorial board at *La Fronde*. In this mock recreation, Durand appears as, above all, interested in her own aging beauty. She is sidetracked at several points, first, to secure some pastilles designed to whiten teeth and offered by a *frondeuse,* second, to turn around so that the others can admire the back of her dress and to correct them when they mistake its most elegant feature for a simple fold, and finally herself to admire the skirt of still another *frondeuse* and to inquire about its designer. Finally turning her attention to the task at hand, Durand laments how "little enthusiasm" was shown for feminism in France, how "it was smiled at, joked about."[126]

Durand's rumored sexual affairs and her use of seduction as a political weapon also presented dangers that feminists were quick to recognize. Durand had a good reason to maintain sprightly relations with the opposite sex, which was to maintain her beauty as a source of power.[127] But as a single mother engaging in a profession outside the home, Durand already risked being labeled a "public" woman of easy virtue. A Marseilles journalist once claimed that Durand's task was "to demonstrate that practically speaking, the woman, contrary to the jest of Proudhon, can be better than a housewife without falling into the shame of prostitution."[128] The statement reveals the narrow framework in which Durand's work and career could be understood by her contemporaries. In a world where work outside the home was deemed shameful for the single middle-class woman, journalism disrupted traditional ideas of female respectability.[129] As a result, the journalist Georges Dubor feared that the *frondeuse* on her beat late at night at the Gare de Lyon would most likely be "confused with a prostitute."[130] Another male journalist called *La Fronde* "*Le Moniteur de Saint-Lazare*" after a Parisian prison for prostitutes.[131]

Even more than her *frondeuses,* Durand — an illegitimate child and a former actress who herself bore *un enfant naturel* — was vulnerable to such charges. Not surprisingly, then, rumors connected the financing of

La Fronde with Durand's so-called secret life as a demimondaine. In exchange for financial support, it was claimed, Durand carried on an affair with any or all of the following: the Baron Gustave de Rothschild, Georges Clemenceau, René Viviani, and even Kaiser Wilhelm II.[132] Fiercely denying it up until her death, Durand melodramatically insisted that she had paid for the paper by selling her pearls — one by one.[133] Still, in December of 1898, Durand was forced to sue *La Libre parole* for a series of attacks on her character and morality.[134] The quarrel consisted of an exchange of insults that began between herself and the editor Gaston Méry when *La Fronde* refused to donate money to a fund sponsored by *La Libre parole* for the widow of Major Henry, the forger in the Dreyfus trial. When Méry accused the *frondeuses* of having no sympathy for "a mother in tears and her baby" (i.e., Major Henry's widow and child), Durand made the mistake of mentioning the incident in which her own child had been taken from her, and of accusing Méry of not being a *galant homme* or gentleman. Méry jumped on the incident to denounce Durand as a bad mother, a *galant femme* and a prostitute with Jewish lovers: "On the field of gallantry, no, really, I am not going to fight with Madame Durand."[135] Méry also accused Durand of coldly turning away an old *comedienne* friend who came for financial help, thus dredging up Durand's acting past and implying that she wanted to bury it.[136]

The danger — very real to some feminists — was that Durand would turn the whole enterprise into a dirty little joke, reinforcing rather than ending "the period of ridicule" for feminists. But there is still another way to look at Durand's feminist aesthetics. The philosopher Luce Irigaray has argued that even as women submit themselves to gender ideologies, the repetition of these opens up a space of difference that can be subversive. In her role as editor and in her self-presentation to the media, Durand flaunted herself as a real woman. But to do so was a misrepresentation inasmuch as she was also a strong, independent new woman. To borrow Irigaray's terms, Durand reenacted traditional notions of femininity within the context of a very untraditional life.[137] Durand was a real woman — *but not quite.*[138] That small space of difference allowed Durand to play with conventional femininity *ironically* rather than be reduced to it. And that parody had an accidentally subversive effect, which was to expose the artifice of the conventional real woman — as an identity that can be embraced by even a very unconventional new woman. In this sense, Durand was like Rousseau's actress who played the virtuous woman. Whether by accident or intention, her embrace of conventional femininity had the effect of trivializing and undermining it.

Looking at some of the ways in which Durand could be said to have mimicked conventional femininity can help us evaluate its subversive potential. Her first goal was to create an exquisite and thoroughly "feminine" aesthetic for *La Fronde* by carefully decorating the paper's offices on the rue St. Georges in Paris. When journalists for *Illustration* arrived there to do a story in January of 1898, they gushed over the flowers, the colors, the decor, and the atmosphere. "A feminine paper," one concluded, "is produced exactly like an ordinary paper; only there are many more green plants and flowers, and the furniture is infinitely more elegant."[139] In this way, Durand used interior decoration to assert the paper's all-important difference in an unthreatening manner. Durand picked blue and green as the predominant colors for the decor because, she felt, they went well with her own coloring. "How feminine it is, this blue-gray," remarked one visitor, "it's a symphony in blue minor. Can you imagine a color that better signifies feminine charm — with its discretion, refinement and mystery?"[140] Durand also equipped the office with extensive dressing room facilities. "Because coquetry is far from banished at *La Fronde*," wrote the *Illustration* reporter, "and because by contrast, fingers stained with ink are unmercifully proscribed, a comfortable powder room is at the disposal of these women."[141]

The elegant, charming, refined, and thoroughly feminine offices of *La Fronde* embodied conventional ideologies of French womanhood and made the paper culturally acceptable to its visitors.[142] But despite all the powder rooms in the world, these women's fingers *were* stained with ink; they were writing their own newspaper.[143]

In this way, Durand transgressed gender conventions without appearing to do so, securing both social acceptance and power. According to her own account, she maneuvered her status as one of the first women to enter the Senate press box in much the same way. Durand was seated in the first row with Gaston Calmette, director of *Le Figaro*, and Arthur Meyer, director of *Le Gaulois*, whom she "happily separated" from Papillaud, an editor for *La Libre Parole*, because the latter "continually riddled (the Jewish Meyer) with insults." The journalists welcomed the first woman in their press box. After about two weeks, for example, the eager-to-please Papillaud began to mark Durand's place with a rose or a little bouquet of violets. Unfortunately for Durand, there were no backs to the seats in the first row, and it was "very tiring" for her "to follow the interminable sessions without having my back supported." But luckily, two "amiable colleagues" behind her (one of them Aristide Briand, then director of *La Lanterne*) offered to help by crossing their arms and forming a sort of cushion against which she could lean back, a gesture she "accepted with gratitude."[144] Once again, Durand's request to press into service old-fashioned gallantry seemed to distract her male colleagues from the fact that she had, in reality, gained some degree of access to institutions of political power.

The offices of *La Fronde* were "feminine" in still another sense, as Durand forbade any man on the premises except the night janitor. Her male colleagues in the press were not happy. As Alexandre Hepp of *Le Journal* hotly put it, the janitor was called upon to be "a specimen of great authenticity so as to embody as best possible the usefulness and honor of the sex that, in a century, has produced only a Napoleon and a Hugo."[145] In order to smooth ruffled feathers, Durand gave several high profile *soirées*, which were attended by the most powerful journalists and politicians in Paris (Joseph Reinach, René Viviani, Raymond Poincaré, to name a few.)[146] In doing so, she again drew on a long tradition of salon sociability continued in the nineteenth century by such female journalists as Delphine de Girardin, whom Durand once named as her historical predecessor.[147] Durand probably learned the importance of such gatherings in the theater, where parties were given in order to secure good press reviews.[148]

Once again, the *soirées* displayed Durand's ability to mimic traditional notions of femininity in a subversive manner. Invitations specified that women wear a *"toilette de soirée décolletée."*[149] Although the parties began as formal literary evenings, they somehow evolved into more uninhibited, *"délicieuses"* affairs with dancing until the wee hours of the morning. They worked brilliantly to correct "false ideas" concerning the *frondeuses*.[150] One morning-after journalist remarked cozily that although he had arrived at *La Fronde*'s offices "an heir to all . . . common prejudices and cliches" concerning "the proverbial ugliness of the *bas-bleus*," he had discovered women who were well-dressed and warm-hearted.[151] "How pretty they are!" exclaimed another journalist after the same party. "At times, in theory or out of habit, we make fun of the *frondeuses* without knowing it." But "yesterday's party proved them to be seductive and pretty." He was happy to discover that "speaking of female rights . . . in no way requires renouncing the joys of seduction."[152]

Durand and the *frondeuses* made no effort to hide their delight in outwitting expectations. They described one 1899 party in this way: "In elegant clothing, adorned with flowers or gems, wedding mind to beauty, the women tried to outdo each other in charm. That to the great astonishment of those who, having come for the first time to a *Fronde* party, expected to meet mostly . . . 'bluestockings' past their prime."[153] According to this account, Durand and her *frondeuses* were using their physical beauty in a conscious way. "Outdoing" each other in charm, they mimicked the real woman, at the same time holding her at a distance both by what they were doing and their own awareness of it. By writing a newspaper, by working outside the home, they disavowed the conventional role they appeared to embrace. And once again, this mimicry itself exposed the fact that the real-woman role, far from being some "essential" attribute of femininity as Rousseau or Michelet had claimed, could be "staged" by even the most unconventional of women.[154] If it could be so effortlessly adopted, even by the most unlikely of women, then it was *nothing but* a role in the first place — and easily rejected as well.

Seen from the perspective of mimicry, Durand's feminist aesthetics, although risky, were at least destabilizing, potentially seditious, and certainly not naive. In an article of July 1899, Louise Debor defended "*la fronde*" (slingshot) of *La Fronde*: "Women are beginning to feel that they would be making a big mistake to neglect their best weapons — beauty and grace." As for critics such as Pelletier, Debor responded in this way: " 'Snobbiness and frivolity,' exclaim our offended old maids. So be it, but cleverness as well. Only in this manner do you attract a large, more open-minded public . . . So let's not pooh-pooh snobs."[155] A snob Durand may have been, but clever as well. She accomplished much during these years: she pioneered female unions when male socialists had little interest in doing so; she published a daily paper for five years that gave unprecedented visibility to the feminist movement and had a cultural impact in all of France.

This impact became clear in 1902, when Durand promised *institutrices* throughout France fifteen days of free subscription if they would write her what they thought of *La Fronde*. (Isolated village *institutrices* were among the paper's most avid readers; they were often called "*frondeuses*" themselves because of their role as enthusiastic readers). The *institutrices* praised the paper's secular and republican spirit, the "powerful support" it gave to "women who work" and most importantly, its ability to educate not only themselves but their male colleagues. One longtime reader, Madame Cadet, wrote Durand that due to *La Fronde*, she had overcome her "long-held belief that politics were not for women." While at first "even very intelligent" gentlemen friends made fun of her for subscribing to the paper, in the end she had gotten her "vengeance" by making them read it: "Because your feminism is made of charm and grace, of goodness and pity, of right and justice, everyone

ends by being persuaded and stopping their mockery."[156] If Madame
Cadet can be believed, then, Durand did help end feminism's "period of
ridicule."

THE AESTHETICS OF THE SPECTACLE

If we are to understand the impact of Durand's feminist aesthetics, it is
important, finally, to recognize it within its fin-de-siècle context of a bur-
geoning mass culture.[157] While it is difficult to speak of one monolithic
mass culture, Durand managed to manipulate successfully the two most
powerful cultural commodities of her time: journalism and theater. To do
this, Durand cultivated an aesthetic precisely attuned to these forms of
mass culture. Her feminist aesthetic was not a traditional glorification of
detail and decoration; on the contrary, it belonged expertly to its own
time. Durand exploited a newer aesthetic of the spectacle; her feminism
was about being *seen*, about visibility and visual beauty. As Vanessa
Schwartz has argued, *le spectacle* was pervasive in fin-de-siècle Paris,
central to mass forms of leisure. It revealed itself in the world exhibition,
(which rendered the world itself as a picture), the popular boulevard
practice of *flânerie*, the creation of the cinema, the unprecedented popularity of the theater, and the journalistic fad of "*faits divers*," based on
the public display of private life. "Morning, noon and night, summer and
winter, there is always something to be seen and a large portion of the
population seems absorbed in the pursuit of pleasure," boasted a *Guide
to Paris* in 1884.[158]

Durand's ability to employ an aesthetics of the spectacle was particularly evident during her 1910 municipal campaign, when she accepted
the gift of a lioness from the governor of French West Africa. Naming her
"Tiger," Durand tried to domesticate her as a household pet. Possibly the
inspiration came from Sarah Bernhardt, who was notorious for keeping
wild animals in her house.[159] Tiger quickly became a media spectacle and
put Durand on the cover of several prominent French journals and newspapers — precisely what she wanted in order to give her campaign publicity.[160] (Because Durand had no legal chance of winning, visibility for
the Cause was her only possible political gain.) Unfortunately, *la petite*
also ruined Durand's garden and terrified her guests, forcing Durand to
end their brief but spectacular affair.

Nevertheless as Durand's portrait on the cover of *Fémina* shows, at
stake here was least of all the "real" animal itself. The caption remarked
on how Durand had undoubtedly named the lioness Tiger "out of love

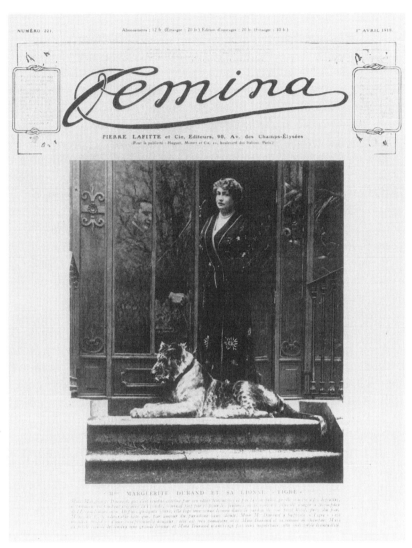

Marguerite Durand and her lion, "Tiger," on the cover of *Fémina*, April 1, 1910. Reproduced with the permission of the Bibliothèque Marguerite Durand.

for paradox." The photograph was obviously posed, with Durand, dressed in an ornate, exotic-looking robe, standing regally in her doorway, holding the lioness by a strong rope. But a closer look reveals that a male figure behind the door, perhaps purposely hidden but nevertheless visible, did the real work of controlling Tiger. The picture, then, rested on a deliberate misrepresentation, grounded in the same contradiction between seduction and power that Durand had played on throughout her life: beautiful and elegant, she also appeared powerful and strong. And the lioness herself served as an appropriate double symbol: like all felines, a traditional image of seduction, she was also seen as a symbol of Durand's power. If Durand raised lions in her home, commented one journalist, she could hardly be cowed by the heckling crowds that greeted her during the campaign.[161]

The media spectacle surrounding Tiger evokes the carnivalesque nature of fin-de-siècle politics. It also illustrates how tuned in Durand's aesthetics were to a mass reading public. According to critics and historians, central to the late nineteenth-century commodification of mass cultural forms such as the newspaper was the disengagement of things, gestures, and activities from a stable, recognizable order of meaning. As they took on a life of their own, consumer commodities increasingly entered into what T. J. Clark has called "the reign of generalized illusion," consisting of images that were arbitrary in their relationship to what they represented.[162] Precisely this arbitrary relation between sign and signified operated in Durand's picture, which noted the "paradox" of a lion named Tiger, and which featured a serene, poised woman restraining an animal several times her strength. In this logic of fantasy, in which the nonreferential image is all that counts, the subject is once again drained of meaning, "obliterated" to use Rousseau's phrase a final time. Inasmuch as the commodification of print culture rested on illusion, it also rested on the theatrical and the performative—qualities that were old hat to Durand and that she didn't hesitate to exploit in the name of feminism.

Finally, this logic of fantasy drew on the exotic and the erotic, qualities that Durand seemed to embrace easily.[163] According to Rosalind Williams, fin-de-siècle merchandisers exploited sexual and orientalist fantasies because they "invite[d] liberation from ordinary conventions and attainment of a more romantic, exciting existence."[164] In the picture, Durand played precisely on these fantasies—making public display of a West African animal given to her by a colonial official and wearing a foreign-looking robe. Her performance converted these consumerist fantasies into feminist capital, in this case, a plea for electoral reform. Once again, it was an ironic and risky business but one attuned to the intensified growth of the mass consumer culture during these years. With foresight, Durand sensed that power in the twentieth century would rest as much with the newspaper and the department store as with the Parliament and suffrage. That was what feminism owed to her blond hair.

CONCLUSION

Durand's theatrics can help us understand how change occurred in French women's lives at the fin-de-siècle — how a group of new women, mostly bourgeois, broke with the traditional domestic ideal and began to construct more unconventional female identities. Feminist historiography has often emphasized the "exceptional," "pioneering" qualities of women such as Durand. But in fact she merely manipulated conventional gender identities (the real woman, the actress) in order to produce a public image that was both culturally acceptable and transgressive. The subversive nature of Durand's theatrics lay not in the creation of a new script but in the strategic reenactment of a conventional script (female seduction in feminist politics).[165]

Durand's biography also suggests that we think in broader terms about both feminism and the fin-de-siècle new woman in order to encompass a wider diversity of women. Clearly the theater world and the acting profession, no less than the feminist movement, served as important arenas for the transgression of conventional gender identities in this period. Durand herself once noted the strong links between feminism and the theater.[166] In fact, it is impossible to imagine the popular images of the new woman and the feminist without thinking of the stage — in particular, the dramas of Ibsen, Strindberg, Wedekind, and, in France, those of Eugène Brieux, Maurice Donnay, and Paul Hervieu.[167] No wonder, then, that the *frondeuses* were sometimes accused of incarnating Hedda Gabler and other "seditious intellectuals" in Ibsen's plays.[168] In 1897, the *frondeuse* Daniel Lesueur (Jeanne Lapauze) also drew a close link between theater and feminism when she defined feminists as authors "who, through the book or *through the theater,* demand the right for the woman to live a full human existence."[169] That year Lesueur's play "Hors du mariage" became the first performed at the Théâtre féministe, founded by the dramatist Marya Chéliga at the old Menus-Plaisirs in Paris. Begun in the same year and for precisely the same purpose as Durand's *La Fronde,* Chéliga's theater aimed to perform plays exclusively written by women in order to "expose their ideas" and "give away the secret of their supposedly indecipherable soul."[170]

Why did the theater serve as a focal point for changes in gender identity at the turn-of-the century? As we have seen, the pariah status of the actress enabled her to enjoy freedom from the restrictions placed on more "respectable" women. Colette's youthful lark as a *vagabonde* is inseparable from her acting career.[171] Like Bernhardt, the actress Gabrielle Réju owned and managed her own theater after her separation from her husband in 1906.[172] The performer Yvette Guilbert (another friend of Durand's) enjoyed an unconventional marriage with her German husband, who left his country and career to accommodate her professional needs. "In public and private," one historian has argued, Guilbert "resisted and challenged the nineteenth-century norms of femininity and established her kinship with the New Woman."[173] And as we have seen with Durand, the path from unconventional lifestyle to feminist consciousness was well trodden. The late-eighteenth-century feminists Olympe de Gouges and Théroigne de Méricourt had earlier careers in the theater, as did the late-nineteenth-century feminist Nelly Roussel. Likewise, Yvette Guilbert and Sarah Bernhardt became outspoken on feminist issues in the 1910s.[174]

But there is another reason that the theater and the acting profession might serve as important sites for gender subversion at the fin de siècle. This one lies in Rousseau's still widespread prejudice that the actress "obliterated" herself by staging an identity that was performative — in the sense of both dramatic and nonreferential.[175] In this period, range was considered the acid test of talent for an actress. As Madame Bartet, an actress at the Comédie-Française, put it in 1903, "One's greatness is measured by the diversity of characters that one can embody." While, Bartet conceded, it was easy to play characters who conform to our own nature, it was much more difficult "to translate passions that are unknown to us, to render true a language which is antipathetic to us, to embody characters radically different from who we are."[176] The actress's real challenge, then, was to become selves different from her own and from each other, from virtuous woman to ingenue to prostitute to domestic mother. In short, her challenge lay in performativity, playing skillfully with identity in a nonreferential sense. For Rousseau, this amounted to the destruction of an essentialized self, and, as we have seen, critics of the theater persisted in their perception of actresses as false, dissembling, fake. When Rousseau saw the so-called immoral actress playing the virtuous woman, he astutely realized theater's threat to society: the potential of the actress not only to grasp but also to expose gender identity as a culturally constructed set of gestures and conventions that one enacted on the stage. Both to act and to watch acting was to appreciate that gender itself was an act rehearsed to perfection, a performative illusion passing itself off as an essential reality.[177]

Actresses like Bernhardt who (in the 1890s) played the virginal Jeanne d'Arc, and who cross-dressed on stage in roles such as "Hamlet," clearly exposed the artifice of gender in the way Rousseau had most feared.[178]

Although these actresses were certainly doing nothing new, their power to enact scripts in subversive ways became politically explosive at the fin de siècle for two reasons. First, the theater arguably reached its greatest cultural impact in modern France during the 1880s and 1890s. In this period, half a million Parisians went weekly to the theater, and more than a million went monthly; in society, it served as the primary topic of conversation. "The population of Paris lives in the theater, for the theater, by the theater," observed one journalist.[179] Second, structural shifts in education and employment created new opportunities for women that destabilized the grip of domestic ideology on the construction of gender and gave rise to a full-scale debate on female identity.[180] In this explosive cultural landscape, the subversive potential of the actress made her an "actor" in a double sense — a key agent in the transformation of gender identity as well as a performer on stage. The example of Marguerite Durand — actress, feminist, journalist, new woman — reveals the volatile cultural stage of the fin de siècle. In her, actress and agent, acting and acting *up* blended in a potent if unstable mix.

NOTES

I am grateful to the American Council of Learned Societies, the National Endowment for the Humanities, the Stanford Institute for Research on Women and Gender, and the Stanford Humanities Center for the financial support that made the research and writing of this article possible. I would like to thank Madame Annie Dizier-Metz and the staff at the Bibliothèque Marguerite Durand for their unerring advice and warm support. I am also grateful to Elinor Accampo, Leora Auslander, Hester Baer, Keith Baker, Edward Berenson, Lenard Berlanstein, Jacqueline Dirks, Paul Friedland, Jan Goldstein, Sheryl Kroen, Joby Margadant, Lissa McLaughlin, Paul Robinson, Aron Rodrigue, Karen Sawislak, Whitney Walton, and most importantly, Joan Scott for their criticism, support, and guidance. Earlier versions of this paper were presented to the European History Workshop at the University of Chicago, to the Stanford Humanities Center, to very helpful audiences at the Alliance Française in Chicago and at Reed College, and to the conference on biography at Santa Clara University. The author thanks these groups for their very helpful comments. Finally, a version of this essay appeared in *French Historical Studies* 24, no. 1 (fall 1996). I am grateful to the journal for permission to reprint.

1. "Confession," *La Fronde*, Oct. 1, 1903

2. See, for example, Durand's interview with *Gil blas* in 1897, "Le Feu à *La Fronde*," *Le Gil blas*, Dec. 7, 1897, Articles parus sur *La Fronde* (hereafter APSF), Bibliothèque Marguerite Durand (hereafter BMD). For a study of the paper *La Fronde* itself, see Mary Louise Roberts, "Copie subversive: Le journal-

isme féministe en France à la fin du siècle dernier," *Clio: Histoires, femmes et sociétés* (fall 1997): 230–49.

3. For an example of the notoriety of Durand's comment, see Jean-Bernard, "Les Femmes du XIXe siècle," *Journal d'ouest,* Nov. 9, 1920, Box 1, Dossier Marguerite Durand, (hereafter DMD), BMD.

4. For Durand's quarrel with other feminists, see Laurence Klejman and Florence Rochefort, *L'Egalité en marche: Le Féminisme sous la Troisième République* (Paris: Presses de la Fondation nationale des sciences politique: Des femmes, 1989), 131; Steven Hause, *Hubertine Auclert: The French Suffragette* (New Haven: Yale University Press, 1987), 175–76, 209. See "Nouvelles de féminisme," *Le Temps,* Sept. 4, 1903, APSF, BMD.

5. Klejman and Rochefort, *L'Egalité en marche,* 131. As Misme once said of Durand: "Her life was a novel." See, no title, *Minerva,* Nov. 9, 1930, Séries 80 Actualités, Biographie, DMD, Fonds Marie-Louise Bouglé, Bibliothèque Historique de la ville de Paris (hereafter FMLB, BHVP).

6. See Bernard Voyenne, *Les Journalistes français: D'où viennent-ils, qui sont-ils? que font-ils?* (Paris: CFPJ, 1985), 201, for this type of treatment of Durand.

7. The two biographies of Durand are Jean Rabaut's, *Marguerite Durand (1864–1936): "La Fronde" féministe ou "Le Temps" en jupons* (Paris: L'Harmattan, 1996) and Sue Helder Goliber's, "The Life and Times of Marguerite Durand: A Study in French Feminism" (Ph.D. diss., Kent State University, 1975). See also Annie Dizier-Metz, *La Bibliothèque Marguerite Durand, Histoire d'une femme, mémoire des femmes* (Paris: Mairie de Paris-Agence Culturelle de Paris, 1992), 77–80, for a brief but illuminating account of Durand's life, as well as a superb bibliography. For *La Fronde,* see Sylvie Cesbron, "Un Journal féministe en 1900: *La Fronde* (1897–1903)" Mémoire dactylographiée, BMD; Irène Jami, "*La Fronde* (1897–1903) et son rôle dans la défense des femmes salariées" (Paris: Université de Paris I, Mémoire de Maîtrise, 1981); Odile Welfelé, "*La Fronde*: Histoire d'une entreprise de presse," (Thèse, École de Chartres, 1982). For Durand's feminist views, see Rabaut, *Marguerite Durand;* Dizier-Metz, *La Bibliothèque Marguerite Durand,* and Klejman and Rochefort, *L'Egalité en marche,* chap. 4.

8. I will be looking specifically at Durand's prewar approach to politics. A comparison of Durand's pre- and postwar writings demonstrates that the Great War was a turning point in terms of her feminism. After the war, Durand became a much more conventional feminist, not only because she began to support the vote, but also because her manuscripts from the twenties and thirties simply repeat the mainstream feminist ideology of more prominent figures such as Maria Vérone, Jane Misme, and Suzanne Grinberg. Hence the truly original phase of Durand's political career was before the war, where I focus.

9. This is how the Belgian paper *Eventail* paraphrased the substance of her talk to a group of German women on the subject of feminism in France in "Les Comédiens français à Berlin," Jan. 26, 1902, Folder "Le Théâtre à Berlin" (hereafter FTB), Box 1, DMD, BMD. The article was originally printed in *Le Temps,* Jan. 19, 1902.

10. Debora Silverman, *Art Nouveau in Fin-de-Siècle France: Politics, Psychology and Style* (Berkeley and Los Angeles: University of California Press, 1989), 70.

11. See Norma Clarke, "From Plaything to Professional: The English Actress, 1660–1990," *Gender and History* 5, no. 1 (spring 1993): 120–24.

12. Georges Lhermitte, "L'Effort," *Le Droit des femmes,* April 1936. Lhermitte was a lawyer and a feminist activist and the husband of the feminist leader Maria Vérone.

13. D. Etchard, "Chronique de fin de décembre," no title or date, APSF, BMD.

14. One exception to this was "Chez les frondeuses," *L'Illustration,* Jan. 15, 1898, Archives La Fronde (hereafter ALF), Box 1, BMD where Durand's journalistic experience is discussed in detail.

15. George Marchant, "Les Femmes journalistes," *L'Intérêt capital,* no date (1898?) APSF, BMD; Jeanne Landre, "Une Feuille féminine," no title or date (1898?) ALF, Box 1, BMD; "Chez les frondeuses." See also Sorgue, "Lysistrata: *La Fronde* journal féminin et féministe," *La Petite République,* no date, APSF, BMD; "Madame Durand Now a Power in France," *New York Journal,* March 1902, ALF, Box 1, BMD; "The Story of *La Fronde,*" *The Young Woman,* Feb. 3, 1901, APSF, BMD; and also Robert Sherard, no title, *Saturday Review,* Dec. 11, 1897, APSF, BMD. The image lingered until her death and is reinscribed in contemporary historiography. See Henry de Forge, "Du Haut du balcon: Vive *la Fronde,*" No place, March 18, 1922, ALF, Box 3, BMD; François Ferrand, "Marguerite Durand," *Le Médical* (?), Sept. 19, 1936, Folder Notices Biographiques, Box 1, DMD, BMD; Jean Rabaut, *Féministes à la Belle Epoque* (Paris: Editions France-Empire, 1985), 115; Evelyne Sullerot, *La Presse féminine* (Paris: Librairie Armand Colin, 1963), 38.

16. Cited in Landre, "Une Feuille féminine." See also "L'Actualité: La Fondation d'un journal exclusivement féminine," no place, no date, APSF, BMD.

17. "Opinions: Vrai féminisme," *L'Éclair,* Sept. 1900, APSF, BMD and cited in D. Etchart, "Chronique de fin de décembre," no place, no date, APSF, BMD. See also Marie Dutoit, "À Travers le féminisme," no place, no date (1899?) APSF, BMD. Like many other eighteenth-century figures, Marie Antoinette was enjoying a popular revival at the end of the century. See Silverman, *Art Nouveau,* chap. 8, particularly 144; and Terry Castle, "Marie Antoinette Obsession," in *The Apparitional Lesbian: Female Homosexuality and Modern Culture* (New York: Columbia University Press, 1993), 107–49.

18. Burke's image was recirculated in fin-de-siècle hagiographic accounts of Marie Antoinette's life. See, for example, Catherine Hyde's *Secret Memoirs of Princess Lamballe* (1901) where she describes Marie Antoinette as "a brilliant star." Quoted in Castle, *Apparitional Lesbian.*

19. Georges Avril, "Les Journalières," *L'Éclaireur* (Nice) Sept. 2, 1903, APSF, BMD.

20. Séverine, "Marguerite Durand," *Volonté,* 12 June 1926, Box 1, DMD, BMD.

21. Dutoit, "À Travers le féminisme."

22. "Portraits de femmes," *Carnet mondial de Jocelyne,* March 31, 1898, APSF, BMD. On fetishistic attention to women in the French Third Republic, see Abigail Solomon-Godeau, "The Legs of the Countess," in *Fetishism as Cultural Discourse,* ed. Emily Apter and William Piete (Ithaca: Cornell University Press, 1993), 266–306.

23. No title, *Le Journal,* June 29, 1898, APSF, BMD; "Courrier de Paris," *Journal de Marseilles,* Dec. 12, 1903, ALF, Box 3, BMD.

24. See Folder "Biographie," Box 1, DMD, BMD, for a copy of the sonnet, dated 1887. See also André Gayot, "Les Comédiennes et le féminisme: Madame Marguerite Durand," *La Rampe,* May 7, 1922, where the sonnet was reprinted.

25. Quoted in Landre, "Une Feuille féminine." See also the remarks of Myriam Harry in Jane Misme, "Les Pionnières: La Vie d'action de Marguerite Durand," *La Française,* Jan. 25, 1936, in Folder Biographie, Box 1, DMD, BMD.

26. "F," "Au jour le jour: Madame Durand de Valfère," *Le Soleil,* Dec. 7, 1897, APSF, BMD.

27. Séverine, "Marguerite Durand."

28. Etchard, "Chronique de fin de décembre"; "Courrier de Paris"; "Portraits de femmes"; Sorgue, "Lysistrata."

29. "F," "Au jour le jour."

30. See also "Chez les frondeuses," *L'Illustration,* and Landre, "Une Feuille féminine." Again, this perspective of Durand has been reproduced in the historiographical literature. See, for example, Sullerot, *La Presse féminine,* 38.

31. Durand was at the Conservatoire two years, and won *Première accessit* her first year, and *Première prix, comédie,* in her second year. She was hired by the Comédie-Française at the age of seventeen. See "Notes autobiographiques adressées à Jane Misme en 1930," Fonds spéciales Jane Misme, BMD; Goliber, "Life and Times," 2–4; Marie-Rose de Labriolle, "Une Femme à l'avant-garde de son époque: Marguerite Durand, 1864–1936," *Femmes diplômées,* 69 (1969), 2. A small dossier on Marguerite Durand exists at the Archives de la Comédie-Française, including documents on her engagement and retirement, a photo, and some press clippings.

32. When writing autobiographical narratives, Durand chose instead to dwell on previous journalistic experience. See, for example, "Les Femmes dans le journalisme," Manuscrits, vol. 3, BMD.

33. On the Berlin trip, see FTB, Box 1, DMD, BMD. The folder includes elaborate financial notes and a printed report detailing start-up costs for the theater. For the publicity surrounding the tour, see particularly "Paris à Berlin," no place or date, this folder. According to this article, Durand created such crowds that the police had to intervene in order to maintain order. The tour, and particularly the performances in Berlin, were heavily reported in the Parisian and provincial press. Durand and Coquelin, accompanied by the troupe of the Théâtre de la Porte-Saint-Martin, performed *Cyrano de Bergerac, Mademoiselle de la Seiglière,* and a Soirée Molière, including *Tartuffe* and *Les Précieuses.*

34. No title, *L'Éclaireur de l'est,* Jan. 14, 1902, and "Les Comédiens français à Berlin," both in FTB, Box 1, DMD, BMD.

35. Letter of Mme. Jules Allix to Marguerite Durand, Aug. 5, 1901, Correspondents to Marguerite Durand, vol. 1, A-G, BMD. See also "La Sainte Marguerite," *La Fronde,* July 21, 1899. Here the (anonymous) author claims that a party gathered in honor of Durand formed around her "a veritable *parterre.*"

36. "F," "Au jour le jour."

37. Séverine, "Marguerite Durand."

38. See Goliber, *Life and Times,* 89–102. The electoral district was the ninth arrondissement in Paris. However, Durand distinguished her type of feminism from that of the British suffragist movement. "Such a campaign is impossible in France," she argued, because "it would quickly be stopped by ridicule." See "Une Campagne féministe: Une Interview de Madame Marguerite Durand," *Gazette du Midi,* Feb. 10, 1910, and "Pas de femmes," *Nouvelliste de Bretagne,* Feb. 8, 1910, both in Folder Candidate aux Élections Legislatives de 1910 (hereafter FCAEL), Box 2, DMD, BMD.

39. Théâtre des Deux Masques is one such theater. See "Les Élections legislatives," *Echo d'Oran,* April 12, 1910, and "Avant les élections: Premières réunions," no place given, March 26, 1910, FCAEL, Box 2, DMD, BMD. For the connection between Durand's training as an actress and her skills as an orator, see her "L'Art oratoire," *Manuscrits,* vol. 3, BMD.

40. *Intransigeant,* March 25, 1910; "La Citoyenne Marguerite Durand," no place, April 9, 1910; and "Avant les élections," all in FCAEL, Box 2, DMD, BMD.

41. Charles Vincent, "Feminisme et politique," no place, March 27, 1910, Box 2, DMD, BMD. Vincent again refers to "cette séduction du verbe et de la personne . . . "

42. See J.-A. Boulanger-Chabrol, "Le Féminisme," *Écho,* April 5, 1902; "Le Féminisme aux élections," *Écho de Paris,* March 24, 1910; "Madame Durand devant ses électeurs," *République de Var,* March 25, 1910; Gaston Derys, "Chronique parisienne," *La Femme chic,* no date given (April 1910); "Madame Durand candidate," *L'Éclair,* April 1, 1910; Vincent, "Feminisme et politique" and "La Citoyenne Marguerite Durand," all in FCAEL, Box 2, DMD, BMD. See also "L'Idiot, le candidat et la suffragette," no place, April 14, 1910, DMD, FMLB, BHVP.

43. The incident is remembered by Maurice Donnay at the time of Durand's death. See his "Nuances," *Paris-Soir,* March 23, 1936, Folder Obséques, Box 3, DMD, BMD.

44. See F. W. J. Hemmings, *The Theatre Industry in Nineteenth-Century France* (Cambridge, Eng.: Cambridge University Press, 1993), 135–43.

45. Jonas Barish, *The Antitheatrical Prejudice* (Berkeley and Los Angeles: University of California Press, 1981), 256–94. For Rousseau's *Lettre à d'Alembert sur les spectacles,* I have relied on the 1896 edition and on the translation by Allan Bloom, *Politics and the Arts: Letter to M. d'Alembert on the Theatre* (Glencoe, Ill.: The Free Press, 1960). In his important dissertation, "Representation and Revolution: The Theatricality of Politics and the Politics of Theater in France, 1789–1794" (Ph.D. diss., University of California, Berkeley, 1995), chap. 4, Paul Friedland makes a distinction between an antitheatricality based on the perceived illicit content of the plays and one that opposed theater as a cultural form altogether.

46. See Barish, *The Antitheatrical Prejudice,* 283, 295, 321–24, 337–43; Rachel Brownstein, *Tragic Muse: Rachel of the Comédie-Française* (New York: Alfred A. Knopf, 1993), 43.

47. Hence, Rousseau said of Molière, "His greatest care is to ridicule good-

ness and simplicity and to present treachery and falsehood so that they arouse our interest and sympathy" and "The most criminal acts are wantonly gathered together here with a playfulness which makes all this pass for nicety." *Lettre,* 54, 71; *Politics and the Arts,* 34, 46.

48. Ibid., *Lettre,* 122; *Politics and the Arts,* 80–81. Bloom uses the word "annihilates" instead of "obliterates." On the notion of Rousseau and the "obliteration" of the self, see particularly David Marshall, "Rousseau and the State of Theater," *Representations* 13 (winter 1986): 90–91.

49. In short, the acting profession challenged Rousseau's ideal of transparency. See Jean Starobinski, *Jean-Jacques Rousseau: La Transparence et l'obstacle* (Paris: Librairie Plon, 1957), 1, 9. In my translation, I rely in part on Jean Starobinski, *Jean-Jacques Rousseau: Transparency and Obstruction,* trans. Arthur Goldhammer (Chicago: University of Chicago Press, 1988). For an important analysis of the theater and Rousseau's ideal of transparency that also brings into account political notions of representation at the time of the revolution, see Friedland, "Representation and Revolution." On this subject, see also James Johnson, "Revolutionary Audiences and the Impossible Imperatives of Fraternity," in *Recreating Authority in Revolutionary France,* ed. Bryant T. Ragan Jr. and Elizabeth A. Williams (New Brunswick, N.J.: Rutgers University Press, 1992), 68–74.

50. Rousseau, *Lettre,* 136. Even an "honest and prudent woman," according to Rousseau, had "great difficulty in keeping a faithful heart." For a helpful analysis of Rousseau's treatment of the actress, see Barish, *Antitheatrical Prejudice,* 282–86; Friedland, "Representation and Revolution," chap. 4. For a brief analysis of the antitheatrical tradition and actresses, see also Brownstein, *Tragic Muse,* 43.

51. Rousseau, *Lettre,* 138; *Politics and Art,* 90–91.

52. For Rousseau's views on the "natural" woman, see Peggy Kamuf de Magnin, "Rousseau's Politics of Visibility," *Diacritics* (winter 1975): 51; Joel Schwartz, *The Sexual Politics of Jean-Jacques Rousseau* (Chicago: University of Chicago Press, 1984); Carol Pateman, *The Sexual Contract* (Stanford: Stanford University Press, 1988).

53. Le Baron Fréderic de Reiffenberg, *Ce que c'est qu'une actrice* (Paris: Ferdinand Sartorius, 1861), 38, 40.

54. Octave Mirbeau, *Gens de théâtre* (1924); cited in Barish, *The Antitheatrical Prejudice,* 340–41.

55. J. Barbey d'Aurevilley, *Les Vieilles actrices* (Paris: Librairie des auteurs modernes, 1884), 5, 45–46, 51–52. See also Reiffenberg, *Ce que c'est.* As late as 1929, a history of eighteenth-century actresses portrayed them as *"donneuses d'illusion"* without sound judgment or virtue. See Henri Lyonnet, *La Vie au dix-huitième siècle: Les Comédiennes* (Paris: Éditions Marcel Seheur, 1929), 220.

56. Léon Bloy, *Le Désespéré* (1887), quoted in Barish, *The Antitheatrical Prejudice,* 321–22.

57. Jules Lemaître, "Jean-Jacques Rousseau et le Théâtre," *Impressions de Théâtre,* Sixième Série (Paris: Lecène, Oudin et Cie, 1892), 139–40

58. Lemaître, *Impressions de Théâtre,* Première Série (Paris: Lecène, Oudin et Cie, 1888), 307–8.

59. As Baudelaire put it in 1859, "The actress comes close to the courtesan," because she "too is a creature of show, an object of public pleasure." See Baudelaire, "The Painter of Modern Life," (1859–1860) *Selected Writings on Art and Literature*, trans. by P. E. Charvet (New York: Penguin Books, 1972), 431.

60. Émile Zola, *Nana, Oeuvres complètes* (Paris: Bernouard, 1928), 32–33; translation in part by George Holden (New York: Penguin Books, 1972), 45–46. Bordenave, the manager of the theater where Nana is performing, describes his establishment as a "brothel," 48.

61. F. Ladevi-Roche, "Confluent d'égouts," 1903, no place, Folder "L'Action", Box 1, DMD, BMD.

62. See Sorgue, "Lysistrata." Durand argued that actresses should organize to force stage managers to pay for their costumes and thus not have to make the cruel choice of "either renouncing theatrical art or becoming prostitutes."

63. Hemmings, *The Theatre Industry*, 201–4. For a contemporary source, see Jeanne Marcya, *La Femme au théâtre* (Paris: Imprimerie G. Jeulin, 1901), 42–45.

64. Bernard Briais, *Au temps des frous-frous* (Paris: Editions France-Empire, 1985), 82–83. See also Arthur Gold and Robert Fizdale, *The Divine Sarah: A Life of Sarah Bernhardt* (New York: Alfred A. Knopf, 1991), a recent biography of Bernhardt that focuses largely on the actress's personal relationships.

65. When Durand was ill in the hospital in March 1899, the papers reported that Bernhardt visited her several times. See *Journal d'Alsace*, March 29, 1899, APSF, BMD. Bernhardt was also lavishly praised in the pages of *La Fronde*. See Daniel LeSueur, "Prêtresse de la beauté," *La Fronde*, Jan. 28, 1898.

66. Cited in Hemmings, *The Theatre Industry*, 147–48. For the popularity of the theater, see Eugen Weber, *France Fin de siècle* (Cambridge, Mass.: Harvard University Press, 1986), chap. 8.

67. Léopold Lacour, *Les Premières actrices françaises* (Paris: Librairie Française, 1921), introduction. Lacour was the husband of *frondeuse* Mary Lacour and a frequenter of Durand's circles. For a similar portrait of the actress, see also the more contemporary Émile Bergerat et al., *Les Actrices de Paris* (Paris: Librairie artistique illustrée, 1882), 2, 16, 49.

68. Rousseau, *Lettre*, 73; *Politics and Art*, 47–48.

69. Sarah Bernhardt, *The Memoirs of Sarah Bernhardt,* (New York: Peebles Press, 1977), 138.

70. For a classic example of this kind of discourse, see Bergerat, *Les Actrices de Paris*. Current historiography reinscribes this idealizing narrative. See, for example, Briais, *Au temps des frous-frous,* 104.

71. See P. Lacome, *Les Étoiles du passé* (Paris: Paul Dupont, 1897), 59. Rachel Brownstein argues that actresses also signified "Woman" herself. They were "artful, artificial and duplicitous" but also "excitingly, transgressively true to the passions and the imagination." Because female sexuality was conceived of "as an excess of either nature or artifice," actresses "were taken to stand for Woman." See her *Tragic Muse*, 43.

72. See, for example, Arthur Pougin, *Acteurs, actrices d'autrefois* (Paris: F. Juven et Cie, 1896), 23.

73. Alfred Mortier, "Les Premières actrices françaises," *La Griffe*, Dec. 15, 1925, Dossier Théâtre, BMD.

74. See, for example, Marcya, *La Femme au théâtre*, particularly 11–18, 45–47. For a more optimistic view, see Camille Le Senne, "Racontars," *L'Evénement*, July 13, 1899, Dossier Comédie-Française, BMD.

75. Hemmings, *The Theatre Industry*, 199. Hemmings also argues, 200, however, that although the world of the theater could be considered in some ways "a world more attuned to the late twentieth than to the nineteenth century," it still "remained firmly anchored in the period," in the sense that many young actresses remained dependent on older male "protectors" who took control over all aspects of their careers from the period of their training onward. See also Viv Gardner and Susan Rutherford, *The New Woman and Her Sisters: Feminism and Theatre, 1850–1914* (New York: Harvester Wheatsheaf, 1992), introduction, 7, considering the emancipatory possibilities of the theater for women. This book focuses mostly on England, not France.

76. See Cornelia Otis Skinner, *Madame Sarah* (Boston: Houghton-Mifflin, 1967), 250.

77. Since Bernhardt was herself the daughter of a *demimondaine*, her hopes for a "respectable" marriage had always been dim.

78. As Jann Matlock has shown, the notion of seduction had a complex, multilayered history in nineteenth-century France, one to which I cannot do justice within the confines of this article. Durand's use of seduction as a political tactic clearly had resonances to other cultural meanings besides that of the actress. For the many associations to the "story" of seduction, see particularly Matlock's epilogue, *Scenes of Seduction: Prostitution, Hysteria and Reading Difference in Nineteenth-Century France* (New York: Columbia University Press, 1994), 307.

79. The man who is believed to be Durand's father, General Alfred Boucher, never recognized her as his daughter. He was a royalist and a grand officer of the legion of honor. See Goliber, "Life and Times," 1; Rabaut, *Féministes à la Belle Epoque*, 116. It is worth noting that Sarah Bernhardt and Marguerite Durand had quite similar early lives. Both were born the illegitimate children of fathers who were of high birth and failed to recognize their daughters. Each spent her childhood at a convent school, sent by mothers who wished to make them more respectable. Both ultimately rebelled against such an education in order to enter into early careers as actresses. Both went to the Conservatoire and then found work on the stage of the Comédie-Française. Finally, both worked with many of the same great actors of their day, namely Coquelin and Mounet-Sully.

80. See also Goliber, "Life and Times," 4, where she argues that while the marriage has been interpreted as a "desire to gain bourgeois respectability," Durand could just as easily have done it to assure her access into politics.

81. For a close look at these years of Durand's life, see her *Carnet*, July 6 to August 1, 1889, BMD. It is clear from this document that Durand was deeply immersed in the Boulangist campaign, that she discussed politics with all the major players in the movement, and that her own private advice was taken seriously. See also X . . . du *Figaro, Les Coulisses du Boulangisme* (Paris: Léopold Cerf, 1890), 219–24. For the term "Madame Roland du Boulangisme," see Bing, "Tête de turc: Mme. Marguerite Durand," *Fantasio*, April 1, 1910, Folder

Notices Biographiques, Box 2, DMD, BMD; and Larent Lasne, *L'Ile aux chiens: La Cimetière des chiens Asnières* (Bois-Colombes: A. Val-Arno, 1988). On the salonnières, see Carolyn Lougee, *"Le Paradis des femmes": Women, Salons, and Social Stratification in Seventeenth-Century France* (Princeton: Princeton University Press, 1976), and Dena Goodman, *The Republic of Letters: A Cultural History of the French Enlightenment* (Ithaca: Cornell University Press, 1994), particularly chap. 3.

82. The anecdote is retold in several places, but one example is Bing, "Tête de turc," and Ferrand, "Marguerite Durand."

83. Bing, "Tête de turc."

84. See, for example, "Les Femmes dans le journalisme," 27–29.

85. Clips of the column are available in a special scrapbook at the BMD. See Goliber, *Life and Times,* 10.

86. See Mss. 31, *Carnet,* Jan. 22 to Dec. 14, 1897, BMD. The incident took place on June 26 when Durand took the infant to see his father. In her words, "le père de mon enfant aidé de deux de ses amis, s'est jeté sur moi, m'a renversée, frappée . . . m'a traînée jusque sur la route. . . ." The reason for the quarrel was not made clear in the *Carnet,* but Durand was clearly traumatized by the incident, which underlined her marginality and powerlessness as a single mother. She received the child back on July 3.

87. See Goliber, *Life and Times,* 11. According to Labriolle, "Une Femme à l'avant-garde," Durand was assigned to report on the conference; Goliber implies that she went to the conference because of an invitation to hear the well-known feminist Maria Pognon. Again according to Labriolle, the article for *Le Figaro* was never written, and indeed, I was unable to find it, although there are several other articles on the conference in these pages. See "Notes autobiographiques adressées à Jane Misme," and see also Huguette Champy, "Résumé de la conférence: Une Grande féministe, Marguerite Durand, 1864–1936," Folder "Notices sur Marguerite Durand," Box 1, DMD, BMD. Here Champy recreates the instructions that Durand's editor at *Le Figaro* gave her concerning "*des folles*" at the Feminist Congress.

88. "Les Femmes dans le journalisme," 26–27. For a contemporary journalist's version of this philosophy, see Daniel Riche, no title, *Littoral,* Jan. 31, 1898, APSF, BMD: "Les hommes luttent avec leur poing et les femmes avec leur sourire. Elles ont là une arme redoutable qu'elles ont bien tort de dédaigner." Durand said much the same thing in an article in *La Fronde,* Dec. 15, 1902: "Aux hommes le forum, aux femmes le foyer . . . Ainsi pensait alors la majorité. J'étais de la majorité."

89. For the ideology of "*la vraie femme*," see Edward Berenson, *The Trial of Madame Caillaux* (Berkeley and Los Angeles: University of California Press, 1992), 92; Bonnie Smith, *Ladies of the Leisure Class: The Bourgeoises of Northern France in the Nineteenth Century* (Princeton: Princeton University Press, 1981); Anne Martin-Fugier's *La Bourgeoise* (Paris: Bernard Grasset, 1983). For the influence of Michelet on the nineteenth-century representation of women, see Thérèse Moreau, *La Sang de l'histoire: Michelet, l'histoire et l'idée de la femme au XIXe siècle* (Paris: Flammarion, 1982).

90. For the new woman, see Silverman, *Art Nouveau;* and Jo B. Margadant,

Madame le Professeur: Women Educators in the Third Republic (Princeton: Princeton University Press, 1990). The phenomenon of the new woman was in great part due to legislation such as the Camille Sée Law of 1880, which established secondary education for women. The number of lycée degrees obtained by women jumped from forty-three hundred to thirteen thousand in the years 1885 to 1900. See Silverman, 66.

91. Jane Misme, "La Femme dans le théâtre nouveau," *La Revue d'art dramatique*, Oct. 1901, 608. After the war, Misme became one of the most prominent feminists in France and editor of the feminist *La Française*. Like many others of her generation, Misme's early career as a journalist and feminist was bolstered by her presence on *La Fronde*'s staff.

92. Durand never directly explained why feminism attracted her in 1896 or what galvanized her to give "this noble cause" a newspaper. But in her "Confession," she once noted that everything feminism meant to her could be found in her preface to the *Congrès international de la condition et des droits des femmes* (Paris: Imprimerie des arts et manufactures, 1901). Here Durand argues that feminist discourse exposed a contradiction between two central discourses in nineteenth-century French bourgeois republican culture: the domestic ideal of the real woman and the liberal ideal of individualism. While most French would not contest the goals of individual self-fulfillment, she argued, they rigidly insisted on defining the female individual in terms of the domestic ideal, thus often abrogating the opportunity for individual self-fulfillment in women. In this sense, the domestic ideal of the real woman is at odds with liberal individualism. By exposing this contradiction, feminist discourse marked the limits of ideological certainty for Durand. Feminism, she argued, "teaches women to get used to counting on themselves, to assert their personality . . . It demands that they prove to be who they really are and not what they are made." For the notion that feminists expose contradictions in republican ideology, see Joan W. Scott, "French Feminists and the Rights of 'Man': Olympe de Gouges's Declarations," *History Workshop* 28 (autumn 1989): 1–21; "Rewriting the History of Feminism," *Western Humanities Review* 58 (fall 1994): 238–51; *Only Paradoxes to Offer: French Feminists and the Rights of Man* (Cambridge, Mass.: Harvard University Press, 1996)

93. Fogg, "Le Feu à '*La Fronde*,'" APSF, BMD. See also Durand, "Les Femmes dans le journalisme," 28–29. Later, Durand recalled that at the time of the congress, she considered feminist ideas to be the "idées de détraquées." For an expression of many of the same ideas, see Durand, "Le Féminisme," Manuscrits, vol. 1, 9–10 (archivist pagination); "Notes autobiographiques adressées à Jane Misme," and Madame Harlor, "Interview de Madame Marguerite Durand préparée pour Radio-Paris," (1935), Manuscript, BMD.

94. Maurice Leudet, "Au jour le jour: Congrès féministe," *Le Figaro*, April 7, 1896. See also the article by Jules Bois, "Quelques silhouettes de féministes," *Le Figaro*, April 8, 1896.

95. "Le Congrès féministe," *Le Figaro*, April 9, 1896. Durand later said, "Les Femmes dans le journalisme," 36: At the time it was fashionable to critique (not sometimes without reason) the tendency among certain women intellectuals to scorn elegance and assume what were then called "*des allures garçonnières*."

For an illuminating interpretation of the discourse of the bluestocking in the early nineteenth century, see Geneviève Fraisse, *Reason's Muse: Sexual Difference and the Birth of Democracy* (Chicago: University of Chicago Press, 1994), particularly chap. 2, and 89–90.

96. Le Passant, "Leur congrès," *Le Figaro,* April 12, 1896.

97. E. Ledrain, "Opinions: Vrai féminisme," *L'Éclair,* Sept. ?, 1900, APSF, BMD.

98. See Silverman, *Art Nouveau,* 63, 69–70.

99. Quoted in Silverman, *Art Nouveau,* 69–70.

100. Naomi Schor, *Reading in Detail: Aesthetics and the Feminine* (New York: Routledge, 1987), particularly chap. 1, "Gender: In the Academy."

101. In *Art Nouveau,* chap. 4, Silverman argues that among the members of the Central Union of the Decorative Arts, the institutional home of French Art Nouveau, the threat of the new woman led to the celebration of the decorative arts and their links to female domesticity. Debates about women and the ornamental (associated with Gustav Klimt and the Viennese Secession) also shaped the response to Art Nouveau in Austria. In 1902, the Viennese art critic Adolf Loos denounced ornament as a sign of cultural decadence and lauded a more functionalist aesthetic. Playing on the traditional links between the female and the decorative, Loos predicted that as women gained economic independence and no longer relied on an appeal to sensuality in order to attract a man and gain power, all female sartorial ornament would become outmoded. For Loos, see Carl Schorske, *Fin-De-Siècle Vienna: Politics and Culture* (New York: Random House, 1981), 339; Schor, *Reading in Detail,* 52–53.

102. Leudet, "Au Jour le jour," *Le Figaro,* April 7, 1896. The word "empire" is frequently used to describe a woman's seductive power. See also Bergerat, *Les Actrices de Paris,* 51.

103. Emphasis mine. Marguerite Durand, "Un Peu de féminisme," *Le Nouveau siècle,* Feb. 27, 1910, Box 2, DMD, BMD.

104. "Confession." For other *frondeuses* who make the same kind of argument, see Raquette, "Sporting notes," *La Fronde,* Dec. 10, 1897; Daniel LeSueur, "A Propos d'une . . . robe," *La Fronde,* March 11, 1898. Durand seemed to be following the advice of Baron Tanneguy de Wogan, who addressed women journalists in this way in 1897: "If your vocation, your means, encourage you to cover paper with writing, eh! My God, do it! That's my advice, but at the same time live like a good *petite bourgeoise* or like a simple *mondaine,* according to your fortune." See his *Manuel des gens de lettres* (Paris: Librairie de Paris, 1897), 33.

105. "Confession." As the feminist Jane Misme later put it, "By her appearance alone, she offered a correction to the obstinate cliches of that time, which portrayed all feminists as ageless, ugly creatures, ridiculously dressed." "Les Pionnières." See also Misme, no title, DMD, BHVP: "Never was there a woman who was more woman with more virile gifts."

106. "Portraits de femmes"; J. L., "Les Cheveux et le féminisme," *Le Républicain,* June 5, 1910, Folder Obséques, Box 3, DMD, BMD. For a similar view of feminists, see also the novel *Emancipées* by Albert Cim (Paris: Flammarion, 1899), 103.

107. "Portraits de femmes."

108. For the centrality of visual propaganda to Boulangism, see Jean-Marie Mayeur and Madeleine Rebérioux, *The Third Republic from its Origins to the Great War* (Cambridge, Eng.: Cambridge University Press, 1984), 127; Michael Burns, *Rural Society and French Politics: Boulangism and the Dreyfus Affair, 1886–1900* (Princeton: Princeton University Press, 1984), 59–69, 115; James Harding, *The Astonishing Adventure of General Boulanger* (New York: Charles Scribner's Sons, 1971), 121–24; Adrien Dansette, *Du Boulangisme à la révolution dreyfusienne: Le Boulangisme, 1886–1890* (Paris: Perrin, 1938), 86–88; Jacques Néré, *Le Boulangisme et la presse* (Paris: Armand Colin, 1964).

109. "Les Femmes dans le journalisme," 3. For the press at the fin de siècle, see the following: Claude Bellanger et al., *De 1871 à 1940*, vol. 3, *L'Histoire de la presse française* (Paris: PUF, 1972); Raymond Manévy, *La Presse de la Troisième Republique* (Paris: Foret, 1955); Michael Palmer, *Des petits journaux aux grandes agences* (Paris: Aubier, 1983); Thomas Ferenczi, *L'Invention du journalisme en France. Naissance de la presse moderne à la fin de XIXè siècle* (Paris: Plon, 1993).

110. See Jules Allix, "Chronique féministe," *Bulletin bimestrial de la Société pour l'amélioration du sort de la femme,* Nov. 15, 1897, APSF, BMD; Paul Lafage, "Souvenirs de 'Frondeuse,'" no place, no date (1903?), ALF, Box 1, BMD.

111. "Les Femmes dans le journalisme," 7. In addition, journalism had always been "a primary school of diplomacy," argued Durand, and men such as Briand, Viviani, and Poincaré had all been journalists. In the same way, then, journalism could serve as an entry point for women into politics. See ibid., 1–2.

112. On feminist journalism as a way to control the production of gender knowledge, see Nina Gelbart's, *Feminine and Opposition Journalism in Old Regime France: Le Journal des dames* (Berkeley and Los Angeles: University of California Press, 1987), 293, where she argues that the editors of *Le Journal des dames* saw journalism "as a way of influencing their public . . . the editors strove to counter misogynistic attitudes in women as well as men and to nurture their female readers' feelings of self-worth." In *Histoire de la presse féminine en France, des origines à 1848* (Paris: Armand Colin, 1966), 211, Evelyne Sullerot calls the feminine press "l'expression d'une prise de conscience collective . . . du monde féminin." And in *À l'aube du féminisme: Les Premières journalistes, 1830–1850* (Paris: Payot, 1979), 75, Laure Adler argues that feminists used journalism in order to "aider, sensibiliser et transformer l'image de la femme dans toutes les couches de la société." For a brief history of women in journalism, see Voyenne, *Les Journalistes français,* 214–22.

113. Emphasis mine. "Les Femmes dans le journalisme," 35. On Feb. 5, 1910, an article in *Gil blas* agreed: "C'est une charmante et jolie Parisienne, qui rend le féminisme attrayant." See Box 2, DMD, BMD.

114. Vincent, "Feminisme et politique." See also "Madame Durand candidate," FCAEL, Box 2, DMD, BMD.

115. "Pour l'honneur," *La Fronde,* Sept. 25, 1898.

116. "Les Comédiens français à Berlin."

117. Hause, *Hubertine Auclert,* 209. For Durand's quarrels with other femi-

nists, see also Rabaut, *Féministes à la Belle Epoque*, 116; Steven Hause with Anne R. Kenney, *Women's Suffrage and Social Politics in the French Third Republic* (Princeton: Princeton University Press, 1984), 290. By contrast, in *Les Filles de Marianne: Histoire de féminismes, 1914–1940* (Paris: Fayard, 1995), 35–36, Christine Bard seems to brush off Durand's troubles with other feminists.

118. Doctoresse Pelletier, *Mémoire d'une féministe* (c. 1933), 10–11; Fonds Madeleine Pelletier, FMLB, BHVP. Joan Scott brought this quotation to my attention.

119. Durand also did this, in part, to avoid trouble with the law. Since *La Fronde* was a morning paper, the typographers had to work late thus breaking a Law of 1892 that forbade women to work at night and that was immediately invoked by the Chambre Syndicale des hommes typographes. According to the Société coopérative de femmes typographes, women became "patronnes associées" who could work when and how they wanted. See Dizier-Metz, *La Bibliothèque Marguerite Durand*, 14. The C.G.T., of course, was suspicious of Durand's position as "patronne" simultaneously of a paper and a *syndicat*. See "Journal à plusieurs voix," *L'Esprit*, (1975), 341, Box 1, DMD, BMD.

120. See Sylvie Cesbron, "Un Journal féministe en 1900," 77, 80–85; Irène Jami, "*La Fronde*, quotidien féministe," particularly 233–40. Jami argues, 233, that "*La Fronde* se fait l'écho des revendications des travailleuses. Elle rend régulièrement compte de leur conditions de travail, de leurs luttes, de leurs grèves." Cesbron quotes the feminist Marie Bonnevial crediting Durand with the growth of women's unions during these years: "Marguerite Durand s'est donnée pour tâche d'aider par tous les moyens . . . les travailleuses à se syndiquer; la propagande est centuplée, méthodisée, rendue permanente par le journal," *La Fronde*, 84.

121. For investigative reporting on women's work, see, for example, the articles by Aline Valette in *La Fronde*, Dec. 19 and 24, 1897; Jan. 1 and Jan. 9, 1898.

122. These ideas are elaborated in Roberts, "Copie subversive: Le journalisme féministe en France à la fin du siècle dernier."

123. See the Dossier Office du travail et des intérêts féminins, BMD. The office was officially created in 1908, sustained by funds by the Ministry of Labor, but it was operative beginning in 1907.

124. See *La Voix de peuple*, April 14, 1907. A copy of the paper appears in the Dossier Office du Travail and on it, Durand has written in large letters that she paid for everything herself. Durand was also attacked for calling the conference in the first place when she had no recognized union position. See also Ernest Bayer, "Féminisme," *Union mutuelle de Bordeaux*, April 1907 in the same dossier and "Journal à plusieurs voix," *L'Esprit*, 341.

125. In a series of lectures after the war, Durand mounted an historical defense of Imperatrice Eugenie. Despite her reputation as "a woman of frivolous spirit, a *coquette* enjoying unbridled luxury," the empress, she argued, was a serious person and an "ardent" feminist. By defending Eugenie, Durand was clearly defending her own brand of feminism and perhaps even sketching out for historians how she might want to be remembered. See "L'Imperatrice Eugenie," *Manuscrits*, vol. 1, BMD. Durand seemed to be using history for the same purpose in her exhibition on "Les Femmes célèbres du XIXe siècle" organized in

Nov. 1922. In this exhibition, women in the theater were "abundantly repre-sented," according to newspaper reports. Actresses such as Rachel were juxta-posed to activists such as Maria Déraismes.

126. "Enfin seules," No place, no date. APSF, BMD.

127. For an example of the warm regard and affection that Durand's male contemporaries held for her, see the letters from Stéphan Liègeard, Aug. 4 and Dec. 6, 1902, Correspondents of Marguerite Durand, vol. 2, BMD.

128. Léo Courbiès, "Les Lois socialists," *Le Sémaphore,* April 5, 1900, APSF, BMD.

129. For the confinement of nineteenth-century women in the home, see Smith, *Ladies of the Leisure Class.*

130. Georges Dubor, "Chronique: Journal féministe," *La Paix,* Oct. 3, 1897, APSF, BMD.

131. See Séverine, "Notes d'une frondeuse: Réponse à Ponchon," *La Fronde,* Dec. 21, 1897. For accusations of prostitution, see also Edmond Deschaumes, "Le Plat de lentilles," *Le Journal,* April 30, 1898, and "La Femme sauvée par la femme," *Le Journal,* May 30, 1898, both APSF, BMD.

132. On Durand's love life, see the informative footnote in Hause with Kenney, *Women's Suffrage,* 289–90; Christine Bard, *Les Filles de Marianne,* 35; and Goliber, *Life and Times,* 33–34, 47–49. For the rumors about Rothschild, see DMD, BHVP. In this dossier are some notes claiming that Durand was the mistress of Gustave de Rothschild at the time of the founding of *La Fronde* and that he gave her 7 million francs to make *La Fronde* a Dreyfusard paper. Such accusations were also consistently made by *La Libre parole* at the time. For the rumored liason with Clemenceau, see Paule Herfort, no title, *Marocain,* Sept. 1936, Folder Notices Biographiques, Box 1, DMD, BMD. According to Jami, "*La Fronde* et son rôle," 13, *La Fronde* began with the considerable capital of Fr 500,000.

133. See Marguerite Durand, "En cinq ans," *La Fronde,* Dec. 15, 1902. For another denial, see "Notes autobiographiques" and her Lettre à Hélène Brion, Nov. 26, 1914, *Correspondance,* vol. 1, BMD. According to Goliber, *Life and Times,* 46, Durand sold only a set of pearl earrings. Goliber's source here is a 1922 article in *La Vie de Paris* by Jean-Bernard. In "Confession," Durand admit-ted that the paper would not have lived fifteen days on the revenue from its sub-scriptions. Durand was also accused by the C.G.T.'s paper *La Voix du peuple* of having accepted funds from Clemenceau and Viviani for the Congress on Women's Work she organized in March of 1907.

134. There were in fact two libel cases against *La Libre parole,* one filed by Durand alone when this paper failed to publish a letter she wrote in response to the editor Gaston Méry, (published in *La Fronde* on Dec. 20) and one filed by Durand and her editors together for libelous remarks made on Dec. 22, 1898 by Méry. Durand lost the first suit on Feb. 1 but won the second on March 15, 1898. Fines totalling Fr 1,000 were imposed on Méry, the manager Millot, and *La Libre parole,* and Durand was able to insert announcement of the court judg-ment in ten papers of her choice, to be paid for by *La Libre parole.* When Durand received the fine money, she donated it to a *syndicat* of women typogra-phers that she was organizing. For other attacks on Durand's morality, see *La Petite république,* Oct. 4, 1897 and *L'Éclair,* Oct. 4, 1897, both APSF, BMD.

135. As a prostitute, the "femme galante" was usually associated with the theater or restaurant; she represented the new, unregulated prostitute that emerged in the late nineteenth century in order to cater to a new middle- and upper-class clientele. See Gaston Méry, "À des femmes," *La Libre parole,* Dec. 17, 1898; Marguerite Durand, "À des hommes," *La Fronde,* Dec. 18, 1898; Méry, "La Morale de Marguerite Durand," *La Libre parole,* Dec. 19, 1898; Gaston Méry, "Au jour le jour," *La Libre parole,* Dec. 21, 1898. See Alain Corbin, *Women for Hire: Prostitution and Sexuality in France after 1850* (Cambridge, Mass.: Harvard University Press, 1990), 132–36. For the accusation that Durand took money from Jewish lovers, see Gaston Méry, "Féministes et féministes," *La Libre parole,* Dec. 22, 1898.

136. Gaston Méry, "Solidarité féminine," *La Libre parole,* Dec. 27, 1898. See the Letters from Dominique Bonnard and Mme. Fautrez (?), Correspondents to Marguerite Durand, vol. 1, BMD, for an example of the kinds of requests Durand received from her connections in the acting world.

137. Luce Irigaray, *This Sex Which Is Not One,* trans. Catherine Porter with Carolyn Burke (Ithaca: Cornell University Press, 1985), "The Power of Discourse and the Subordination of the Feminine," 76. Nancy Miller cited this quotation and brought it to my attention. See her "Emphasis Added: Plots and Plausibilities in Women's Fiction" *PMLA* 96 (1981), 38. In my notion of mimicry here, I have also relied on Homi Bhabha in "Of Mimicry and Man: The Ambivalence of the Colonial Discourse," most recently anthologized in *The Location of Culture* (New York: Routledge, 1994) and the film critic Mary Anne Doane's notion of the "masquerade" of femininity (adapted from the psychoanalyst Joan Rivière) as the "wearing" of womanhood as a "mask." Like Irigaray, Doane uses the notion of distance to explain the subversive nature of masquerade: "The masquerade, in flaunting femininity, holds it at a distance. Womanliness is a mask which can be worn or removed. The masquerade's resistance to patriarchal positioning would therefore lie in its denial of the production of femininity as closeness, as presence-to-itself." See her "Film and the Masquerade," 25–26, 32 and "Masquerade Reconsidered: Further Thoughts on the Female Spectator," 33–38, both in *Femme Fatales: Feminism, Film Theory, Psychoanalysis* (New York: Routledge, 1991). Durand's "masquerade" in this way could explain the prominent journalist Arthur Meyer's somewhat cryptic description of her in 1914, at the time she was editor of *Les Nouvelles:* "Sometimes she likes to wear a hooded dress [*domino* (eq) attire for a masked ball] as she did at *La Fronde,* and sometimes a mask, as at *Les Nouvelles.*" See Arthur Meyer, *Ce que mes yeux ont vu* (Paris: Plon, 1914), 393.

138. For the phrase "but not quite," see also Homi Bhabha, "Of Mimicry and Man." In this essay, Bhabha explores the mimicry of conventions of race, whereas I am more interested in ideologies of gender.

139. "Chez les frondeuses."

140. Dutoit, "À Travers le féminisme."

141. "Chez les frondeuses," *Illustration.* On the lack of stained fingers, see also Jean Bernard, "Chez les frondeuses" no periodical or date APSF, BMD. See also the British view in *Truth* (London), Dec. 16, 1897, APSF, BMD; no author or title, *The African Review,* Oct. 22, 1898, APSF, BMD; and "The Story of *La Fronde.*"

142. One exception to the "feminine" character of the office was the gym that Durand installed for fencing, her favorite sport. The gym caused controversy because at the time fencing was considered to be a supremely masculine sport, associated with male virility, honor, and patriotism. In *L'Escrime et la femme* (Paris: M. Désirée Benoist, 1896), A. Bergès argues for female fencing because it will allow women to teach their sons to be fierce fighters for the republic. Since fencing was also a *mondaine* sport, the gym might have expressed class pretensions on Durand's part. For more on fencing in the primary literature, see Dossier Escrime, BMD and "Sporting notes: L'Escrime féminine," *La Fronde*, Jan. 7, 1898. In the secondary literature, see Robert Nye, *Masculinity and Male Codes of Honor in Modern France* (New York: Oxford University Press, 1993), particularly 160–71.

143. One contemporary described the new women as "rebels with ink on their fingers." See M. Reader, "La Position de la femme en France," no place, Nov. 10, 1892, Dossier Féminisme, XIXe siècle, BMD.

144. Durand, "Causerie sur la maison des journalistes et 'La Fronde,'" Faite à la Société pour l'amélioration du sort de la femme" (1933) Manuscrits, vol. 2, BMD, 29.

145. Alexandre Hepp, "La Bataille de dames," *Le Journal*, Dec. 7, 1897, APSF, BMD. Durand later defended such a position by arguing that even if one man had been employed by *La Fronde*, its doubters could claim that the paper was really written by men and that women simply signed the articles. See "Notes autobiographiques" and Dizier-Metz, *La Bibliothèque*, 10.

146. R.S.V.P. notes from famous journalists and politicians are evidence of the high-powered nature of these parties. See Correspondents to Marguerite Durand, vols. 1, 2, BMD. The star-studded invitation lists were also often commented upon in the press. See, for example, *Le Gil blas*, Dec. 11, 1899, APSF, BMD. The rough dates of some of these parties were: Dec. 1897, June 1898, Dec. 1898, and Dec. 1899.

147. See "Notes autobiographiques" and "Les Femmes dans le journalisme," 18. On Delphine de Girardin see Henri Malo, *La Gloire du vicomte de Launay, Delphine Gay de Girardin* (Paris: Émile-Paul frères, 1925) and Pierre Pellissier, *Émile de Girardin, Prince de la presse* (Paris: Éditions Denoël, 1985), chaps. 3, 5. For the connection to Girardin, I am indebted to Jo Burr Margadant. See her "Comment on Session 'Gender and Mass Culture in France: 1880–1930,'" Meeting of the American Historical Association, San Francisco, Jan. 1994, 9.

148. Margadant, "Comment on Session," 9. For the importance of sociability to an actress's career, see also Briais, *Au temps des frous-frous*, 20–27, 83.

149. Cesbron, "Un Journal féministe, 14.

150. For the description of Durand's *soirées* as "*délicieuses*," see the letter from Jozereau, Correspondents of Marguerite Durand, vol. 2, BMD. In the same collection, see also the letter by Hugues Le Roux, Dec. 1, 1899.

151. *Le Journal*, 29 June 1898, no author or title, APSF, BMD.

152. Bernard, "Chez les frondeuses." Like the *Illustration* journalist, he was astonished by the lack of ink stains on their fingers, which he found "tapered and aristocratic." On another occasion, the British *Pall Mall Gazette* remarked that the greatest surprise for the visitors was the appearance of the "blue-stockings":

"To the popular imagination the literary lady is a fearful and wonderful object, a creature of forbidding looks and of strenuous eccentricity in the matter of clothes. The staff of *La Fronde* offer none of these characteristics. Were you to meet them in a drawing-room you might suppose them innocent of printers' ink." "Women Journalists in Paris: The First Anniversary of '*La Fronde*,'" *Pall Mall Gazette*, Dec. 12, 1898. See also M. de Arbeaumont, "Petits échos," *Triboulet*, Jan. 18, 1899, and no title or author, *Le Gil blas*, Dec. 11, 1899, both APSF, BMD.

153. *La Fronde*, Dec. 11, 1899. Durand later wrote how she believed that the journalists expected the worst — "certain animals that one encounters more frequently in the desert . . . than on the boulevards . . . On this point, still, what surprise!" See Durand, "Causerie sur la maison des journalistes."

154. Even the far-flung *Grand Rapids Herald* in Michigan sang their praises: "The brilliant and cultured French women who conduct *La Fronde* know well how to combine utility and beauty, grace of manner and shrewd business ability." See "New Woman in Paris," *Grand Rapids Herald*, April 17, 1899, APSF, BMD.

155. Louise Debor, "Le Féminisme en dentelles," *La Fronde*, July 19, 1899.

156. "Enquêtes de *La Fronde*," ALF, Box 1, BMD. See, in particular, the letters of P. Stuart, Marguerite Bodier, Madame Loubirau, C. Pascal, Madame Deleuze, and H. Soulabaille.

157. On the growth of mass culture in this period, see Patrick Brantlinger, "Mass Media and Culture in Fin-de-siècle Europe," in *Fin de Siècle and its Legacy*, ed. Mikulas Teich and Roy Porter (Cambridge, Mass.: Cambridge University Press, 1990), 98–114, 151.

158. Quoted from Vanessa Schwartz, *Spectacular Realities: Early Mass Culture in Fin-de-Siècle Culture* (Berkeley and Los Angeles: University of California Press, 1998), 1. For more on the aesthetic of the spectacle, see T. J. Clark, *The Painting of Modern Life: Paris in the Art of Manet and his followers* (Princeton: Princeton University Press, 1984), and Charles Rearick, *Pleasures of the Belle Epoque: Entertainment and Festivity in Turn-of-the-Century France* (New Haven, Conn.: Yale University Press, 1985). For a brilliant analysis of the world exhibitions as spectacles, see Timothy Mitchell, *Colonizing Egypt* (Berkeley and Los Angeles: University of California Press, 1988), particularly 1–33.

159. See Ruth Brandon, *Being Divine: A Biography of Sarah Bernhardt* (London: Secker and Warburg, 1991), 187. Bernhardt was particularly fond of pumas and lion cubs. She once decided to have a tiger's tail grafted onto the base of her spine, and had even persuaded a doctor to do the operation when her friends talked her out of it.

160. See Folder "Divers," Box 3, DMD, BMD, particularly a letter from "Rapide: Agence Internationale de Reportage Photographique," dated Feb. 14, 1910.

161. The journalist Bing said of the lion: She "is at once a great spoiler of carpets and a symbol." See "Madame Marguerite Durand," *Fantasio*, April 1, 1910, FCAEL, Box 2, DMD, BMD. For the lioness as a symbol of seduction, see Margadant, "Comment on Session," 12. For the journalists who saw the lion as a symbol of power, see Yvonne Sarcey, no title, *Les Annales*, April 10, 1910; *Dépêche marocaine*, Tanger, Feb. 24, 1910 and "La Candidate," *La Vie parisi-*

enne, all in FCAEL, Box 2, DMD, BMD. Rumor also had it that Durand wanted to take Tiger to her rallies and that she would take the animal to the Chamber if elected.

162. Clark, *Painting of Modern Life,* 49. For cultural critics, see Guy Debord, *La Société du spectacle* (Paris: Éditions Buchet-Chastel, 1967); and Jean Baudrillard, *Le Système des objets* (Paris: Gallimard, 1968). For a historian, see Rachel Bowlby, *Just Looking: Consumer Culture in Dreiser, Gissing and Zola* (New York: Methuen, 1985), 2, 6–8, 25, 34. Richard Terdiman argues in *Discourse/Counter-discourse: The Theory and Practice of Symbolic Resistance in Nineteenth-Century France* (Ithaca: Cornell University Press, 1985), 120, that "the daily paper was arguably the *first* consumer commodity: made to be perishable, purchased to be thrown away."

163. Rosalind Williams, *Dream Worlds: Mass Consumption in Late Nineteenth-Century France* (Berkeley and Los Angeles: University of California, 1982), 70–71, 88–89, 90–91. On the commodification of female desire in mass culture, see also Émile Zola, *Au Paradis des femmes* (1883), and Bowlby, *Just Looking,* 11, 76–77.

164. Williams, *Dream Worlds,* 90.

165. In thinking about the issues of subjectivity, agency, and change, I have found the following particularly helpful: Paul Smith, *Discerning the Subject* (Minneapolis: University of Minnesota Press, 1988); Felicity Nussbaum, *The Autobiographical Subject: Gender and Ideology in Eighteenth-Century England* (Baltimore: The Johns Hopkins University Press, 1989), particularly 30–31; Joan Scott, "The Evidence of Experience," *Critical Inquiry* 17 (summer 1991): 793; Catherine Belsey, *The Subject of Tragedy: Identity and Difference in Renaissance Drama* (London: Methuen, 1985), particularly 6; Wendy Holloway, "Gender Difference and the Production of Subjectivity," in *Changing the Subject: Psychology, Social Regulation and Subjectivity,* ed. Julian Henriques et al. (London: Methuen, 1984), 252; Judith Butler, "Contingent Foundations: Feminism and the Question of 'Postmodernism'" in *Feminists Theorize the Political,* ed. Judith Butler and Joan W. Scott (New York: Routledge 1992); Sarah Mills, *Discourses of Difference: An Analysis of Women's Travel Writing and Colonialism* (London: Routledge, 1991), 12–19. For an intelligent and compelling analysis of these issues within a biographical context, see Kali A. K. Israel, "Style, Strategy, and Self-Creation in the Life of Emilia Dilke," in *Constructions of the Self,* ed. George Levine (New Brunswick: Rutgers University Press, 1992), 213–45, and her "Writing inside the Kaleidoscope: (Re)Representing Victorian Women Public Figures," *Gender and History* 2 (spring 1990): 40–48.

166. See Gayot, "Les Comédiennes et le féminisme."

167. According to Weber, *Fin de siècle,* Ibsen and Strindberg were both played on the French stage in the 1880s and 1890s. For more on French popular drama and the image of the new woman, see Jane Misme, "La Femme dans le théâtre nouveau." For the links between feminism and the theater in England, see Gardner and Rutherford, eds., *The New Woman and Her Sisters,* and Jan McDonald, "New Women in the New Drama," *New Theatre Quarterly* 21 (Feb. 1990): 31–42, and particularly 32.

168. Maurice le Blond, "Études sur la presse," *Revue naturiste,* April 1900, ALF, BMD.

169. Emphasis mine. See Daniel LeSueur, "Nos idylles," *La Fronde*, Dec. 10, 1897.

170. See Mary Chéliga, "Le Féminisme au théâtre," *Revue d'art dramatique*, Oct. 1901. The *Théâtre féministe* was fiercely defended in the pages of *La Fronde*. See, for example, "Chronique féministe," Jan. 28, 1898. See also Geraldine Harris, "Yvette Guilbert: *La Femme Moderne* on the British Stage," in *The New Woman*, ed. Gardner and Rutherford, 118.

171. On Colette, see Michèle Sarde, *Colette: Free and Fettered* (New York: William Morrow, 1980); Herbert Lottman, *Colette, A Life* (Boston: Little-Brown, 1991); Elaine Marks, *Colette* (New Brunswick: Rutgers University Press, 1960); Joanna Richardson, *Colette* (London: Methuen, 1983).

172. Briais, *Au temps des frous-frous*, 96–97.

173. Harris, "Yvette Guilbert," 129; Briais, *Au temps des Frous-Frous*, 111–20, and Bettina Knapp, *That was Yvette: The Biography of the Great Diseuse* (London: Friedrich Muller, 1966). For Marguerite Durand's friendship with Guilbert, see her letter to Harlor, April 11, 1933, *Correspondance*, BMD, and her invitation to Marie-Louise Bouglé to a conference given by Guilbert, DMD, BHVP.

174. For Roussel, see the essay in this volume by Elinor Accampo, "Private Life, Public Image: Motherhood and Militancy in the Self-Construction of Nelly Roussel, 1900–1922." See also Jennifer Waelti-Walters and Steven Hause, *Feminisms of the Belle Epoque: A Historical and Literary Anthology* (Lincoln: University of Nebraska Press, 1994), 17. For Guilbert, see "Les Comédiennes et le féminisme: Madame Yvette," *La Rampe*, May 14, 1922. For Bernhardt, see also Jill Edmonds, "Princess Hamlet" in *The New Woman and Her Sisters*, ed. Gardner and Rutherford, 74.

175. For this notion of "performative" identity, see Judy Butler, "Performative Acts and Gender Constitution: An Essay in Phenomenology and Feminist Theory," in *Performing Feminisms: Feminist Critical Theory and Theatre*, ed. Sue-Ellen Case (Baltimore: The Johns Hopkins University Press, 1990) and Judith Butler, *Gender Trouble: Feminism and the Subversion of Identity* (New York: Routledge, 1990), 134–41.

176. Madame Bartet, *Causerie sur l'art dramatique* (Paris: Edouard Pelletan, 1903), 22–23.

177. As Butler argues in "Performative Acts," 273, gender is a "construction that regularly conceals its genesis."

178. For an interesting discussion of Bernhardt's cross-dressing, see Brandon, *Being Divine*, 339–43; Jill Edmonds, "Princess Hamlet," in Gardner and Rutherford, *The New Woman*, 59–76; and Lenard Berlanstein, "Britches and Breeches: Cross-Dressed Theater and the Culture of Gender Ambiguity in Modern France," *Comparative Studies in Society and History* 38 (1996): 338–70.

179. Weber, *France Fin de siècle*, 159

180. See Annelise Maugue, *L'Identité masculine en crise au tournant du siècle* (Paris: Editions Rivages, 1987).

Private Life, Public Image

Motherhood and Militancy in the Self-Construction of Nelly Roussel, 1900–1922

ELINOR A. ACCAMPO

INTRODUCTION

In 1901, at age twenty-three, Nelly Roussel launched a public speaking and writing career as a feminist and advocate of birth control. A talented orator whom the press frequently described as "conquering" her audiences, Roussel earned instant success and indeed, notoriety. She captivated the imaginations of her listeners by turning her lectures into dramatic performances, but she also intrigued them with a persona that embodied contradiction: her dynamism and energy contrasted with her slight stature, and the power of her words belied an appearance of fragility. Contemporaries employed superlatives to describe her voice, whose timbre conveyed at once weakness and strength, passion and reason, femininity and masculinity. It sounded like music, one of her supporters recollected, a "pure crystal whose pathetic vibrations filled huge rooms"; her "large, profound eyes had flames," and the "strange impression of energy and of fragility which emanated . . . from her frail silhouette, always clothed in black, and from her luminous pallor, . . . rendered her all at once touching and domineering."[1] Press descriptions of her lectures repeated frequently these binary sets of adjectives, conveying the sense that Roussel disarmed her audiences because they could not easily categorize, and thus dismiss, her. They also repeatedly remarked upon the sincerity and authenticity with which she expressed her convictions and, by endorsing her public voice, challenged notions that women could

Photograph of Nelly Roussel. Bibliothéque Marguerite Durand.

only dissimulate, especially when "performing" before large audiences.[2] Establishing such credibility in public, and especially in public speaking, was no small challenge for women of the Belle Époque.[3]

In both her private and public lives, Nelly Roussel ruptured boundaries of gender and of Victorian bourgeois propriety. Although feminism and the rise of the "New Woman" had already destabilized traditional notions of gender as Roussel came of age in the 1880s and 1890s, her public career pushed those boundaries further than those of most other feminists and independent women. Even as bourgeois women began to participate in public life, to see a woman speak before large audiences still provoked disapproval and cat calls, particularly when, as in the case of Roussel, she spoke of issues that implicitly or explicitly addressed sexuality, as did the topic of birth control. How did Nelly Roussel manage to have a public life centered on giving voice to issues that were taboo at a time when female public speakers were still very rare? How might we measure her impact?

By illustrating the intricate relationship between Roussel's private and public lives this essay will argue that a careful and deliberate presentation of her public image contributed to the subversive power of her challenge to state authority and the moral assumptions that underpinned it. With the cooperation and unwavering support of her husband, Roussel packaged an extremely radical message in the conservative image of bourgeois wife and mother. While at first glance her life seems replete with contradiction, if not hypocrisy, in fact she created a coherent self that enabled her to achieve, at least in her personal life, the goals she advocated.[4] Three principal topics under consideration here are how Roussel perceived herself as a public figure and her husband's role in helping create that image; how her private life, particularly her identity as individual, wife, and mother reflected her ideology and fueled her ability to challenge the state; and how the image she created facilitated her subversive politics, particularly in an environment that became increasingly hostile to them.

BECOMING A MILITANT

Roussel's husband, Henri Godet, played a pivotal role in her intellectual and emotional development. Indeed, it was her marriage that enabled Roussel to become unorthodox and to pursue the path from which her parents had thwarted her. Raised in a proper Parisian bourgeois family with a traditional education and Catholic upbringing, she felt impassioned about religion in her youth and wrote religious poetry during her late adolescence and early adulthood in the 1890s.[5] But her character also contained less conventional elements. Her grandfather, who wrote plays for the family to perform from the time she was very young, passed on to her a passion for tragic drama. At age six she began writing her own plays and performing them with her friends. To her enormous disappointment, her family would not permit her to pursue an acting career. Nor would they allow her to continue her education past age fifteen, another stinging blow to her own desires and one that nourished an "instinctive" feminism that grew with her increased awareness about differences in the way boys and girls were raised.[6]

From about age thirteen, another aspect of her character — a taste for logic — began to compete with Roussel's religious sentiment, leading her to question Catholic dogma. Her doubts grew as she "devoured" her grandfather's library once her formal education ended. By the time she met Henri Godet when she was twenty years old, she had begun to doubt even the existence of God. Moreover, her incipient feminism, her passion for acting, her religious doubts all led her to the conclusion that she would be unsuitable for marriage to anyone in her milieu. Henri Godet — a sculptor, free thinker, socialist militant, and atheist — had also given up hope of meeting a "girl" who would suit his "ideal" when he met Roussel at age thirty-five. They married in 1898, less than five months after their first encounter. According to Godet, their marriage gave Roussel a "whole new birth of ideas," and a "complete blossoming of her own faculties."[7]

Free of her parents, Roussel initially wished to pursue her theatrical vocation and was encouraged to do so by all those "who had been able to appreciate her great talent as a tragedian," including Godet. But she discovered the power of her voice in public speaking when she gave her first lecture on feminism in 1901. She quickly recognized this "new path" to be her true calling, one more "noble and interesting" than the theater because it was based on conviction and authenticity rather than on performance alone.[8]

This "marriage of feminism and freethinking," as Godet called it, anchored Roussel in a radical milieu. She rejected completely all religion, as well as dogma of any kind, and came to sympathize with anarchism. In 1900 Godet's sister married Fritz Robin, the son of Paul Robin, founder of the French birth-control movement. Through that marriage Roussel came to know Paul Robin and dubbed him a "new Christ"; birth control then became the centerpiece of her feminism.[9] Although she retained the trappings of a bourgeois lifestyle in her manners and her tastes, Roussel's life after marriage hardly reflected that for which her background had groomed her. Leaving her husband and children for weeks at a time, she traveled alone to unfamiliar destinations and was usually received by male lecture organizers neither she nor her husband had ever met. Even in Paris she seemed to spend relatively little time with her children.

If Roussel's personal comportment after marriage exhibited considerable independence, so did the ideology she brought to her public. Her feminism exceeded most others of the Belle Époque because it subverted the very definitions of womanhood upon which the latter were based. More importantly her arguments, when combined with her image, worked to challenge notions of womanhood that formed the basis of Third Republic social policy. Belief systems about gender during this era evolved in an atmosphere of near-hysteria that low French birth rates betokened a diseased "social body," a degenerating French "race," and a declining military capability. Women were viewed not as individuals, but as mothers or potential mothers who could replenish the French nation.[10] Joshua Cole has recently described the official consensus that placed women and reproduction at the center of French social debate. He argues convincingly that the language that demographers used in their study of declining fertility conflated individual women with the "reproductive potential of the nation's female population as a whole," thus reinforcing an already overdetermined connection between womanhood and motherhood.[11] The collapsing of these two concepts also had certain political consequences. In a now classic article, Karen Offen argued that motherhood became the very basis upon which moderate feminists sought to raise the civil and political status of women.[12] The conception of womanhood among both mainstream feminists and social reformers thus focused on women's identities as mothers. Although feminists sought to use maternity as a justification for increasing women's roles in the public sphere, their logic did little to challenge traditional views of domesticity or to reconceptualize women as individuals in their own right, independent of relationships with men and with children.

By adding reproductive rights to demands for civil and political rights, Roussel, along with a tiny minority of other feminists, changed completely the parameters of feminist debate. For Roussel, women's control over their bodies became the very foundation of their ability to be independent, and thus to have political and civil rights. She believed that birth control would not only improve marriages, but it would also liberate women from the worst physical, emotional, and economic burdens of motherhood and provide them with the means to have genuine equity with men in both private and public life. Inherent in her demand for women's access to birth control was an insistence on their right to enjoy sex without the fear and suffering associated with pregnancy and childbirth. Social reformers, Roussel was always quick to point out, never discussed the burdens motherhood imposed on women — nor did mainstream feminists. To convey her message, Roussel used some interesting rhetorical tactics. Evoking the knowledge, passion, and sentiment of her Catholic upbringing, she frequently used religious metaphor to tap into a pervasive cultural perception that, either because they were descendants of Eve, or because "Nature" deemed it so, women were meant to suffer and to endure their suffering; "self-abasement and love of suffering" were considered "essential elements of the female identity."[13] She thus titled one of her most famous and most frequently presented lectures "L'Éternelle sacrifiée," "she who is eternally sacrificed." In another key lecture, "Liberté de maternité," she compared the stages of childbirth and motherhood to Christ's Calvary.[14]

During a twenty-year period, Roussel delivered various versions of this message in 236 lectures and speeches throughout France, Austria, Hungary, Switzerland, and Belgium. Many of her lectures drew audiences in the hundreds and some even in the thousands; those who did not attend her lectures could read them or read about them in the Parisian and provincial newspapers, which summarized them or quoted them verbatim. Edited versions of her lectures and articles appeared in five collections published between 1907 and 1932.[15] Again drawing on religious metaphor, Roussel viewed herself as an "apostle" and her public career as a "mission." Not unlike "a new Christ" in her own right, in her self-perception she gave up the "fortune and glory" that her "natural gifts" for acting would have brought her with a career in the theater. But demanding nothing for herself, "she put [her gifts] at the service of her unfortunate sisters," and "she gave herself as a mission spreading the feminist idea, making it penetrate distant regions where it is . . . almost unknown."[16] She particularly targeted working-class and rural communities on her speaking tours, traveling to places such as Bourg-Argental (Loire), Firminy (Loire), and Le Puy (Haute-Loire). In larger cities such as Paris and Lyon, her audiences tended to be more middle class, often school teachers. Women usually comprised one-third to one-half her audiences.[17]

Roussel's lengthy trips away from Paris resulted in an abundant correspondence with her husband and other family members. Analyzed in conjunction with other sources in her private papers, this correspondence shows clearly that her marriage and her extended family relations made her public career possible. Indeed, this correspondence served as a site in which public image and private identity intersected, where one helped form the other, and it provides the basis for the first part of this essay. As Michelle Perrot has cautioned, the contents of private letters are often "dictated by rules of propriety and a need for self-dramatization. Nothing is less spontaneous than a letter . . . which is designed to conceal as much as it reveals."[18] But the frequency with which this couple corresponded during a twenty-year period resulted in a large quantity of letters, which lends itself to seeking patterns in subjects as well as in structure, making it possible for one to read between lines and detect what these letters conceal as well as what they reveal, particularly when read alongside other sources such as Roussel's daily agendas and newspaper accounts of her speaking tours.

Of the two correspondents, Roussel remained much closer to bourgeois convention than did Godet. Her letters exhibit more grammatical accuracy, restraint, structure, and propriety. During one period of strained communication about her lecture schedule, she wrote, "I should respond to you about this subject, but I am too well brought up for that . . ." and in another communication noted that her letter was "poorly written" precisely because it had come "from the heart." Godet's letters, far more spontaneous, even sloppy in grammar, spelling, and especially handwriting, incurred Roussel's chiding comments about his "elegant language as a sculptor" and comparisons of his language skills with those of their young children.[19]

Sensitivity to patterns and habits in letter writing and awareness of the stylistic differences between correspondents enables the unintended reader to understand better the author's use of language as a way of ordering experience and as a way of imagining his or her self at that particular moment. Roussel's letters allow us to view her self-consciousness about her fame as it grew. Her correspondence with Godet gave her the opportunity to describe to a trusted intimate her own estimation of her success, both positive and negative. In April 1905, for example, after delivering "L'Éternelle Sacrifiée" and performing her short "symbolic" play, *Par la révolte*, Roussel wrote of her success at reaching her predominantly working-class audience in Bourg-Argental, some of whom she had moved to tears: " . . . everybody was talking about me [the day after the lecture], all the women in the region, [but] especially in the silk-weaving factories. All those who had not dared attend the lecture declared themselves terribly sorry, and asked if 'this lady' would come again another time. Even the women who support clericalism regretted their abstention. I am told that *Par la révolte* circulated from hand to hand." She recounted how she had shamed men in the audience — a tactic she would frequently use when talking to and about men — and how she had succeeded in making them repent: "As for the male listeners, they avowed the next day that when I had looked at them . . . during the course of the lecture, they felt ashamed and wished they could hide . . . Many of the women workers are, it seems, abandoned single mothers . . . And their seducers, who were also in the room, admitted responsibility for their actions."[20] Roussel experienced her success in many different ways and often expressed its impact on her in melodramatic terms. In 1907 she wrote from Belgium, "Rejoice my dear barnum! Your phenomenon just carried off two great successes. It is with a hand still trembling from emotion and noble fatigue that traces for you these blue lines. Last night . . . the audience was attentive and curious; but at the beginning, cold, skeptical and suspicious; then, little by little conquered, and by the end vibrant and enthusiastic. Today, in the theater, about 500 local residents listened to me and applauded in a very satisfactory fashion."

Roussel also measured her success with the number of brochures she sold after her lectures. At the exit of the two lectures she referred to in the letter above, she sold respectively fifty and sixty copies of *Par la révolte,* good numbers in her estimation.[21] Similarly, two months later she wrote from Annecy, " . . . the lecture was a great success. I felt joy, and the glory of conquering little by little a suspicious and cold, almost jeering audience. Today, all over the city, one heard only enthusiastic exclamations of those 'who were there' and the regrets of 'those who were not there.' Borrel assured me that the public of Annecy is expert and knows very well how to appreciate oratory form."[22] She delighted in being compared with the famous anarchist and neo-Malthusian speaker Sebastian Faure, who could draw audiences of four thousand, and with the more famous socialist leader when a worker referred to her as "a Jaurès in skirts." But having entered the man's world of public speaking, she remained very aware of her own femininity and the purposes it served, remarking for example, "Yesterday, everything went as wished, my new dress produced its little effect." Indeed, Roussel was quite aware of her beauty. Christine Bard noted "The black hair of Nelly-Roussel — like the blond hair of Marguerite Durand — also had its place in the gallery of charms put in the service of the cause."[23]

Roussel also used her missives to Godet as an occasion for reflecting on her shortcomings and failures. "Last evening," she wrote two days after one of her great successes, "I harangued about a thousand people in a huge cold room with very bad acoustics, which made the lecture fairly tiring. Moreover, I was poorly disposed and I am not happy with myself. But it is necessary to believe I am wrong, since these gentlemen showered me with congratulations, declaring that I had 'surpassed' myself. There were many more people [in the audience] than last year; and the organizers claim that the lecture was even more pleasing. This is not my opinion. On the contrary, I had the sensation of being less understood."[24] Similarly, from a speaking tour in Switzerland she wrote, "Yesterday, there was a crowd. These gentlemen are very happy; not I, because I found myself very inferior [to my own expectations]. Never perhaps have I spoken with so little animation. Never, above all, have I been so unable to control the trouble caused by fatigue. The end was completely ruined. And this annoyed me all the more since I am really 'someone' in Lausanne . . . I would have wanted to surpass myself, to be sublime, to force admiration from the adversaries. Friends were nice enough to congratulate me. I remain furious." But she also discovered that her passion for propagandizing, her love for travel, and the rush of adrenaline at the moment she started speaking often enabled her to overcome the fatigue that plagued her.[25]

These letters served as more than occasions for Roussel to reflect on her successes and failures as a public speaker. As their recipient, Henri Godet had great investment in his wife's personal and professional well-being. Nearly every letter from her brought requests of a practical nature. Routinely she asked him to mail her more brochures to sell, to answer her correspondence, to set up contacts for her publications, to send money and forgotten articles of clothing, to arrange and publicize future lectures, to see to it that each lecture was reviewed in the local presses, to assure that local reviews of her lectures would reach the Paris press, to arrange for and send train permits, and to try to figure out whether, when, and where they could meet if her tour were to keep her away from Paris for several weeks or even several months.

Somewhat surprisingly, Roussel did not establish her itineraries prior to her tours, but instead they evolved as she traveled. In fact the radical, anticlerical, daily newspaper *L'Action,* which systematically announced and covered her lectures, invited readers to set up additional lectures as she toured.[26] The proceeds from her lectures, usually somewhere from fifty to three hundred francs, as well as the sale of her brochures, supported her travels to further destinations. What determined those destinations, in addition to publicity from *L'Action,* appears to have been word of her successes in the networks of organizers, usually groups of freemasons, freethinkers, feminists, anarchists, or neo-Malthusianists. Such lack of planning created practical difficulties and communication gaps. Godet often did not know when she would reach a particular destination or how long she would stay there. Consequently many of his letters had to be forwarded from one location to the next, resulting in his frustrated complaint that he needed a more precise idea of her plans so that his letters would not "remain *en panne* [broken down] like vulgar automobiles."[27]

Godet did all he could to comply with her requests, and sometimes seemed to organize his life around them. Unable to earn a living through sculpture, in 1908 he established, with the financial assistance of Roussel's stepfather, a joint-stock company for the extraction and sale of marble from a quarry in Italy. Until that point he seemed to have plenty of time to devote himself to the promotion of his wife's career, which explains why one of her pet names for him was "Barnum." This moniker originated with one of his own trips away from Paris early in Roussel's career in which he encountered the traveling circus of Barnum and Bailey and became deeply impressed with their methods of publicity: "The city of Châlons is getting ready in a worthy manner to receive Barnum and Bayley *[sic]* — the walls are covered as though by magic with multi-colored posters — there isn't a single shop that doesn't have posters in its windows. All the surrounding villages are covered. A special wagon brought the pasters and their material, wagons wait at the station to carry each team armed with paste and paper toward the designated places — and all this only for a day. The following day it will be Reims which will have the honor to receive these . . . charlatans — [then in English:] *All Right.*"[28] Godet's observations of this spectacle impressed upon him the impact publicity could have, and the experience no doubt inspired him to publicize more extensively and with greater care Roussel's lectures. That she called him "Barnum" throughout the height of her career also suggests the manner in which she conceived of her own performances.

Even after Godet's business affairs consumed his time and required travel on his part, he continued to make practical arrangements while she toured and to supply considerable intellectual and emotional support. He routinely advised Roussel on the content of her lectures and gave editorial advice as she prepared them for publication. He also overtly helped her formulate the public image that promoted her success. Her identity as a bourgeois wife and mother became a key element in this image. Friendly press coverage of her lectures and testimony from her supporters frequently noted this aspect of her persona, for it legitimated and lent further credibility to her message. For these sympathetic commentators he offered living proof that a feminist could have a loving relationship with a man, and her marriage was portrayed as a model of companionship. In this manner she differed significantly from other radical feminists who advocated birth control, such as Gabrielle Petit who was not bourgeois and "lacked culture," or Aria Ly who openly hated men and advocated permanent virginity, or Madeleine Pelletier whose celibacy, disgust for sexuality of any kind, and lack of femininity many found offputting.[29] With Godet's assistance, images of Roussel's marriage and motherhood became part of her published works and public image.

For example, while Roussel toured in 1907, she and Godet exchanged several letters discussing the publication of her first collection of lectures, a volume entitled *Quelques discours,* which appeared that same year. They debated the title, the dedication, and the photograph that would accompany it. This exchange of letters particularly reveals the public image they wished to convey as well as at least one dynamic of their relationship. On April 23, Godet wrote, "I just re-read the dedication and permit myself some reflections: it has the fault of most dedications concerning women; I would have preferred that it make clear that I opened this horizon of activity to you, [a horizon] that you did not consider, that at least I showed you the way, encouraged you to follow it. It's very difficult to explain what I mean to say — and I am tired, I am going to bed. I will add something Wednesday the 24th that will perhaps be less idiotic."[30] For all the difficulty he had in expressing himself, Godet clearly desired more public and private credit for the role he had played in Roussel's political and intellectual development. Just as interesting as his desire for acknowledgment is his confusion about expressing it and the labeling of his attempt as "idiotic," for it reveals not only a sense of diffidence in his relationship with her, but at least in comparison with her letters, a relative lack of self-censorship.

Roussel's response to Godet's comments about her dedication came four days later at the end of her letter, crammed into the margins almost as an afterthought: "I'm thinking of the dedication. It's upsetting that you don't like it, my little dedication, that I was happy with! . . . it is necessary, above all, that you like it. We'll talk about it more." Three days later she offered him this revision: "To my husband, to my best friend; he who understood and encouraged my apostolate".[31] But this version also left Godet frustrated and confused. On May 4 he wrote that he had "plunged his head in his hands" to try to figure out what it was he did not like about her proposed revision: "Why does your dedication resemble an epitaph? . . . it's because you speak in the past tense . . . here is what I propose, but the man proposes, the woman disposes and even sometimes indisposes. 'To my dear husband, who understands me and encourages me.' It is less romantic, but you know, Victor [referring to their mutual hero, Victor Hugo] is dead, and we must not raise the dead . . . in fact I don't know if one says it, but I suppose that many would find it bad — come on, I am saying a bunch of stupid things, it's the effect of the *tilleul* that I just drank." Again Godet's letter conveys pain, frustration, and insecurity. But more than anything else, he expresses here a desire for a patrimony of his own in the form of his initiatory and continuing contribution to his wife's career. Perhaps too, Godet was trying to protect Roussel: he might have supposed "many would find it bad" that she used the word "apostolate," which he had eliminated from his suggested version. Given his atheism and anticlericalism, he might have found her use of religious metaphor inappropriate, if not embarrassing. The remainder of this letter returns to practical matters: he pleaded with her to send dates, places, names of theaters for where she would be speaking so that he could make posters to publicize her lectures — otherwise he had no means of doing so. In spite of his being ever ready to serve her, she neglected on her part to provide him with the necessary information then chastised him for his tardiness.[32]

The final version of the dedication was indeed that of her last suggestion, only changed to the present tense. But another issue remained unresolved. Letters they each wrote May 2, thus crossing in the mail, referred to the photograph of Roussel that would appear in the book. She wanted her portrait on the cover, saying with emphasis, "you know which one." At the same time Godet suggested that he would make the decision alone, and use a photograph of himself and their son. If his intention was facetious, he no doubt also meant to remind her that she was neglecting half her family in both her affection and in her self-image. The photograph that did serve as the frontispiece for the collection is that shown on page 230, Roussel with her daughter in their bourgeois domestic setting, with Godet's sculptures in the background. That Roussel chose this photograph rather than a family portrait was quite self-conscious and deliberate. It perhaps reflected a strictly feminine sense of her "apostolate"; it framed the hard logic of her written word in a soft image, lending a strictly female ownership and female voice to the subjects between the

Photograph of Nelly Roussel with her daughter, frontispiece for *Quelques discours* (1907 edition). Bibliothèque Marguerite Durand.

covers, all the while giving the maternal relationship political authority and agency.[33]

Godet's own ideal of maternity appeared in a photograph in the second collection of Roussel's lectures, *Quelques lances rompues pour nos libertés*, published in 1910. The photograph portrays the bust of Roussel and her daughter that Godet sculpted in 1904. It became the frontispiece

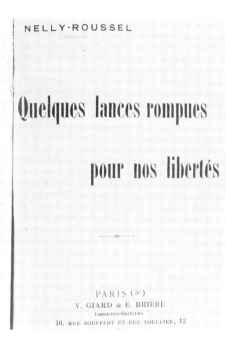

NELLY-ROUSSEL

Quelques lances rompues

pour nos libertés

PARIS (5ᵉ)
V. GIARD & E. BRIÈRE
LIBRAIRES-ÉDITEURS
16, RUE SOUFFLOT ET RUE TOULLIER, 12

Sculpture of Nelly Roussel and her daughter by Henri Godet, Roussel's husband (1904), frontispiece for *Quelques lances rompues* (1910 edition).

as well as the front cover of this volume. Here the maternal figure, with the child emerging from her mother's body, appears more radiant than the photo of flesh-and-blood mother and daughter. The imagery again provides a strong counterpoint to the "broken lances" of the title, as well as to metaphors of militarism and the "masculine" logic within the book. Like the previous image, this one reminds the reader that the subjects of reproduction, sexuality, and feminism belong to women. Roussel dedicated the volume to her then ten-year-old daughter: "To my dear little Mireille, so that later she remembers that her mother was among those who battled to conquer liberties she will perhaps enjoy." This dedication also reflects Godet's input, and in fact, his effort to temper what her audience might have perceived as hubris or over abundant confidence; the previous year he had written, "I just glanced at your manuscript — you write in the dedication . . . liberties which she *will* enjoy. Don't you think it would be prudent to add . . . *maybe* or *I hope* . . . write me a word on this subject."[34]

Whether or not it was always his conscious intent, Godet's interven-

tions tempered Roussel's vanity and emphasized her identity as wife and
mother.[35] So too did the prefaces to some of her published volumes
emphasize these domestic roles. Émile Darnaud, a fervent octogenarian
feminist and admirer of hers, carefully noted Roussel's virtues as a spouse
and young mother in the preface to *Quelques lances*. The photographs of
Roussel and her daughter and of Godet's bust reappeared in press coverage of her lectures, as did frequent commentary about the authority her
experience as wife and mother gave her as she spoke of neo-Malthusian
issues. Coverage of a lecture she delivered at the annual festival of the
Society for Freethinking in September 1908, thus described her: "Enemy
not of maternity, but only of imposed maternity, she is herself mother of
two small children, of which one is a delicious little girl of eight who
responds to the pretty name of Mireille. Her husband . . . is like her, a
militant of socialism and of freethinking, at the same time a convinced
feminist. He accompanies her in her propaganda tours. Nothing [is]
more charming than this household, united by such a complete community of ideas." The identical quotation (with Mireille's age updated),
authored by Roussel's friend and supporter Odette Laguerre, reappeared
three years later in a Toulouse newspaper on the occasion of another
tour.[36]

Remarkable about this description is the manner in which its very
feminine language embeds Roussel and her ideology within marriage and
family life, when in fact so much of her own life and her ideology embodied individual freedom and independence. The description lacks accuracy
in even less subtle ways, for more often than not Roussel toured alone —
rarely did Godet join her. Other notable examples of press coverage that
stressed how family life legitimized her message stated, "Nelly Roussel
. . . as wife and many times a mother [twice not being enough] is better
placed to uphold the neo-Malthusian thesis," and "Especially men
applauded her, even if veritably attacked, because she knows how to talk
about love of two beings united in order to form a home, create a family
and raise children with mother and father being equal." Roussel's marriage as portrayed here fit squarely that of the republican ideal, which
most often meant "equality in difference."[37]

Roussel's image as wife and mother continued to serve her feminist
message through her career and after her premature death from tuberculosis in 1922 and clearly influenced her audience. For example, after
one of her lectures in 1907, a female postal employee sent her compliments because she was sure "that your husband and your children are
happy to possess a wife and mother such as you."[38] But the image also

had inherent contradictions, for how could a woman who left her husband and children for weeks at a time be such an ideal wife and mother?
The preface a friend wrote to *Quelques discours* attempted to address
this paradox: "The spectacle is assuredly very rare of a happy woman, a
happy spouse, a happy mother, leaving the warm shadow of the hearth
in order to go off on great roads, free, uncertain roads, to serve a cause.
You abandon a soft quietude for the austere joy of speaking according to
your heart and your faith, and you accept in advance the danger of being
misinterpreted . . . "[39] This preface seeks to reconcile Roussel's qualities
as bourgeois wife and mother with her absence from the home by construing the latter as personal sacrifice to a cause. Without question,
Roussel experienced loneliness and physical discomforts of insomnia,
fatigue, and increasingly frequent ill health, and she particularly missed
Godet and Paris when she toured. Typical was her complaint of having
to lodge with people she did not know, rather than staying in a hotel: "I
will probably be an inconvenience to them, without being better off
myself . . . because I am rather unwell. Ah, it isn't always rosy, this *métier
d'apôtre* (profession of apostle)."[40] But it is also clear from her correspondence while on tour that the joy in conquering audiences was hardly
"austere" and that the "soft quietude" of the warm hearth offered her little temptation. The language in the preface and her own language, moreover, implicitly justify Roussel's departure from her "happy home" by
evoking the image of an apostolate, referring to her "cause," her "faith,"
"danger of being misinterpreted," and the sacrifices she must make for
her "profession" as an "apostle." [41]

But another tension is at play in the language Roussel and her supporters used, for while she portrayed herself as a mother and wife, she
also employed military metaphors, as exemplified by the title *Quelques
lances rompues* (literally, "a few broken lances"). Having been called to
Auxerre by militant neo-Malthusian workers to confront a conservative
philosopher at a public meeting, Roussel wrote to Godet: "Here I am, my
noble warrior, again in this extremely vibrant city, after twelve and a half
years of the noise of your glorious armed feats. This evening is going to
be a battlefield for me as well."[42] The language of battle pervaded much
of her performance and rhetoric. An article she published in *L'Action*,
"Après la bataille," called the elections in 1906 "the battle that mobilizes
the lively forces of the army of militants." In "L'Éternelle sacrifiée" she
referred to the "war between the sexes" and the men who "violently bar
the route" against women "marching for the conquest of our liberties."
In a speech at a protest meeting against the centennial celebration of the

Civil Code, she said, "One does not find honors too big, nor words too laudatory for the 'courageous' mutilated on the field of battle. But on our battlefield, to us, mothers, there is no glory to collect. The Society calling itself *civilized* has placed the work of death above the work of life, reserving, by an inconceivable aberration, its homage for the destructive soldier, its disdainful indifference for the creative woman!"[43]

Her play, *Par la révolte,* offers a particularly rich example of Roussel's use of metaphor, both religious and military. The play opens with "Eve" plaintively seeking someone to free her from her slavery. She turns to the Church for comfort, but is told that because she has sinned, she must suffer in silence and humility. She then turns to "Republican Society," "born of the blood of heroes." Society responds that the words "liberty, equality, and fraternity" were not written for her. Woman's duty is to procreate, for Society needs citizens. "Revolt," who identifies herself as "the sublime daughter of pain," then appears on the scene. She is proud, draped in scarlet, hair blowing in the wind. "It's not on knees that one marches to justice," she announces. Breathing power into Eve, the latter stands up and defies Church and Society, telling them to be silent. Eve tells her "sore flanks" to close themselves "until the hour of triumph; the glorious hour when the antiquated fortresses will crumble beneath my exasperated shouts! Where, in the place at last conquered, I will enter, trembling from heroic battles, in order to make more love and beauty germinate there."[44]

This play, of course, has several levels of meaning, not least of which is that writing and performing it allowed Roussel to fulfill her youthful acting ambitions. As she often did, Roussel turned religious metaphor on its head: the "Eve" here is victim rather than sinner; she escapes her condition rather than resigning herself to it. Perhaps most interesting is the character "Revolt," the daughter of what is no doubt *maternal* pain. Does her scarlet robe signify blood, the perpetual mutilation of the "eternally sacrificed woman," or perhaps the republican icon Marianne? Does it signify revolution? Here as elsewhere, Roussel employed multiple images and discourses, mixing them in unexpected but effective ways in order to forge an alternate female identity, while at once transfixing members of her diverse audiences and disturbing the assumptions they held.

With these rhetorical tactics, especially shaming and the implicit call to civil disorder when neither the Church nor the Third Republic would stop "sacrificing" women, Roussel appropriated and mimicked the language of public life — male language — that had become militarized during the course of the nineteenth century.[45] This strategy is all the more ironic given the recurrent distinction she made between soldiers and mothers. Elsewhere she criticized the figurative placement of mothers in a "battlefield," when she pejoratively quoted a doctor who stated, "Maternity is the battlefield of the woman; she must not desert it."[46] She opened up contradictions and paradoxes in French society and republican ideology with her rhetoric, but she also often mixed her metaphors, such as when she figuratively called women to arms, all the while contending that motherhood should be a priesthood.[47] On the surface Roussel's rhetoric had a compelling logic, and her use of both militaristic and religious metaphor drew her audiences in. The internal linguistic contradictions, the contending images of mothers and militants, and her talent for evoking shame, destabilized the world of her audiences. Therein lay her oratory power.

BEING A MOTHER

The slippage between the public image of an apostle/warrior who is also an ideal mother and wife, and the private reality of family life is more apparent in one gaping silence that permeates the Roussel-Godet correspondence: amid the terms of endearment with which Roussel closed her letters to Godet, she only occasionally told him to hug or even to say hello to her children. Otherwise she rarely mentioned them. Such silence also characterized the letters she wrote from home while he was away on business. Godet did write frequently about the children, initially mostly about Mireille when she was very young, and then about their son Marcel, nicknamed "Nono" (as in *Non! Non!*). Born respectively in 1899 and 1904, the children were quite young during the busiest years of Roussel's career, 1901 to 1910. Within just a few months of Marcel's birth, she left home for two months for a speaking tour in which she gave thirty-four lectures in fifteen departments.[48]

Godet wrote during these years of how much Marcel in particular missed his mother. He would act on her behalf to try to placate him, for example buying pastries for the boy and telling him that his mother had sent them.[49] Marcel frequently asked whether and when his mother might come home, and whether she would bring her trunk, suggesting he feared she would never return, and if she did, she would soon depart again. Godet used her absence as a disciplinary tool, responding that his mother would return only if he were a good boy.[50] But a good boy he was not, for Marcel seemed particularly recalcitrant in the matter of toilet training, and by Godet's complaints, seemed generally disobedient. One of the rare occasions that Roussel responded specifically to comments Godet made about the children, she wrote, referring first to her own accomplishments, "And there, my dear barnum, the detailed recital of the latest exploits of your 'international phenomenon.' They are worth more than those of your son. Dirty little Nono! Ignoble kid! Who always profits from my absence to do such things, because he knows that I am the only one who whips him conscientiously. Hug him for me . . . after having washed him."[51] Expressions of genuine affection for both children did appear in these letters and in letters she wrote directly to them, but the complaints were ultimately more serious than routine grumbling about a child in his "terrible two's."[52] In the summer of 1908, Godet joined Roussel after one of her lecture tours for a second honeymoon to celebrate their tenth wedding anniversary. He returned to Paris while she continued to travel. After his return he wrote to her of his efforts to find a new apartment and to hire a new maid. He then added,

> Another question, not less brilliant and every bit as perplexing — Paul and Andrée [Roussel's sister] proposed to me that I leave Nono with them — my heart as a father is doubtlessly stone because it is not torn at the terms of this proposition — understood that we would pay for his room and board and this would be on condition that they declared themselves absolutely satisfied with the circumstances and that we would accept moreover their propositions in this regard — without discussion — the question is knowing if your heart as a mother is as untearable as my heart as a father — I have already reflected on this and I estimate that we would have a lot of trouble becoming re-accustomed to Nono's roguish tricks judging by the first days of my return.[53]

Roussel responded briefly in the fourth paragraph of her letter, "We have time to talk about this more. My heart as a mother does not seem to me to present any serious wound, . . . [her ellipse] but there are other questions at play."[54]

Roussel's reactions to her children as expressed in these letters correspond with evidence from other letters and from her daily agendas indicating that even while in Paris she spent relatively little time with them. Marcel lived his first three years in a *pouponnière,* a home that kept children until they reached age three. Between age three and four, when Roussel and Godet seemed to have so much difficulty with him, they did give him over to Roussel's sister, where he mostly lived for the next several years. Mireille lived primarily with Roussel's mother and stepfather. Otherwise, both children found themselves in the care of domestics and other extended family. Godet did frequently care for both children, but the time spent as a complete nuclear family of all four together was rather rare.[55] Marcel and Mireille would join Roussel for at least part of her three- or four-month summer vacations in the country. But she spent a good portion of these months away from both Godet and her children, partly to recover her health. When the children were present, she complained a great deal of noise and contracting colds from them. For example when Marcel was nearly five and with her at a summer home, she suffered exhaustion, and wrote, "Clearly I am in the process of losing again the little improvement I gained with such difficulty. I feel as bad as possible. And Nono only contributes to this wonderful result. This child will kill me *(me fera mourir)*. I don't have the strength to write any more."[56]

In short, the reality of Roussel's private life did not fit the public image she and Godet created in order to market her ideology. Although it may be unfair to read too much into the moment captured by an early twentieth-century camera, the pose of Roussel and her daughter conveys a message other than "a happy mother in the warm shadow of her hearth." Roussel has the viewer gazing into the privacy of her home, with her child by her side and her husband's work in the background. But her gaze goes beyond the frame, looking outward to where her "mission" and her "apostolate" await her. In one world, but looking out to another one, she suggests maternal detachment and distance. But framed in a feminized "missionary" context, she understood that such detachment would be accepted by her family and by her public.[57] Leaving her children to the care of Godet, her extended family, domestics, and in the case of Marcel, even a *pouponnière*, motherhood for Roussel was a part-time occupation despite the image she successfully imparted to her audiences. If in her public addresses she extolled motherhood while arguing for woman's ability to control it, in her private life she succeeded in largely escaping it. Her apparent self-perception about her maternal role was profoundly ironic. In the "biography" she penned about herself, she wrote, "At last, to terminate, let's say that Madame Nelly Roussel gives, through her private life, a striking denial *[démenti]* to those who want the emancipation of women necessarily to mean defeminization . . . loving and loved spouse, she is the happy mother of two charming children, and her last book is dedicated to her daughter, to her 'little Mireille,' in order that she remembers."[58] The *"démenti"* here was clearly Roussel's.

No doubt when Roussel married Godet in 1898 she wanted children; like most women of her time, it had never occurred to her not to have them or not to want them. But her own experiences with motherhood did as much to awaken her feminism — which for her included an intense sense of individualism — as did her husband's convictions, which may explain why Godet had to remind her to give him credit. Though her first experience with childbirth left her with indelibly painful memories, particularly brutal was her second experience with labor, which came very close to killing her, as well as the loss at age four months of the child she bore from that labor. Her third pregnancy produced the "enfant terrible" Marcel, whose very conception had been quite unintended and much resented.[59] These experiences set her consciousness and her life on a new course. Physically and emotionally debilitated, she became almost obsessed with articulating the pains of motherhood in contrast to its purported joys. Maternal suffering not only awakened in her feminist issues based on control over reproduction — they propelled her to articulate her experience and gave her the language to do so.[60]

In this interpretation of Roussel's correspondence, I do not intend to suggest that she did not love her children; if her feelings about Marcel understandably reflected ambivalence, no evidence suggests that her love for Mireille was less than unqualified. She at once loved her children and wished to be unfettered by them. Her marriage to Godet made both love and freedom possible. Their relationship promoted and sustained her career and allowed her to practice her feminist ideology of fulfilling her own potential as an individual. Given his more frequent writing, the emotional and sometimes emotionally confused tone of his letters, his care of the children, his inability to support the family financially, and his role as her secretary, it would be quite tempting to suggest that their gender positions represented a reversal of the norm. I would prefer to view their relationship as Roussel no doubt saw it, above the binary divisions of male and female, as two unusually different and complementary individuals each of whom exhibited characteristics of "masculinity" and "femininity." Nonetheless, if either of them was ambivalent about their role, it was Godet. Although he claimed never to have any fights with his wife, the confusion in his letters reveals not only deep frustration, but psychological stress about the unusual position in which she continually placed him, both in practical and in symbolic terms.[61]

It is a considerable irony that Roussel's marriage as well as the financial, emotional, and practical support of her bourgeois family allowed her to transcend the usual dictates of gender and class, fulfill her potential as an individual, and bring a very radical message to tens of thousands of listeners and an unknown number of readers throughout Europe. Although she could never publicly reveal, let alone advocate, her private means of reconciling her maternal self with her individualist self, she preached *liberté de maternité* — "freedom of motherhood" — while she practiced and implicitly fought for "freedom *from* motherhood," and in so doing she parted ways with the vast majority of other feminists.

Noteworthy about Roussel's private conduct with regard to her family life is that it did not provoke commentary, let alone criticism, either from the more traditionally oriented members of her family, such as her mother and her conservative stepfather, or from any of her friends, feminist or otherwise. Even Odette Laguerre, who helped portray Roussel's public image as wife and mother, and for whom motherhood had enormous importance, apparently did not think Roussel's extended absences from her children the least abnormal.[62] This silence might indeed indicate that despite the emphasis on feminine domesticity through the Victorian era and the increased political importance that motherhood assumed, maternal practices themselves had not yet become what they would be after World War II. The continued presence of domestics and extended families allowed mothers to separate themselves from their children on a daily basis. Certainly Roussel's behavior suggests a gap between maternal rhetoric and bourgeois reality.[63] The absence of criticism about her behavior among family and friends, as well as the majority of her public, also speaks to the success of the image she created as "apostle," which justified for her supporters her absence from the home. One of the many elegies using the words "apostle" or "apostolate" summarizes well the image she achieved: "Nelly Roussel, who added the charms of the woman to the faith of the apostle, was an accomplished spouse and mother."[64]

Another reason no one in her family criticized Roussel is that its members, even though they did not all share her views, enjoyed remarkable intimacy and manifested fierce loyalty to her. For their entire marriage, Roussel and Godet lived no more than a block away from her mother and stepfather's house in the twelfth arrondissement. When Roussel was in Paris, they both saw her mother several times a week, often having lunch or dinner with her. Although her conservative stepfather, whom she and Godet never liked, certainly opposed her politics, he never expressed such opposition until the end her life, and he consistently provided them with financial support and well-intended, if unwanted, advice. The entire family attended many of her lectures in Paris. Roussel, Godet, and their children also had an extremely close relationship with Godet's sister and the Robin family into which she married, spending most Sundays in the Bois de Vincennes and sharing summer homes when Roussel was not traveling. Though politics cemented solidarity with the

Robin family, both sides of the family collectively spent an enormous amount of time together.[65]

BEING SUBVERSIVE

Roussel's image as bourgeois wife and mother served her in a multitude of ways. It enabled her to deliver a radical message that would have otherwise offended her audiences and ostracized her from other feminists. In their history of women's suffrage during the Third Republic, Steven Hause and Anne Kenney noted Roussel's ability to cooperate with moderates and even serve in executive positions in moderate organizations. Though her ideas about female sexual emancipation were every bit as radical as Madeleine Pelletier's, and just as intolerable among feminists and nonfeminists alike, her persona as wife and mother enabled her to enter a wide variety of social and political circles. Very early in her career, feminists of all types considered her to be their most effective orator. During a counter-celebration on the one-hundredth anniversary of the Napoleonic Code, "between 800 and 1,000 women — a huge crowd for the feminist movement in 1904 — " paid to hear her speak against the code for establishing the legal oppression of women. The variety of organizations that collaborated in sponsoring her tours, moreover, testifies to her wide appeal despite the radicalism of her message. In addition to free-thinkers, neo-Malthusian, and feminist groups already mentioned, teachers, pacifists, socialists, and Masonic lodges also invited her to lecture.[66]

Even some of Roussel's fiercest opponents admitted admiration of her, but others lost no time in vilifying her as a danger to society for undermining its moral fabric, as well as to the state for undermining national security. Indeed, Roussel quite deliberately intended to thwart what she perceived as the French government's goal to "repopulate" for purposes of providing additional "cannon fodder." From the outset of the neo-Malthusian movement in 1896, pronatalists pressured the Third Republic government to take action against advocates of birth control. Moral conservatives throughout the political spectrum condemned the movement for blurring gender boundaries, undermining family values, reinforcing the culture of individualism over community and social responsibilities, and perhaps most important, provoking sexual debauchery and the further degeneration of the French "race."[67]

With no laws specifically prohibiting birth-control propaganda, beginning in 1909 several neo-Malthusianists were convicted on grounds of obscenity; they served prison terms of several months and were fined.

Prosecutions resulted in self-silencing, circumscribed language, and a virtual end to public instruction on the use of birth control.[68] Nelly Roussel never became subject to this particular sort of persecution, in part because she did not speak explicitly about birth-control methods, and in part because of the public image she presented. Her bourgeois and her female status no doubt protected her from such treatment. The images she created of herself desexualized issues that were implicitly sexual and would have been perceived as more explicitly sexual if treated by a man. Despite her visibility in the press, Roussel escaped police scrutiny even as agents produced voluminous reports on other neo-Malthusians. They primarily focused on the anarchists who dominated the movement and whom they viewed as revolutionary. While police reports occasionally mentioned Roussel, they covered only very few of the lectures she delivered — the ones in which she accompanied male anarchist speakers such as Sebastian Faure. Police generally remained unaware of her charisma and the role the press played in enhancing it.[69]

Although not persecuted by the state, Roussel did lose a telling court battle, the content of which reveals the subversive power of her message. The case involved press coverage of a lecture she delivered in Paris at a neo-Malthusian meeting in November 1905. She lectured on "Liberty and Procreative Prudence in Maternity," (a title far more precise than that which had been advertised as "Many Children") to an audience of six hundred, among whom were many women.[70] She opened her lecture with the observation that woman is eternally sacrificed, the constant victim of all religions, and of society in general. She argued against the dogmatic religious dictum "to increase and multiply," as well as against the increasingly pervasive social dogma of fecundity characteristic of pronatalists. Not only did excessive population growth lead to economic disaster, she continued, but woman had to have liberty of maternity, and as in every other social function, the right to go on strike with her womb in order to end the procreation of "slaves, cannon fodder, and pleasure fodder." The police report carefully noted that Roussel "only spoke of the theoretical question, avoiding the great peril of practice," and "averted any hint of obscenity or ridicule."[71]

Guy de Cassagnac, director of the newspaper *L'Autorité*, published an article two months later that criticized Roussel's lecture and attempted to refute the neo-Malthusian theory upon which it was based. Roussel responded with a letter rebutting Cassagnac. The latter published only part of Roussel's letter, which provoked her to sue him. Her case rested on Article 13 of the law of July 29, 1881, which obligated a journal to publish, in its entirety, any letter of response from anyone named or designated in a newspaper. Exceptions could be made only for letters containing a "direct provocation to debauchery" by "exposing an immoral and antisocial doctrine" that was "contrary to laws and good morals."[72] The court decided in favor of Cassagnac claiming that although Roussel's letter did not include any direct provocation to debauchery, it did assert that women had a right to voluntary sterility. Her letter invoked reasons of health, which the court found legitimate, but it also used as its reasoning women's "fear of suffering and the desire for well-being"; and instead of recommending chastity, neo-Malthusian theory "invit[ed] its disciples, not to abstain from sexual pleasures, but to seek after them by taking necessary precautions to avoid procreation." The court found this theory to be "immoral and antisocial"; its practice would "stop the progress of humanity" and cause "national weakness and decadence."[73] Significant about this court decision is not its anticipated condemnation of birth control, but the distinction it made between avoiding procreation for reasons of physical health and avoiding it for reasons of psychological or emotional well-being. The court only recognized women's right to protect their bodies through chastity, but did not endorse their right to engage in sexual activity "without fear of suffering." Obviously of religious origin, this moral precept justifying female pain continued to influence justice in a secular society. It was also the very precept against which Roussel ceaselessly fought.

Witnessing the arrests and imprisonment of her neo-Malthusian colleagues, Roussel exercised great caution in her public speaking and continued to evade any police repression, though the meaning of her message remained the same. She carried on her public career of speaking and writing newspaper articles, but after 1910 the frequency of her lectures diminished as tuberculosis slowly but progressively deteriorated her body. In 1911, she spent five painful months in a *maison de santé* in Switzerland, during which Godet seemed lonelier and yearned for her more than ever.[74] In subsequent years, Roussel would again take "rest cures" either in privately rented country homes or in institutions. The key turning point in both her private and public lives — as was true for anyone in Europe — came with the First World War. Fortunately for their family, Godet was too old to be conscripted and Marcel too young. Nonetheless they suffered the ravages of war as close friends lost family members, as stories of atrocities filtered back to the home front, and as they experienced daily material deprivations along with everyone else. Their situation became particularly precarious when Godet's business collapsed and he had difficulty finding another livelihood. The expenses incurred by Roussel's illness became ever less affordable, and she and Godet became more dependent on assistance from her stepfather. Hardship seemed to make the family closer; Marcel returned from boarding school and lived at home permanently. Despite adversity, Roussel continued her "mission" as best she could.

The war fundamentally transformed the political context for Roussel's intellectual thought and rhetoric in two ways: it completely crippled the feminist movement and increased vocal support for pronatalism. Radical feminists, by incorporating any variety of socialist, anarchist, pacifist, or neo-Malthusian ideas had assumed a political stance opposing the government prior to the war. When the war broke out, like other left-wing groups who had previously opposed the state, radical feminists suddenly dropped their demands, and joined the "sacred union" of patriotic sentiment that war and fear had so effectively tapped throughout the nation. Both feminist and nonfeminist women shed their private concerns and undertook a host of voluntary, as well as paid, war-related activities. Feminism as a movement became completely moribund.[75]

As feminism dissipated, pronatalist sentiment intensified. Pronatalist leagues expanded in number from one to four, and their collective membership to more than a million; they diffused anti-Malthusian propaganda through the popular press, in newspapers, and journals that had not previously treated this question. Much of French society, including most feminists, came to share the opinion that women who wished to avoid childbearing exhibited selfishness and shirked their patriotic duty. Indeed, as the war dragged on, fears that the French "race" would disappear intensified; more than ever procreation became an issue of patriotism. Though feminists continued to use motherhood as a basis for increasing the status of women's social functions, the image of woman as mother and homemaker became ever more powerful and pervasive.[76]

Roussel numbered among a very small minority whose political sentiments did not change or soften with the outbreak of war; indeed, they were intensified. Understandably her attentions turned toward the war and away from many of the specific issues that had previously preoccupied her. Her ideas often bordered on sedition and had the effect of isolating her from other feminists and socialists. Never once abandoning her convictions, she was forced to repackage them. The war itself horrified and disgusted her from its beginning, and so too did the attitudes of most French people, including some of her closest friends and family. She felt no patriotism, but her profound sense of humanitarianism led her to tread lightly on the sentiments of others, and like other women, to work on behalf of the French war effort. She never, however, abandoned pacifism. And when she did not censor herself on that passion, the French government did.

The one topic Roussel did remain silent about after the war broke out was that which was dearest to her: freedom of motherhood. Associated with the cause of neo-Malthusianism, this feminist issue found the least sympathetic hearing and might well have been construed as the most seditious of all her campaigns because of its implications for public morale. Privately, its cause and effect encouraged selfish individualism among women and undermined marriage, male prerogative, and familial bonds. But publicly, neo-Malthusians also intended to reduce the availability of "cannon fodder," and thereby end war. Here the incompatibility between "liberty of motherhood" and national well-being was most clearly evident, particularly in the height of a war whose outcome remained in doubt and whose end was nowhere in sight.[77]

For reasons of both censorship and ill health, Roussel did not resume her campaign for freedom of motherhood until well after the end of the war when she no longer had any use for packaging her messages in bourgeois or patriotic images. Once again, the context for her rhetoric had changed. In some respects the war had improved women's public position, but it also proved to be an irreversible setback for feminism, having killed its prewar momentum and further divided the movement.[78] Although Roussel remained consistent in her ideals, the war had at least momentarily destroyed the veneer of bourgeois gentility for most everyone. She thus no longer crossed boundaries among groups throughout the political spectrum; instead, she committed herself exclusively to socialist feminism. She did so primarily through the new journal, *La Voix des femmes,* founded in 1917 partly as an idealistic response to the Bolshevik Revolution. Soon approaching a circulation of five thousand, this newspaper became the "loudest voice on the women's left." [79] A member of the editorial board, Roussel described the paper as "an oasis, a refuge of hope," because it offered a tribune for the most radical of feminists, as well as for neo-Malthusian theory.[80]

It was here that Roussel published most of her articles in the last years of her life, and it was under the newspaper's sponsorship that she continued to lecture. The emphasis of her content shifted, however, from women's individual freedom to the social connections between overpopulation and war, and to men's responsibility for war. Indeed, her rhetoric became distinctly more "essentialist" in highlighting men's tendencies toward brutality and the need to bring women into the public sphere in order to combat and compensate for that brutality with their "natural" life-creating tendencies. The war had convinced her more than ever that civilized society required the participation of women in public affairs, and she devoted many of her articles, lectures, and activities to that end.[81]

In 1919, Roussel published a new edition of the 1907 *Quelques discours*. This version included lectures she had given through 1916 and in many ways captures the impact that war had on her public and private identity, and on the content and tone of her expression. She gave this volume a new title, *Paroles de combat et d'espoir;* in the foreword she stated that "facts had clearly given her reason to remain faithful to her ideal, and that she had not changed fields in the battle of her ideas." In keeping with her previous publications, this one too had her portrait on the front cover, but it bore little relation to its antecedents. Shed of all bourgeois pretense, this artistic sketch portrays a woman of beauty, but also of working-class simplicity, with an imploring posture. This figure needs no accompanying child to legitimize its demands; their intensity is conveyed in the implied movement of the arms, hands, and fingers, and in the impetuous eyes. Gone too is the *femme fatale* of the figure on page 219. Postwar economies in the expense of printing could partly explain the simplicity of this cover, but clearly it conveys the transformation in Roussel's own selfhood by the end of the war. Included in that transformation was the tuberculosis that had invaded her body, creating a new personal "battlefield" as well. Her preface also represents a major change from that of the 1907 version, as well as from the 1910 preface to *Quelques lances rompues:*

> I dedicated, in 1907, the first edition of some of my speeches:
>
>> To my husband, my best friend,
>> To him who encourages my apostolate.
>
> I add today:
>
>> And to those who will perhaps continue it,
>> To my children, Mireille and Marcel.

Gone was the notion in her publication of 1910 that Mireille would "perhaps" enjoy the fruits of her mother's career; instead, knowing its limits, Roussel humbly requested that both children, now respectively twenty and fifteen years old, carry on her mission. But significant too is her inclusion of Marcel here, the unwanted "Nono" whom her mission had so often pushed to the margins of her life.

Portrait of Nelly Roussel, frontispiece for *Paroles de combat et d'espoir* (1919).

The period following the end of the war gave Roussel no reason for complacency. Despite the support of *La Voix des femmes* and the women associated with it, bitter disappointment plagued the last years of her life. Passage of the law of 1920, which finally criminalized the sale of and propaganda for all female forms of contraception and which facilitated penalties for abortion, might have made her feel that all her efforts of the previous twenty years had failed.[82] In the spring of 1920 as the National Assembly prepared this law, Roussel vigorously spoke against it at meetings of *La Voix des femmes* and the French socialist party, the S.F.I.O. The latter meeting took place in St. Ouen, where she spoke to a working-class audience of one thousand. She stressed two themes in these meetings: first, the importance of women's participation in the "administration of public affairs and in the study of the great social problems," for the latter would "never be resolved as long as only a fraction of the human species is looking for the solution"; second, the "sacred" freedom of woman "to dispose of her womb, to love as she wishes, and to be a mother only by choice . . . a human mother and not a female animal." The impact of the war and of her own illness on her rhetoric became apparent in the brittleness of her tone: "At the hour when capitalist and nationalist eaters of men reclaim their spoils, is it necessary to extract from our aching wombs that which feeds future battlefields? Humanity is exhausted from war, from alcohol, tuberculosis, syphilis: the race needs to take care of itself and to heal before it expands, and our refusal to bear children by chance and without limits is no longer the first of our rights; it becomes the most urgent and the most imperious of our duties."[83] Roussel concluded that the law would be inoperable because "the truth cannot be suppressed; one can hide it for a long time, [but] it always reappears."[84]

Most disappointing to Roussel and other radical feminists who shared her views was not simply the passage of this law two months later, but the fact that most of their male feminist allies in the National Assembly, as well as feminist and nonfeminist women throughout France, supported it. As Christine Bard has recounted, feminists did not oppose abortion and contraception for religious reasons; their opposition came from their sensitivity to the populationist theories, according to which national security and prosperity were measured by the number of children born. Not wishing women to suffer from repetitive pregnancies, reformist feminists somewhat paradoxically recommended sexual abstinence. But feminist support for the law of 1920 also had an underlying strategic motivation: allied with the Radical Party that also supported this law, suffragists did not want to weaken their political position by protesting a law Radicals supported.[85]

Under the law of 1920, Nelly Roussel would have been imprisoned for six months to three years and fined one hundred to three thousand francs for many of the lectures she had given and articles she had published throughout her career. After the passage of this law, she continued to voice her radical feminist politics, though she did not address the issue of birth control directly. She attacked "repopulators" and revolutionaries alike for not addressing women's issues and for not including women in their deliberations. She wrote of revolution as a process and its relationship to feminism, and she wrote against war and militarism. If she could not write about liberty of motherhood, she wrote extensively on the burdens of motherhood and how they remained unrecognized by men on both the left and the right. One of the last articles she published in *La Voix des femmes* did, however, proclaim that women had the right not to be mothers, indeed sometimes even the duty not to be. Not being a mother, woman "remains no less a human individual equal to a masculine individual . . . whose faculties are as necessary for universal harmony."[86]

Though the law of 1920 muted Roussel's campaign for maternal liberty and virtually destroyed the neo-Malthusian movement, it inspired her to pursue a new path. Convinced more than ever that women had to participate in public life, she also realized that such participation depended upon their ability to speak, and helping them do so by sharing her own talents and expertise became her new mission. To that end, and with the sponsorship of *La Voix des femmes,* she created a "School of Propagandists" to teach women how to speak in public, to debate as well as to lecture.[87] Roussel taught in this school with Alice Jouenne and Madeleine Pelletier until her voice failed her in 1922.[88]

CONCLUSION

It was not, finally, the government that silenced Nelly Roussel, but tuberculosis. On June 9, 1922, her mother and Marcel, then seventeen years old, accompanied her on the train to the "Sanatorium of the Pines" in Lamotte-Beuvron (Loire-et-Cher). Panicked at witnessing his wife's rapid decline, losing faith in Roussel's doctor who deprived patients of heat, not for therapeutic purposes, but to save money, Godet moved Roussel to the sanatorium of Buzenval, just west of Paris. There she died on December 18, 1922, after an excruciatingly painful illness, detailed in her diary and in Godet's memoir.[89] Her death came less than a month before her forty-fifth birthday. In numerous respects, the family seems never to have recovered from her death. Godet, nearly sixty years old when she died, survived Roussel another fourteen years, never remarrying and never overcoming the loss of the wife to whom he had been completely devoted. But he also suffered another insurmountable injury; Marcel died of stomach cancer only six years later just after having married. Mireille lived until age eighty-three, maintaining close ties with her mother's friends such as Odette Laguerre and with the descendants of Paul Robin, founder of the neo-Malthusian movement in France, whose son had married Godet's sister.

Mireille Godet, who in print often referred to herself as "Mireille Nelly-Roussel," never married and devoted her life to keeping alive the memory of her mother. Close to her until her death, Michel Robin noted that Mireille never had any interest in men or in sexuality, and though she had close friends of both genders, never had interest in marriage or in physical intimacy of any kind—indeed, she was "repelled" by the thought of it. This life of sensual/sexual isolation in Mireille suggests other ways of thinking about her mother. Did Roussel's tragic pregnancies create a fear of sex, a fear that she conveyed to her daughter despite a life-long effort to liberate sex from its "natural consequences" and from its culture-bound moral precepts?[90]

Several points emerge from this analysis of Roussel's private life, public image, and public impact. Her private life allowed her the freedom and flexibility to create an image—that did indeed have a basis in the reality of her background and lifestyle—of a "proper woman" whose "acceptability" gave her the means to publicize unacceptable ideas. One noteworthy impression from reading her private papers is that she harbored no sense of guilt or of hypocrisy in casting herself as the ideal bourgeois mother and wife. In her manners and in her sensibilities, she was indeed bourgeois—a term whose inherent meaning does, after all, include the importance of appearance and impression making. Her motherhood extended well beyond the biological sense, even if her maternal practices did not fit Victorian prescriptions. She loved and cared for her children, though others so frequently "took care" of them, and because of her career and her disease, she ultimately marginalized them. Her own physical, emotional, and psychological experiences with motherhood gave her the language to make maternity a political issue, whether she extolled it as a "sacrament" or emphasized its burdens.

Such experiences also gave Roussel reason to argue that women had

a right to sexual pleasure and such pleasure could only be attained if sex
were separated from reproduction. This message would not be officially
accepted until well after France had recovered from World War II, a fact
that provides no small hint about what the law of 1920 meant. Though
the passage of this law can be easily explained — and thus dismissed —
within the context of postwar hysteria regarding France's admittedly piti-
ful demographic condition, the law was about far more than demogra-
phy, since it did nothing to restrict male forms of contraception. The law
sought to control only female sexuality.[91] The French government, and
much of French society, could not tolerate a female sexuality untem-
pered by maternity — which is why they made certain sexuality and
maternity would not become disassociated in official discourse. But the
great irony of Roussel's career is that to a large extent she was preaching
to the already converted. Perhaps she gained such popularity by soothing
individual consciences, providing them with a justification for what they
were already doing.[92] Birthrates had begun to decline before she "took to
the pulpit" and continued to do so until after World War II. They fell
from 21.4 per 1,000 in 1920, to 18.3 in 1928, and to 14.6 in 1938.[93]
This continued gap between the official rhetoric of pronatalism and the
reality of what went on in bedrooms throughout France is a cultural phenomenon itself worth exploring, for it reflects a persistent secular and
civic need for moral precepts founded upon religion.[94] Birth control as a
topic of discussion — like many other topics in French and Western culture — remained taboo despite its practice. The fact remains, however,
that we do not know exactly what people did. Because of the anticon-
traceptive laws, birth control may have continued to depend on male prerogative — withdrawal and condoms — and on clandestine abortion, as it
had in the past. To endorse female methods of contraception would have
accomplished precisely what Guy de Cassagnac — the newspaper director
to whom Roussel lost the lawsuit over women's "right not to suffer"
from sex — and others like him were trying to prevent. It would have
meant open admission of behavior still considered to be immoral and
antisocial, therefore unvirtuous — and it would have rendered impossible
the collective self-deception upon which French "honor" was based.[95]

NOTES

I wish to thank the University of Southern California for a Zumberge Faculty
Research and Innovation Grant and a College Award for Research Excellence,
as well as the American Council of Learned Societies for a summer grant-in-aid,
all of which made research for this essay possible. The project would have been

impossible without the extraordinary — indeed unparalleled — generosity of Mme. Annie Metz, *Conservatrice* of the Bibliothèque Marguerite Durand, and my indebtedness to her extends well beyond the parameters of this particular essay. I thank her also for permission to publish photographs of Nelly Roussel obtained from the BMD. I am grateful to Michel Robin for his time, hospitality, and insights about the Roussel-Godet family. This essay was originally presented as a paper at the Society for French Historical Studies in Boston, March 1996. Then and many times since, it has benefited from the careful critique of Robert A. Nye, Rachel Fuchs, Sharif Gemie, Yves Lequin, Mauricio Mazón, John Merriman, Karen Offen, Lou Roberts, and David Troyansky, all of whom read various versions of this essay and gave invaluable suggestions. I wish most especially to thank Joby Margadant, not only for putting this collection together, but for the insights and suggestions that have helped reshape my thinking about Nelly Roussel. I also wish to thank the other contributors to this collection, as well as Sheila Levine and the anonymous referees of the University of California Press.

1. Odette Laguerre, preface to Nelly Roussel, *Trois Conférences de Nelly Roussel* (Paris: Marcel Giard, 1930), 5.

2. The following is a typical description of Roussel while on one of her tours: "Tall, slender, with a brow of elevated thoughts, of dreamy eyes, of a simple elegance, dressed in black, the lecturer speaks with a captivating, warm, trembling voice, with lyrical, poetic amplifications, with a voice which moves and which reveals the sincerity of expressed convictions. Throughout the length of her talk, one feels that the citizeness Nelly-Roussel does not just speak in any way about any subject, but [speaks] with all her heart and all her soul, about doctrines that are dear to her and to which she is completely devoted"; quoted from "Une Conférence de Mme. Nelly-Roussel" in *Le Petit Var* of Toulon, April 29, 1907. Similar press descriptions from 1902 to 1922 can be found in Roussel's scrapbook in Fonds Roussel, Bibliothèque Marguerite Durand.

3. With the expansion of the bourgeois public sphere in the eighteenth century, especially as manifested with the French Revolution, women were systematically excluded from public life because they were deemed inherently untrustworthy. Jean-Jacques Rousseau, among others, established the moral and theoretical basis for this attitude, which French revolutionaries implemented in 1793. See Lieselotte Steinbrugge, *The Moral Sex: Woman's Nature in the French Enlightenment*, trans. Pamela E. Selwyn (New York: Oxford University Press, 1995); Joan Landes, *Women and the Public Sphere in the Age of the French Revolution* (Ithaca: Cornell University Press, 1988); Christine Fauré, *Democracy without Women: Feminism and the Rise of Liberal Individualism in France*, trans. Claudia Gorbman and John Berks (Bloomington: Indiana University Press, 1991); Carol Blum, *Rousseau and the Republic of Virtue: The Language of Politics in the French Revolution* (Ithaca: Cornell University Press, 1986); William H. Sewell Jr., "Le citoyen/la citoyenne: Activity, Passivity, and the Revolutionary Concept of Citizenship," in *The Political Culture of the French Revolution*, ed. Colin Lucas, vol. 2 (New York: Pergamon Press, 1988), 105–23; Lynn Hunt, *The Family Romance of the French Revolution* (Berkeley and Los

Angeles: University of California Press, 1992). Attitudes cemented during the revolution persisted in a multitude of ways through the nineteenth century. See for example, Geneviève Fraisse, *Muse de la raison: Démocratie et exclusion des femmes en France* (Paris: Gallimard, 1989). Robert A. Nye, and more recently, William M. Reddy have studied male codes of honor in nineteenth-century French society, noting that women could not participate in public life because they could not physically defend their honor; honor is a masculine concept necessary to regulation of public life. See Nye, *Masculinity and Male Codes of Honor in Modern France* (Oxford: Oxford University Press, 1993) and Reddy, *The Invisible Code: Honor and Sentiment in Postrevolutionary France, 1814–1848* (Berkeley and Los Angeles: The University of California Press, 1997). See also Edward Berenson, *The Trial of Madame Caillaux* (Berkeley and Los Angeles: University of California Press, 1992).

4. The research for this essay is based on Roussel's private papers, located in Fonds Roussel, Bibliothèque Marguerite Durand (henceforth BMD). They are in the process of being systematically catalogued, and it is not always possible to provide specific catalogue numbers for each citation given here. For this essay, biographical information has also been drawn from Marbel, "Les Femmes d'aujourd'hui" (c. 1923); Marie-Jo Bonnet, "La Belle Époque du féminisme," *Flair* (January 1979), both in "dossier Roussel." I have used other private papers to interpret the correspondence between Nelly Roussel (henceforth, NR) and Henri Godet (henceforth, HG), such as letters to and from other people, her daily agendas, her speaking agenda, and the press clippings of reviews of her lectures. Further published biographical information on Roussel appears in the following: Anne Cova, "Féminisme et natalité: Nelly Roussel (1878–1922)," *History of European Ideas* 15, nos. 4–6 (1992): 663–72; Nelly Roussel, *L'Éternelle sacrifiée* with preface, notes, and commentary by Daniel Armogathe and Maité Albistur (Paris: Syros, 1979); and prefaces to Roussel's other works, such as *Paroles de combat et d'espoir* (Epone, 1919); *Trois Conférences* (Paris, 1930); *Derniers Combats: recueil d'articles et de discours (1911–1922)* (Paris, 1932). This essay is part of a book-length study, in progress, of Roussel and the neo-Malthusian movement.

5. Her religious poetry is located in "documents relatifs à la biographie de Nelly Roussel et Henri Godet," dossier 07 in Fonds Roussel, BMD. Poems reflecting her conservative religious and political sensibililties in her youth are "Sur la Mort de Sadi Carnot," June 24, 1894; "Souvenir de mon inoubliable voyage à Marseilles," June 1895; "Sur la Cathédrale de Paris," April 1898.

6. See the very short, handwritten "biographies" penned respectively by Henri Godet (c. 1903) and Nelly Roussel (c. 1911), both written in the third person, in Fonds Roussel. These points about her youth are also mentioned in the preface to Armogathe and Albistur, 9. These authors also had the benefit of interviewing Mireille Godet, Roussel's daughter, who died in 1982.

7. Roussel and Godet, manuscript biographies. Armagathe and Albistur noted that she "devoured" her grandfather's library, 9.

8. Godet, biography.

9. Roussel recalled her feelings upon meeting Robin in a eulogy she wrote when he committed suicide in 1912. See Nelly Roussel, "Petite gerbe sur une

grande tombe," *Génération consciente,* October 1, 1912. On Paul Robin, see Christiane Demeulenaere-Douyère, *Paul Robin: Un Militant de la liberté et du bonheur* (Paris: Publisud, 1994); Gabriel Giroud, *Paul Robin: Sa vie. Ses idées. Son action.* (Paris: G. Mignolet & Storz, 1937). On the neo-Malthusian movement (and Paul Robin), see Elinor A. Accampo, "The Rhetoric of Reproduction and the Reconfiguration of Womanhood in the French Birth Control Movement, 1890–1920," *Journal of Family History* 21, no. 3 (1996): 351–71; Angus McLaren, *Sexuality and Social Order: The Debate over the Fertility of Women and Workers in France, 1770–1920* (New York: Holmes & Meier, 1983); Françis Ronsin, *La Grève des ventres: propagande néo-Malthusienne et baisse de la natalité on France, 19e et 20e siècles* (Paris: Aubier Montaigne, 1980); Roger-Henri Guerrand, *La libre maternité, 1896–1969* (Paris: Caasterman, 1971).

10. See Elinor A. Accampo, Rachel G. Fuchs, and Mary Lynn Stewart, *Gender and the Politics of Social Reform in France, 1870–1914* (Baltimore: The Johns Hopkins University Press, 1995). Instilling appropriate values of motherhood and domesticity were also the goals of the massive reform in girls' education that began in the 1880s. See Jo Burr Margadant, *Madame le Professeur: Women Educators in the Third Republic* (Princeton: Princeton University Press, 1990). For an excellent discussion of degeneration theory and its translation into social theory, see Robert A. Nye, *Crime, Madness, and Politics in Modern France: The Medical Concept of National Decline* (Princeton: Princeton University Press, 1984), 119–70.

11. Joshua Cole, " 'There Are Only Good Mothers': The Ideological Work of Women's Fertility in France before World War I," *French Historical Studies* 19 (spring 1996): 653.

12. Karen Offen, "Depopulation, Nationalism, and Feminism in Fin-de-Siècle France," *The American Historical Review* 89 (June 1984): 648–76. More recently Anne Cova, in her study of the history of legislative debates and measures to protect motherhood, has documented the enormous influence "depopulation" and the debates surrounding it had on the role that motherhood played in French feminism. Anne Cova, *Maternité et droits des femmes en France (XIXe–XXe siècles)* (Paris: Anthropos, 1997).

13. David Barnes makes this point about cultural perceptions during the Belle Époque in his analysis of the relationship between female suffering and tuberculosis in *The Making of a Social Disease: Tuberculosis in Nineteenth-Century France* (Berkeley and Los Angeles: University of California Press, 1995), 60.

14. The actual quote is "ce sont les étapes douloureuses, et meurtrières parfois, ce sont les échelons du calvaire qu'il faut gravir lentement pour en arriver là . . . " in Nelly Roussel, "Liberté de Maternité," reproduced in *Trois Conférences* (Paris: Marcel Giard, 1930), 42. It is also translated and published as "Freedom of Motherhood" in *Feminisms of the Belle Époque: A Historical and Literary Anthology,* ed. Jennifer Waelti-Walters and Steven C. Hause, trans. Jette Kjaer, Lydia Willis, and Jennifer Waelti-Walters (Lincoln: University of Nebraska Press, 1994), 241–51. They translate this particular line somewhat differently: " . . . the rungs of martyrdom that must slowly be climbed before getting there . . . " (245). I prefer to interpret the religious reference more literally because, given other religious metaphors throughout her work, I think that is what Roussel intended.

Regardless, the meaning is the same: women are sacrificed, indeed, martyred as they labor in childbirth and motherhood. "L'Éternelle sacrifiée" is also translated in Waelti-Walters and Hause as "She Who Is Eternally Sacrificed," 18–37. For another bold example of Roussel's use of religious metaphor, see her play *La Faute d'Eve*, first published in *Le mouvement féminine*, September 15, 1913.

15. These include *Quelques Discours* (Paris, 1907); *Quelques lances rompues pour nos libertés* (Paris, 1910); *Paroles de combat et d'espoir* (Epone, 1919); *Trois Conférences* (Paris, 1930); and *Derniers Combats: receuil d'articles et de discours* (Paris, 1932). She also published a one-act play that she frequently performed after lectures, *Par la révolte: scène symbolique* (Paris, c. 1903).

16. Quoted from Roussel's autobiographical sketch, written in third person, c. 1911–1913. References by others to her "mission" and her "apostolate" were very frequent, especially in numerous postmortem eulogies.

17. Information about her audiences — size, composition, and reaction to her lectures — is obtained from her letters to Godet and from newspaper coverage. For her reception in Bourg-Argental in April 1905, see for example NR to HG, April 13 and 27, 1905; *La Tribune de Saint Étienne*, April 14, 1905; *Le Progrès du Lyon*, April 14, 1905; *Lyon républicain*, April 14, 1905. Roussel also received testimonial letters from her listeners, documenting the impact she had on them. The most prominent example of working-class woman Roussel "converted" is Charlotte Davy, who became a militant feminist and contributor to *La Voix des femmes* after hearing one of Roussel's lectures. See her autobiographical account in Charlotte Davy, *Une femme . . .* (Paris: Eugene Figuiere, 1927).

18. *A History of Private Life, V–IV: From the Fires of Revolution to the Great World War*, ed. Michelle Perrot, trans. Arthur Goldhammer (Cambridge, Mass.: Belknap Press of Harvard University Press, 1990), 3–4. On the use of letters as a historical source, see also Roger Chartier (under the direction of Roger Chartier), *La correspondance: Les usages de la lettre au XIXe siècle* (Paris: Fayard, 1991), 451–58.

19. NR to HG, May 9, 1907, and NR to HG, February 11, 1911, Fonds Roussel.

20. NR to HG, April 13, 1905. Robert Nye's work on male codes of honor and William Reddy's more recent *Invisible Code* both suggest how powerful this tactic could be, given the pervasiveness and importance of male honor. And that she, a woman, shamed these men publicly was of no small significance.

21. NR to HG, February 24, 1907.

22. NR to HG, April 19, 1907.

23. She compares herself with Sebastian Faure in letters to HG written April 3 and 19, 1905, April 30, 1907; May 9, 1911; the reference to Jaurès is in NR to HG, May 7, 1911; her comment about the effect of her new dress is in NR to HG, April 2, 1911; examples of other letters in which Roussel emphasizes her own successes include NR to HG, March 1, 1907; April 10, 17, 30, 1907; February 10, 15, 18, 1908; March 1, 2, 1908; September 8, 14, 1908; February 8, 15, 1909; February 25, 28, March 12, May 26, 1910; February 19, April 5, 1911. Bard's quote is from Christine Bard, *Les Filles de Marianne: Histoire des féminismes, 1914–1940* (Paris: Fayard, 1995), 213.

24. NR to HG, February 26, 1907.

25. NR to HG, April 13, 1907; April 5, May 2, 1911; March 16, November 30, 1913.

26. In her early career, Roussel contributed more articles to this newspaper than to any other. Founded in March 1903, it was an "independent organ of rejuvenated radicalism" that supported free thinking and feminism. Later that year, it merged with Marguerite Durand's *La Fronde,* whose circulation had declined. See Claude Bellanger et al., *L'Histoire de la presse française,* vol. 3 (Paris: Presses Universitaires de France, 1972); Godet informed Roussel of this merger and discussed it in HG to NR, August 23, 1903.

27. HG to NR, May 4, 1907.

28. HG to NR, September 11, 1902. Godet's observations also accurately reflect the modernization and commercialization of leisure and entertainment during the Belle Époque. See for example, Charles Rearick, *Pleasures of the Belle Époque* (New Haven, Conn.: Yale University Press, 1985) and Rosalind Williams, *Dream Worlds* (Berkeley and Los Angeles: University of California Press, 1982).

29. Laurence Klejman and Florence Rochefort, *L'Égalité en marche: Le Féminisme sous la Troisième République* (Paris: Presses de la Fondation Nationale des Sciences Politiques, 1989), 218; on women neo-Malthusianists, see Angus McLaren, 161–66; Francis Ronsin, 158–63; Bard, 209–15. For Madeleine Pelletier, see Charles Sowerwine and Claude Maignien, *Madeleine Pelletier, une féministe dans l'arène politique* (Paris: Les Éditions Ouvrières, 1992); Felicia Gordon, *The Integral Feminist: Madeleine Pelletier, 1874–1939* (Minneapolis: University of Minnesota Press, 1990); Christine Bard, ed., *Madeleine Pelletier: Logique et infortunes d'un combat pour l'égalité* (Paris: Côté-Femmes Éditions, 1992), especially Marie-Victoire Louis, "Sexualité et prostitution," 109–25; Joan Wallach Scott, *Only Paradoxes to Offer: French Feminists and the Rights of Man* (Cambridge, Mass.: Harvard University Press, 1996), 125–60.

30. HG to NR, April 23, 1907.

31. NR to HG, April 27 and 30, 1907.

32. HG to NR, May 4, 1907.

33. I am most grateful to Joby Margadant for her insightful suggestions about these photographs, as well as for her suggestions regarding Roussel's use of language.

34. Nelly-Roussel, *Quelques lances;* HG to NR, 2 August 1909; my emphasis added for clarity.

35. Godet very deliberately used this image when, in a case of mistaken identity involving Roussel, he wrote to the editor of the errant newspaper to defend her honor, describing her as "an orator of grand talent and an irreproachable mother of a family," *La Justice,* June 7, 1910.

36. "Manifestation Anticléricale," *Le Démocrate Soissonnais,* October 4, 1908; *Le Midi Socialiste* of Toulouse, May 4, 1911.

37. *Le Travailleur socialist* of Sens, May 27, 1911; *Le Progrès du Nord,* November 21, 1911. For other examples of this image and for the use of the photographs, see "Madame Nelly Roussel," *Revista do Bem* of Lisbon, July 31, 1907 and the edition of *La Mère éducatrice* commemorating the anniversary of Roussel's death, December 1923. Jane Misme, whose feminist ideas were far

more conservative than those of Roussel, emphasized the compatibility of marriage and motherhood with feminism and how the former two qualities legitimized the latter, using Roussel as an example: " . . . par une générosité téméraire à notre avis, et au grand scandale d'une partie du public qui ne l'a point comprise, le champion de ce qu'on appelle la maternité consentie . . . — j'ai nommé Mme. Nelly Roussel — qui ne soit pas très bourgeoisement mère de trois enfants et parfaite épouse," in "Épouses et Mères," *La Française*, September 22, 1907. On the republican ideal of marriage, see Margadant, *Madame le Professeur*, 25–28; Philip Nord, *The Republican Moment: Struggles for Democracy in Nineteenth-Century France* (Cambridge, Mass.: Harvard University Press, 1995), 220–22; Judith F. Stone, "The Republican Brotherhood: Gender and Ideology" and Theresa McBride, "Divorce and the Republican Family," in Accampo, Fuchs, Stewart, *Gender and the Politics of Social Reform*, 28–58, 59–81.

38. Letter to NR from Mme. Moine, 16 February 1907, in letters responding to lectures, 1907, Fonds Roussel.

39. J. Hellé, preface to Roussel, *Quelques discours,* 6.

40. NR to HG, May 7, 1911.

41. In some respects her self-image here is not unlike that required of another secular "mission" underway in the Third Republic — that of teacher-training and teaching, which did indeed model itself on the cloister and sought to create a worldly role for women who were required to leave their families, without losing an identity based on feminine domesticity. See Margadant, *Madame le Professeur*, especially 39. See also Michela De Giogio, "The Catholic Model," in *A History of Women: Emerging Feminism from Revolution to World War I,* ed. Geneviève Fraisse and Michelle Perrot (Cambridge, Mass.: Belknap Press of Harvard University Press, 1993), 166–97.

42. NR to HG, May 24, 1911; the "twelve and a half years" refers to the duration of their marriage and no doubt his role in converting her to a "militant."

43. Roussel, "Après la Bataille," *L'Action*, May 26, 1906, reprinted in Nelly-Roussel, *Quelques lances rompues pour nos libertés,* 59–66; "Meeting de Protestation contre la célébration du Centenaire du Code civil, 24 octobre 1904," in *Quelques discours de Nelly-Roussel,* "L'Éternelle sacrifiée," 37–39. In this last lecture, Roussel also makes the distinction between the soldier who takes life and the mother who gives life, 55.

44. Nelly Roussel, *Par la révolte: scène symbolique,* 4th ed., with speech by Sebastian Faure. Original edition was published c. 1903. Roussel often referred to women's "flanks," no doubt to emphasize her contention that repeated, uncontrolled, unwanted pregnancies made women animal-like. For example, in "L'Éternelle sacrifiée," she states, " . . . it is *from this procreation alone that we aspire to escape* as long as our painful flanks can only call to life sons who despise us, or daughters who suffer like us . . . ," (61). In "La Libre maternité," she wrote, "[Our fatherland] dares to say 'Be mothers'! This fatherland which, by its laws, reduces our maternity to a purely physical function, robs it of its noble, moral prerogatives, treating the aching creator *(créatrice)* as a negligible quantity who cannot even be consulted, and reducing the human mother below the female animal, from whom no "right of the father" comes to tear away her young" (41).

45. This analysis draws on Reddy, *Invisible Code*. For example, when discussing the influence of Cicero being taught in schools, he notes "Political courage, probity, and patriotism were linked with public speech that . . . sought to shame and humiliate political opponents; and such speech often called implicitly for civil violence to restore legitimacy and defend civic honor" (31). See also his discussion of the relationship between shame and honor, 6–9.

46. Roussel, "Les Tortureurs," *Quelques lances rompues*, 113. Christine Bard points out that a large number of moderate feminists, radicals, and antimilitarists, believed that motherhood was the "battlefield" of women. In a footnote she goes on to remark that the equation between motherhood and militarism was "recuperated" by antifeminists, then took a dramatic turn with the Nazis. See Bard, 141, 141n4.

47. In "Liberté de Maternité," she argued that "conscious and voluntary motherhood" will be "like a priesthood" (51). Although I do not draw from Roussel's life and work the same conclusions as Joan Scott does from the feminists she studies in *Only Paradoxes to Offer*, in her own "paradoxes" and in those she unveiled regarding the Church and the Third Republic, Roussel is similar to them.

48. Roussel's speaking agendas and daily diaries through 1922 reflect the pace and fluctuations in her activities, as well as indicating the timing and destinations of her travels. In 1910, her health took a permanent turn for the worse, and though she remained very active the subsequent twelve years of her life, she made many fewer public appearances. She did, however, continue to travel for reasons of her health, spending several months each year in the countryside, often away from both Godet and her children. Her agendas and diaries are located in Fonds Roussel, BMD.

49. HG to NR, February 18, 1908.

50. HG to NR, February 9, 1908.

51. NR to HG, March 1, 1907. Other letters complaining about Marcel include March 2, April 14, 22, 26, 1907; February 14, 19, 20, September 8, 1908; June 29, July 6, August 3, 1909; January 13, April 8, 26, 1911.

52. For example, Roussel mentions how well behaved Marcel was when they were on vacation and that she took pleasure in his appreciation of the forest. NR to HG, June 21, 1909. Other examples of lightheartedness and expressions of affection toward one or both of the children can be found in correspondence dated July 24, 28, August 20, 22, 25, 1902; August 21, 1903; August 13, September 1, 1909; March 12, 1910; February 11, 19, 1911. The vast majority of comments expressing affectionate concern for the children are from Godet.

53. HG to NR, September 8, 1908.

54. NR to HG, September 10, 1908.

55. Roussel's diaries in Fonds Roussel merely list her daily activities with no embellishment. She noted about twice a week that she visited Marcel in the *pouponnière* and that she would see Mireille for lunch or dinner at her mother's house.

56. NR to HG, August 3, 1909. Especially touching is Mireille's letter to HG while away with Roussel, when she assumes responsibility and painful guilt for having transmitted a cold to her mother; Mireille to HG, September 9, 1910.

Roussel added to this letter her anger at having caught the cold precisely at the moment when she was beginning to feel "almost good." Such ruminations might have less meaning and could be dismissed as rudimentary family exchanges if Roussel had lived with her children routinely and if her health had not been so precarious.

57. I am indebted to Joby Margadant for her suggestive ideas about this photograph.

58. Nelly Roussel, untitled manuscript "biography," Fonds Roussel, BMD.

59. Comments about her difficult labor and the death of her son appear in biographical information in note 4 above, particularly the piece by Marbel. Her feelings about her third pregnancy have not been published but appear in her correspondence of 1904.

60. Two of Roussel's most famous lectures develop these themes: "L'Éternelle sacrifiée" and "Liberté de maternité," both of which are translated and published in Waelti-Walters and Hause, *Feminism of the Belle Epoque*, 18–37, 242–50.

61. Godet claimed, and there is no evidence to the contrary save the relatively minor strains expressed in their letters, that during their twenty-five years of marriage "at no moment did the least dispute trouble our perfect accord." See Henri Godet, "Nelly Roussel: souvenirs," *La Mère éducatrice*, no. 11 (November 1923). One can certainly expect such idealization in a printed eulogy, but throughout their correspondence Godet would often ruminate about their marriage and how it compared favorably with other marriages. For example, in the twelfth year of their marriage, he wrote: "Me too, I want to write to you today. I have not been able to do it early enough for my letter to leave before tomorrow — what does it matter, after twelve years a day won't make any difference — whatever happens now, we each have our savings of happiness; they are extremely rare, those who can say without any reservation that a woman gave them a dozen years of complete love, women who can say that of their husbands are also rare — I am becoming profoundly idiotic [and] fortunately I perceive it on time — I have always told you it is very difficult to speak of love without professing transcendental stupidities . . . ," HG to NR, June 6, 1910. But if it was difficult to talk about love, it was not so difficult for Godet to express himself romantically. Thirteen years into their marriage, for example, he wrote, "Then I looked at the moon, thinking that you were looking at it too, and that our two regards meeting in infinity would create a new star, which would upset the astronomers." HG to NR, February 1, 1911. Though somewhat more formal and deliberate than Godet, Roussel also expressed herself romantically throughout this correspondence.

62. Odette Laguerre, as a journalist, sometimes reported on Roussel's speaking tours and in describing her, emphasized Roussel's domestic role. She also sponsored some of her lectures, and on at least one occasion, in introducing Roussel, gave homage to Godet and Mireille as well, even telling stories about the latter. This was recounted in NR to HG, April 14, 1905. Laguerre also wrote the preface to the posthumously published volume *Trois Conférences de Nelly Roussel*, in which she wrote, "I knew Nelly Roussel in her beautiful years of ardent battles and fertile activity. I saw her in her happy and welcoming hearth, among her husband and her beautiful children: Mireille and Marcel" (11).

Roussel's years of most fertile activity were the same years neither Mireille nor Marcel lived in the Roussel-Godet household. The absence of any comment about this on Laguerre's part, as well as the importance that motherhood held for her is notable in her correspondence to both Roussel and Mireille Godet in Fonds Roussel and in her own memoirs in Dossier Laguerre, BMD.

63. I thank Karen Offen and Charlotte Furth for suggestive comments they made about maternal practices and domestic servants respectively.

64. "Necrologie," *Le Petit Provençal,* December 23, 1922. The following articles also used the words "apostle" or "apostolate": "Une féministe qui s'en va," *La Mère éducatrice,* Nov.-Dec. 1922; "Nos Pierres noires," *La Voix des femmes,* December 13, 1923; "Un Anniversaire du féminism," *La Mère éducatrice,* November 1924; *Pages féminines,* August 1, 1930; "Une Apôtre du féminisme: Nelly Roussel," *La Française,* March 14, 1931. It is noteworthy that I have not found thus far any use of the term "apostolate" by Godet.

65. Roussel's letters (1902–1922) and diaries (1904–1922) reveal patterns of sociability. Paul Robin's great-grandson, Michel Robin (son of Juliette Godet and Fritz Robin), grew up knowing the Roussel family, especially Mireille Godet. I interviewed him on June 6, and June 9, 1997. When I asked how the family viewed Roussel's continual absences from the home, he responded that they viewed it as her "mission" and that there was no question about what was required of her. Certainly the Robin side of the family believed in the mission for ideological reasons, but Roussel's side of the family apparently did not question it either.

66. For the respect Roussel enjoyed among other feminists, see Steven Hause with Anne R. Kenney, *Women's Suffrage and Social Politics in the French Third Republic* (Princeton: Princeton University Press, 1984), 76, 92.

67. A significant portion of the left-wing and organized labor movement opposed birth control because of its implications for gender roles, because they felt the proletariat needed to populate its own "army," and because it gave the proletariat false hopes, diverted them from socialist tactics, and turned them into reformists. See Ronsin, *La Grève des ventres,* 121–48, 171–79; McLaren, *Sexuality and Social Order,* 77–89, 169–83.

68. Ronsin, *La Grève des ventres,* 138–40.

69. This point is developed more fully in Elinor A. Accampo's, "Dissemblance and Dissemination: Birth Control Debate and the French Press, 1900–1914," *Proceedings: Western Society for French History* 23 (1996): 384–93.

70. Report of the Second Police Brigade, November 21, 1905, APP Ba 381.

71. Ibid., and Foureur report of November 21, 1905, APP Ba 381.

72. "La Citoyenne Roussel à Fontenay-Trésigny," *La Tribune Briarde,* March 27, 1907, and "Cour d'Appel de Paris," *Gazette du Palais,* April 10, 1907, in press clippings, Fonds Roussel, BMD. I have not yet found a copy of Roussel's letter to *L'Autorité* among her papers.

73. "Cour d'Appel de Paris," *Gazette du Palais,* April 10, 1907.

74. See Godet's correspondence from May to October, 1911. These letters contain more explicit reference to his sexual desire for her than the correspondence of previous years. Unfortunately, her letters to him were not saved or not included in the papers deposited in the BMD.

75. The logic behind feminist responses to the outbreak of the war is far more complex than there is space to deal with here but is covered thoroughly in Bard, chap. 2. See also Hause with Kenny, chap. 7, and Charles Sowerine, *Sisters or Citizens? Women and Socialism in France since 1876* (Cambridge, Eng.: Cambridge University Press, 1982), chap. 7. For the experience of women during the war, see Françoise Thébaud, *La Femme au temps de la guerre de 14* (Paris: Éditions Stock, 1986), and James F. McMillan, *Housewife or Harlot: The Place of Women in French Society, 1870–1940* (New York: Saint Martin's Press, 1981).

76. Thébaud, *La Femme au temps de la guerre de 14*, 275–83; Hause with Kenny, *Women's Suffrage*, 195. Moderate or reformist, feminists had long been very sensitive to the depopulation issue and had created an antiabortion league prior to 1914. In 1916, one among them, Cécile Brunschvicg declared that after the war, women's first duty would be to have many children. See Bard, 64–66.

77. On the cultural impact of the war and its aftermath on concepts of gender, see Mary Louise Roberts, *Civilization without Sexes: Reconstructing Gender in Postwar France, 1917–1927* (Chicago: University of Chicago Press, 1994); on the issue of depopulation especially, see 100. See also Cova, *Maternité et droits des femmes*, chaps. 3 and 4.

78. Hause and Kenny are particularly insightful about the impact of war on feminism; see *Women's Suffrage*, 197–206. See also Hause, "More Minerva than Mars: The French Women's Rights Campaign and the First World War," and Michelle Perrot, "The New Eve and the Old Adam: French Women's Condition at the Turn of the Century," in *Behind the Lines: Gender and the Two World Wars*, Margaret Randolph Higonnet et al. (New Haven, Conn.: Yale University Press, 1987), 51–60, 99–113.

79. Hause with Kenny, *Women's Suffrage*, 216–17.

80. Nelly Roussel, "Le Front unique des Femmes," *La Voix des femmes*, May 25, 1922.

81. As Mary Louise Roberts has effectively portrayed, the culture to which she brought this message was one in which concepts of gender had become destabilized. Men were perceived as having been "emasculated" by the war, and women were blamed for their selfish indulgence during and after the war, in their consumerism and their promiscuous sexuality.

82. On this law, see Roberts, *Civilization without Sexes*, 93–119, and Cova, "Feminisme et natalité," 254–65. The justification for not outlawing condoms was the prevention of venereal disease.

83. Quoted from the summary of the meeting of April 10, 1920 in *La Voix des femmes*, April 15, 1920. See also summaries of the May 9, 1920, S.F.I.O. meeting in St. Ouen in *L'Action française*, May 10, 1920, and *La Voix des femmes*, May 13, 1920.

84. *La Voix des femmes*, May 13, 1920.

85. Bard, *Les Filles de Marianne*, 209–12; Cova, "Feminisme et natalité," 259–61.

86. Nelly Roussel, "Charges militaires, Charges maternelles," *La Voix des femmes*, March 16, 1922.

87. On this school see, *L'Humanité*, December 12, 1920; *La Voix des femmes,* December 2, 1920; February 3, 10, 1921, and March 2, 16, 23, 1922.

88. *La Voix des femmes,* May 13, 1920. Fewer than three weeks prior to her death, on December 1, 1922, *La Voix des Femmes* published her last article, "Du Rêve à la réalité" ("From the Dream to the Reality") in which she emphasized the importance of keeping this newspaper and its program alive.

89. Godet, "Sanatorium des Pins," "Buzenval," Fonds Roussel, BMD. See Roussel's daily agendas, and Roussel's, Godet's, and Mireille Godet's correspondence in Fonds Roussel.

90. Robin's grandson and great-grandson, Michel Robin, took care of Mireille at the end of her life. Michel Robin's comments about Mireille Godet come from the interview with him on June 6, 1997.

91. Angus McLaren also made this point, though arguing more broadly that the legislators sought to "discipline" workers and women through this law. See 181–82. See also Roberts, who analyzes this law in the context of a "master narrative of postwar economic, military, political, and gender anxiety," *Civilization without Sexes,* 107.

92. It is true, however, that the working class to whom she wanted most to deliver her message, was the last to limit their fertility. Police reports in the Department of the Yonne specifically blamed the neo-Malthusian movement when fertility among workers began to drop prior to World War I. In 1911, the prefect of the Yonne reported that since the census of 1906, the population of the department had decreased by twelve thousand. He claimed that one of the principal causes of this decrease was the spread of neo-Malthusian theory among the working class, the result of frequent lectures organized by the neo-Malthusian group of Auxerre. See AN F7 13955, report from the prefect to the president of the Council of the Ministry of the Interior, November 2, 1911. Roussel had just given a lecture in Auxerre (Yonne) the previous May, to a very enthusiastic audience of five hundred. See AN F7 13955, police report to the Minister of Interior, May 25, 1911.

93. Françoise Thébaud, *Quand nos grand-mères donnaient la vie: La maternité en France dans l'entre-deux-guerres* (Lyon: Presses Universitaires de Lyon, 1986), 13.

94. Robert Nye's observations about the persistence of what appeared to be anachronistic male codes of honor are relevant here: "Anachronisms must be explained as conscientiously as historical novelties. The historian cannot simply invoke tradition to account for the persistence of earlier beliefs or practices. Even the most 'vestigial' social and cultural practices serve some useful purpose and convey meaning to contemporaries." *Masculinity and Male Codes of Honor,* 135.

95. See Reddy, *The Invisible Code,* 13.

Bibliography

Accampo, Elinor A. "Dissemblance and Dissemination: Birth Control Debate and the French Press, 1900–1914." *Proceedings: Western Society for French History* 23 (1996): 384–93.

———. "The Rhetoric of Reproduction and the Reconfiguration of Womanhood in the French Birth Control Movement, 1890–1920." *Journal of Family History* 21, no. 3 (1996): 351–71.

Accampo, Elinor A., Rachel G. Fuchs, and Mary Lynn Stewart. *Gender and the Politics of Social Reform in France, 1870–1914.* Baltimore: Johns Hopkins University Press, 1995.

Adler, Laure. *À l'Aube du féminisme: Les Premières journalistes, 1830–1850.* Paris: Payot, 1979.

D'Agoult, Comtesse Marie. "Correspondance." Bibliothèque Nationale de France, Manuscrits, Fonds Daniel Ollivier, N.A.F., 25181, 25185.

———. [Stern, Daniel] *Essai sur la liberté considérée comme principe et fin de l'activité humaine.* Paris: Aymot, 1847.

———. *Histoire de la Révolution de 1848.* 2 vols. 2d ed. Paris: Charpentier, 1868.

———. *Histoire des commencements de la république aux Pays-bas, 1581–1615.* Paris: Michel Lévy Frères, 1872.

———. *Lettres républicaines.* Paris: Edouard Proux, 1848.

———. *Mémoires, 1833–1854.* Introduction by Daniel Ollivier. Paris: Calmann-Lévy, 1927.

———. *Mémoires, souvenirs et journaux de la comtesse d'Agoult (Daniel Stern).* Edited by Charles F. Dupêchez. 2 vols. Paris: Mercure de France, 1990.

———. *Mes Souvenirs, 1806–1833.* Paris: Calmann Lévy, 1877.

Albistur, Maïté, and Daniel Armogathe. *Histoire du féminisme français.* Paris: Editions des femmes, 1977.

Allart, Hortense. *Histoire de la République d'Athènes.* Paris: n.p., 1866.
————. [Hortense Allart de Méritens] *Histoire de la république de Florence.* Paris: Moutardier, 1837.
————. [Hortense Allart de Méritens] *La Femme et la démocratie de nos temps.* Paris: Delaunay, 1836.
————. [Mme P. de Saman] *Les Enchantements de Prudence.* 2d ed. Paris: Michel Lévy Frères, 1873.
————. [Mme P. de Saman] *Les Nouveaux Enchantements.* Paris: Michel Lévy Frères, 1873.
————. [Hortense Allart de Méritens] *Lettres inédites à Sainte-Beuve (1841–1848).* Edited by Léon Séché. 2d. ed. Paris: Société du Mercure de France, 1980.
————. *Lettres sur les ouvrages de Madame de Staël.* Paris: Bossauge père, 1824.
————. *Nouvelles Lettres à Sainte-Beuve (1832–1864).* Edited by Lorin A. Uffenbeck. Geneva: Droz, 1965.
————. [Hortense Allart de Méritens] *Second petit livre. Études diverses.* Paris: Renault, 1850.
————. *Settimia.* 2 vols. Brussels: Ad. Wahlen et Cie, 1836.
————. [Hortense Allart de Méritens] *Troisième petit livre. Études diverses.* Paris: Renault, 1851.
Amar, André. "The National Convention Outlaws Clubs and Popular Societies of Women." In *Women in Revolutionary Paris, 1789–1795,* ed. Darline Gay Levy, Harriet Branson Applewhite, and Mary Durham Johnson. Urbana: University of Illinois Press, 1979.
Aminzade, Ronald. "Class Analysis, Politics and French Labor History." In *Rethinking Labor History: Essays on Discourse and Class Analysis,* ed. Lenard R. Berlanstein. Urbana: University of Illinois Press, 1993.
Anne, Théodore. *La Prisonnière de Blaye.* Paris, 1832.
Appleby, Joyce. "The Power of History." Presidential address. *American Historical Review* 103, no. 1 (1988): 1–14.
Appleby, Joyce, Lynn Hunt, and Margaret Jacob. *Telling the Truth about History.* New York: Norton, 1994.
Apponyi, Rodolphe. *Vingt-cinq ans à Paris, 1826–1850. Journal du comte Rodolphe Apponyi.* Vol. 1, 2d ed. Paris, 1829.
Baelen, Jean. *La Vie et l'oeuvre de Flora Tristan: socialisme et féminisme au XIXe siècle.* Paris: Seuil, 1972.
Balzac, Honoré de. *La Duchesse de Langeais.* Paris: Librarie générale française, 1983.
Barbey d'Aurevilley, J. *Les Vieilles Actrices.* Paris: Librairie des auteurs modernes, 1884.
Barbier, Pierre, and France Vernillat, eds. *Histoire de France par les chansons.* Vol. 4, 3d ed. *La Restauration.* Paris: Gallimard, 1958.
Bard, Christine. *Les Filles de Marianne: Histoire des féminismes, 1914–1940.* Paris: Fayard, 1995.
Barish, Jonas. *The Antitheatrical Prejudice.* Berkeley and Los Angeles: University of California Press, 1981.
Barnes, David. *The Making of a Social Disease: Tuberculosis in Nineteenth-Century France.* Berkeley and Los Angeles: University of California Press, 1995.
Barry, Joseph. *Infamous Woman: The Life of George Sand.* Garden City, N.Y.: Doubleday, 1977.

Baudelaire, Charles. "The Painter of Modern Life." In *Selected Writings on Art and Literature (1859–1860)*, trans. P. E. Charvet. New York: Penguin Books, 1972.

Baudrillard, Jean. *Le Système des objets*. Paris: Gallimard, 1968.

Bell, Susan Groag, and Karen M. Offen, eds. *Women, the Family, and Freedom: The Debate in Documents* (Stanford: Stanford University Press, 1983).

Bellanger, Claude, et al. *De 1871 à 1940*. Vol. 3 of *L'Histoire de la presse française*. Paris: Presses universitaires de France, 1972.

Bellet, Roger. "Masculin et féminin dans les pseudonyms des femmes de lettres au XIXe siècle." In *Femmes des lettres au XIXe siècle*, ed. Roger Bellet. Lyon: Presses universitaires de Lyon, 1982.

Belsey, Catherine. *The Subject of Tragedy: Identity and Difference in Renaissance Drama*. London: Methuen, 1985.

Benstock, Shari, ed. *The Private Self: Theory and Practice of Women's Autobiographical Writing*. Chapel Hill: University of North Carolina, 1994.

Berenson, Edward. "A New Religion of the Left: Christianity and Social Radicalism in France, 1815–1848." In *The French Revolution and the Creation of Modern Political Culture*, ed. François Furet and Mona Ozouf. Vol. 3. *The Transformation of Political Culture, 1789–1848*. Oxford: Pergamon Press, 1989.

———. *The Trial of Madame Caillaux*. Berkeley and Los Angeles: University of California Press, 1992.

Bergerat, Émile, et al. *Les Actrices de Paris*. Paris: Librairie artistique illustrée, 1882.

Bergès, A. *L'Éscrime et la femme*. Paris: M. Désirée Benoist, 1896.

Bergman-Carton, Janis. *The Woman of Ideas in French Art, 1830–1848*. New Haven, Conn.: Yale University Press, 1995.

Berlanstein, Lenard R. "Britches and Breeches: Cross-Dressed Theater and the Culture of Gender Ambiguity in Modern France." *Comparative Studies in Society and History* 38 (1996): 338–70.

———. "Women and Power in Eighteenth-Century France: Actresses at the Comédie-Française." *Feminist Studies* 20, no. 3 (1996): 474–506.

Bernhardt, Sarah. *The Memoirs of Sarah Bernhardt*. New York: Peebles Press, 1977.

Bertier, Ferdinand de. *Souvenirs d'un ultra-royaliste*. Paris: Tallandier, 1933.

Bertier de Sauvigny, Guillaume de. *Documents inédits sur la conspiration légitimiste de 1830 à 1832*. Paris: A. Hatier, 1951.

Bethel, Lorraine. "What Chou Mean *We* White Girl? or, The Colored Lesbian Feminist Declaration of Independence (Dedicated to the Proposition that All Women Are Not Equal, i.e. Identically Oppressed)." *Conditions: Five* 2 (1979): 86–92.

Bezucha, Robert J. *The Lyon Uprising of 1834: Social and Political Conflict in the Early July Monarchy*. Cambridge, Mass.: Harvard University Press, 1974.

Bhabha, Homi. "Of Mimicry and Man: The Ambivalence of the Colonial Discourse." In *The Location of Culture*. New York: Routledge, 1994.

Billy, André. *Hortense et ses amants*. Paris: Flammarion, 1961.

Bled, Jean-Paul. *Les Lys en exil ou la seconde mort de l'Ancien Régime*. Paris: Fayard, 1992.

Bloch, Jean H. "Women and the Reform of the Nation." In *Woman and Society in Eighteenth-Century France: Essays in Honour of John Stephenson Spink*, ed. Eva Jacobs et al. London: The Athlone Press, 1979.

Bloom, Allan. *Politics and the Arts: Letter to M. d'Alembert on the Theatre.* Glencoe, Ill.: The Free Press, 1960.

Blum, Carol. *Rousseau and the Republic of Virtue. The Language of Politics in the French Revolution.* Ithaca: Cornell University Press, 1986.

Boigne, Comtesse de. *Mémoires de la comtesse de Boigne. Récits d'une tante.* Vol. 2. Paris: Mercure de France, 1986.

Bonnemaison, F. *Galerie de Son Altesse Royale Madame, duchesse de Berry: École française, peintres modernes et lithographies par d'habiles artistes.* 2 vols. Paris, 1828.

Bowlby, Rachel. *Just Looking: Consumer Culture in Dreiser, Gissing and Zola.* New York: Methuen, 1985.

Bowman, Frank Paul. *Eliphas Lévi visionnaire romantique.* Paris: Presses universitaires de France, 1969.

———. "Religion, Politics, and Utopia in French Romanticism." *Australian Journal of French Studies* 11, no. 3 (1974): 307–24.

Brantlinger, Patrick. "Mass Media and Culture in Fin-de-siècle Europe." In *Fin de Siècle and its Legacy,* ed. Mikulas Teich and Roy Porter. Cambridge, Eng.: Cambridge University Press, 1990.

Briais, Bernard. *Au Temps des frous-frous.* Paris: Editions France-Empire, 1985.

Brodski, Bella, and Celeste Schenck, eds. *Life/Lines: Theorizing Women's Autobiography.* Ithaca: Cornell University Press, 1988.

Brooks, Peter. *The Melodramatic Imagination: Balzac, Henry James, Melodrama, and the Mode of Excess.* New Haven, Conn.: Yale University Press, 1976.

Brownstein, Rachel. *Tragic Muse: Rachel of the Comédie-Française.* New York: Alfred A. Knopf, 1993.

Buijs, Gina, ed. *Migrant Women: Crossing Boundaries and Changing Identities.* Oxford: Berg, 1993.

Burns, Michael. *Rural Society and French Politics: Boulangism and the Dreyfus Affair, 1886–1900.* Princeton: Princeton University Press, 1984.

Busst, A. J. L. "The Image of the Androgyne in the Nineteenth Century." In *Romantic Mythologies,* ed. Ian Fletcher. London: Routledge & Kegan Paul, 1967.

Butler, Judith. *Bodies That Matter: On the Discursive Limits of "Sex."* New York: Routledge, 1993.

———. *Gender Trouble: Feminism and the Subversion of Identity.* New York: Routledge, 1990.

———. "Performative Acts and Gender Constitution: An Essay in Phenomenology and Feminist Theory." In *Performing Feminisms: Feminist Critical Theory and Theater,* ed. Sue-Ellen Case. Baltimore: Johns Hopkins University Press, 1990.

———. *The Psychic Life of Power: Theories in Subjection.* Stanford: Stanford University Press, 1997.

Butler, Judith, and Joan W. Scott, eds. *Feminists Theorize the Political.* New York: Routledge, 1992.

Canning, Kathleen. "Feminist History after the Linguistic Turn: Historicizing Discourse and Experience." *Signs* 19 (1994): 368–404.

Castelot, André. *Le Duc de Berry et son double mariage d'après des documents inédits.* Paris: S.F.E.L.T., 1950.

———. *La Duchesse de Berry d'après des documents inédits.* Paris: Librairie académique Perrin, 1963.

Castle, Terry. "Marie Antoinette Obsession." In *The Apparitional Lesbian: Female Homosexuality and Modern Culture.* New York: Columbia University Press, 1993.

Cate, Curtis. *George Sand. A Biography.* Boston: Houghton Mifflin, 1975.

Cesbron, Sylvie. "Un Journal féministe en 1900: *La Fronde,* (1897–1903)." Mémoire dactylographiée. Bibliothèque Marguerite Durand.

Chaline, Jean-Pierre. "Sociabilité féminine et 'maternalisme': les sociétés de charité maternelle au XIXe siècle." In *Femmes dans la cité, 1815–1871,* ed. Alain Corbin, Jacqueline Lalouette, Michèle Riot-Sarcey. Paris: Créaphis, 1993.

Changy, Hugues de. *Le Soulèvement de la duchesse de Berry, 1830–1832: Les Royalistes dans la tourmente.* Paris: Albatros and Diffusion-Université-Culture, 1986.

Chartier, Roger. *La Correspondance: Les Usages des lettres au XIXe siècle.* Paris: Fayard, 1991.

Chateaubriand, François-René, Vicomte de. *Mémoires, lettres et pièces authentiques touchant à la vie et la mort de S.A.R. monseigneur Charles-Ferdinand-d'Artois, fils de France, duc de Berry.* Paris, 1820.

Childers, Mary, and Bell Hooks. "A Conversation about Race and Class." In *Conflicts in Feminism,* ed. Marianne Hirsch and Evelyn Fox Keller. New York: Routledge, 1990.

Cim, Albert. *Emancipées.* Paris: Flammarion, 1899.

Clark, T. J. *The Painting of Modern Life: Paris in the Art of Manet and His Followers.* Princeton: Princeton University Press, 1984.

Clarke, Norma. "From Plaything to Professional: The English Actress, 1660–1990." *Gender and History* 5, no. 1 (1993): 120–24.

C. L. *Religion Saint-Simonienne. Église de Talouse. Enseignement de l'Athénée. Avenir de la Femme.* Toulouse: A. Hènault, 1831.

Cole, Joshua. " 'There Are Only Good Mothers': The Ideological Work of Women's Fertility in France before World War I." *French Historical Studies* 19, no. 3 (1996).

Colley, Linda. *Britons: Forging the Nation, 1707–1837.* New Haven, Conn.: Yale University Press, 1992.

Comaroff, Jean, and John L. Comaroff. *Of Revelation and Revolution: Christianity, Colonialism and Consciousness in South Africa.* Chicago: University of Chicago Press, 1991.

Cominos, Peter T. "Innocent Femina Sensualis in Unconscious Conflict." In *Suffer and Be Still: Women in the Victorian Age,* ed. Martha Vicinus. Bloomington: Indiana University Press, 1972.

Comte, Auguste. *Correspondance générale et confessions.* Edited by Paulo E. de Berrêdo Carneiro, Pierre Arnaud, Paul Arbousse-Bastide, and Angèle Kremer-Marietti. 8 vols. Paris: Écoles des Hautes Études en Sciences Sociales, 1973–1990.

———. *Physique sociale: Cours de philosophie positive, leçons 46 à 60.* Edited by Jean-Paul Enthoven. Paris: Hermann, 1975.

———. *Testament d'Auguste Comte avec les documents qui s'y rapportent: Pièces justificatives, prières quotidiennes, confessions annuelles, correspondance avec Mme de Vaux.* 2d ed. Paris, 1896.

Connell, R. W. "The Big Picture: Masculinities in Recent World History." *Theory and Society* 22 (1993): 597–623.

Constant, Alphonse-Louis. Epilogue to *L'Émancipation de la femme ou le testament de la paria,* a posthumous work by Mme Flora Tristan, completed

from her notes and published by A.-L. Constant. Paris: au Bureau de la
Direction de *La Vérité*, 1846.

Corbin, Alain. *The Lure of the Sea: The Discovery of the Seaside in the Western World, 1750–1840.* Translated by Jocelyn Phelps. Berkeley and Los Angeles: University of California Press, 1994.

———. *Women for Hire: Prostitution and Sexuality in France after 1850.* Cambridge, Mass.: Harvard University Press, 1990.

Courtivron, Isabelle de. "Weak Men and Fatal Women: The Sand Image." In *Homosexualities and French Literature: Cultural Contexts/Critical Texts,* ed. George Stambolian and Elaine Marks. Ithaca: Cornell University Press, 1979.

Cova, Anne. "Féminisme et natalité: Nelly Roussel (1878–1922)." *History of European Ideas* 15, no. 4–5 (1992): 663–72.

———. *Maternité et droits des femmes en France (XIXe–XXe siècles).* Paris: Anthropos, 1997.

Crecelius, Kathryn J. *Family Romances: George Sand's Early Novels.* Bloomington: Indiana University Press, 1987.

"Critical Pragmatism, Language, and Cultural History: Forum on Roger Chartier's *On the Edge of the Cliff.*" *French Historical Studies* 21, no. 2 (1998): 213–64.

Cross, Máire, and Tim Gray. *The Feminism of Flora Tristan.* Oxford: Berg, 1992.

Crossley, Ceri. *French Historians and Romanticism: Thierry, Guizot, the Saint-Simonians, Quinet, Michelet.* London: Routledge, 1993.

D'Alméras, Henri. *La Vie parisienne sous la Restauration.* Paris: A. Michel, 1910.

Dansette, Adrien. *Du Boulangisme à la révolution dreyfusienne: Le Boulangisme, 1886–1890.* Paris: Perrin, 1938.

Darrow, Margaret H. "French Noblewomen and the New Domesticity, 1750–1850." *Feminist Studies* 5, no. 1 (1979): 41–65.

———. *Revolution in the House: Family, Class and Inheritance in Southern France, 1775–1825.* Princeton: Princeton University Press, 1989.

Daumard, Adeline. *La Bourgeoisie parisienne de 1815 à 1848.* Paris: S.E.V.P.E.N., 1963.

Davidoff, Leonore. "Regarding Some 'Old Husbands' Tales': Public and Private in Feminist History." In *Worlds between: Historical Perspectives on Gender and Class.* New York: Routledge, 1995.

Davis, Natalie Zemon. "On the Lame." *American Historical Review* 93 (1988): 572–603.

———. *The Return of Martin Guerre.* Cambridge, Mass.: Harvard University Press, 1983.

Davy, Charlotte. *Une femme . . .* Paris: Eugene Figuiere, 1927.

Debord, Guy. *La Société du spectacle.* Paris: Editions Buchet-Chastel, 1967.

Demeulenaere-Douyère, Christiane. *Paul Robin: Sa vie. Ses idées. Son action.* Paris: G. Mignolet & Storz, 1937.

Dermoncourt, General. *La Vendée et Madame.* Paris, 1833.

Derrida, Jacques. *Of Grammatology.* Translated by Gayatri Chakravorty Spivak. Baltimore: Johns Hopkins University Press, 1974.

Desan, Suzanne. " 'War between Brothers and Sisters': Inheritance Law and Gender Politics in Revolutionary France." *French Historical Studies* 20, no. 4 (1997): 632–34.

Desanti, Dominique. *Daniel, ou le visage secret d'une comtesse romantique, Marie d'Agoult.* Paris: Stock, 1980.

————. *Flora Tristan: Vie et oeuvres mêlées.* Paris: Union générale d'éditions, 1973.

Desmarais, Cyprien. *La Révolution de juillet à S.A.R. la duchesse de Berry, captive à Blaye.* Paris, 1832.

Devance, Louis. "Femme, famille, travail et morale sexuelle dans l'idéologie de 1848." *Romantisme* 13–14 (1976): 79–103.

De Vaux, Clotilde. *Willelmine.* Paris: Edition Positiviste, 1929.

Dewald, Jonathan. *Aristocratic Experience and the Origins of Modern Culture: France, 1570–1715.* Berkeley and Los Angeles: University of California Press, 1993.

D'Haussez, Baron. *Mémoires de baron d'Haussez.* Vol. 2. Paris, 1896.

Dijkstra, Sandra. *Flora Tristan: Pioneer Feminist and Socialist.* Berkeley: Center for Socialist History, 1984.

Dizier-Metz, Annie. *La Bibliothèque Marguerite Durand, Histoire d'une femme, mémoire des femmes.* Paris: Mairie de Paris–Agence Culturelle de Paris, 1992.

Doane, Mary Anne. *Femmes Fatales: Feminism, Film Theory, Psychoanalysis.* New York: Routledge, 1991.

Donzelot, Jacques. *The Policing of Families.* Translated by Robert Hurley. New York: Pantheon, 1979.

Dorléans, Ferdinand-Philippe. *Souvenirs, 1810–1830.* Edited by Hervé Robert. Geneva: Droz, 1993.

Downs, Laura Lee. "If 'Woman' Is Just an Empty Category, Then Why Am I Afraid to Walk Alone at Night? Identity Politics Meets the Postmodern Subject." *Comparative Studies in Society and History* 35 (1993): 438–43.

————. "Reply to Joan Scott." *Comparative Studies in Society and History* 35 (1993): 444–51.

Dupêchez, Charles. *Marie d'Agoult, 1805–1876.* Paris: Perrin, 1989.

Duprat, Catherine. "Le Silence des femmes: Associations féminines du premier XIXe siècle." In *Femmes dans la cité, 1815–1871,* ed. Alain Corbin, Jacqueline Lalouette, Michèle Riot-Sarcey. Paris: Créaphis, 1993.

Elias, Norbert. *The Court Society.* Translated by Edmund Jephcott. New York: Pantheon Books, 1983.

Elshtain, Jean Bethke. *Public Man, Private Woman: Women in Social and Political Thought.* Princeton: Princeton University Press, 1981.

Farrell, Michèle Longino. *Performing Motherhood: The Sévigné Correspondence.* Hanover, N.H.: University Press of New England, 1991.

Faure, Alain. *Paris Carême-prenant: du carnaval à Paris au XIXe siècle.* Paris: Hachette, 1978.

Fauré, Christine. *Democracy without Women: Feminism and the Rise of Liberal Individualism in France.* Translated by Claudia Gorbman and John Berks. Bloomington: Indiana University Press, 1991.

Ferenczi, Thomas. *L'Invention du journalisme en France. Naissance de la presse moderne à la fin de XIXe siècle.* Paris: Plon, 1993.

Folkenflik, Robert, ed. *The Culture of Autobiography: Constructions of Self-Representation.* Stanford: Stanford University Press, 1993.

Fortescue, William. "Divorce Debated and Deferred: The French Debate on Divorce and the Failure of the Crémieux Divorce Bill in 1848." *French History* 7 (1993): 137–62.

Foucault, Michel. *Discipline and Punish: The Birth of the Prison.* Translated by Alan Sheridan. New York: Pantheon Books, 1979.

———. *The History of Sexuality.* Vol. 1. *An Introduction.* Translated by Robert Hurley. New York: Pantheon Books, 1978.

———. *Language, Counter-Memory Practice.* Translated by Donald F. Bouchard and Sherry Simon. Ithaca: Cornell University Press, 1977.

———. *The Order of Things: An Archaeology of the Human Sciences.* New York: Vintage, 1973.

———. *Power/Knowledge: Selected Interviews and Other Writings, 1972–1977.* Translated by Colin Gordon. New York: Pantheon Books, 1980.

Fraisse, Geneviève. *Reason's Muse: Sexual Difference and the Birth of Democracy.* Translated by Jane Marie Todd. Chicago: University of Chicago Press, 1995.

Fraisse, Geneviève, and Michelle Perrot, eds. *A History of Women in the West.* Vol. 4. *Emerging Feminism from Revolution to World War.* Cambridge, Mass.: Harvard University Press, 1993.

Friedland, Paul. "Representation and Revolution: The Theatricality of Politics and the Politics of Theater in France, 1789–1794." Ph.D. diss., University of California, Berkeley, 1995.

Friedman, Susan Stanford. "Women's Autobiographical Selves: Theory and Practice." In *The Private Self: Theory and Practice of Women's Autobiographical Writing,* ed. Shari Benstock. Chapel Hill: University of North Carolina Press, 1988.

Fuchs, Rachel G. *Poor and Pregnant in Paris: Strategies for Survival in the Nineteenth Century.* New Brunswick, N.J.: Rutgers University Press, 1992.

Gardner, Viv, and Susan Rutherford. *The New Woman and Her Sisters: Feminism and Theatre, 1850–1914.* New York: Harvester Wheatsheaf, 1992.

Geertz, Clifford. "Blurred Genres: The Refiguration of Social Thought." In *Local Knowledge: Further Essays in Interpretive Anthropology.* New York: Basic Books, 1983.

———. "Deep Play: Notes on the Balinese Cockfight." In *The Interpretation of Cultures; Selected Essays.* New York: Basic Books, 1973.

Gelbart, Nina. *Feminine and Opposition Journalism in Old Regime France: Le Journal des dames.* Berkeley and Los Angeles: University of California Press, 1987.

Gender and History. Special Issue on Autobiography and Biography. 2, no. 1 (1990): 1–78.

Gikandi, Simon. *Maps of Englishness: Writing Identity in the Culture of Colonialism.* New York: Columbia University Press, 1996.

Godet, Henri. "Nelly Roussel: Souvenirs." *La Mère éducatrice* 11 (Nov. 1923).

Godineau, Dominique. *The Women of Paris and Their French Revolution.* Translated by Katherine Streip. Berkeley and Los Angeles: University of California Press, 1998.

Gold, Arthur, and Robert Fizdale. *The Divine Sarah: A Life of Sarah Bernhardt.* New York: Alfred A. Knopf, 1991.

Goliber, Sue Helder. "The Life and Times of Marguerite Durand: A Study in French Feminism." Ph.D. diss., Kent State University, Manhattan, Kan., 1975.

Gontaut-Biron, Marie Joséphine, duchesse de. *Mémoires de madame la duchesse de Gontaut; gouvernante des enfants de France.* Paris: E. Plon, Nourrit & Cie, 1891.

Goodman, Dena. *The Republic of Letters: A Cultural History of the French Enlightenment*. Ithaca: Cornell University Press, 1994.

———. "Women and the Enlightenment." In *Becoming Visible: Women in European History*, ed. Renate Bridenthal, Susan Mosher Stuard, and Merry E. Weisner. 3d ed. Boston: Houghton Mifflin, 1998.

Gordon, Felicia. *The Integral Feminist: Madeleine Pelletier: Logique et infortunes d'un combat pour l'égalité*. Paris: Côte-Femmes Editions, 1992.

Gordon, Felicia, and Máire Cross. *Early French Feminists, 1830–1940: A Passion for Liberty*. Cheltenham: Edward Elgar, 1996.

Greenblatt, Stephen. *Renaissance Self-Fashioning: From More to Shakespeare*. Chicago: Chicago University Press, 1990.

Grewal, Inderpal, and Caren Kaplan. "Introduction: Transnational Feminist Practices and Questions of Postmodernity." In *Scattered Hegemonies: Postmodernity and Transnational Feminist Practices*. Minneapolis: University of Minnesota Press, 1994.

Grogan, Susan. *Flora Tristan: Life Stories*. London: Routledge, 1998.

———. *French Socialism and Sexual Difference: Women and the New Society, 1803–1844*. Basingstoke, Eng.: Macmillan, 1992.

Guerrand, Robert-H. *La Libre maternité, 1896–1969*. Paris: Caasterman, 1971.

Habermas, Jürgen. *Transformation of the Public Sphere*. Translated by Thomas Burger. Cambridge, Mass.: M.I.T. Press, 1989.

Hall, Jacqueline Dowd. *Revolt against Chivalry: Jesse Daniel Ames and the Women's Campaign against Lynching*. New York: Columbia University Press, 1974.

Halperin, David M. "Is There a History of Sexuality?" In *The Lesbian and Gay Studies Reader*, ed. Henry Abelove, Michèle Aina Barale, and David M. Halperin. New York: Routledge, 1993.

Hanley, Sarah. "Engendering the State: Family Formation and State Building in Early Modern France." *French Historical Studies* 16, no. 1 (1989): 4–27.

———. "Les Visages de la loi salique dans la quête pour le droit des hommes et l'exclusion des femmes du gouvernement monarchique." In *Les Droits des femmes et la Loi Salique*. Paris: Indigo & Côte-femmes 1994.

———. "Mapping Rulership in the French Body Politic: Political Identity, Public Law and the *King's One Body*." *Historical Reflections/Réflections historiques* 23, no. 1 (1997): 129–49.

———. "The Monarchic State in Early Modern France: Marital Regime Government and Male Right." In *Politics, Ideology and the Law in Early Modern Europe*, ed. Adrianna E. Bakos. Rochester: University of Rochester Press, 1994.

Harding, James. *The Astonishing Adventure of General Boulanger*. New York: Charles Scribner's Sons, 1971.

Harteman, Jean. "Une maternité inopinée de Marie-Caroline, duchesse de Berry." Paper presented at l'Académie de Stanislas de Nancy, May 16, 1969.

Hause, Steven. *Hubertine Auclert: The French Suffragette*. New Haven, Conn.: Yale University Press, 1987.

———. "More Minerva than Mars: The French Women's Rights Campaign and the First World War." In *Behind the Lines: Gender and the Two World Wars*, ed. Margaret Randolph Higonnet et al. New Haven, Conn.: Yale University Press, 1987.

Hause, Steven, with Anne R. Kenney. *Women's Suffrage and Social Politics in the French Third Republic*. Princeton: Princeton University Press, 1984.

Hawkes, Jean, ed. *The London Journal of Flora Tristan 1842, or the Aristocracy and the Working Class of England: A Translation of Promenades dans Londres*. London: Virago, 1982.

Heilbrun, Carolyn G. *Writing a Woman's Life*. New York: Norton, 1988.

Hellerstein, Erna Olafson. "French Women and the Orderly Household, 1830–1870." *Proceedings of the Annual Meeting of the Western Society for French History*. Denver, 1975.

Hemmings, F. W. J. *Culture and Society in France, 1789–1848*. Leicester, Eng.: Leicester University Press, 1987.

———. *The Theatre Industry in Nineteenth-Century France*. Cambridge, Eng.: Cambridge University Press, 1993.

Hesse, Carla. "Reading Signatures: Female Authorship and Revolutionary Law in France, 1750–1850." *Eighteenth-Century Studies* 22 (spring 1989): 469–87.

Higgs, David. *Nobles in Nineteenth-Century France: The Practice of Inegalitarianism*. Baltimore: Johns Hopkins University Press, 1987.

Hill, Mary A. *Charlotte Perkins Gilman: The Making of a Radical Feminist, 1860–1896*. Philadelphia: University of Pennsylvania Press, 1980.

Hirsch, Marianne, and Evelyn Fox Keller. *Conflicts in Feminism*. New York: Routledge, 1990.

Hoffmann, Paul. *La Femme dans la pensée des lumières*. Paris: Editions Ophrys, 1977.

Holland, Claude. "Mademoiselle Merquem: De-Mythifying Woman by Rejecting the Law of the Father." In *The World of George Sand*, ed. Natalie Datlof, Jeanne Fuchs, and David A. Powell. New York: Greenwood Press, 1991.

Holloway, Wendy. "Gender Difference and the Production of Subjectivity." In *Changing the Subject: Psychology, Social Regulation and Subjectivity*, ed. Julian Henriques et al. London: Methuen, 1984.

Hovey, Tamara. *A Mind of Her Own. A Life of the Writer George Sand*. New York: Harper & Row, 1977.

Hufton, Olwen H. *Women and the Limits of Citizenship in the French Revolution*. Toronto: University of Toronto Press, 1992.

Hunt, Lynn. "Deconstruction of Categories and Reconstruction of Narratives in Gender History." In *Gender History and General History*, ed. Anne-Charlotte Trepp and Hans Medick. Göttinger Gespräche zur Geschichtswissenschaft. Forthcoming.

———. *The Family Romance of the French Revolution*. Berkeley and Los Angeles: University of California Press, 1992.

———. "Reading the French Revolution: A Reply." *French Historical Studies* 19, no. 2 (1995): 289–98.

Hunt, Lynn, and Margaret Jacob. *Telling the Truth about History*. New York: Norton, 1994.

Hunt, Lynn, and Victoria Bonnell. *Beyond the Cultural Turn*. Berkeley and Los Angeles: University of California Press, 1999.

Irigaray, Luce. *This Sex Which Is Not One*. Translated by Catherine Porter with Carolyn Burke. Ithaca: Cornell University Press, 1985.

Israel, Kali A. K. "Kaleidoscopic Lives and Genres of Biography." In "Drawing from Life: Art, Work and Feminism in the Life of Emilia Dilke (1840–1940)." Ph.D. diss. Graduate School-New Brunswick, Rutgers, the State University of New Jersey, 1992.

———. "Style, Strategy, and Self-Creation in the Life of Emilia Dilke." In

Constructions of the Self, ed. George Levine. New Brunswick, N.J.: Rutgers University Press, 1992.

————. "Writing Inside the Kaleidoscope: Re-Representing Victorian Women as Public Figures." *Gender and History* 2 (spring 1990): 40–48.

Jami, Irène. "*La Fronde* (1897–1903) et son rôle dans la défense des femmes salariées." Mémoire de Maîtrise. Paris: Université de Paris I, 1981.

Johnson, Christopher. *Utopian Communism in France.* Ithaca: Cornell University Press, 1974.

Johnson, James. "Revolutionary Audiences and the Impossible Imperatives of Fraternity." In *Recreating Authority in Revolutionary France,* ed. Bryant T. Ragan Jr. and Elizabeth A. Williams. New Brunswick, N.J.: Rutgers University Press, 1992.

Jones, Gareth Stedman. *Languages of Class: Studies in English Working-Class History, 1832–1982.* Cambridge, Eng.: Cambridge University Press, 1983.

Jordan, Ruth. *George Sand. A Biographical Portrait.* New York: Taplinger, 1976.

Kaiser, Thomas E. "Madame de Pompadour and the Theaters of Power." *French Historical Studies* 19, no. 4 (1996): 1025–44.

Kantorowicz, E. H. *The King's Two Bodies.* Princeton: Princeton University Press, 1957.

Karenine, Wladimir. *George Sand: Sa vie et ses oeuvres.* 4 vols. Paris: Plon, 1926.

Kelly, Gary. *Women, Writing, and Revolution, 1790–1827.* Oxford, Eng.: Clarendon Press, 1993.

King, Katie. "Producing Sex, Theory, and Culture: Gay/Straight Remappings in Contemporary Feminism." In *Conflicts in Feminism,* ed. Marianne Hirsch and Evelyn Fox Keller. New York: Routledge, 1990.

Klejman, Laurence, and Florence Rochefort. *L'Egalité en marche: Le Féminisme sous la Troisième République.* Paris: Presses de la Fondation nationale des sciences politiques: Des Femmes, 1989.

Knapp, Bettina. *That Was Yvette: The Biography of the Great Diseuse.* London: Friedrich Muller, 1966.

Kofman, Sarah. *Aberrations: Le devenir-femme d'Auguste Comte.* Paris: Aubier-Flammarion, 1978.

Krakovitch, Odile. *Les Pièces de théâtre soumises à la censure (1800–1830).* Paris: Archives nationales, 1982.

Kramer, Lloyd. *Lafayette in Two Worlds: Public Cultures and Personal Identities in an Age of Revolutions.* Chapel Hill: University of North Carolina Press, 1996.

Lacome, P. *Les Étoiles du passé.* Paris: Paul Dupont, 1897.

Lacour, Léopold. *Les Premières actrices françaises.* Paris: Librairie Française, 1921.

Landes, Joan. *Women and the Public Sphere in the Age of the French Revolution.* Ithaca: Cornell University Press, 1988.

Lanser, Susan Sniader. "Toward a Feminist Poetics of Narrative Voice." In *Fictions of Authority: Women Writers and Narrative Voice,* ed. Susan Sniader Lanser. Ithaca: Cornell University Press, 1992.

Lascar, Fabrice. "Cris et chuchotements. Démonstrations séditieuses et injures au roi ou à la famille royale sous la Monarchie de Juillet (août 1830 – février 1848)." Maîtrisse, University of Paris I, 1990.

Lasne, Larent. *L'Île aux chiens: La Cimetière des chiens Asnières.* Bois-Colombes: A. Val-Arno, 1988.

Lauretis, Teresa de, ed. *Feminist Studies/Critical Studies*. Bloomington: Indiana University Press, 1986.

———. *La Vendée et Madame, deuxième édition véritable*. Paris, 1834.

Lefranc, Émile. *La Duchesse de Berri en dix-sept tableaux*. Paris, 1832.

Legouvé, Ernest. *Histoire morale des femmes*. 10th ed. Paris: J. Hetzel et Cie, 1896.

Le Hir, Marie-Pierre. "La Représentation de la famille dans le mélodrame du début du dix-neuvième siècle de Pixerécourt à Ducange." *Nineteenth-Century French Studies* 18 (1989/1990): 15–24.

Lemaître, Jules. "Jean-Jacques Rousseau et le théâtre." *Impressions du théâtre*. Sixième Série. Paris: Lecène, Oudin et Cie, 1892.

Leo, Gerhard. *Flora Tristan: La Révolte d'une paria*. Paris: Éditions de l'Atelier, 1994.

Lerner, Gerda. *The Creation of Patriarchy*. New York: Oxford University Press, 1986.

LeSueur, Daniel. *Manuel des gens de lettres*. Paris: Librairie de Paris, 1897.

Levine, George, ed. *Constructions of the Self*. New Brunswick, N.J.: Rutgers University Press, 1992.

Levy, Darline Gay, Harriet Branson Applewhite, and Mary Durham Johnson, eds. *Women in Revolutionary Paris, 1789–1795: Selected Documents*. Urbana: University of Illinois Press, 1979.

Lewis, Jan. "Motherhood and the Construction of the Male Citizen in the United States, 1750–1850." In *Constructions of the Self*, ed. George Levine. New Brunswick, N.J.: Rutgers University Press, 1992.

Liszt, Franz. *Correspondance de Liszt et de la comtesse d'Agoult, 1833–1864*. 2 vols. Edited by Daniel Ollivier. Paris: Éditions Bernard Grasset, 1934.

Lottman, Herbert. *Colette, A Life*. Boston: Little-Brown, 1991.

Lougee, Carolyn C. *"Le Paradis des Femmes": Women, Salons and Social Stratification in Seventeenth-Century France*. Princeton: Princeton University Press, 1976.

Lucas-Dubreton, Jean. *La Duchesse de Berry*. Paris, 1835.

———. *La Princesse captive, la duchesse de Berry, 1832–1833*. Paris: Perrin, 1925.

Lynch, Katherine A. *Family, Class, and Ideology in Early Industrial France: Social Policy and the Working-Class Family, 1825–1848*. Madison: University of Wisconsin Press, 1988.

Lyonnet, Henri. *La Vie au dix-huitième siècle: Les Comédiennes*. Paris: Éditions Marcel Seheur, 1929.

Magnin, Peggy Kamuf de. "Rousseau's Politics of Visibility." *Diacritics* (winter 1975): 51–56.

Maillé, Duchesse de. *Souvenirs des deux restaurations*. Paris: Perrin, 1984.

Malo, Henri. *La Gloire du vicomte de Launay, delphine Gay de Girardin*. Paris: Émile-Paul Frères, 1925.

Manévy, Raymond. *La Presse de la Troisième République*. Paris: Forêt, 1955.

Mansel, Philip. *The Eagle in Splendour: Napoleon I and his Court*. London: G. Philip, 1987.

———. *The Court of France, 1789–1830*. Cambridge, Eng.: Cambridge University Press, 1988.

Marcya, Jeanne. *La Femme au théâtre*. Paris: Imprimerie G. Jeulin, 1901.

Margadant, Jo Burr. "The Duchesse de Berry and Royalist Political Culture in Postrevolutionary France." *History Workshop Journal* 43 (1997): 23–52.

———. *Madame le Professeur: Women Educators in the Third Republic.* Princeton: Princeton University Press, 1990.

———. "The New Biography in Historical Practice." *French Historical Studies* 19, no. 4 (1996): 1045–58.

Marie-Amélie, *Journal de Marie-Amélie, reine des français.* Edited by Suzanne d'Huart. Paris: Perrin, 1981.

Marks, Elaine. *Colette.* New Brunswick, N.J.: Rutgers University Press, 1960.

Marrinan, Michael. *Painting Politics for Louis-Philippe.* New Haven, Conn.: Yale University Press, 1988.

Martin-Fugier, Anne. *La Bourgeoise.* Paris: Bernard Grasset, 1983.

———. *La Vie élégante ou la formation du Tout-Paris, 1815–1848.* Paris: Fayard, 1990.

———. *La Vie quotidienne de Louis-Philippe et de sa famille, 1830–1848.* Paris: Hachette, 1992.

Matlock, Jann. *Scenes of Seduction: Prostitution, Hysteria, and Reading Difference in Nineteenth-Century France.* New York: Columbia University Press, 1994.

Maugue, Annelise. *L'Identité masculine en crise au tournant du siècle.* Paris: Éditions Rivages, 1987.

Maurois, André. *Lélia: The Life of George Sand.* Translated by Gerard Hopkins. New York: Harper & Row, 1953.

Mayeur, Jean-Marie, and Madeleine Rebérioux. *The Third Republic from its Origins to the Great War.* Cambridge, Eng.: Cambridge University Press, 1984.

Mazedier, René. *Histoire de la presse parisienne de Théophraste Renaudot à la IVe République, 1631–1945.* Paris: Éditions du Pavois, 1945.

McDonald, Jan. "New Women in the New Drama." *New Theatre Quarterly* 21 (Feb. 1990): 31–42.

McLaren, Angus. *Sexuality and Social Order: The Debate over the Fertility of Women and Workers in France, 1770–1920.* New York: Holmes & Meier, 1983.

McMillan, James F. *Housewife or Harlot: The Place of Women in French Society, 1870–1940.* New York: St. Martin's Press, 1981.

Ménière, Prosper. *La Captivité de madame la duchesse de Berry à Blaye, 1833: Journal du Docteur P. Ménière, médecin envoyé par le gouvernement auprès de la princesse.* Vol. 1. Paris: J. C. Levy, 1882.

Mesnard, Louis-Charles, Comte de. *Souvenirs intimes de M. le Cte de Mesnard. Premier écuyer et chevalier d'honneur de S.A.R. Mme la duchesse de Berry.* 3 vols. Paris, 1844.

Metcalf, Barbara D. "What Happened in Mecca: Mumtaz Mufti's 'Labbaik.'" In *The Culture of Autobiography: Constructions or Self-Representation,* ed. Robert Folkenflik. Stanford: Stanford University Press, 1993.

Michaud, Stéphane. *Muse et Madone. Visages de la femme de la Révolution française aux apparitions de Lourdes.* Paris: Seuil, 1985.

———. "Se choisir paria: Brève note sur Flora Tristan." *Romantisme* 58 (1987): 39–45.

Middlebrook, Diane Wood. "Postmodernism and the Biographer." In *Revealing Lives: Autobiography, Biography and Gender,* ed. Susan Groag Bell and Marilyn Yalom. New York: State University of New York Press, 1990.

Mill, John Stuart. *Auguste Comte and Positivism.* Ann Arbor: University of Michigan Press, Ann Arbor Paperback, 1961.

———. *The Earlier Letters of John Stuart Mill, 1812–1848.* Edited by Francis E. Mineka. 2 vols. (vols. 12 and 13 of *The Collected Works*). Toronto: University of Toronto Press and Routledge & Kegan Paul, 1963.

Miller, Nancy K. "Emphasis Added: Plots and Plausibilities in Women's Fiction." *PMLA* 96 (1981): 36–48.

———. "Writing Fictions: Women's Autobiography in France." In *Life/Lines: Theorizing Women's Autobiography,* ed. Bella Brodzki and Celeste Schenck. Ithaca: Cornell University Press, 1988.

Mills, Sarah. *Discourses of Difference: An Analysis of Women's Travel Writing and Colonialism.* London: Routledge, 1991.

Mitchell, Timothy. *Colonizing Egypt.* Berkeley and Los Angeles: University of California Press, 1988.

M.L.C. *Mystère dévoilé ou les géoliers de Blaye confondus par eux-memes,* 2d ed. (Paris, 1839)

Moon, S. Joan. "Feminism and Socialism: The Utopian Synthesis of Flora Tristan." In *Socialist Women: European Socialist Feminism in the Nineteenth and Early Twentieth Centuries,* ed. Marilyn Boxer and Jean Quataert. New York: Elsevier, 1978.

Moote, Lloyd. "New Bottles and New Wine: The Current State of Early Modernist Biographical Writing." *French Historical Studies* 19, no. 4 (1996): 911–26.

Moreau, J. (de Tours). *La psychologie morbide dans ses rapports avec la philosophie de l'histoire ou de l'influence des neuropathies sur le dynamisme intellectuel.* Paris, 1859.

———. *De la folie hystérique et de quelques phénomènes nerveux propres à l'hystérie.* Paris, 1865.

Moreau, Thérèse. *Le Sang de l'histoire: Michelet, l'histoire et l'idée de la femme au XIXe siècle.* Paris: Flammarion, 1982.

Morel, T. *La Vérité sur l'arrestation de Madame, duchesse de Berry, et les mensonges de Deutz dévoilés, . . . augmentée de l'homme qui livre une femme par Victor Hugo.* Paris, 1836.

Moses, Claire Goldberg. *French Feminism in the Nineteenth Century.* Albany: State University of New York Press, 1984.

Moses, Claire Goldberg, and Leslie Wahl Rabine. *Feminism, Socialism and French Romanticism.* Bloomington: Indiana University Press, 1993.

Mosse, George L. *Nationalism and Sexuality: Middle-Class Morality and Sexual Norms in Modern Europe.* Madison: University of Wisconsin Press, 1985.

Nadel, Ira Bruce. *Biography: Fact, Fiction and Form.* New York: St. Martin's Press, 1984.

Nagle, Jean. *Luxe et charité: le Faubourg Saint-Germain et l'argent.* Paris: Perrin, 1994.

Naginski, Isabelle Hoog. *George Sand: Writing for Her Life.* New Brunswick, N.J.: Rutgers University Press, 1991.

Néré, Jacques. *Le Boulangisme et la presse.* Paris: Armand Colin, 1964.

Nettement, Alfred [Baron Étienne Léon Lamothe-Langon]. *Mémoire historique de S.A.R. Madame, duchesse de Berri depuis sa naissance jusqu'à ce jour.* 3 vols. Paris: Allidin, 1837.

Nicolet, Claude. *L'Idée républicaine en France, (1789–1924): Essai d'histoire critique.* Paris: Gallimard, 1982.

Noiriel, Gérard. *Sur la "crise" de l'histoire.* Paris: Belin, 1996.

Nord, Philip. *The Republican Moment: Struggles for Democracy in Nineteenth-Century France.* Cambridge, Mass.: Harvard University Press, 1995.

Nordau, Max. *Psycho-physiologie du génie et du talent.* Translated by Auguste Dietrich. Paris, 1897.

———. *Dégénération.* 7th ed. New York, 1895.

Nussbaum, Felicity. *The Autobiographical Subject: Gender and Ideology in Eighteenth-Century England.* Baltimore: Johns Hopkins University Press, 1989.

Nye, Robert A. *Crime, Madness, and Politics in Modern France: The Medical Concept of National Decline.* Princeton: Princeton University Press, 1984.

———. *Masculinity and Male Codes of Honor in Modern France.* New York: Oxford University Press, 1993.

O'Brien, Sharon. "Feminist Theory and Literary Biography." In *Contesting the Subject: Essays in the Postmodern Theory and Practice of Biography and Biographical Criticism,* ed. William H. Epstein. West Lafayette, Ind.: Purdue University Press, 1991.

Offen, Karen. "Defining Feminism: A Comparative Historical Approach." *Signs* 14 (fall 1988): 119–57.

———. "Depopulation, Nationalism, and Feminism in Fin-de-Siècle France." *The American Historical Review* 89 (June 1984): 648–76.

———. "Ernest Legouvé and the Doctrine of 'Equality in Difference' for Women: A Case Study of Male Feminism in Nineteenth-Century French Thought." *Journal of Modern History* 58 (June 1968): 452–84.

———. *European Feminisms, 1799–1950: A Political History.* Stanford: Stanford University Press. Forthcoming.

———. "Women's History as French History." *Journal of Women's History* 8 (spring 1996): 147–54.

Ortner, Sherry B. *Making Gender: The Politics and Erotics of Culture.* Boston: Beacon Press, 1996.

———, ed. "The Fate of 'Culture': Geertz and Beyond." Special Issue. *Representations* 59 (1997).

Outram, Dorinda. *The Body and the French Revolution. Sex, Class, and Political Culture.* New Haven, Conn.: Yale University Press, 1989.

Ozouf, Mona. *Women's Words: Essay on French Singularity.* Translated by Jane Marie Todd. Chicago: University of Chicago Press, 1997.

Palmer, Michael. *Des Petits journaux aux grandes agences.* Paris: Aubier, 1983.

Pateman, Carole. *The Sexual Contract.* Stanford: Stanford University Press, 1988.

Pellissier, Pierre. *Émile de Girardin, Prince de la presse.* Paris: Éditions Denoël, 1985.

Perrot, Michelle. "The Family Triumphant." In *A History of Private Life,* ed. Philippe Ariès and Georges Duby. Vol. 4. *From the Fires of the Revolution to the Great War.* Edited by Michelle Perrot. Cambridge, Mass.: The Belknap Press of Harvard University Press, 1990.

———. "The New Eve and the Old Adam: French Women's Condition at the Turn of the Century." In *Behind the Lines: Gender and the Two World Wars,* ed. Margaret Randolph Higonnnet et al. New Haven, Conn.: Yale University Press, 1987.

The Personal Narratives Group, Joy Webster Barbre et al. *Interpreting Women's Lives: Feminist Theory and Personal Narratives.* Bloomington: Indiana University Press, 1989.

Petitpierre, Lieutenant Ferdinand. *Journal de la captivité de la duchesse de Berry à Blaye, 1832–1833.* Paris, 1904.

Phillips, Roderick. *Putting Asunder: A History of Divorce in Western Society.* Cambridge, Eng.: Cambridge University Press, 1988.

Pickering, Mary. "Angels and Demons in the Moral Vision of Auguste Comte." *Journal of Women's History* 8 (summer 1996): 10–40.

———. *Auguste Comte: An Intellectual Biography.* Vol 1. Cambridge, Eng.: Cambridge University Press, 1993.

———. "Rhetorical Strategies in the Works of Auguste Comte." *Historical Reflections/Réflexions Historiques* 23 (spring 1997): 151–75.

Pilbeam, Pamela M. *Republicanism in Nineteenth-Century France, 1814–1871.* New York: St. Martin's Press, 1995.

Pilkington, Hilary. *Migration, Displacement and Identity in Post-Soviet Russia.* New York: Routledge, 1998.

Pitts, Jesse R. "Continuity and Change in Bourgeois France." In *In Search of France: The Economy, Society and Political System in the Twentieth Century,* ed. Stanley Hoffmann et al. New York: Harper & Row, 1963.

Planté, Christine. *La petite soeur de Balzac: Essai sur la femme auteur.* Paris: Seuil, 1989.

Pope, Barbara Corrado. "Immaculate and Powerful: The Marian Revival in the Nineteenth Century." In *Immaculate and Powerful. The Female in Sacred Image and Social Reality,* ed. Clarissa W. Atkinson, Constance H. Buchanan, and Margaret R. Miles. Boston: Beacon Press, 1985.

———. "Revolution and Retreat: Upper-Class French Women after 1789." In *Women, War and Revolution,* ed. Carol R. Berkin and Clara M. Lovett. London: Holmes and Meier, 1980.

Pougin, Arthur. *Acteurs, actrices d'autrefois.* Paris: F. Juven et Cie, 1896.

Prassoloff, Annie. "Le Statut juridique de la femme auteur." *Romantisme* 77 (1992): 9–14.

Puech, Jules-L. *La Vie et l'oeuvre de Flora Tristan.* Paris: Marcel Rivière, 1925.

Rabaut, Jean. *Féministes à la Belle Epoque.* Paris: Editions France-Empire, 1985.

———. *Marguerite Durand (1864–1936): "La Fronde" féministe ou "Le Temps" en jupons.* Paris: L'Harmattan, 1996.

Rabine, Leslie Wahl. "Feminist Texts and Feminine Subjects." In *Feminism, Socialism, and French Romanticism,* ed. Claire Goldberg Moses and Leslie Wahl Rabine. Bloomington: Indiana University Press, 1993.

Rearick, Charles. *Pleasures of the Belle Epoque: Entertainment and Festivity in Turn-of-the-Century France.* New Haven, Conn.: Yale University Press, 1985.

Reddy, William M. "Condottieri of the Pen: Journalists and the Public Sphere in Postrevolutionary France (1815–1850)." *American Historical Review* 99, no. 5 (1994): 1546–70.

———. "The Concept of Class." In *Social Orders and Social Classes in Europe since 1500: Studies in Social Stratification,* ed. M. L. Bush. London: Longman, 1992.

———. *The Invisible Code: Honor and Sentiment in Postrevolutionary France, 1814–1848.* Berkeley and Los Angeles: University of California Press, 1997.

Reiffenberg, Le Baron Fréderic de. *Ce que c'est qu'une actrice.* Paris: Ferdinand Sartorius, 1861.

Reiset, Tony Henri Auguste, Vicomte de. *Les Enfants du duc de Berry: d'après de nouveaux documents.* 3d ed. Paris: Émile-Paul, 1905.

Revel, Jacques, and Lynn Hunt, eds. *Histories: French Constructions of the Past.* Vol 1. *Postwar French Thought.* Translated by Arthur Goldhammer et al. New York: New Press, 1995.

Reynolds, Siân. "Marianne's Citizens? Women, the Republic and Universal Suffrage in France." In *Women, State and Revolution: Essays on Power and Gender in Europe since 1789.* Amherst: University of Massachusetts Press, 1987.

Richardson, Joanna. *Colette.* London: Methuen, 1983.

Riley, Denise. *Am I That Name? Feminism and the Category of "Women" in History.* Minneapolis: University of Minnesota Press, 1988.

Riot-Sarcey, Michèle. *La Démocratie à l'épreuve des femmes. Trois figures critiques du pouvoir, 1830–1848.* Paris: Albin Michel, 1994.

Roberts, Mary Louise. "Acting Up: The Feminist Theatrics of Marguerite Durand." *French Historical Studies* 19, no. 4 (1996): 1103–38.

———. *Civilization without Sexes: Reconstructing Gender in Postwar France, 1917–1927.* Chicago: University of Chicago Press, 1994.

———. "Copie subversive: Le Journalisme féministe en France à la fin du siècle dernier." *Clio: Histoires, femmes et sociétés* (fall 1997): 230–49.

Rogers, Rebecca. "Boarding Schools, Women Teachers and Domesticity: Reforming Girls' Secondary Education in the First Half of the Nineteenth Century." *French Historical Studies* 19, no. 1 (spring 1995): 153–81.

Ronsin, Françis. *La Grève des ventres: Propagande néo-Malthusienne et baisse de la natalité en France, 19e et 20e siècles.* Paris: Aubier Montaigne, 1980.

Rosanvallon, Pierre. *L'État en France de 1789 à nos jours.* Paris: Éditions du Seuil, 1990.

Rousseau, Jean-Jacques. *Lettre à d'Alembert sur les spectacles.* Paris: Hachette, 1896.

Roussel, Nelly. "Charges militaires, charges maternelles." *La Voix des femmes* (March 16, 1922).

———. *Derniers combats: recueil d'articles et de discours (1911–1922).* Paris, 1932.

———. *L'Eternelle sacrifiée.* Preface, notes, and commentary by Daniel Armogathe and Maité Albistur. Paris: Syros, 1979.

———. "La Faute d'Eve." *Le Mouvement féminine* (Sept. 15, 1913).

———. "Freedom of Motherhood." In *Feminisms of the Belle Epoque: A Historical and Literary Anthology,* ed. Jennifer Waelti-Walters and Steven C. Hause. Translated by Jette Kjaer, Lydia Willis, and Jennifer Waelti-Walters. Lincoln: University of Nebraska Press, 1994.

———. "Le Front unique des femmes." *La Voix des femmes* (May 25, 1922).

———. *Par la révolte: scène symbolique.* c. 1903.

———. *Paroles de combat et d'espoir.* Epone, 1919.

———. *Quelques lances rompues pour nos libertés.* Paris, 1910.

———. "Petite gerbe sur une grande tombe." *Génération consciente* (Oct. 1, 1912).

———. "Du Rêve à la réalité." *La Voix des femmes* (Dec. 1, 1922).

———. *Trois Conférences de Nelly Roussel.* Preface by Odette Laguerre. Paris: Marcel Giard, 1930.

Rouvre, Charles de. *L'Amoureuse Histoire d'Auguste Comte et de Clotilde de Vaux.* Paris: Calmann-Lévy, 1917.

Sahlins, Marshall. *Islands of History.* Chicago: University of Chicago Press, 1985.

Sahlins, Peter. *Boundaries: The Making of France and Spain in the Pyrenees.* Berkeley and Los Angeles: University of California Press, 1989.

Sand, George. *Correspondance*. 25 vols. Edited by Georges Lubin. Paris: Garnier, 1964–1991.

———. *Histoire de ma vie*. In *Oeuvres autobiographiques*, ed. Georges Lubin. 2 vols. Paris: Gallimard, 1970–1971.

———. *Lettres à Marcie*. In *Les Sept Cordes de la lyre*. New ed. Paris: Michel Lévy Frères, 1869.

———. *Lettres d'un voyageur*. New ed. Paris: Calmann-Lévy, 1927.

———. *Politique et polémiques, 1843–1850*. Introduction by Michelle Perrot. Paris: Imprimerie Nationale, 1997.

———. *Story of My Life: The Autobiography of George Sand*. A group translation. Edited by Thelma Jurgrau. Albany: State University of New York Press, 1991.

Sarde, Michèle. *Colette: Free and Fettered*. New York: William Morrow, 1980.

Schiebinger, Londa. *The Mind Has No Sex? Women in the Origins of Modern Science*. Cambridge, Mass.: Harvard University, 1989.

Schor, Naomi. *George Sand and Idealism*. New York: Columbia University Press, 1993.

———. *Reading in Detail: Aesthetics and the Feminine*. New York: Routledge, 1987.

Schorske, Carl. *Fin-de-Siècle Vienna: Politics and Culture*. New York: Random House, 1981.

Schwartz, Joel. *The Sexual Politics of Jean-Jacques Rousseau*. Chicago: University of Chicago Press, 1984.

Schwartz, Vanessa. *Spectacular Realities: Early Mass Culture in Fin-de-Siècle Culture*. Berkeley and Los Angeles: University of California Press, 1998.

Scott, Joan. "The Evidence of Experience." *Critical Inquiry* 17, no. 4 (1991): 773–97.

———. "French Feminists and the Rights of 'Man': Olympe de Gouges's Declarations." *History Workshop* 28 (autumn 1989): 1–21.

———. "Introduction," "Gender: A Useful Category of Historical Analysis," and "On Language, Gender, and Working-Class History." In *Gender and Politics of History*, ed. Judith Butler and Joan Scott. New York: Columbia University Press, 1995.

———. *Only Paradoxes to Offer: French Feminists and the Rights of Man*. Cambridge, Mass.: Harvard University Press, 1996.

———. "Rewriting the History of Feminism." *Western Humanities Review* 58 (fall 1994): 238–51.

———. "The Tip of the Volcano." *Comparative Studies in Society and History* 35 (1993): 438–51.

Scribe, Eugène, and Roger de Rougemont. "Avant, pendant et après, esquisses historiques." Paris, 1828.

Séché, Léon. *Hortense Allart de Méritens*. Paris: Société de Mercure de France, 1908.

Seigel, Jerrold. *Bohemian Paris: Culture, Politics, and the Boundaries of Bourgeois Life, 1830–1930*. New York: Viking, 1987.

Sewell, William H. Jr. "Le citoyen/la citoyenne: Activity, Passivity and the Revolutionary Concept of Citizenship." In *The Political Culture of the French Revolution*, ed. Colin Lucas. Vol 2. New York: Pergamon Press, 1988.

Shama, Simon. "The Domestication of Majesty: Royal Family Portraiture, 1500–1850." *The Journal of Interdisciplinary History* 17 (1986): 155–84.

Shapiro, Ann-Louise. "History and Feminist Theory." In *Feminists Revision*

History, ed. Ann-Louise Shapiro. New Brunswick, N.J.: Rutgers University Press, 1994.

Silverman, Debora. *Art Nouveau in Fin-de-Siècle France: Politics, Psychology and Style.* Berkeley and Los Angeles: University of California Press, 1989.

Skinner, Cornelia Otis. *Madame Sarah.* Boston: Houghton-Mifflin, 1967.

Sklar, Kathryn Kish. *Catharine Beecher: A Study in American Domesticity.* New Haven, Conn.: Yale University Press, 1973.

Smith, Bonnie. *Changing Lives: Women in European History since 1700.* Lexington, Va.: D. C. Heath, 1989.

———. *The Gender of History: Men, Women and Historical Practice.* Cambridge, Mass.: Harvard University Press, 1998.

———. "History and Genius: The Narcotic, Erotic, and Baroque Life of Germaine de Staël." *French Historical Studies* 19, no. 4 (1996): 1059–81.

———. *Ladies of the Leisure Class: The Bourgeoises of Northern France in the Nineteenth Century.* Princeton: Princeton University Press, 1981.

Smith, Paul. *Discerning the Subject.* Minneapolis: University of Minnesota Press, 1988.

Smith, Sidonie. "Autobiography Criticism and the Problematics of Gender." In *A Poetics of Women's Autobiography: Marginality and the Fictions of Self-Representation.* Bloomington: Indiana University Press, 1987.

———. *A Poetics of Women's Autobiography: Marginality and the Fictions of Self-Representation.* Bloomington: Indiana University Press, 1987.

Solomon-Godeau, Abigail. "The Legs of the Countess." In *Fetishism as Cultural Discourse,* ed. Emily Apter and William Piete. Ithaca: Cornell University Press, 1993.

Sowerwine, Charles. *Sisters or Citizens? Women and Socialism in France since 1876.* Cambridge, Eng.: Cambridge University Press, 1982.

Sowerwine, Charles, and Claude Maignien. *Madeleine Pelletier, une féministe dans l'arène politique.* Paris: Les Éditions Ouvrières, 1992.

Spitzer, Alan. *The French Generation of 1820.* Princeton: Princeton University Press, 1987.

Starobinski, Jean. *Jean-Jacques Rousseau: La Transparence et l'obstacle.* Paris: Librairie Plon, 1957.

———. *Jean-Jacques Rousseau: Transparency and Obstruction.* Translated by Arthur Goldhammer. Chicago: University of Chicago Press, 1988.

Steedman, Carolyn. *Childhood, Culture and Class in Britain: Margaret McMillan, 1860–1931.* New Brunswick, N.J.: Rutgers University Press, 1990.

———. "La Théorie qui n'en est pas une: or Why Clio Doesn't Care." In *Feminists Revision History,* ed. Ann-Louise Shapiro. New Brunswick, N.J.: Rutgers University Press, 1994.

Steinbrugge, Lieselotte. *The Moral Sex: Woman's Nature in the French Enlightenment.* Translated by Pamela E. Selwyn. New York: Oxford University Press, 1995.

Stock-Morton, Phyllis. "Daniel Stern, Historian." *History of European Ideas* 8 (1987): 489–501.

Struminger, Laura. "L'Ange de la Maison. Mothers and Daughters in Nineteenth-Century France." *International Journal of Women's Studies* 2, no. 1 (1979): 51–61.

———. "Looking Back: Women of 1848 and the Revolutionary Heritage of 1789." In *Women and Politics in the Age of the Democratic Revolution,* ed.

Harriet B. Applewhite and Darline G. Levy. Ann Arbor: University of Michigan, 1990.

———. *The Odyssey of Flora Tristan*. New York: Peter Lang, 1988.

———. *What Were Little Girls and Boys Made of?: Primary Education in Rural France, 1830–1880*. Albany: State University of New York Press, 1983.

Sullerot, Evelyne. *Histoire de la presse féminine en France, des origines à 1848*. Paris: Armand Colin, 1966.

———. *La Presse féminine*. Paris: Librairie Armand Colin, 1963.

Sussman, George D. *Selling Mothers' Milk. The Wet-Nursing Business in France, 1715–1914*. Urbana: University of Illinois Press, 1982.

Taillandier, Isabelle. "La Villégiature à Dieppe sous la Restauration." Maîtrise, University of Paris I, 1988.

Talbot, Margaret. "An Emancipated Voice: Flora Tristan and Utopian Allegory." *Feminist Studies* 17, no. 2 (1991): 219–39.

Taussig, Michael T. *Mimesis and Alterity: A Particular History of the Senses*. New York: Routledge, 1993.

Terdiman, Richard. *Discourse/Counter-discourse: The Theory and Practice of Symbolic Resistance in Nineteenth-Century France*. Ithaca: Cornell University Press, 1985.

Terry, Jennifer. "Theorizing Deviant Historiography." In *Feminists Revision History*, ed. Ann-Louise Shapiro. New Brunswick, N.J.: Rutgers University Press, 1994.

Thébaud, Françoise. *La Femme au temps de la guerre de 14*. Paris: Éditions Stock, 1986.

———. *Quand nos grand-mères donnaient la vie: La Maternité en France dans l'entre-deux-guerres*. Lyon: Presses universitaires de Lyon, 1986.

Thérive, André. *Clotilde de Vaux ou la déesse morte*. Paris: Albin Michel, 1957.

Thibert, Marguerite. *Le Féminisme dans le socialisme français de 1830 à 1850*. Paris: Giard, 1926.

Thirria, Hippolyte. *La Duchesse de Berry (S.A.R. Madame), 1798–1870*. Paris: T. J. Plange, 1900.

Thompson, E. P. *The Making of the English Working Class*. New York: Vintage, 1966.

Thompson, Victoria. "Creating Boundaries: Homosexuality and the Changing Social Order in France, 1830–1870." In *Homosexuality in Modern France*, ed. Jeffrey Merrick and Bryant T. Ragan Jr. New York: Oxford University Press, 1996.

Tolédano, A.-D. *La Vie de famille sous la Restauration et la Monarchie de Juillet*. Paris: A. Michel, 1943.

Tomaselli, Sylvana, "The Enlightenment Debate on Women." *History Workshop Journal* 20 (1985): 101–24.

Tristan, Flora. *Flora Tristan la paria et son rêve: Correspondance établie par Stéphane Michaud*. Fontenay/Saint-Cloud: ENS Editions, 1995.

———. *Flora Tristan Lettres*. Réunies, présentées, et annotées par Stéphane Michaud. Paris: Seuil, 1980.

———. *Méphis*. 2 vols. Paris: Ladvocat, 1838.

———. *Pérégrinations d'une paria, 1833–1834*. 2 vols. Paris: Arthus Bertrand, 1838. Reprint. Paris: Maspero, 1980.

———. *Promenades dans Londres, ou l'aristocratie et les prolétaires anglais*. Edition prepared and annotated by François Bédarida. Paris: Maspero, 1978.

————. *Le Tour de France: État actuel de la classe ouvrière sous l'aspect moral, intellectuel et matériel.* 2 vols. Paris: Maspero, 1980.

————. *Union ouvrière.* 2d ed. Paris: chez tous les libraires, 1844.

Uffenbeck, Lorin A. *The Life and Writings of Hortense Allart, (1801–1879).* Ph.D. diss. University of Wisconsin-Madison, 1957.

Valette, Jacques. "Utopie sociale et les utopismes sociaux en France vers 1848." In *1848. Les Utopismes sociaux,* ed. J. Bartier et al. Paris: Éditions SEDES: CDU, 1981.

Vareille, Kristina Wingård. *Socialité, sexualité et les impasses de l'histoire: l'évolution de la thématique sandienne d'Indiana (1832) à Mauprat (1837).* Stockholm: Uppsala, 1987.

Varikas, Eleni. "Paria: une métaphore de l'exclusion des femmes." *Sources: Travaux historiques* 12 (1987): 37–43.

Vicinus, Martha. " 'Helpless and Unfriended': Nineteenth-Century Domestic Melodrama." *New Literary History* 13, no. 1 (autumn 1981): 127–43.

————. *Suffer and Be Still: Women in the Victorian Age.* Bloomington: Indiana University Press, 1972.

Vidal de la Blanche, Jacques. *Marie-Caroline duchesse de Berry.* Paris: France-Empire, 1980.

Vier, Jacques. *La Comtesse d'Agoult et son temps.* 6 vols. Paris: Albin Michel, 1955–1963.

Voyenne, Bernard. *Les Journalistes français: D'Où viennent-ils, qui sont-ils? que font-ils?* Paris: CFPJ, 1985.

Waelti-Waters, Jennifer, and Steven Hause, eds. *Feminisms of the Belle Epoque: A Historical and Literary Anthology.* Translated by Jette Kjaer, Lydia Willis, and Jennifer Waelti-Walters. Lincoln: University of Nebraska Press, 1994.

Wagner-Martin, Linda. *Telling Women's Lives: The New Biography.* New Brunswick, N.J.: Rutgers University Press, 1994.

Wahrman, Dror. *Imagining the Middle Class: The Political Representation of Class in Britain, c. 1780–1840.* Cambridge, Eng.: Cambridge University Press, 1995.

Walton, Whitney. *Eve's Proud Descendants: Four Women Writers and Republican Politics in Nineteenth-Century France.* Stanford: Stanford University Press, 2000.

————. "Literary Production and the Rearticulation of Home Space in the Works of George Sand, Marie d'Agoult, and Hortense Allart." *Women's History Review* 6 (1997): 115–32.

————. "Sailing a Fragile Bark: Rewriting the Family and the Individual in Nineteenth-Century France." *Journal of Family History* 22 (April 1997): 150–75.

————. "Writing the 1848 Revolution: Politics, Gender, and Feminism in the Works of French Women of Letters." *French Historical Studies* 18, no. 2 (1994): 1001–24.

Waquet, Françoise. *Les Fêtes royales sous la Restauration ou l'ancien régime retrouvé.* Geneva: Droz, 1981.

Weber, Eugen. *France Fin de Siècle.* Cambridge, Mass.: Harvard University Press, 1986.

Weil, Kari. *Androgyny and the Denial of Difference.* Charlottesville: University Press of Virginia, 1992.

Welfelé, Odile. "*La Fronde:* Histoire d'une entreprise de presse." Thèse: École de Chartres, 1982.

White, Hayden. *The Content of the Form: Narrative Discourse and Historical Representation.* Baltimore: Johns Hopkins University Press, 1987.

Williams, Patrick, and Laura Chrismen, eds. *Colonial Discourse and Post-Colonial Theory: A Reader.* New York: Harvester Wheatsheaf, 1993.

Williams, Rosalind. *Dream Worlds: Mass Consumption in Late Nineteenth-Century France.* Berkeley and Los Angeles: University of California Press, 1982.

Winegarten, Renée. *The Double Life of George Sand. Woman and Writer. A Critical Biography.* New York: Basic Books, 1978.

Witkowski, G.-J. *Les Accouchements à la Cour.* Paris, n.d.

Zeldin, Theodore. *France, 1848–1945.* Vol. 1. *Ambition, Love and Politics.* Oxford: Oxford University Press, 1977.

Zola, Émile. *Nana, Oeuvres complètes.* Paris: Bernouard, 1928.

———. *Nana.* Translated in part by George Holden. New York: Penguin Books, 1972.

Contributors

Elinor A. Accampo is an associate professor of history at the University of Southern California. She is author of *Industrialization, Family Life, and Class Relations: Saint Chamond, 1815 to 1914*, and coauthor of *Gender and the Politics of Social Reform in France, 1870–1914*. She is currently working on a biography of Nelly Roussel.

Susan Grogan is currently a Senior Lecturer in history at Victoria University of Wellington, New Zealand. Her primary publications are *French Socialism and Sexual Difference: Women and the New Society, 1803–1844* and *Flora Tristan: Life Stories*.

Jo Burr Margadant is associate professor at Santa Clara University. Her first book, *Madame le Professeur: Women Educators in the Third Republic,* won four national awards including the 1990 David Pinkney Prize for the best book in French History (co-recipient). She coedited with Professor A. Lloyd Moote a special issue on biography for *French Historical Studies* and has published two articles on representations of the d'Orléans royal family during the July monarchy. She is currently working on a book on that subject. Beginning July 2000, she will serve as coeditor of *French Historical Studies*.

Mary Pickering received her Ph.D. from Harvard University in 1988 and is associate professor at San Jose State University. The publication of her first book, *Auguste Comte: An Intellectual Biography,* will soon be followed by a second volume, which she is currently writing. Her articles on Auguste Comte's thought, intellectual trajectory, and rhetorical strategies have appeared in several leading journals and as chapters in edited collections.

Mary Louise Roberts is an associate professor at Stanford University. Her first book, *Civilization without Sexes: Reconstructing Gender in Postwar France, 1917–1927,* won the American Historical Association's Joan Kelly Award for the Best Book in Women's History, 1994. At present, she is working on a study of the fin-de-siècle "new woman" in France, including the reporter Séverine and "La Divine," Sarah Bernhardt.

Whitney Walton is the author of *France at the Crystal Palace: Bourgeois Taste and Artisan Manufacture in the Nineteenth Century* and of several articles in French social and gender history. Her new book is entitled *Eve's Proud Descendants: Four Women Writers and Republican Politics in Nineteenth-Century France.* She is an associate professor of history at Purdue University and is exploring some possibilities in comparative history for her next project.

Index

Accampo, Elinor A., 8–9, 15–16, 218–61

acting career, 19–20, 174–80, 197–99, 205nn59,71, 206n75; Durand's, 19, 171, 173, 174–80, 184, 190, 192, 197, 202nn31,33, 206n79; male, 82, 175, 177, 206n79; prostitutes and, 177–79, 205n59, 213n135; Roussel ambitions for, 19, 198, 221, 223, 234; social prejudices against, 19, 176–80, 197–98, 203–4nn45,47,49. *See also* Bernhardt, Sarah; performances

L'Action, 226–27, 233

Adler, Laure, 210n112

aesthetics: feminist, 172–76, 183–96, 208n95, 209n101. *See also* beauty; dress

d'Agoult, Charles, 105

d'Agoult, Marie (1805–1876), 13, 17, 19, 99–136, 140; autobiography, 13, 100, 103, 107, 110–12, 114–15, 121, 123, 126; and duchesse de Berry, 65n71; *Essay on Liberty,* 121; family, 13, 104–7, 110–12, 114–15, 123, 124, 126; *History of the 1848 Revolution,* 105, 121; Lehmann portrait, 111*illus;* salon, 18, 105, 120, 121, 126; Stern pseudonym, 99, 105–6

d'Albret, Jeanne, 64n52

d'Albuféra, duc, 46

d'Alembert, Jean le Rond, 176–77

Allart, Hortense (1801–1879), 13, 17, 18, 99–136; authorial names, 106; autobiography, 13, 100, 103, 107,

112–15, 122, 123, 125; family, 13, 105–7, 112–15, 123–25, 135n90; Gabriac portrait, 113*illus;* "Marpé," 125; meritocracy, 122, 134n74; *Settimia,* 125

Allix, Mme. Jules, 175

Amar, André, 127–28n4

Amis de l'ordre, 53

d'Angoulême, duc (Dauphin), 38, 48, 70n129

d'Angoulême, duchesse (Dauphine), 38–39, 42, 48, 50, 51–52, 70n129

"apostolate," female, 22–23; Roussel, 8, 22–23, 223, 228–30, 233, 237, 239, 254n16. *See also* messianism

Apponyi, Rudolphe, 52

"Après la bataille" (Roussel), 233

aristocracy: d'Agoult's family, 110, 112; de Vaux, 139; domesticity, 33, 36, 58, 61n10, 70n127; Old Regime, 36, 40–41, 76; and public birthing, 46; rivalries among, 39–40; in Scribe play, 50; theatrical pastimes, 19. *See also* elite

d'Artois, comte, 38, 39, 132n24. *See also* Charles X

"Assemblée Législative de la mode" (*La Mode*), 51

Auclert, Hubertine, 128–29n8, 187

authority: domestic ideal and, 72, 76–79, 84, 91, 143, 145, 163, 232; female moral, 72, 76, 77, 79, 83–91, 93, 143, 145, 163; feminine critique of, 79–84; male domestic, 11, 18, 77, 101, 106, 107; male political, 76–79, 86–89,

Studies on the History of Society and Culture
Victoria E. Bonnell and Lynn Hunt, Editors

Text:	10/13 Sabon
Display:	Sabon
Composition:	BookMatters
Printing and binding:	Thomson-Shore
Index:	Barbara Roos